PENGUIN MODERN CLASSICS

LOOK AT ME NOW
AND HERE I AM

Gertrude Stein died in France in 1946 at the age of seventy-two. She had become one of the century's most publicized but least read authors and she had influenced three generations of writers, including Hemingway and Thornton Wilder.

She was born in Pennsylvania but spent her earliest years in Austria and then Paris. When the family returned to America, it was this time to California. At the age of eighteen, with both parents dead, Gertrude Stein moved to Baltimore where, in 1893, she registered at the Harvard Annex. She graduated in 1898 and continued her studies at the Johns Hopkins Medical School – leaving without a degree because she was 'bored, frankly and openly bored'.

From 1903, Gertrude Stein and her brother settled in Paris and began to collect paintings and, in her case, to write. In these years before the First World War, she met and grew to know the group of painters and writers who were to be her friends. Alice Toklas joined this group in 1907 and stayed to become a faithful friend and helper. During both wars, the two friends remained in France in spite of danger and Gertrude continued to write with increasing recognition until she died just after the Second World War.

Her *Autobiography of Alice B. Toklas* is also available in Penguin Modern Classics.

GERTRUDE STEIN

LOOK AT ME NOW AND HERE I AM

Writings and Lectures
1909–45

———

EDITED BY PATRICIA MEYEROWITZ
WITH AN INTRODUCTION BY
ELIZABETH SPRIGGE

PENGUIN BOOKS

Penguin Books Ltd, Harmondsworth, Middlesex, England
Penguin Books Inc., 7110 Ambassador Road, Baltimore,
Maryland 21207, U.S.A.
Penguin Books Australia Ltd, Ringwood, Victoria, Australia

—

This selection first published by Peter Owen 1967
Published in Penguin Books 1971

—

—

Printed in the United States of America
Set in Monotype Fournier

CONTENTS

EDITOR'S FOREWORD

WHEN Gertrude Stein was lecturing at the University of Chicago a young student in her seminar asked her for the meaning of 'rose is a rose is a rose'. This was her reply:

Now listen. Can't you see that when the language was new – as it was with Chaucer and Homer – the poet could use the name of a thing and the thing was really there. He could say 'O moon', 'O sea', 'O love', and the moon and the sea and love were really there. And can't you see that after hundreds of years had gone by and thousands of poems had been written, he could call on those words and find that they were just wornout literary words. The excitingness of pure being had withdrawn from them; they were just rather stale literary words. Now the poet has to work in the excitingness of pure being; he has to get back that intensity into the language. We all know that it's hard to write poetry in a late age; and we know that you have to put some strangeness, as something unexpected, into the structure of the sentence in order to bring back vitality to the noun. Now it's not enough to be bizarre; the strangeness in the sentence structure has to come from the poetic gift, too. That's why it's doubly hard to be a poet in a late age. Now you all have seen hundreds of poems about roses and you know in your bones that the rose is not there. All those songs that sopranos sing as encores about 'I have a garden! oh, what a garden!' Now I don't want to put too much emphasis on that line, because it's just one line in a longer poem. But I notice that you all know it; you make fun of it, but you know it. Now listen! I'm no fool. I know that in daily life we don't go around saying '... is a ... is a ... is a ...'. Yes, I'm no fool; but I think that in that line the rose is red for the first time in English poetry for a hundred years.[1]

Gertrude Stein was sixty-one years old when she answered the young student in Chicago; she had been writing for over thirty years. This anthology presents her startling achievements in creative writing, both during that period and the ten years that remained to her.

[1] Quoted by Thornton Wilder in his introduction to *Four In America*.

Gertrude Stein lived in France for over forty years. Her home in Paris was famous as a meeting place for artists and writers. Some came to speak and listen to her, while others came to see her large collection of contemporary paintings.

During all these years, Gertrude Stein was writing continuously. She developed an important habit of meditating each day, and through writing and meditation the methods in her work underwent changes as she made discoveries. Her life was a full working life with at least twenty-six books published, and during the twelve years following her death in July 1946, another twelve books were published.

A great deal has already been said and written about Gertrude Stein both during her lifetime and subsequently. She once said that even well meaning people sometimes did her work more harm than good by writing about it. It is with this in mind that I do not offer here anyone's opinions or assessments but present Gertrude Stein accompanied by her own explanations of what she was doing.

The lectures in the first part of the book constitute almost all the major lectures on writing given by Gertrude Stein in England and the United States.[2] The works in the second part of the book, with the exception of the last eight items, are related to the lectures and references are given in the accompanying notes. *Henry James* was chosen because of its relationship to the piece immediately preceding it and also because of its position in the chronology of Gertrude Stein's work. The last two items were written after all the lectures were given and show Gertrude Stein's return to a narrative derived from years of creative work and meditation on writing and its content. Since there are no references to them in the lectures, relevant quotations from other work are given.[3]

Much information about the life and work of Gertrude Stein will emerge through reading the lectures, the work itself and the notes, but for greater detail about her life, or for opinions, interpretations

2. The lectures entitled 'Narration' have been excluded because of their length. They retrace some of the ideas already stated in other lectures but mostly concern the subject of narrative. See footnote on p. 273.

3. For this Penguin edition, Gertrude Stein's lively articles on money have been included among the later works: see p. 331.

and assessments of her work, the reader should refer to the bibliography on page 443. Particularly recommended are Thornton Wilder's introductions to *The Geographical History of America* and *Four In America*.

Finally, if we still cannot understand all of Gertrude Stein after reading her own explanations, we must always keep in mind what she said to a group of journalists who greeted her in New York when she arrived for a lecture tour in 1934. After astonishing them by asking: 'Suppose there were no questions what would the answer be,' she went on to answer their questions lucidly and in good humour. This prompted one of the journalists to ask: 'Why don't you write the way you talk?' To which she replied: 'Why don't you read the way I write?'

INTRODUCTION

Steins were called Steins in the time of Napoleon before that any name was a name but in the time of Napoleon in any country he went through the name of any one had to be written and so they took the name they gave them and Stein was an easy one.

Everybody's Autobiography

My father's name was Daniel he had a black beard he was not tall not at all tall, he had a black beard his name was Daniel.

The Mother of Us All

THE Stein family came from Bavaria; Gertrude's uncle Meyer having crossed the Atlantic in 1841 – at the age of eighteen – to seek his fortune. Soon afterwards he persuaded his family to join him. Within a few years he and his four brothers, who included the young Daniel, were running a successful clothing store in Baltimore. Presently, the Steins being a quarrelsome family, this partnership broke up. Daniel married Amelia Keyser, a Baltimore girl from another German-Jewish family, earlier settlers in America than the Steins, and moved to Allegheny, now a suburb of Pittsburgh, but in those days a small separate town. Here Daniel and his brother Solomon built themselves twin houses and proceeded to raise their families – Daniel's children being Michael, Simon, Bertha, Leo, and then on 3 February 1874, the baby of the family, Gertrude.

In the year of her birth Allegheny was devastated by flood and fire and Daniel took his family to Austria. He was an ardent educationalist and had decided that his elder children would benefit by some European teaching. Rachel, one of Mrs Stein's unmarried sisters, went with them, and they had a most comfortable establishment, first at Gemünden and then in Vienna, including a nurse, a tutor, a governess and a full domestic staff. Music and dancing-lessons, riding, skating and sight-seeing were all part of the programme, as befitted a well-to-do middle-class family in the seventies.

The letters written home by the two sisters, and the little diaries kept by Mrs Stein, give us many pictures of the small Gertrude, as do the photographs of the period. She was already plump, 'the darling little dumpling', and obviously intelligent, prattling mostly in German, toddling around copying everything that was said or done, 'she beats them all', and delighting to play with stones and pebbles. She always rejoiced that she was the youngest child and '... there you are you are privileged,' she wrote at the beginning of *Wars I Have Seen*, 'nobody can do anything but take care of you, that is the way I was and that is the way I still am ...'

The eldest brother, Michael, was a very bright boy, Simon and Bertha were of low intelligence and Leo, who for many years was to be Gertrude's dearest counsellor and companion, was exceptionally clever.

Living at a loose end in Europe did not suit Daniel Stein, so presently he left his family and returned to America to consider new ways of making money. In 1878, when Gertrude was four, Mrs Stein moved the family to Paris, and a little later on Gertrude and Bertha went for a while to a small boarding-school there. Although she was so young, the sights and sounds and smells of Paris impressed themselves on Gertrude's senses, so that when twenty-five years later she returned to make Paris her home, it was at once familiar. Presently Mr Stein joined his family again and took them all back to America, where in 1880 they settled in Oakland, across the Bay from San Francisco. Daniel had now abandoned the clothing trade in favour of street railroads, cable cars, mines and the Stock Exchange.

Here, as Gertrude Stein described in *The Making of Americans*, the children lived a life of true Californian freedom and at the same time their education continued both with governesses at home and at local schools. Nor was their religious training as orthodox Jews neglected, although as an adult Gertrude Stein never practised the Jewish religion. She seldom referred to her Jewish heritage, but as Adele in *Things As They Are* she observed:

I have the failing of my tribe. I believe in the sacred rites of conversation even when it is a monologue.

All through her childhood Gertrude Stein read. 'She read anything that came her way, and a great deal came her way,' she was to write in *The Autobiography of Alice B. Toklas*, for as she grew older she made extensive use of the local and San Francisco libraries and acquired a wide knowledge of English literature.

When she was fourteen her mother, long an invalid, died. The household became quite disorganized and Daniel grew more and more morose and eccentric. Three years later he too died and Gertrude, Leo and their sister went back to Baltimore to make their home with one of their mother's sisters. During these vicissitudes Gertrude had been plunged in adolescent gloom, increased by her parting with Leo, who had gone to Harvard. In 1893, when she was nineteen, she herself went off to register at the Harvard Annex, soon to be renamed Radcliffe College, and although she had not taken the usual entrance examinations, was accepted as a student.

When I was at Radcliffe I was of course very interested in psychology. I was interested in biology and I was interested in psychology and philosophy and history, that was all natural enough, I came out of the nineteenth century you had to be interested in evolution and biology, I liked thinking so I had to be interested in philosophy and I liked looking at every one and talking and listening so I had to be interested in history and psychology.

For these subjects she attended the post-graduate courses of William James, another tribute to her intelligence and personality. James, after the publication of his *Principles of Psychology*, was now at the height of his fame, and Gertrude Stein also studied under the brilliant young psychologist Hugo Münsterberg, whom James called 'the Rudyard Kipling of Psychology' and had brought over from Germany to work at Harvard.

William James delighted her. His personality and his way of teaching and his way of amusing himself and his students all pleased her.

In her admiration of James, as in so much else, Gertrude was emulating her brother Leo, who had also been his pupil for a while. Both James and Münsterberg simply repeated their Harvard lectures to the young women at Radcliffe, and they both appreciated this clever rollicking girl – she had now exchanged melancholy for very high spirits. Indeed Münsterberg used her as his model when describing an ideal student.

It would be difficult to overrate William James's influence on Gertrude Stein. The conscious, just before it was superseded, through the influence of Freud, by the unconscious – although never for Gertrude Stein – was a main concern of thinking people, and she was a thinker. James's conception of the 'stream of consciousness' awoke an immediate response in her. 'Within each personal consciousness, thought is sensibly continuous,' he had already written in the *Principles*. 'Consciousness . . . is nothing jointed: it flows.' And so-called interruptions 'no more break the flow of the thought that thinks them than they break the time and space in which they lie'. James was also interested in parts of speech:

We ought to say a feeling of *and*, a feeling of *if*, a feeling of *but*, and a feeling of *by*, quite as readily as we say a feeling of *blue* or a feeling of *cold*. Yet we do not: so inveterate has our habit become of recognizing the existence of the substantive parts alone, that language almost refuses to lend itself to any other use.

There are many other similarities between William James's and Gertrude Stein's principles of the use of language. James, for instance, observed that while we are contemplating the present, 'it has melted in our grasp . . . gone in the instant of becoming'.

Here are the seeds of Gertrude Stein's 'continuous present', the 'immediate existing', on which she was to base her own writing.

During this period Gertrude Stein, collaborating with Leo Solomons, a graduate student who was a close friend of hers, made a series of experiments which were recorded in *The Psychological Review* for September 1896 under the title 'Normal Motor Automatism', the first piece of Gertrude Stein's writing to be published. For one of the experiments, at William James's suggestion, they used a planchette to produce automatic writing. After Gertrude Stein became famous, critics discovered this early article and tried to prove that its contents explained the origins of her individual style. This was a complete error. As she herself stated:

Gertrude Stein never had subconscious reactions, nor was she a successful subject for automatic writing.

The origins were in the encouragement given to her own bent by William James's ideas, although having nothing of the mystic in her, she could not follow him into the twentieth century, any more than he could follow her.

That he appreciated her brains is clear from this famous anecdote:

It was a very lovely spring day, Gertrude Stein had been going to the opera every night and going also to the opera in the afternoon and had been otherwise engrossed and it was the period of the final examinations, and there was the examination in William James's course. She sat down with the examination paper before her and she just could not. 'Dear Professor James', she wrote at the top of her paper. 'I am so sorry but really I do not feel a bit like an examination paper in philosophy today,' and left.

The next day she had a postal card from William James saying, Dear Miss Stein, I understand perfectly how you feel. I often feel like that myself. And underneath it he gave her work the highest mark in his course.

The psychological experiments Gertrude Stein made with Leo Solomons were not confined to automatic writing and they used their fellow-students as guinea-pigs. What emerges from Gertrude Stein's own comments is that while indifferent to the results of these experiments, she was deeply interested in the characters of the students and took great pains to analyse them.

Having graduated *magna cum laude*, although a year later than her class, Gertrude Stein took William James's second recommendation – his first was to take up Philosophy – and joined Leo in Baltimore, where he was taking a second degree in Biology, in order to read Psychology herself at the Johns Hopkins Medical School. The Steins took a largish house, hung up their Japanese prints, and entertained their friends, though not in the usual Baltimore fashion, for, as Gertrude observed, she and Leo were 'born Bohemians'.

As a medical student Gertrude Stein's work was very varied – she made a study of brain tracts and she assisted in the delivery of infants, particularly in the Negro quarter, which gave her fine material for her early story *Melanctha Herbert*. None the less, during the first two years at Johns Hopkins, she was, she declared, 'bored, frankly and openly bored'. The exciting times for her now were the vacations which she spent in Europe, chiefly Italy, with her brother Leo, who had finished with schools and had begun to paint and to study aesthetics.

In the spring of 1902 Gertrude and Leo visited England and lived for a while in Bloomsbury, she becoming an habituée of the British Museum Reading Room. After another short spell in New York, she joined Leo to live in their famous *pavillon* and studio at 27 rue de Fleurus.

America is my country and Paris is my home town and it is as it has come to be.

Paris was the place that suited those of us that were to create the twentieth century art and literature, naturally enough . . .

And now the picture-buying began. Under the influence of Bernard Berenson, Leo Stein had already bought a Cézanne landscape and soon their collection would include paintings by Renoir, Gauguin, Manet, Toulouse-Lautrec and other contemporary artists, among whom Picasso was to rise as the new star.

Gertrude Stein was now writing. First came the novel *Q.E.D.*, posthumously published as *Things As They Are*, a good analytical work of conventional fiction. Next came her translation of Flaubert's *Trois Contes*, which led to her own book of stories: *Three Lives*. By the time she met Picasso, with whom she immediately became friends, as she and Leo bought his paintings and she sat to him for her portrait, she was at work on this book, with a Cézanne painting before her eyes:

Finished or unfinished it always was what it looked like the very essence of an oil painting because everything was there . . . this then was a great relief to me and I began my writing.

And behind her still was William James with his knowledge of consciousness and of states of mind, and in her life was Pablo Picasso, the great exponent of the present, that continuous present that she was to make her own trademark. The exciting difference between him and the other masters who had influenced her was that Picasso was a contemporary, younger than herself, and she could watch him at work. They were both full of inspiration.

One of the pleasantest things those of us who write or paint do is to have a daily miracle. It does come.

In 1909 Alice B. Toklas joined the Stein ménage in rue de Fleurus.

She was a young Californian who knew the Michael Steins and it was they who introduced her to Gertrude, whose close friend and helper she became for the rest of the writer's life. Gertrude was then writing *The Making of Americans* and Alice Toklas taught herself to type while copying the enormously long manuscript.

The close relationship between Leo and Gertrude had already begun to slacken, chiefly as a result of his inability to appreciate her writing. Before long he departed, leaving the famous studio and *pavillon* to the friends.

Gertrude Stein and Alice Toklas were in England when the war broke out and their one thought was to get back to France, where later they distributed hospital supplies in a car driven by Gertrude.

Between the wars, rue de Fleurus became a famous meeting-place for writers and artists, and Gertrude Stein continued to write steadily and to have a certain amount published, although without winning the literary recognition she longed for. Fame came, however, in the thirties, and she and Alice Toklas went off to the States for a lecture tour, Gertrude Stein thoroughly enjoying being a celebrity. Later she also lectured in England at both Oxford and Cambridge.

During the second war, although Gertrude Stein and Alice Toklas left Paris, they once more refused to leave France, in spite of the special dangers during the Occupation for those of Jewish origin. They came through unscathed and so did Gertrude Stein's now valuable collection of pictures, left hanging in Paris in the apartment in rue Christine to which the friends had moved the year before the war. And here they lived a rich and fruitful life until Gertrude Stein's death on 27 July 1946.

Her last words were splendidly characteristic: 'What is the answer?' she asked, and when no answer came she laughed and said: 'Then what is the question?'

ELIZABETH SPRIGGE

PART ONE

LECTURES

Gertrude Stein received invitations from the Oxford and the Cambridge literary societies to lecture to them. She wrote this lecture in January 1926 and went to England in the spring. After giving the lecture she read out four examples of her work: 'Preciocilla', 'A Saint in Seven', 'Sitwell Edith Sitwell', and 'Jean Cocteau'.

The lecture was first published by the Hogarth Press, London, 1926.

I

COMPOSITION AS EXPLANATION

THERE is singularly nothing that makes a difference a difference in beginning and in the middle and in ending except that each generation has something different at which they are all looking. By this I mean so simply that anybody knows it that composition is the difference which makes each and all of them then different from other generations and this is what makes everything different otherwise they are all alike and everybody knows it because everybody says it.

It is very likely that nearly every one has been very nearly certain that something that is interesting is interesting them. Can they and do they. It is very interesting that nothing inside in them, that is when you consider the very long history of how every one ever acted or has felt, it is very interesting that nothing inside in them in all of them makes it connectedly different. By this I mean this. The only thing that is different from one time to another is what is seen and what is seen depends upon how everybody is doing everything. This makes the thing we are looking at very different and this makes what those describe it make of it, it makes a composition, it confuses, it shows, it is, it looks, it likes it as it is, and this makes what is seen as it is seen. Nothing changes from generation to generation except the thing seen and that makes a composition. Lord Grey remarked that when the generals before the war talked about the war they talked about it as a nineteenth-century war although to be fought with twentieth-century weapons. That is because war is a thing that decides how it is to be done when it is to be done. It is prepared and to that degree it is like all academies it is not a thing made by being made it is a thing prepared. Writing and painting and all that, is like that, for those who occupy themselves with it and don't make it as it is made. Now the few who make it as it is made, and it is to be remarked that the most decided of them usually are prepared just as the world around them is preparing, do it in this way and so I if you do not mind I will tell you how it happens. Naturally one does not know how it happened until it is well over beginning happening.

To come back to the part that the only thing that is different is what is seen when it seems to be being seen, in other words, composition and time sense.

No one is ahead of his time, it is only that the particular variety of creating his time is the one that his contemporaries who also are creating their own time refuse to accept. And they refuse to accept it for a very simple reason and that is that they do not have to accept it for any reason. They themselves that is everybody in their entering the modern composition and they do enter it, if they do not enter it they are not so to speak in it they are out of it and so they do enter it; but in as you may say the non-competitive efforts where if you are not in it nothing is lost except nothing at all except what is not had, there are naturally all the refusals, and the things refused are only important if unexpectedly somebody happens to need them. In the case of the arts it is very definite. Those who are creating the modern composition authentically are naturally only of importance when they are dead because by that time the modern composition having become past is classified and the description of it is classical. That is the reason why the creator of the new composition in the arts is an outlaw until he is a classic, there is hardly a moment in between and it is really too bad very much too bad naturally for the creator but also very much too bad for the enjoyer, they all really would enjoy the created so much better just after it has been made than when it is already a classic, but it is perfectly simple that there is no reason why the contemporary should see, because it would not make any difference as they lead their lives in the new composition anyway, and as every one is naturally indolent why naturally they don't see. For this reason as in quoting Lord Grey it is quite certain that nations not actively threatened are at least several generations behind themselves militarily so aesthetically they are more than several generations behind themselves and it is very much too bad, it is so very much more exciting and satisfactory for everybody if one can have contemporaries, if all one's contemporaries could be one's contemporaries.

There is almost not an interval.

For a very long time everybody refuses and then almost without a pause almost everybody accepts. In the history of the refused in the arts and literature the rapidity of the change is always startling. Now the only difficulty with the *volte-face* concerning the arts is this. When the acceptance comes, by that acceptance the thing created becomes a classic. It is a natural phenomena a rather extraordinary natural phenomena that a thing accepted becomes a classic. And what is the characteristic quality of a classic. The characteristic quality of a classic is that it is beautiful. Now of course it is perfectly true that a more or less first rate work of art is beautiful but the trouble is that when that first rate work of art becomes a classic because it is accepted the only thing that is important from then on to the majority of the acceptors the enormous majority, the most intelligent majority of the acceptors is that it is so wonderfully beautiful. Of course it is wonderfully beautiful, only when it is still a thing irritating annoying stimulating then all quality of beauty is denied to it.

Of course it is beautiful but first all beauty in it is denied and then all the beauty of it is accepted. If every one were not so indolent they would realize that beauty is beauty even when it is irritating and stimulating not only when it is accepted and classic. Of course it is extremely difficult nothing more so than to remember back to its not being beautiful once it has become beautiful. This makes it so much more difficult to realize its beauty when the work is being refused and prevents every one from realizing that they were convinced that beauty was denied, once the work is accepted. Automatically with the acceptance of the time sense comes the recognition of the beauty and once the beauty is accepted the beauty never fails any one.

Beginning again and again is a natural thing even when there is a series.

Beginning again and again and again explaining composition and time is a natural thing.

It is understood by this time that everything is the same except composition and time, composition and the time of the composition and the time in the composition.

Everything is the same except composition and as the composition is different and always going to be different everything is not the same. Everything is not the same as the time when of the composition and the time in the composition is different. The composition is different, that is certain.

The composition is the thing seen by every one living in the living that they are doing, they are the composing of the composition that at the time they are living is the composition of the time in which they are living. It is that that makes living a thing they are doing. Nothing else is different, of that almost any one can be certain. The time when and the time of and the time in that composition is the natural phenomena of that composition and of that perhaps every one can be certain.

No one thinks these things when they are making when they are creating what is the composition, naturally no one thinks, that is no one formulates until what is to be formulated has been made.

Composition is not there, it is going to be there and we are here. This is some time ago for us naturally.

The only thing that is different from one time to another is what is seen and what is seen depends upon how everybody is doing everything. This makes the thing we are looking at very different and this makes what those who describe it make of it, it makes a composition, it confuses, it shows, it is, it looks, it likes it as it is, and this makes what is seen as it is seen. Nothing changes from generation to generation except the thing seen and that makes a composition.

Now the few who make writing as it is made and it is to be remarked that the most decided of them are those that are prepared by preparing, are prepared just as the world around them is prepared and is preparing to do it in this way and so if you do not mind I will again tell you how it happens. Naturally one does not know how it happened until it is well over beginning happening.

Each period of living differs from any other period of living not in the way life is but in the way life is conducted and that authentically speaking is composition. After life has been conducted in a certain way everybody knows it but nobody knows it, little by little, nobody knows it as long as nobody knows it. Any one creating the composition in the arts does not know it either, they are conducting life and that makes their composition what it is, it makes their work compose as it does.

Their influence and their influences are the same as that of all of their contemporaries only it must always be remembered that the analogy is not obvious until as I say the composition of a time has become so pronounced that it is past and the artistic composition of it is a classic.

And now to begin as if to begin. Composition is not there, it is going to be there and we are here. This is some time ago for us naturally. There is something to be added afterwards.

Just how much my work is known to you I do not know. I feel that perhaps it would be just as well to tell the whole of it.

In beginning writing I wrote a book called *Three Lives* this was written in 1905. I wrote a negro story called *Melanctha*. In that there was a constant recurring and beginning there was a marked direction in the direction of being in the present although naturally I had been accustomed to past present and future, and why, because the composition forming around me was a prolonged present. A composition of a prolonged present is a natural composition in the world as it has been these thirty years it was more and more a prolonged present. I created then a prolonged present naturally I knew nothing of a continuous present but it came naturally to me to make one, it was simple it was clear to me and nobody knew why it was done like that, I did not myself although naturally to me it was natural.

After that I did a book called *The Making of Americans* it is a long book about a thousand pages.

Here again it was all so natural to me and more and more complicatedly a continuous present. A continuous present is a continuous present. I made almost a thousand pages of a continuous present.

Continuous present is one thing and beginning again and again is another thing. These are both things. And then there is using everything.

This brings us again to composition this the using everything.

The using everything brings us to composition and to this composition. A continuous present and using everything and beginning again. In these two books there was elaboration of the complexities of using everything and of a continuous present and of beginning again and again and again.

In the first book there was a groping for a continuous present and for using everything by beginning again and again.

There was a groping for using everything and there was a groping for a continuous present and there was an inevitable beginning of beginning again and again and again.

Having naturally done this I naturally was a little troubled with it when I read it. I became then like the others who read it. One does, you know, excepting that when I reread it myself I lost myself in it again. Then I said to myself this time it will be different and I began. I did not begin again I just began.

In this beginning naturally since I at once went on and on very soon there were pages and pages and pages more and more elaborated creating a more and more continuous present including more and more using of everything and continuing more and more beginning and beginning and beginning.

I went on and on to a thousand pages of it.

In the meantime to naturally begin I commenced making portraits of anybody and anything. In making these portraits I naturally made a continuous present an including everything and a beginning again and again within a very small thing. That started me into composing anything into one thing. So then naturally it was natural that one thing an enormously long thing was not everything an enormously short thing was also not everything nor was it all of it a continuous present thing nor was it always and always beginning again. Naturally I would then begin again. I would begin again I would naturally begin. I did naturally begin. This brings me to a great deal that has been begun.

And after that what changes what changes after that, after that what changes and what changes after that and after that and what changes and after that and what changes after that.

The problem from this time on became more definite.

It was all so nearly alike it must be different and it is different, it is natural that if everything is used and there is a continuous present and a beginning again and again if it is all so alike it must be simply different and everything simply different was the natural way of creating it then.

In this natural way of creating it then that it was simply different everything being alike it was simply different, this kept on leading one to lists. Lists naturally for a while and by lists I mean a series. More and more in going back over what was done at this time I find that I naturally kept simply different as an intention. Whether there was or whether there was not a continuous present did not then any longer trouble me there was or there was not, using everything no longer troubled me if everything is alike using everything could no longer trouble me and beginning again and again could no longer trouble me because if lists were inevitable if series were inevitable and the whole of it was inevitable beginning again and again could not trouble me so then with nothing to trouble me I very completely began naturally since everything is alike making it as simply different naturally as simply different as possible. I began doing natural phenomena what I call natural phenomena and natural phenomena naturally everything being alike natural phenomena are making things be naturally simply different. This found its culmination later, in the beginning it began in a center confused with lists with series with geography with returning portraits and with particularly often four and three and often with five and four. It is easy to see that in the beginning such a conception as everything being naturally different would be very inarticulate and very slowly it began to emerge and take the form of anything, and then naturally if anything that is simply different is simply different what follows will follow.

So far then the progress of my conceptions was the natural progress entirely in accordance with my epoch as I am sure is to be quite easily realized if you think over the scene that was before us all from year to year.

As I said in the beginning, there is the long history of how every one ever acted or has felt and that nothing inside in them in all of them makes it connectedly different. By this I mean all this.

The only thing that is different from one time to another is what is seen and what is seen depends upon how everybody is doing every thing.

It is understood by this time that everything is the same except

composition and time, composition and the time of the composition
and the time in the composition.

Everything is the same except composition and as the composition is different and always going to be different everything is not
the same. So then I as a contemporary creating the composition in
the beginning was groping toward a continuous present, a using
everything a beginning again and again and then everything being
alike then everything very simply everything was naturally simply
different and so I as a contemporary was creating everything being
alike was creating everything naturally being naturally simply different, everything being alike. This then was the period that brings me
to the period of the beginning of 1914. Everything being alike
everything naturally would be simply different and war came and
everything being alike and everything being simply different brings
everything being simply different brings it to romanticism.

Romanticism is then when everything being alike everything is
naturally simply different, and romanticism.

Then for four years this was more and more different even though
this was, was everything alike. Everything alike naturally everything was simply different and this is and was romanticism and this
is and was war. Everything being alike everything naturally everything is different simply different naturally simply different.

And so there was the natural phenomena that was war, which had
been, before war came, several generations behind the contemporary
composition, because it became war and so completely needed to be
contemporary became completely contemporary and so created the
completed recognition of the contemporary composition. Every one
but one may say every one became consciously became aware of the
existence of the authenticity of the modern composition. This then
the contemporary recognition, because of the academic thing known
as war having been forced to become contemporary made every one
not only contemporary in act not only contemporary in thought
but contemporary in self-consciousness made every one contemporary with the modern composition. And so the art creation of the
contemporary composition which would have been outlawed norm-
ally outlawed several generations more behind even than war, war
having been brought so to speak up to date art so to speak was
allowed not completely to be up to date, but nearly up to date, in

other words we who created the expression of the modern composition were to be recognized before we were dead some of us even quite a long time before we were dead. And so war may be said to have advanced a general recognition of the expression of the contemporary composition by almost thirty years.

And now after that there is no more of that in other words there is peace and something comes then and it follows coming then.

And so now one finds oneself interesting oneself in an equilibration, that of course means words as well as things and distribution as well as between themselves between the words and themselves and the things and themselves, a distribution as distribution. This makes what follows what follows and now there is every reason why there should be an arrangement made. Distribution is interesting and equilibration is interesting when a continuous present and a beginning again and again and using everything and everything alike and everything naturally simply different has been done.

After all this, there is that, there has been that that there is a composition and that nothing changes except composition the composition and the time of and the time in the composition.

The time of the composition is a natural thing and the time in the composition is a natural thing it is a natural thing and it is a contemporary thing.

The time of the composition is the time of the composition. It has been at times a present thing it has been at times a past thing it has been at times a future thing it has been at times an endeavour at parts or all of these things. In my beginning it was a continuous present a beginning again and again and again and again, it was a series it was a list it was a similarity and everything different it was a distribution and an equilibration. That is all of the time some of the time of the composition.

Now there is still something else the time-sense in the composition. This is what is always a fear a doubt and a judgement and a conviction. The quality in the creation of expression the quality in a composition that makes it go dead just after it has been made is very troublesome.

The time in the composition is a thing that is very troublesome. If the time in the composition is very troublesome it is because there must even if there is no time at all in the composition there must be time in the composition which is in its quality of distribution and equilibration. In the beginning there was the time in the composition that naturally was in the composition but time in the composition comes now and this is what is now troubling every one the time in the composition is now a part of distribution and equilibration. In the beginning there was confusion there was a continuous present and later there was romanticism which was not a confusion but an extrication and now there is either succeeding or failing there mus be distribution and equilibration there must be time that is distributed and equilibrated. This is the thing that is at present the most troubling and if there is the time that is at present the most troublesome the time-sense that is at present the most troubling is the thing that makes the present the most troubling. There is at present there is distribution, by this I mean expression and time, and in this way at present composition is time that is the reason that at present the time-sense is troubling that is the reason why at present the time-sense in the composition is the composition that is making what there is in composition.

And afterwards.

Now that is all.

In 1934 Gertrude Stein was invited to the United States on a lecture tour. In October she and Alice Toklas left France by ship and lived in America until May 1935. During these months they toured the country and Gertrude Stein lectured at various universities and other institutions. The following five lectures, written in 1934, were originally published in a book called *Lectures in America* (Random House, New York, 1935), and included one other lecture: 'Pictures'.

2

WHAT IS ENGLISH LITERATURE

ONE cannot come back too often to the question what is knowledge and to the answer knowledge is what one knows.

What is English literature that is to say what do I know about it, that is to say what is it. What is English literature, by English literature I mean American literature too.

Knowledge is the thing you know and how can you know more than you do know. But I do know a great deal about literature about English literature about American literature.

There is a great deal of literature but not so much but that one can know it. And that is the pleasant the delightful the fascinating the peaceful thing about literature that there is a great deal of it but that one can all one's life know all of it. _1934_

One can know all of it and one can know it all one's life and at any moment in one's life one can know all of it. There it is right in you right inside you right behind you. Perhaps in front of you but this you do not know. To be sure it has been more or less truly said about English literature that until about fifty years ago a first class English writer appeared almost every ten years, since that time it has been necessary to very much help if not to replace it by American literature. And so I say one can have at any one moment in one's life all of English literature inside you and behind you and what you do not yet know is if it is in front of you, you do not know if there is going to be any more of it. However very likely there is, *

time sequence

there is at any rate going to be more American literature. Very likely.

At any rate it is a pleasure to know that there is so much English literature and that any any moment in one's life it is all inside you. At any rate it is all inside me. At any rate that is what I know. And now what is it that I do know about the English literature that is inside me, that is in me completely in me any moment of my living.

English literature has been with us a long time, quite a few hundreds of years, and during all that time it has had a great deal to do and also it has had a great deal to not do.

This as a whole thing could be told in a couple of sentences but it is necessary to make it a great deal longer. Anybody, even I, can understand that necessity.

What has it had to do and what has it had not to do and how does one know one from the other, know what it has had to do from what it has had not to do.

In English literature there is a great deal of poetry and there is a great deal of prose and sometimes the poetry and the prose has had something to do one with the other and very often not. Besides this there has been again and again in English literature the question can one serve god and mammon, and the further question if one can should one. But the important question can remain and does remain what is god and mammon insofar as it concerns English literature. Has this question to do with prose and with poetry as both or as either one. I wish to very largely go into this because in it is the whole description of the whole of English literature and with it and after it although not entirely out of it comes American literature.

But to begin at any beginning at least as a beginning is.

There are two ways of thinking about literature as the history of English literature, the literature as it is a history of it and the literature as it is a history of you. Any one of us and anyway those of us that have always had the habit of reading have our own history of English literature inside us, the history as by reading we have come to know it. Then there is the history as the English people came to do it. Every one's own history of English literature is their own until they tell it to somebody else as I am now telling mine. The history of English literature as it was written is English

Literature's History and that too most of any of us who have to
read do know.

There is then also the English people's history of their English
literature but then after all that is their affair as far as I am concerned, as I am deeply concerned, it is none of my business. GS

It is awfully important to know what is and what is not your
business. I know that one of the most profoundly exciting moments
of my life was when at about sixteen I suddenly concluded that I
would not make all knowledge my province.

And so my business is how English literature was made inside me
and how English literature was made inside itself.

What does literature do and how does it do it. And what does
English literature do and how does it do it. And what ways does it
use to do what it does do.

If it describes what it sees how does it do it. If it describes what it
knows how does it do it and what is the difference between what it
sees and what it knows. And then too there is what it feels and then
also there is what it hopes and wishes and then too there is what it
would see if it could see and then there is what it explains. To do any
or all of these things different things have to be done. Most of them
are being done all the time by literature. And how has English
literature done it.

As you come slowly to become acquainted with English Literature there are two things that at first do not interest you, explanations, that is one thing, and what it is that is felt, that is another
thing. Most people all their later lives like these things the best in
literature those of them who concern themselves with English
literature by reading it.

They like explanations and they like to know how they felt, how
they felt by the others feeling but anyway and principally how they
felt.

The thing that has made the glory of English literature is description simple concentrated description not of what happened nor
what is thought or what is dreamed but what exists and so makes
the life the island life the daily island life. It is natural that an island
life should be that. What could interest an island as much as the
daily the completely daily island life. And in the descriptions the
daily, the hourly descriptions of this island life as it exists and it does

exist it does really exist English literature has gone on and on from Chaucer until now. It does not go on so well now for several reasons, in the first place they are not so interested in their island life because they are in short they are not so interested. And in the next place it is not as much an island life.

But in the beginning and then for an endless long going on there was there is the steady description of the daily life the daily island life. That makes a large one third of the glory of English literature.

Then there is the poetry that too comes out of a daily island life, because granted that a daily island life is what it is and the English daily island life has always been completely what it is, it is necessary that poetry is not what they lose or what they feel but is the things with which they are shut up, that is shut in, in the daily the simply daily island life. And so the poetry of England is so much what it is, it is the poetry of the things with which any of them are shut in in their daily, completely daily island life. It makes very beautiful poetry because anything shut in with you can sing. There are the same things in other countries but they are not mentioned not mentioned in that simple intense certain way that makes English poetry what it is.

It is easy to know all that.

So that is something that has made several sides of English literature what it is.

And so to begin again to go on.

When anybody at any time comes to read English literature it is not at all necessary that they need to know that England is an island, what they need to know and that in reading any real piece of English literature they do know is that the thing written is completely contained within itself.

That is one of the reasons why in English literature there has been less question as to whether one should serve God and Mammon. There may inevitably be a question as to whether there is any god and mammon in respect to the inner existence of English literature. Because of there being really no vital question as to the God and Mammon and which is which in serving literature in English literature English literature has existed each piece of it inside itself in a perfectly extraordinary degree compared with other literatures that is other modern literatures and this gives it at once its complete solidity, its complete imagination, its complete existence.

⑦ When I was a child I was always completely fascinated by the sentence, he who runs may read. In England running and reading is one because any one can read, and since any one can read does it make any difference how or why they run. Not on an island. In fact insofar as they run they are there there where they read just as much as not.

I am trying not to give to myself but to you a feeling of the way English literature feels inside me.

I have been thinking a great deal as to the question of serving God or mammon, and that in the case of most peoples, certainly peoples who live on continents it is not possible to do both not in making literature, but in English literature generally in English literature the question does not arise, because since the life of the island the daily life of the island goes on so completely and daily and entirely, there is no possibility, granting that it is all included and it always is, there is no possibility that in satisfying anybody there is not the satisfying everybody and so there is no question as between serving God and Mammon. There is enormously such a question for anybody living on a continent and the reason why I will go into largely as English literature connects with American literature. Not that it really does connect and yet not that it really does not. But this again is another matter.

To begin again then not begin again but just to state how English literature has come to be, came to be in me. In short what English literature is.

As I say description of the complete the entirely complete daily island life has been England's glory. Think of Chaucer, think of Jane Austen, think of Anthony Trollope, and the life of the things shut up with that daily life is the poetry, think of all the lyrical poets, think what they say and what they have. They have shut in with them in their daily island life but completely shut in with them all the things that just in enumeration make poetry, and they can and do enumerate and they can and do make poetry, this enumeration. That is all one side of English literature and indeed anybody knows, where it grows, the daily life the complete daily life and the things shut in with that complete daily life.

The things being shut in are free and that makes more poetry so very much more poetry. It is very easy to understand that there has been so much poetry written in England.

On a continent even in small countries on a continent, the daily life is of course a daily life but it is not held in within as it is on an island and that makes an enormous difference, and I am quite certain that even if you do not see it as the same anybody does see that this if it is the truth is the truth. If it is the truth about English literature it is the truth about English literature.

It is a comparatively early thing to know English literature as English literature to those of us who read as naturally as we read that is as we run.

It begins if it begins it begins with Lamb's tales of Shakespeare. And how are they the island daily life the English island daily life. But they are. And they are because of their poetry, and the poetry is because of the reality of all the life that is shut in, so completely sweetly, so delicately really shut in with their daily life.

I remember well I cannot say I do remember but I do feel and I did feel as if I did feel and did remember and do remember this.

And in the poetry of that time in their poetry is there any question of the difference in literature between its serving god and mammon.

Yes perhaps a little somewhat of that time. They knew their style knew that there were two styles. There was a style that those who run may read and there was a style too a style that those who read do not run. They need not run because there is nothing to run with or from.

That is the difference between serving god and serving mammon, and the period after the Chaucer time to the Pope Gibbon Johnson time was such a time. And how does one, how does one not run.

As I talk of serving god and mammon I do not of course mean religion in any sense excepting the need to complete that which is trying to fill itself up inside any one. And this may be part of the same inside in one or it may not. If it is then it is a complete daily life, if it is not then it is not.

As I say in that period from Chaucer to Pope Gibbon and John-son and Swift, a great many things filled up everybody that had to be filled, of course it is only those who have an active need to be completely completed who have all this as a bother.

As I say during this long period, the daily island life was there completely literally and daily and simply there, the poetry of the things shut in with that daily life were there but other things were there too and these other things were due to other origins and all these origins at that time were just sufficiently disturbing to make it possible for style to know that there is a serving god a serving mammon for those who write as they write. What else can they do.

During this long period and it was a long period, a very strongly long period a great many things happened in England and as they happened inside England they to a certain extent destroyed or at least confused the daily island life.

When the confusion comes to an island from the outside it is soon over and if not over then absorbed, that is what happened in the beginning of this period the norman conquest but when the confusion comes from the inside then it is a very confused confusion because it is a confusion inside the daily island life. This is what happened in all the latter part of this long period the English civil wars the period from Chaucer to Swift Gibbon Pope and Johnson and then again it settled down to being an island daily life only there were things left over from the late confusion and that was then the eighteenth century English literature and then there was the nineteenth century and then there was not any more a confusion but a complete settling in into the daily island life. What was outside was outside and what was inside was inside, and how could there be a question of god and mammon, when what is inside is inside and what is outside is outside there can be no confusing god and mammon.

Perhaps and perhaps not but that is at any rate one way in which living can be lived, literature can be made.

So the history of English literature is beginning to be clear, the history of English literature. Of course if the English people had not been what they were they would not have made out of the daily island life the literature they did make. That is true enough. Anything is true enough. But that certainly is.

The thing that happened before Chaucer, the norman conquest coming as it did from the outside was one of those things which as I say do not produce confusion. They upset things for a while but they do not confuse things, a very different matter. And so when all that was over the thing English literature had still to do was to describe the daily island life and Chaucer did it, and the making of poetry of the things shut in with that daily island life and Chaucer certainly did it. Anybody that knows can certainly remember that. But and that must not be forgotten, words were in that daily island life which had not been there before and these words although they did not make for confusion did make for separation.

This separation is important in making literature, because there are so many ways for one to feel oneself and every new way helps, and a separating way may help a great deal, indeed it may, it may, it may help very much. And this did.

As you may or may not know I read a great deal of Elizabethan prose and poetry and in this period I felt the culmination of all of this. There was no confusion but there still was left over separation and this left over separation made a division in the writer of writing. He knew that there were two things to do and which of the things did he have to do. There was a choice at that time a choice as to how a writer should write. And this choice when there is a choice a writer can and does feel as a choice between serving god and mammon. This choice has nothing to do with religion, it has nothing to do with success. It has to do with something different than that, it has to do with completion.

How is anything completed. And if it is not might it, and is there a choice.

In the whole of the Elizabethan literature one feels this something.

There is no confusion but there is a separation and to any one doing it that is writing, I am speaking of the Elizabethans to themselves inside them, there was this bother.

And it was natural that there should be this bother. God and Mammon, god and mammon, it was left over and it was there and in all the Elizabethans it was there this bother, this choice, in every minute in their writing. There was the daily island life and it made poetry and it made prose but also there was this separation and it made poetry and it made prose but the choice the choice was the thing. In a true daily island life a choice is not the thing. It was the outside separation that had come to be an inside separation that made this thing. Think about it in any Elizabethan, any Elizabethan writing, in any Elizabethan who was writing.

And words had everything to do with it.

And now perhaps I had better explain a little more clearly what I mean by serving god and mammon in literature that is as a writer making literature.

When I say god and mammon concerning the writer writing, I mean that any one can use words to say something. And in using these words to say what he has to say he may use those words directly or indirectly. If he uses these words indirectly he says what he intends to have heard by somebody who is to hear and in so doing inevitably he has to serve mammon. Mammon may be a success, mammon may be an effort he is to produce, mammon may be a pleasure he has from hearing what he himself has done, mammon may be his way of explaining, mammon may be a laziness that needs nothing but going on, in short mammon may be anything that is done indirectly. Now serving god for a writer who is writing is writing anything directly, it makes no difference what it is but it must be direct, the relation between the thing done and the doer must be direct. In this way there is completion and the essence of the completed thing is completion. I have had a very great deal to say about this in the life of Henry James[1] in my *Four In America* and I am not going to say any more about this now. But slowly you will see what I mean. If not why not.

But to return to English literature.

English literature when it is directly and completely describing the daily island life beginning with Chaucer and going on to now did have this complete quality of completeness. The lyric poets of England who described the things that are shut in with that daily island life also had this directness of completion.

But and this is very important during just before and the Elizabethan period there was another bother there was separation, separation between completion and incompletion and everybody dimly knew something of such a thing inside them.

If you like it was because the two languages were just coming to be one it was if you like because, although they were living the daily

1. See p. 291.

island life, they still, a considerable part of them, still had a memory of not having been living a daily island life. And this made a strange bother that any one can feel in the writing, the writing of any one writing during all that time. And that is a natural enough thing.

It is in all the prose and all the poetry of that long period. It all moves so much, and that is its most characteristic quality it all moves so much, it moves up and down and forward and back and right and left and around and around. And that is what makes it so exciting. And also what makes it inside itself so separating.

If you think in detail of the writing of any one writing in that long period you will know what I mean. Think of the one you know the best and you will see what I mean. There was no confusion, as I say the trouble had come from the outside and had been absorbed in the inside and in the process of absorption as there is in any healthy digestion there was no confusion but inevitably in concluding digestion there was separation.

And this is very much to be seen in the writing and there was very much writing, in that period. It was natural that there would be a great deal of writing because liveliness and choice inevitably produces a great deal of writing.

There was then at this period constant choice constant decision and the words have the liveliness of being constantly chosen.

That is what makes that the literature that it is.

And as there was all during that period the necessity of choice and the liveliness of choosing there was also all through that period the necessity of completing. Because why choose if there is not to be completion. And so they knew they quite knew the difference between being serving god and serving mammon, the difference between direct and indirect, the difference between separation and completion. They knew. And they knew it as they knew it. That too is a very real thing. And so although all through that period there was the daily island life, they were digesting there being that and it not always having been.

And that made for the writing that was being done then by everybody writing.

Then came the period after a period when they did not write so very much, because first it was all confused the disturbing of the daily island life having come from within, English Civil War, it was confused, and then we come to the beginning when everything was clear again and the daily island life was being lived with so much clarity that there could be nothing but the expression of that being that thing. That was the period that made Swift and Gibbon and Pope and Johnson and they had no longer to choose their words they could have all the pleasure in their use. And they did. No one ever enjoyed the use of what they had more than they did. There was no separation anywhere, the completeness was in the use.

As one says this one feels that.

As I say the pleasure of a literature is having it all inside you. It is the one thing that one can have all inside one.

This makes literature words whether you choose them whether you use them, whether they are there whether or not you use them and whether they are no longer there even when you are still going on using them. And in this way a century is a century. One century has words, another century chooses words, another century uses words and then another century using the words no longer has them.

All this as you have it inside you settles something it settles what you have when you write anything, it settles what you complete if you complete anything, it settles whether you address something as you express anything. In short it settles what you do as you proceed to write which you certainly do, that is which I certainly do.

As I say then each century has its way and by century of course one may mean a longer or shorter time but generally speaking a century is generally and almost always somewhere about a hundred years.

And so although and all through there was in England in English literature the complete and direct and simple and real description of their daily life, their daily life as they lived it every day on their island and which made their real solid body of writing and there was always too the description which made their lyric poetry the description of all the daily life of everything that was shut in inside their daily living, of all the things that grew and flew and were there to be in their daily living, in each century because of the outside coming to penetrate inside and then having become inside became inside, or because the inside caused confusion in the inside or because the decision of inside made all the inside as settled as if there never had been an outside or again later and this was in the nineteenth century when the inside had become so solidly inside that all the outside could be outside and still the inside was all inside, in each generation it effected writing because after all the way you write has everything to do with where you are insofar as you are anywhere, and of course and inevitably you are somewhere.

So once again all English literature being all inside you or inside me let me see how each century did as they were to see, that is as they were to say.

It is nice thinking how different each century is and the reason why. It is also nice to think about how differently the words sound one next to each other in each century and the reason why.

It is nice to feel the sound as the words next each other sound so differently.

I have always been very fond of the books that have little quotations at the head of each chapter. I like it particularly when the quotations are very varied and many of them of more or less important writers. I like it too sometimes when the quotations are only from one or two writers. It brings out with great clearness the way words sound next to each other even the same words when the century is different and the writer is different. I am very fond in that way of coming to feel how completely what is written comes to say what it does.

But to begin again as to what the different centuries do and how they do it and familiar as it is because it all is so familiar, it is all different. English literature then is very solid, and its reality is real and its poetry very poetry. And it did change in each century.

I am not very good at dates but there were generally speaking five centuries and now we are in the twentieth century which makes a sixth century and for this we go to America. And so to begin now. That is to begin again with any of them any of the five of them of English literature.

I wish I could make it as real to you the difference in which words phrases and then the gradual changes in each century were and as I realize them. I wish I could. I really wish I could. Because if I could well after that words and the way they say that for which they use them would make no difference or not any difference or all the difference.

You do remember Chaucer, even if you have not read him you do remember not how it looks but how it sounds, how simply it sounds as it sounds. That is as I say because the words were there. They had not yet to be chosen, they had only as yet to be there just there.

That makes a sound that gently sings that gently sounds but sounds as sounds. It sounds as sounds of course as words but it sounds as sounds. It sounds as sounds that is to say as birds as well as words. And that is because the words are there, they are not chosen as words, they are already there. That is the way Chaucer sounds.

And then comes the long period. In that long period there were so many words that were chosen. Everybody was busy choosing words. In the poetry of that long period as well as in the prose everybody was livelily busy choosing words. And as the words were chosen, the sounds were very varied. And that is natural because each one liked what they liked. They did not care so much about what they said although they knew that what they said meant a great deal but they liked the words, and one word and another word next to the other word was always being chosen. Think well of the English literature of the sixteenth century and see how they chose the words, they chose them with so much choice that everything made the song they chose to sing. It was no longer just a song it was a song of words that were chosen to make a song that would sound like the words they were to sing. There is no use giving examples because it is true of everything that was written then. As they chose so early and often so late and often as they were everlastingly choosing and choosing was a lively occupation you have an infinite variety of length and shortness of words chosen of vowels and consonants of words chosen and and that is the important thing it was the specific word next to the specific word next it chosen to be next it that was the important thing. That made the glory that culminated in what is called Elizabethan. Just have it in your head and then go and look at it and you will have to see what I mean. There was no confusion then, things could be long that is words next to each other could be long and go on and very often they were short the words next to each other and they did go on but they were short, but each one was as it was chosen. There was no losing choosing in what they were saying. Never no never.

Confusion comes when they confuse what they are saying with the words they are choosing. And they knew. They knew, and a little one sees it coming even in the end of Shakespeare one sees it coming a little that there is confusion. This confusion comes when there is a giving up choosing, words next to each other are no longer so strictly chosen because there is intention to say what they are saying more importantly than completely choosing the words next each other which are to be chosen.

When that commences then there is confusion.

As I said at the end of the long period before the eighteenth century there was confusion, there was inside confusion. Something that had meant everything meant something but it no longer meant something in meaning everything and they all began to think what they wanted to say and how they wanted to say it.

The minute they all begin to think what they want to say and how they want to say it they no longer choose. And when they no longer choose then as far as writing goes they are no longer serving god they are serving mammon. No matter what it is or how fine it is or how religious it is the thing they want to say.

What is the use unless everybody knows what I want to say and what is the use if everybody does want to know everything that I want to say.

Well anyway at the end of the great epoch they began to think more of what they wanted to say as well as how they wanted to say it. Perhaps that should be turned around, they began to think more of how they wanted to say what they had come to decide to say than they did of choosing words to say what they chose the words to say the words next to each other to say.

That is pretty nearly what I do want to say.

And so we come to the confusion of which I spoke and which shows in Milton and lasted pretty well to Pope and Gibbon and Swift and Johnson.

Then as I say the confusion cleared. Nobody was any longer really interested in what anybody else was saying. They no longer chose the words to be one next to each other but they did choose and clearly chose all the words that were to go together.

By this time there was no confusion and no interest in what there was to say nor how they were to say it. There was no confusion. There was choosing but there was the choosing of a completed thing and so as there was no completing it as being chosen being in as much as it was there to choose being already a completed thing, they naturally had no separation inside in them, nothing was separated from anything. That made it all come as clearly as it came that made it all as completed as it was, that made it a whole thing chosen, and so the words were not next to each other but all the words as they followed each other were all together.

And that was all that.

If you think of the eighteenth century in English literature you will see how clear it was. But never forget that always it was an island life they lived and as they lived that daily island life they described daily that daily island life.

They wrote very much.

And now slowly there was coming something. The daily island life was still the daily island life, it would be more than ever that thing, because slowly a complete thing was nothing anybody was interested in choosing, because all they all lived as they only could live the daily island life and they came to own everything, and so although they brought nothing that they owned to be within the island life, as they owned everything outside and brought none of this inside they naturally were no longer interested in choosing complete things. That was the beginning of the nineteenth century.

Anybody can understand how natural this is.

If you live a daily island life and live it every day and own everything or enough to call it everything outside the island you are naturally not interested in completion, but you are naturally interested in telling about how you own everything. But naturally more completely are you interested in describing the daily island life, because more completely as you are describing the daily island life the more steadily and firmly are you owning everything you own which being practically everything could be called anything and everything.

Oh yes you do see.

You do see that.

And what has it to do with writing.

It has a great deal to do with writing.

And in this century in this nineteenth century anything could be a bother and was.

So now you see that up to the nineteenth century a number of things had been and gone and each time something had been and gone there had been a great deal of writing. That is again inevitable in a daily island life, if they write at all they write a great deal. Either nothing is worth writing about or everything is worth writing about. That anybody can understand.

And the daily life had always been worth writing about and so they always wrote a great deal. What else could they do. Granted that they lived this daily island life and realized it every day and were shut in every day with all of that daily island life every day what could they do but say it every day and as they said it every day they wrote it every day practically every day.

There had then as everybody knows been a great deal of English writing a great great deal of English writing, and it was poetry and it was prose.

The use of words whether the words were there as in Chaucer, whether they were livelily chosen to be next to each other one next to the other as in the long period after, and there were so many words chosen during that long period so many words chosen to be next to each other that there never can be a greater pleasure.

At the end of that long period when the words chosen to be next to each other gradually became troubled by the intention of how something was to be said rather than something that was something other than that something and how was the way that they had decided it should be said. That was the period of fashion and confusion the period of the restoration.

And then came the time after when everything was so complete that choosing or not choosing was not really any bother. They knew what to do because it was all so well done.

And then came the wars of Napoleon and England then came to own everything. And what happened.

As I say what happened was that the daily island life was more a daily life than ever. If it had not been it would have been lost in their owning everything and if it had been lost in their owning everything they would naturally have then ceased to own everything. Anybody can understand that.

They needed to be within completely within their daily island life in order to own everything outside as they were then really owning everything.

And what happened, what happened to their writing. Oh that is very interesting. It is interesting because it is very important about serving god and mammon, it is interesting because of what it did to words and phrases. It is interesting because we are still in the shadow of this thing. It is interesting.

In the first place did it change quickly.

And there is something you must always remember about wars that is about catastrophes, they make a change which is a change which is about to be a change go faster as much faster as a war can go, and even a slow war a slow catastrophe goes quite fast.

To be sure anything goes quite fast, that is changes quite fast. It is always an astonishment to me even in country family lives how much has changed how much a family life has changed, how completely a family life has changed say in five years.

This is always true but a catastrophe makes one say so more.

At any rate it was true although they did not in their daily life say that was true it was true in the life of English Literature.

After all it has not lasted so very long English literature and it has passed through so very much. And now came the nineteenth century and a great many things were gone.

That the words were there by themselves simply was gone. That the words were livelily chosen to be next one to the other was gone.

That the confusion of how and what was the way that any one at that time had to find was the way to say what they had to say was gone.

And the clarity of something having completion that too was gone completely gone.

And now what had they to do and how did they do it.

They were living their daily life and they owned everything, everything that existed anywhere outside.

And everybody wrote everybody always had written and how did they do it.

As I say we are still in the shadow of it.

One of the first things to notice is that the time now had come when they began to explain.

Before that in all the periods before things had been said been known been described been sung about, been fought about been destroyed been denied been imprisoned been lost but never been explained.

So then they began to explain. And we may say that they have been explaining ever since.

And as I say we are still in the shadow of it.

And what did they explain and why and what did it do to words and phrases.

And what did they do beside and what did living their island life inside and owning everything outside have to do with it.

There is explanation, the nineteenth century discovered explanation and what is the relation between explanation and sentimental emotion, such as the nineteenth century wrote. Is there any. Yes there is. There is a very distinct connection.

Of course I have read always read did nothing but read everything that was ever written in the nineteenth century. That is natural enough since I was born in the nineteenth century. What else could I do but read everything there was to read that was or had been written in the nineteenth century.

I had read almost read everything that was written in English in the eighteenth century, poetry prose and history, philosophy memoirs and novels, very long novels and I have read them all, I have read practically read and I was always reading, everything that was written in English in the eighteenth century. Of the long period that went before from Chaucer to the eighteenth century I read a good deal quite a good deal but of course not all, not all as I read what was written in the eighteenth century. In the nineteenth century I read more I read more than all and by that I mean that I read a great deal written in the nineteenth century that was just anybody's writing. And so it is easy to see that I having read so much that was written have a liking for reading writing. If not why not. But there is no if not, I do like reading writing. Now what did I slowly or not at all or very often or very well find out.

I have already told about some of the things I have found out and now to tell about what I more than found out what I knew every day as every day I read pretty nearly anything every day. And so to go on with explanation and how it came about and sentimental emotion and how it came about.

Some day I would like to be able to realize everything I feel about sentimental writing and what it is to each one who hears or writes or reads it. But first everything to tell everything about how differently the nineteenth century explained anything from the other times and what makes English nineteenth century literature what it is.

In the first place remember, I remember that words and then choice or not choice, knowing what there is to say or saying what they do say has been changing.

In the nineteenth century what they thought was not what they said but they said what they thought and they were thinking about what they thought.

This was different than the time that went before.

And now how do phrases come to be phrases and not sentences, that is the thing to know. Because in the nineteenth century it does. And that makes everything that makes the nineteenth century. And in order to understand, it must be understood that explaining was invented, naturally invented by those living a daily island life and owning everything else outside. They owned everything inside of course but that they had always done, but now they owned everything outside and that reinforced their owning everything inside, and that was as it was only more so but as they owned everything outside, outside and inside had to be told something about all this owning, otherwise they might not remember all this owning and so there was invented explaining and that made nineteenth century English literature what it is. And with explaining went emotional sentimental feeling because of course it had to be explained all the owning had to be told about its being owned about its owning and anybody can see that if island daily life were to continue its daily existing there must be emotional sentimental feeling.

To like to tell it like that again, and to remember all the books that were written and read, read by any one read by me, oh yes read, and still read.

As I say in the nineteenth century what they thought was not what they said, but and this may sound like the same thing only it is not, they said what they thought and they were thinking about what they thought. This made the nineteenth century what it was.

If you live a daily life and it is all yours, and you come to own everything outside your daily life beside and it is all yours, you naturally begin to explain. You naturally continue describing your daily life which is all yours, and you naturally begin to explain how you own everything beside. You naturally begin to explain that to yourself and you also naturally begin to explain it to those living your daily life who own it with you, everything outside, and you naturally explain it in a kind of a way to some of those whom you own. All this leads you to that what you think is not what you say but you say what you think and you are thinking about what you think. Do you understand, if not it is perhaps because after all you have not read all English nineteenth century literature, but perhaps you have and if you have then you do understand. You must also then understand what explaining is and how it came to be.

Perhaps we are still under its shadow a little bit.

I am thinking of all the nineteenth century English literature that I have always read. There is so much of it and I have read so much of it and I have read it so often and I have so read it over and over again. And I am still reading it. I read it in long pieces and little pieces, it is a natural thing to do because after all when one picks up a book to read and if you read a great deal as I read a great deal books every day and many books every week of course inevitably I read many books I have read, and as I have read everything written in the nineteenth century, important unimportant, prose, poetry, history, science and some essays why naturally I read it again. What else can I do.

And so I know what it is.

That is natural enough.

What is it.

I have already said what it is and I think that is what it is. And in its being that, it is necessary that it was written in the way it was.

As I said the eighteenth century was clear and so there was a choice and the choice was a completed thing and what is a completed thing. A sentence is a completed thing and so the eighteenth century chose the completed sentence as a completed thing. Now what did the nineteenth century do.

As I explained it did not choose a completed thing. Anybody can understand that if you explain and the thing to be explained is that you leading your daily inside life own everything outside, it is not possible to choose a completed sentence a completed thing. That manifestly is not possible because if you have to explain the inside to the inside and the owning of the outside to the inside that has to be explained to the inside life and and the owning of the outside has to be explained to the outside it absolutely is not possible that it is to be done in completed sentences. Anybody can see that, anybody can. And so then how did the nineteenth century write.

They did not write in words that were simply words as Chaucer did. That would not help explain anything, it was too simple a thing to need or to be employed to make explaining. They did not choose words to be next to each other and to be lively just in being that in being next to each other because anything as lively as that could not own everything. Anybody can understand that. And as I have already said they could not content themselves with a completed thing that is choosing a whole sentence, because if a thing is a completed thing then it does not need explanation.

So what did they do and gradually if you think how from the eighteenth century to the nineteenth century the language gradually changed you will see that it proceeded to live by phrases, words no longer lived, sentences and paragraphs were divisions because they always are but they did not mean particularly much, but phrases became the thing. Think of the English writing in the height of the nineteenth century and you will see that it is so.

They thought about what they were thinking and if you think about what you are thinking you are bound to think about it in phrases, because if you think about what you are thinking you are not thinking about a whole thing. If you are explaining the same thing is true, you cannot explain a whole thing because if it is a whole thing it does not need explaining, it merely needs stating. And then the emotional sentiment that any one living their daily living and owning everything outside needs to express is again something that can only be expressed by phrases, neither by words nor by sentences. Anybody ought to be able to realize this thing.

I do really definitely know that although some may think there are some exceptions there were really not except in the beginning when the eighteenth century was still lingering or toward the end when the twentieth century was beginning. There were really no exceptions.

Think really think about any big piece or any little piece of nineteenth century writing and you will see that it is true that it exists by its phrases. Its poetry does as well as its prose. Compare Jane Austen with Anthony Trollope and you will see what I mean and how the volume of the phrasing gradually grew and when you read Dickens, compare it with and they are both sentimental with Clarissa Harlowe and you will see what I mean. One lives by its whole the eighteenth-century thing and the nineteenth-century thing lives by its parts. You can see what I mean that this connects itself with explaining. The same thing is true with nineteenth-century poetry. The lake poets had other ideas, they felt that it was wrong to live by parts of a whole and they tried and they tried they wanted to serve god not mammon, but they too inevitably as they wrote longer and longer live by parts of the whole, because after all mammon and god were interchangeable since in the nineteenth century England lived its daily island life and owned everything outside. Oh yes you do see this. And so it goes on and on and think of Tennyson. There you completely see what I mean. And now we come to a new thing. I hope you thoroughly understand that the nineteenth century wrote by its phrases and it wrote a great great great deal and I have read it all and so have a good many others. It is a soothing thing to rest upon, it is more soothing than other things in spite of the fact that a great many people who wrote it did not like it as they knew they wrote. But it is a soothing thing to write phrases, the sentiment of phrases is a soothing thing and so we all of us always like reading nineteenth-century writing, those of us who like to feel soothed by something that touches feeling.

Do you feel the nineteenth-century writing as it is. I hope so. I do.

And toward the end of the nineteenth century there was bound to be a change because after all nothing goes on longer than it can.

And this quite naturally could not go on any longer than it could any more than anything else did. And this is where it connects on with American literature.

American literature all the nineteenth century went on by itself and although it might seem to have been doing the same thing as

English literature it really was not and it really was not for an excellent reason it was not leading a daily island life. Not at all nothing could be more completely not a daily island life than the life the daily life of any American. It was so completely not a daily island life that one may well say that it was not a daily life at all.

That is fundamental that is what the American writing inevitably is, it is not a daily life at all.

But before going on with this at all I am going on with English literature and although nothing much happened in the way of changes something did happen and this does help to connect with American writing.

As the time went on to the end of the nineteenth century and Victoria was over and the Boer war it began to be a little different in England. The daily island life was less daily and the owning everything outside was less owning, and, and this should be remembered, there were a great many writing but the writing was not so good. I remember very well, I was quite young then being very worried about England because there had been, one might quite say Kipling was the last one no really first class writing. The other writing of that period was the second class writing of the last generation, the young generation were doing the second class writing of the past generation, Wells, Galsworthy, Bennett, etc. And since then it has not changed.

But before this happened there was something else that connected itself with what was to be American, American writing, one might say Meredith, Swinburne, etc. and this had to do with the fact that the daily living was ceasing to be quite so daily and besides that they were beginning not to know everything about owning everything that was existing outside of them outside of their daily living. And this had to do with phrasing.

Slowly the phrasing, you see it in Browning you see it in Swinburne and in Meredith and its culmination was in Henry James who being American knew what he was doing, it is to be seen that even phrases were no longer necessary to make emotion emotion to make explaining explaining.

As I say as daily living was no longer being so positively lived every day and they were not all of them so certainly owning everything outside them, explaining and expressing their feeling was not

any longer an inevitable thing and so the phrase no longer sufficiently held what a phrase had to hold and they no longer said what
they thought and they were beginning not to think about what they
thought.

This brought about something that made neither words exist for
themselves, nor sentences, nor choosing, it created the need of
paragraphing, and the whole paragraph having been being made
the whole paragraph had rising from it off of it its meaning.

If you think of the writers I have mentioned you will see what I
mean.

As I say Henry James being an American knew best what he was
doing when he did this thing.

Do you quite clearly see that now there has commenced really
commenced paragraphing.

I once said in *How To Write* a book I wrote about Sentences and
Paragraphs, that paragraphs were emotional and sentences were not.
Paragraphs are emotional not because they express an emotion but
because they register or limit an emotion. Compare paragraphs with
sentences any paragraph or any sentence and you will see what I mean.

Paragraphs then having in them the quality of registering as well
as limiting an emotion were the natural expression of the end of the
nineteenth century of English literature. The daily island life was
not sufficient any more as limiting the daily life of the English, and
the owning everything outside was no longer actual or certain and
so it was necessary that these things should be replaced by something and they were replaced by the paragraph. Do you quite see
what I mean. I know quite completely what I mean. Think of
Browning Meredith and Henry James and Swinburne and you will
see what I mean. The phrases the emotion of phrases, the explaining
in phrases that made the whole nineteenth century adequately felt
and seen no longer sufficed to satisfy what anybody could mean.
And so they needed a paragraph. A phrase no longer soothed,
suggested or convinced, they needed a whole paragraph. And so
slowly the paragraph came to be the thing, neither the words of the
earlier period, the sentence of the eighteenth century, the phrases
of the nineteenth century, but the paragraphs of the twentieth
century, and, it is true, the English have not gone on with this thing
but we have we in American literature. In English literature they

just went back to the nineteenth century and made it a little weaker, and that was because well because they were a little weaker. What else can I say.

And so we come to American literature and why they went on and we are the twentieth century literature.

I will not tell a great deal about what I will tell just a little about that.

I said I certainly have said that daily life was not the daily life in America. If you think of the difference between England and America you will understand it.

In England the daily island life was the daily life and it was solidly that daily life and they generally always simply relied on it. They relied on it so completely that they did not describe it they just had it and told it. Just like that. And then they had poetry, because everything was shut in there with them and these things birds beasts woods flowers, roses, violets and fishes were all there and as they were all there just telling that they were all there made poetry for any one. And there was a great deal of poetry there. That was English literature and it has lasted for some five hundred years or more and there is a great deal of it. All this now has been everything.

In America as I was saying the daily everything was not the daily living and generally speaking there is not a daily everything. They do not live every day. And as they do not live every day they do not have the daily living and so they do not have this as something that they are telling.

To be sure a number of them who have learned to write by reading and naturally they have learned to write by reading what English literature has been telling, a number of them tried to turn it into a telling of daily living daily American living but these even these although they did it as much as they could did not really succeed in doing it because it is not an American thing, to tell a daily living, as in America there is not any really not any daily daily living. So of course it is not to be told.

And now think how American literature tells something. It tells something because that anything is not connected with what would be daily living if they had it.

This is quite definitely not the same not the same as in English writing.

It has often been known that American literature in a kind of a way is more connected with English Elizabethan than with later and that if you remember was at a time when words were chosen to be next one to the other and because in a kind of a way at that time it was a bother to feel inside one that one was a writer because things were separated away one thing from another thing, one way of choosing anything from another way of choosing.

Now all this is sufficiently different from what is American but still it has something to do with it.

What there is to say is this.

Think about all persistent American writing. There is inside it as separation, a separation from what is chosen to what is that from which it has been chosen.

Think of them, from Washington Irving, Emerson, Hawthorne, Walt Whitman, Henry James. They knew that there is a separation a quite separation between what is chosen and from what there is the choosing. You do see that.

This makes what American literature is, something that in its way is quite alone. As it has to be, because in its choosing it has to be, that it has not to be, it has to be without any connection with that from which it is choosing.

Now you can see how different this is from English writing, which almost completely makes that from which it is chosen, indeed it makes it so completely that there is no choice there does not have to be any choosing.

You do see what I say.

And so, and this is the thing to know, American literature was ready to go on, because where English literature had ceased to be because it had no further to go, American literature had always had it as the way to go.

You understand that I tell you so. And it is so, as you can easily see, if you see what American literature always really has been and has had to be.

To go back to where Henry James, and Browning, and Swinburne and Meredith had come.

I told you they had come where they needed a whole paragraph to give off something that did come. And this they all did.

The others all stayed where they were, it was where they had come but Henry James knew he was on his way. That is because this did connect with the American way. And so although they did in a way the same thing, his had a future feeling and theirs an ending. It is very interesting.

And now do you see what I mean.

English literature then had a need to be what it had become. Browning Swinburne Meredith were no longer able to go on, they had come where they had come, because although island daily living was still island daily living every one could know that this was not what it was to be and if it was not to be this with all the outside belonging to it what was it to be. They Swinburne Browning and Meredith were giving the last extension, they were needing a whole paragraph to make it something that they could mention and in doing so the paragraph no longer said what all English literature had always said that alive or dead the daily life the daily island life was always led.

This is where they were.

And so as I say since everything one cannot say had gone away, but was no longer there to stay, it was necessary to have a whole paragraph to hold anything there at all. And so that ended that.

In the meantime Henry James went on. He too needed the whole paragraph because he too was just there, but, and that is the thing to notice, his whole paragraph was detached what it said from what it did, what it was from what it held, and over it all something floated not floated away but just floated, floated up there. You can see how that was not true of Swinburne and Browning and Meredith but that it was true of Henry James.

And so this makes it that Henry James just went on doing what American literature had always done, the form was always the form of the contemporary English one, but the disembodied way of disconnecting something from anything and anything from something was the American one. The way it had of often all never having any daily living was an American one.

Some say that it is repression but no it is not repression it is a lack of connection, of there being no connection with living and daily living because there is none, that makes American writing what it always has been and what it will continue to become.

And so there we are.

And now, the paragraph having been completely become, it was a moment when I came and I had to do more with the paragraph than ever had been done. So I thought I did. And then I went on to what was the American thing the disconnection and I kept breaking the paragraph down, and everything down to commence again with not connecting with the daily anything and yet to really choose something. But this is another story and I have told enough.

And now about serving god and mammon. The writer is to serve god or mammon by writing the way it has been written or by writing the way it is being written that is to say the way the writing is writing. That is for writing the difference between serving god and mammon. If you write the way it has already been written the way writing has already been written then you are serving mammon, because you are living by something some one has already been earning or has earned. If you write as you are to be writing then you are serving as a writer god because you are not earning anything. If anything is to be earned you will not know what earning is therefore you are serving god. But really there is no choice. Nobody chooses. What you do you do even if you do not yield to a temptation. After all a temptation is not very tempting. So anyway you will earn nothing. And so this is the history of English literature of all the writing written in English as I understand it.

3

PLAYS

IN a book I wrote called *How To Write* I made a discovery which I considered fundamental, that sentences are not emotional and that paragraphs are. I found out about language that paragraphs are emotional and sentences are not and I found out something else about it. I found out that this difference was not a contradiction but a combination and that this combination causes one to think endlessly about sentences and paragraphs because the emotional paragraphs are made up of unemotional sentences.

I found out a fundamental thing about plays. The thing I found out about plays was too a combination and not a contradiction and it was something that makes one think endlessly about plays.

That something is this.

The thing that is fundamental about plays is that the scene as depicted on the stage is more often than not one might say it is almost always in syncopated time in relation to the emotion of anybody in the audience.

What this says is this.

Your sensation as one in the audience in relation to the play played before you your sensation I say your emotion concerning that play is always either behind or ahead of the play at which you are looking and to which you are listening. So your emotion as a member of the audience is never going on at the same time as the action of the play.

This thing the fact that your emotional time as an audience is not the same as the emotional time of the play is what makes one endlessly troubled about a play, because not only is there a thing to know as to why this is so but also there is a thing to know why perhaps it does not need to be so.

This is a thing to know and knowledge as anybody can know is a thing to get by getting.

And so I will try to tell you what I had to get and what perhaps

I have gotten in plays and to do so I will tell you all that I have ever felt about plays or about any play.

Plays are either read or heard or seen.

And there then comes the question which comes first and which is first, reading or hearing or seeing a play.

I ask you.

What is knowledge. Of course knowledge is what you know and what you know is what you do know.

What do I know about plays.

In order to know one must always go back.

What was the first play I saw and was I then already bothered bothered about the different tempo there is in the play and in yourself and your emotion in having the play go on in front of you. I think I may say I may say I know that I was already troubled by this in that my first experience at a play. The thing seen and the emotion did not go on together.

This that the thing seen and the thing felt about the thing seen not going on at the same tempo is what makes the being at the theatre something that makes anybody nervous.

The jazz bands made of this thing, the thing that makes you nervous at the theatre, they made of this thing an end in itself. They made of this different tempo a something that was nothing but a difference in tempo between anybody and everybody including all those doing it and all those hearing and seeing it. In the theatre of course this difference in tempo is less violent but still it is there and it does make anybody nervous.

In the first place at the theatre there is the curtain and the curtain already makes one feel that one is not going to have the same tempo as the thing that is there behind the curtain. The emotion of you on one side of the curtain and what is on the other side of the curtain are not going to be going on together. One will always be behind or in front of the other.

Then also beside the curtain there is the audience and the fact that they are or will be or will not be in the way when the curtain goes up that too makes for nervousness and nervousness is the certain proof that the emotion of the one seeing and the emotion of the thing seen do not progress together.

Nervousness consists in needing to go faster or to go slower so as to get together. It is that that makes anybody feel nervous.

And is it a mistake that that is what the theatre is or is it not.

There are things that are exciting as the theatre is exciting but do they make you nervous or do they not, and if they do and if they do not why do they and why do they not.

Let us think of three different kinds of things that are exciting and that make or do not make one nervous. First any scene which is a real scene something real that is happening in which one takes part as an actor in that scene. Second any book that is exciting, third the theatre at which one sees an exciting action in which one does not take part.

Now in a real scene in which one takes part at which one is an actor what does one feel as to time and what is it that does or does not make one nervous.

And is your feeling at such a time ahead and behind the action the way it is when you are at the theatre. It is the same and it is not. But more not.

If you are taking part in an actual violent scene, and you talk and they or he or she talk and it goes on and it gets more exciting and finally then it happens, whatever it is that does happen then when it happens then at the moment of happening is it a relief from the excitement or is it a completion of the excitement. In the real thing it is a completion of the excitement, in the theatre it is a relief from the excitement, and in that difference the difference between completion and relief is the difference between emotion concerning a thing seen on the stage and the emotion concerning a real presentation that is really something happening. I wish to illustrate this from a bit of *The Making of Americans*.

This one, and the one I am now beginning describing is Martha Hersland and this is a little story of the acting in her of her being in her very young living, this one was a very little one then and she was running and she was in the street and it was a muddy one and she had an umbrella that she was dragging and she was crying. I will throw the umbrella in the mud, she was saying, she was very little then, she was just beginning her schooling, I will throw the umbrella in the mud, she said and no one was near her and she was dragging the umbrella and bitterness possessed her, I will throw the umbrella in the mud, she was saying and nobody heard her, the others had run ahead to get home and they had left her, I will throw the umbrella in the mud, and there was desperate anger in her, I have throwed the umbrella in the mud, burst from her, she had thrown the umbrella in the mud and that was the end of it all in her. She had thrown the umbrella in the mud and no one heard her as it burst from her, I have throwed the umbrella in the mud, it was the end of all that to her.[1]

This then is the fundamental difference between excitement in real life and on the stage, in real life it culminates in a sense of completion whether an exciting act or an exciting emotion has been done or not, and on the stage the exciting climax is a relief. And the memory of the two things is different. As you go over the detail that leads to culmination of any scene in real life, you find that each time you cannot get completion, but you can get relief and so already your memory of any exciting scene in which you have taken part turns it into the thing seen or heard not the thing felt. You have as I say as the result relief rather than culmination. Relief from excitement, rather than the climax of excitement. In this respect an exciting story does the same only in the exciting story, you so to speak have control of it as you have in your memory of a really exciting scene, it is not as it is on the stage a thing over which you have no real control. You can with an exciting story find out the end and so begin over again just as you can in remembering an exciting scene, but the stage is different, it is not real and yet it is not within your control as the memory of an exciting thing is or the reading of an exciting book. No matter how well you know the end of the stage story it is nevertheless not within your control as the memory of an exciting thing is or as the written story of an exciting thing is or even in a curious way the heard story of an exciting thing is. And what is the reason for this difference and what does it do to the stage. It makes for nervousness that of course, and the cause of nervousness is the fact that the emotion of the one seeing the play is always ahead or behind the play.

Beside all this there is a thing to be realized and that is how you are being introduced to the characters who take part in an exciting action even when you yourself are one of the actors. And this too has to be very much thought about. And thought about in relation

1. *The Making of Americans*, Harcourt, Brace, New York, p. 232.

to an exciting real thing to an exciting book, to an exciting theatre. How are you introduced to the characters.

There are then the three ways of having something be exciting, and the excitement may or may not make one nervous, a book being read that is exciting, a scene in which one takes part or an action in which one takes part and the theatre at which one looks on.

In each case the excitement and the nervousness and the being behind or ahead in one's feeling is different.

First anything exciting in which one takes part. There one progresses forward and back emotionally and at the supreme crises of the scene the scene in which one takes part, in which one's hopes and loves and fears take part at the extreme crisis of this thing one is almost one with one's emotions, the action and the emotion go together, there is but just a moment of this coordination but it does exist otherwise there is no completion as one has no result, no result of a scene in which one has taken part, and so instinctively when any people are living an exciting moment one with another they go on and on and on until the thing has come together the emotion the action the excitement and that is the way it is when there is any violence either of loving or hating or quarreling or losing or succeeding. But there is, there has to be the moment of it all being abreast the emotion, the excitement and the action otherwise there would be no succeeding and no failing and so no one would go on living, why yes of course not.

That is life the way it is lived.

Why yes of course and there is a reasonable and sometimes an unreasonable and very often not a reasonable amount of excitement in everybody's life and when it happens it happens in that way.

Now when you read a book how is it. Well it is not exactly like that no not even when a book is even more exciting than any excitement one has ever had. In the first place one can always look at the end of the book and so quiet down one's excitement. The excitement having been quieted down one can enjoy the excitement just as any one can enjoy the excitement of anything having happened to them by remembering and so tasting it over and over again but each time less intensely and each time until it is all over. Those who like to read books over and over get continuously this

sensation of the excitement as if it were a pleasant distant thunder
that rolls and rolls and the more it rolls well the further it rolls the
pleasanter until it does not roll any more. That is until at last you
have read the book so often that it no longer holds any excitement
not even ever so faintly and then you have to wait until you have
forgotten it and you can begin it again.

Now the theatre has still another way of being all this to you, the
thing causing your emotion and the excitement in connection with
it.

Of course lots of other things can do these things to lots of other
people that is to say excite lots of people but as I have said knowledge is what you know and I naturally tell you what I know, as I
do so very essentially believe in knowledge.

So then once again what does the theatre do and how does it do
it.

What happens on the stage and how and how does one feel about
it. That is the thing to know, to know and to tell it as so.

Is the thing seen or the thing heard the thing that makes most of
its impression upon you at the theatre. How much has the hearing
to do with it and how little. Does the thing heard replace the thing
seen. Does it help or does it interfere with it.

And when you are taking part in something really happening
that is exciting, how is it. Does the thing seen or does the thing heard
effect you and effect you at the same time or in the same degree or
does it not. Can you wait to hear or can you wait to see and which
excites you the most. And what has either one to do with the completion of the excitement when the excitement is a real excitement
that is excited by something really happening. And then little by
little does the hearing replace the seeing or does the seeing replace
the hearing. Do they go together or do they not. And when the
exciting something in which you have taken part arrives at its
completion does the hearing replace the seeing or does it not. Does
the seeing replace the hearing or does it not. Or do they both go on
together.

All this is very important, and important for me and important,
just important. It has of course a great deal to do with the theatre
a great deal.

In connection with reading an exciting book the thing is again more complicated than just seeing, because of course in reading one sees but one also hears and when the story is at its most exciting does one hear more than one sees or does one not do so.

I am posing all these questions to you because of course in writing, all these things are things that are really most entirely really exciting. But of course yes.

And in asking a question one is not answering but one is as one may say deciding about knowing. Knowing is what you know and in asking these questions although there is no one who answers these questions there is in them that there is knowledge. Knowledge is what you know.

And now is the thing seen or the thing heard the thing that makes most of its impression upon you at the theatre, and does as the scene on the theatre proceeds does the hearing take the place of seeing as perhaps it does when something real is being most exciting, or does seeing take the place of hearing as it perhaps does when anything real is happening or does the mixture get to be more mixed seeing and hearing as perhaps it does when anything really exciting is really happening.

If the emotion of the person looking at the theatre does or does not do what it would do if it were really a real something that was happening and they were taking part in it or they were looking at it, when the emotion of the person looking on at the theatre comes then at the climax to relief rather than completion has the mixture of seeing and hearing something to do with this and does this mixture have something to do with the nervousness of the emotion at the theatre which has perhaps to do with the fact that the emotion of the person at the theatre is always behind and ahead of the scene at the theatre but not with it.

There are then quite a number of things that any one does or does not know.

Does the thing heard replace the thing seen does it help it or does it interfere with it. Does the thing seen replace the thing heard or does it help or does it interfere with it.

I suppose one might have gotten to know a good deal about these things from the cinema and how it changed from sight to sound, and how much before there was real sound how much of the sight was sound or how much it was not. In other words the cinema undoubtedly had a new way of understanding sight and sound in relation to emotion and time.

I may say that as a matter of fact the thing which has induced a person like myself to constantly think about the theatre from the standpoint of sight and sound and its relation to emotion and time, rather than in relation to story and action is the same as you may say general form of conception as the inevitable experiments made by the cinema although the method of doing so has naturally nothing to do with the other. I myself never go to the cinema or hardly ever practically never and the cinema has never read my work or hardly ever. The fact remains that there is the same impulse to solve the problem of time in relation to emotion and the relation of the scene to the emotion of the audience in the one case as in the other. There is the same impulse to solve the problem of the relation of seeing and hearing in the one case as in the other.

It is in short the inevitable problem of anybody living in the composition of the present time, that is living as we are now living as we have it and now do live in it.

The business of Art as I tried to explain in *Composition as Explanation* is to live in the actual present, that is the complete actual present, and to completely express that complete actual present.

But to come back to that other question which is at once so important a part of any scene in real life, in books or on the stage, how are the actors introduced to the sight, hearing and consciousness of the person having the emotion about them. How is it done in each case and what has that to do with the way the emotion progresses.

How are the actors in a real scene introduced to those acting with them in that scene and how are the real actors in a real scene introduced to you who are going to be in an exciting scene with them. How does it happen, that is, as it usually happens.

And how are the actors in a book scene introduced to the reader of the book, how does one come to know them, that is how is one really introduced to them.

And how are the people on the stage that is the people the actors act how are they introduced to the audience and what is the reason why, the reason they are introduced in the way that they are introduced, and what happens, and how does it matter, and how does it affect the emotions of the audience.

In a real scene, naturally in a real scene, you either have already very well known all the actors in the real scene of which you are one, or you have not. More generally you have than you have not, but and this is the element of excitement in an exciting scene, it quite of course is the element of excitement in an exciting scene that is in a real scene, all that you have known of the persons including yourself who are taking part in the exciting scene, although you have most probably known them very well, what makes it exciting is that insofar as the scene is exciting they the actors in the scene including yourself might just as well have been strangers because they all act talk and feel differently from the way you have expected them to act feel or talk. And this that they feel act and talk including yourself differently from the way you would have thought that they would act feel and talk makes the scene an exciting scene and makes the climax of this scene which is a real scene a climax of completion and not a climax of relief. That is what a real scene is. Would it make any difference in a real scene if they were all strangers, if they had never known each other. Yes it would, it would be practically impossible in the real scene to have a really exciting scene if they were all strangers because generally speaking it is the contradiction between the way you know the people you know including yourself act and the way they are acting or feeling or talking that makes of any scene that is an exciting scene an exciting scene.

Of course there are other exciting scenes in peace and in war in which the exciting scene takes place with strangers but in that case for the purpose of excitement you are all strangers but so completely strangers, including you yourself to yourself as well as the others to each other and to you that they are not really individuals and inasmuch as that is so it has the advantage and the disadvantage that you proceed by a series of completions which follow each other so closely that when it is all over you cannot remember that is you cannot really reconstruct the thing, the thing that has happened. That is something that one must think about in relation to the theatre and it is a very interesting thing. Then in a case like that where you are all strangers in an exciting scene what happens as far as hearing and seeing is concerned. When in an exciting scene where you are all strangers you to yourself and you to them and they to you and they to each other and where no one of all of them including yourself have any consciousness of knowing each other do you have the disadvantage of not knowing the difference between hearing and seeing and is that a disadvantage from the standpoint of remembering. From that standpoint the standpoint of remembering it is a serious disadvantage.

But we may say that that exciting experience of exciting scenes where you have really no acquaintance with the other actors as well as none with yourself in an exciting action are comparatively rare and are not the normal material of excitement as it is exciting in the average person's experience.

As I say in the kind of excitement where you have had no normal introduction to the actors of the scene the action and the emotion is so violent that sight sound and emotion is so little realized that it cannot be remembered and therefore in a kind of a way it has really nothing to do with anything because really it is more exciting action than exciting emotion or excitement. I think I can say that these are not the same thing. Have they anything to do with the way the theatre gets you to know or not to know what the people on the stage are. Perhaps yes and perhaps no.

In ordinary life one has known pretty well the people with whom one is having the exciting scene before the exciting scene takes place and one of the most exciting elements in the excitement be it love or a quarrel or a struggle is that, that having been well known that is familiarly known, they all act in acting violently act in the same way as they always did of course only the same way has become so completely different that from the standpoint of familiar acquaintance there is none there is complete familiarity but there is no proportion that has hitherto been known, and it is this which makes the scene the real scene exciting, and it is this that leads to completion, the proportion achieves in your emotion the new proportion therefore it is completion but not relief. A new proportion cannot be a relief.

Now how does one naturally get acquainted in real life which makes one have a familiarity with some one. By a prolonged familiarity of course.

And how does one achieve this familiarity with the people in a book or the people on the stage. Or does one.

In real life the familiarity is of course the result of accident, intention or natural causes but in any case there is a progressive familiarity that makes one acquainted.

Now in a book there is an attempt to do the same thing that is, to say, to do a double thing, to make the people in the book familiar with each other and to make the reader familiar with them. That is the reason in a book it is always a strange doubling, the familiarity between the characters in the book is a progressive familiarity and the familiarity between them and the reader is a familiarity that is a forcing process or an incubation. It makes of course a double time and later at another time we will go into that.

But now how about the theatre.

It is not possible in the theatre to produce familiarity which is of the essence of acquaintance because, in the first place when the actors are there they are there and they are there right away.

When one reads a play and very often one does read a play, anyway one did read Shakespeare's play a great deal at least I did, it was always necessary to keep one's finger in the list of characters for at least the whole first act, and in a way it is necessary to do the same when the play is played. One has one's programme for that and beside one has to become or has become acquainted with the actors as an actor and one has one's programme too for that. And so the introduction to the characters on the stage has a great many different sides to it. And this has again a great deal to do with the nervousness of the theatre excitement.

Anybody who was as I was, brought up and at the time that I was brought up was brought up in Oakland and in San Francisco inevitably went to the theatre a lot. Actors in those days liked to go out to the Coast and as it was expensive to get back and not expensive to stay there they stayed. Besides that there were a great many foreign actors who came and having come stayed and any actor who stays acts and so there was always a great deal to see on the stage and children went, they went with each other and they went alone, and they went with people who were older, and there was twenty-five cent opera to which anybody went and the theatre was natural and anybody went to the theatre. I did go a great deal in those days. I also read plays a great deal. I rather liked reading plays, I very much liked reading plays. In the first place there was in reading plays as I have said the necessity of going forward and back to the list of characters to find out which was which and then insensibly to know. Then there was the poetry and then gradually there were the portraits.

I can remember quite definitely in the reading of plays that there were very decidedly these three things, the way of getting acquainted that was not an imitation of what one usually did, but the having to remember which character was which. That was very different from real life or from a book. Then there was the element of poetry. Poetry connected with a play was livelier poetry than poetry unconnected with a play. In the first place there were a great many bits that were short and sometimes it was only a line.

I remember *Henry the Sixth* which I read and re-read and which of course I have never seen played but which I liked to read because there were so many characters and there were so many little bits in it that were lively words. In the poetry of plays words are more lively words than in any other kind of poetry and if one naturally liked lively words and I naturally did one likes to read plays in poetry. I always as a child read all the plays I could get hold of that were in poetry. Plays in prose do not read so well. The words in prose are livelier when they are not a play. I am not saying anything about why, it is just a fact.

So then for me there was the reading of plays which was one thing and then there was the seeing of plays and of operas a great many of them which was another thing.

Later on so very much later on there was for me the writing of plays which was one thing and there was at that time no longer any seeing of plays. I practically when I wrote my first play had completely ceased going to the theatre. In fact although I have written a great many plays and I am quite sure they are plays I have since I commenced writing these plays I have practically never been inside of any kind of a theatre. Of course none of this has been intentional, one may say generally speaking that anything that is really inevitable, that is to say necessary is not intentional.

But to go back to the plays I did see, and then to go on to the plays I did write.

It was then a natural thing in the Oakland and San Francisco in which I was brought up to see a great many plays played. Beside there was a great deal of opera played and so all of it was natural enough and how did I feel about it.

Generally speaking all the early recollections all a child's feeling of the theatre is two things. One which is in a way like a circus that is the general movement and light and air which any theatre has, and a great deal of glitter in the light and a great deal of height in the air, and then there are moments, a very very few moments but still moments. One must be pretty far advance in adolescence before one realizes a whole play.

Up to the time of adolescence when one does really live in a whole play up to that time the theatre consists of bright filled space and usually not more than one moment in a play.

I think this is fairly everybody's experience and it was completely mine.

Uncle Tom's Cabin may not have been my first play but it was very nearly my first play. I think my first play really was *Pinafore* in London but the theatre there was so huge that I do not remember at all seeing a stage I only remember that it felt like a theatre that is the theatre did. I doubt if I did see the stage.

In *Uncle Tom's Cabin* I remember only the escape across the ice, I imagine because the blocks of ice moving up and down naturally would catch my eye more than the people on the stage would.

The next thing was the opera the twenty-five cent opera of San Francisco and the fight in *Faust*. But that I imagine was largely because my brother had told me about the fight in *Faust*. As a matter of fact I gradually saw more of the opera because I saw it quite frequently. Then there was *Buffalo Bill* and the Indian attack, well of course anybody raised where everybody collected arrow heads and played Indians would notice Indians. And then there was *Lohengrin*, and there all that I saw was the swan being changed into a boy, our insisting on seeing that made my father with us lose the last boat home to Oakland, but my brother and I did not mind, naturally not as it was the moment.

In spite of my having seen operas quite often the first thing that I remember as sound on the stage was the playing by some English actor of Richelieu at the Oakland theatre and his repeated calling out, Nemours Nemours. That is the first thing that I remember hearing with my ears at the theatre and as I say nothing is more interesting to know about the theatre than the relation of sight and sound. It is always the most interesting thing about anything to know whether you hear or you see. And how one has to do with the other. It is one of the important things in finding out how you know what you know.

Then I enormously remember Booth playing Hamlet but there again the only thing I noticed and it is rather a strange thing to have noticed is his lying at the Queen's feet during the play. One would suppose that a child would notice other things in the play than that but that is what I remember and I noticed him there more than I did the play he saw, although I knew that there was a play going on there, that is the little play. It was in this way that I first felt two things going on at one time. That is something that one has to come to feel.

Then the next thing I knew was adolescence and going to the theatre all the time, a great deal alone, and all of it making an outside inside existence for me, not so real as books, which were all inside me, but so real that it the theatre made me real outside of me which up to that time I never had been in my emotion. I had largely been so in an active daily life but not in any emotion.

Then gradually there came the beginning of really realizing the great difficulty of having my emotion accompany the scene and then moreover I became fairly consciously troubled by the things over which one stumbles over which one stumbled to such an extent that the time of one's emotion in relation to the scene was always interrupted. The things over which one stumbled and there it was a matter both of seeing and of hearing were clothes, voices, what they the actors said, how they were dressed and how that related itself to their moving around. Then the bother of never being able to begin over again because before it had commenced it was over, and at no time had you been ready, either to commence or to be over. Then I began to vaguely wonder whether I could see and hear at the same time and which helped or interfered with the other and which helped or interfered with the thing on the stage having been over before it really commenced. Could I see and hear and feel at the same time and did I.

I began to be a good deal troubled by all these things, the more emotion I felt while at the theatre the more troubled I became by all these things.

And then I was relieved.

As I said San Francisco was a wonderful place to hear and see foreign actors as at that time they liked it when they got there and they stayed and they played.

I must have been about sixteen years old and Bernhardt came to San Francisco and stayed two months. I knew a little french of course but really it did not matter, it was all so foreign and her voice being so varied and it all being so french I could rest in it untroubled. And I did.

It was better than the opera because it went on. It was better than the theatre because you did not have to get acquainted. The manners and customs of the french theatre created a thing in itself and it existed in and for itself as the poetical plays had that I used so much to read, there were so many characters just as there were in those plays and you did not have to know them they were so foreign, and the foreign scenery and actuality replaced the poetry and the voices replaced the portraits. It was for me a very simple direct and moving pleasure.

This experience curiously enough and yet perhaps it was not so curious awakened in me a desire for melodrama on the stage, because there again everything happened so quietly one did not have to get acquainted and as what the people felt was of no importance one did not have to realize what was said.

This pleasure in melodrama and in those days there was always one theatre in a theatrically inclined town that played melodrama, this pleasure in melodrama culminated for me in the civil war dramas of that period and the best of them was of course *Secret Service*. Gillette[2] had conceived a new technique, silence stillness and quick movement. Of course it had been done in the melodrama already by the villains particularly in such plays as the *Queen of Chinatown* and those that had to do with telegraph operators. But Gillette had not only done it but he had conceived it and it made the whole stage the whole play this technique silence stillness and quick movement. One was no longer bothered by the theatre, you

2. William Hooker Gillette (1855–1937), American playwright and actor.

had to get acquainted of course but that was quickly over and after that nothing bothered. In fact Gillette created what the cinema later repeated by mixing up the short story and the stage but there is yet the trouble with the cinema that it is after all a photograph, and a photograph continues to be a photograph and yet can it become something else. Perhaps it can but that is a whole other question. If it can then some one will have to feel that about it. But to go on.

From then on I was less and less interested in the theatre.

I became more interested in opera, I went one went and the whole business almost came together and then finally, just finally, I came not to care at all for music and so having concluded that music was made for adolescents and not for adults and having just left adolescence behind me and beside I knew all the operas anyway by that time I did not care any more for opera.

Then I came to Paris to live and there for a long time I did not go to the theatre at all. I forgot the theatre, I never thought about the theatre. I did sometimes think about the opera. I went to the opera once in Venice and I liked it and then much later Strauss' *Electra* made me realize that in a kind of a way there could be a solution of the problem of conversation on the stage. Beside it was a new opera and it is quite exciting to hear something unknown really unknown.

But as I say I settled down to Paris life and I forgot the theatre and almost forgot opera. There was of course Isadora Duncan and then the Russian ballet and in between Spain and the Argentine and bull-fights and I began once more to feel something about something going on at a theatre.

And then I went back, not in my reading but in my feeling to the reading of plays in my childhood, the lots of characters, the poetry and the portraits and the scenery which was always of course and ought always to be of course woods that is forests and trees and streets and windows.

And so one day all of a sudden I began to write Plays.

I remember very well the first one I wrote. I called it *What Happened, a Play*, it is in *Geography and Plays* as are all the plays I wrote at that time. I think and always have thought that if you write a play you ought to announce that it is a play and that is what I did. *What Happened. A Play.*

I had just come home from a pleasant dinner party and I realized then as anybody can know that something is always happening.

Something is always happening, anybody knows a quantity of stories of people's lives that are always happening, there are always plenty for the newspapers and there are always plenty in private life. Everybody knows so many stories and what is the use of telling another story. What is the use of telling a story since there are so many and everybody knows so many and tells so many. In the country it is perfectly extraordinary how many complicated dramas go on all the time. And everybody knows them, so why tell another one. There is always a story going on.

So naturally what I wanted to do in my play was what everybody did not always know nor always tell. By everybody I do of course include myself but always I do of course include myself.

And so I wrote, *What Happened, A Play*.

Then I wrote *Ladies Voices* and then I wrote a Curtain Raiser. I did this last because I wanted still more to tell what could be told if one did not tell anything.

Perhaps I will read some of these to you later.

Then I went to Spain and there I wrote a lot of plays. I concluded that anything that was not a story could be a play and I even made plays in letters and advertisements.

I had before I began writing plays written many portraits. I had been enormously interested all my life in finding out what made each one that one and so I had written a great many portraits.

I came to think that since each one is that one and that there are a number of them each one being that one, the only way to express this thing each one being that one and there being a number of them knowing each other was in a play. And so I began to write these plays. And the idea in *What Happened, A Play* was to express this without telling what happened, in short to make a play the essence of what happened. I tried to do this with the first series of plays that I wrote.

A tiger a rapt and surrounded overcoat securely arranged with spots old enough to be thought useful and witty quite witty in a secret and in a blinding flurry.[3]

3. *What Happened*, a five-act play, in *Geography and Plays*, Four Seas, Boston, 1922, p. 205.

ACT TWO

(Three)

Four and nobody wounded, five and nobody flourishing, six and nobody talkative, eight and nobody sensible.

One and a left hand lift that is so heavy that there is no way of pronouncing perfectly.

A point of accuracy, a point of a strange stove, a point that is so sober that the reason left is all the chance of swelling.

(The same three.)

A wide oak a wide enough oak, a very wide cake, a lightning cooky, a single wide open and exchanged box filled with the same little sac that shines.

The best the only better and more left footed stranger.

The very kindness there is in all lemons oranges apples pears and potatoes.

(The same three.)

A same frame a sadder portal, a singular gate and a bracketed mischance.

A rich market where there is no memory of more moon than there is everywhere and yet where strangely there is apparel and a whole set.

A connection, a clam cup connection, a survey, a ticket and a return to laying over.

ACT THREE

(Two)

A cut, a cut is not a slice, what is the occasion for representing a cut and a slice. What is the occasion for all that.

A cut is a slice, a cut is the same slice. The reason that a cut is a slice is that if there is no hurry any time is just as useful.[4]

I have of course always been struggling with this thing, to say what you nor I nor nobody knows, but what is really what you and I and everybody knows, and as I say everybody hears stories but the thing that makes each one what he is is not that. Everybody hears stories and knows stories. How can they not because that is what anybody does and what everybody tells. But in my portraits I had tried to tell what each one is without telling stories and now in my

4. *Geography and Plays*, p. 206.

early plays I tried to tell what happened without telling stories so that the essence of what happened would be like the essence of the portraits, what made what happened be what it was. And then I had for the moment gone as far as I could then go in plays and I went back to poetry and portraits and description.

Then I began to spend my summers in Bilignin in the department of the Ain and there I lived in a landscape that made itself its own landscape. I slowly came to feel that since the landscape was the thing, I had tried to write it down in *Lucy Church Amiably* and I did but I wanted it even more really, in short I found that since the landscape was the thing, a play was a thing and I went on writing plays a great many plays. The landscape at Bilignin so completely made a play that I wrote quantities of plays.

I felt that if a play was exactly like a landscape then there would be no difficulty about the emotion of the person looking on at the play being behind or ahead of the play because the landscape does not have to make acquaintance. You may have to make acquaintance with it, but it does not with you, it is there and so the play being written the relation between you at any time is so exactly that that it is of no importance unless you look at it. Well I did look at it and the result is in all the plays that I have printed as *Opera and Plays*.

MARIUS: I am very pleased I am indeed very pleased that it is a great pleasure.

MARTHA: If four are sitting at a table and one of them is lying upon it it does not make any difference. If bread and pomegranates are on a table and four are sitting at the table and one of them is leaning upon it it does not make any difference.

MARTHA: It does not make any difference if four are seated at a table and one is leaning upon it.

MARYAS: If five are seated at a table and there is bread on it and there are pomegranates on it and one of the five is leaning on the table it does not make any difference.

MARTHA: If on a day that comes again and if we consider a day a week day it does come again if on a day that comes again and we consider every day to be a day that comes again it comes again then when accidentally when very accidentally every other day and every other day every other day and every other day that comes again and every day comes again when accidentally every other day comes again, every other day comes again and every other and every day comes again and accidentally and every day and it comes again, a day comes again and a day in that way comes again.

MARYAS: Accidentally in the morning and after that every evening and accidentally every evening and after that every morning and after that accidentally every morning and after that accidentally and after that every morning.

MARYAS: After that accidentally. Accidentally after that.

MARYAS: Accidentally after that. After that accidentally.

MARYAS AND MARTHA: More Maryas and more Martha.

MARYAS AND MARTHA: More Martha and more Maryas.

MARTHA AND MARYAS: More and more and more Martha and more Maryas.

MARIUS: It is spoken of in that way.

MABEL: It is spoken of in that way.

MARIUS AND MABEL: It is spoken in that way and it is spoken of in that way.

MARIUS AND MABEL: It is spoken of in that way.

MABEL: I speak of it in that way.

MARIUS: I have spoken of it in that way and I speak it in that way. I have spoken of it in that way.

MABEL: I speak of it in that way.[5]

The landscape has its formation and as after all a play has to have formation and be in relation one thing to the other thing and as the story is not the thing as any one is always telling something then the landscape not moving but being always in relation, the trees to the hills the hills to the fields the trees to each other any piece of it to any sky and then any detail to any other detail, the story is only of importance if you like to tell or like to hear a story but the relation is there anyway. And of that relation I wanted to make a play and I did, a great number of plays.

SAY IT WITH FLOWERS

A PLAY

George Henry, Henry Henry and Elisabeth Henry.
Subsidiary characters.
Elisabeth and William Long.

5. 'A List' in *Operas and Plays*, Plain Edition, Random House, p. 92.

Time Louis XI

Place Gisors.
Action in a cake shop and the sea shore.
Other interests.
The welcoming of a man and his dog and the wish that they would
come back sooner.
George Henry and Elisabeth Henry and Henry Henry
ruminating.
Elisabeth and William Long.

Waiting.
Who has asked them to be amiable to me.
She said she was waiting.
George Henry and Elisabeth Henry and Henry Henry.
Who might be asleep if they were not waiting for me.
She.
Elisabeth Henry and Henry Henry and George Henry.
She might be waiting with me.
Henry Henry absolutely ready to be here with me.
Scenery.
The home where they were waiting for William Long to ask them
to come along and ask them not to be waiting for them.
Will they be asleep while they are waiting.
They will be pleased with everything.
What is everything.
A hyacinth is everything.
Will they be sleeping while they are waiting for everything.
William Long and Elisabeth Long were so silent you might have
heard an egg shell breaking. They were busy all day long with every-
thing.
Elisabeth and William Long were very busy waiting for him to come
and bring his dog along.
Why did they not go with him.
Because they were busy waiting.[6]

LOUIS XI AND MADAME GIRAUD

SCENE II

Louis the XI loved a boat
A boat on the Seine

6. *Operas and Plays*, p. 331.

Sinks and leaves.
Leaves which have patterns
They with delight.
Make it be loaned
To administer their confinement
They will go away
Without which it will matter.

Louis XI

Has won gold for France
And in this way.
He has settled she and a girl
He and a wife
He and a friend
They and their mother
The mother and the son Percy.[7]

MADAME RECAMIER

Yvonne Marin

Out loud is when the mother wishes
When the brother fishes
When the father considers wishes
When the sister supposes wishes
She will change to say I say I say so.
Let her think of learning nothing.
Let her think of seeing everything
Let her think like that.

Florence Descotes

Never to be restless
Never to be afraid
Never to ask will they come
Never to have made
Never to like having had
Little that is left then
She made it do
One and two
Thank her for everything.

7. *Operas and Plays*, p. 352.

Madame Recamier

It is not thoughtless to think well of them.

Louis Raynal

A place where she sits
Is a place where they were.[8]

The only one of course that has been played is *Four Saints*. In *Four Saints* I made the Saints the landscape. All the saints that I made and I made a number of them because after all a great many pieces of things are in a landscape all these saints together made my landscape. These attendant saints were the landscape and it the play really is a landscape.

A landscape does not move nothing really moves in a landscape but things are there, and I put into the play the things that were there.

Magpies are in the landscape that is they are in the sky of a landscape, they are black and white and they are in the sky of the landscape in Bilignin and in Spain, especially in Avila. When they are in the sky they do something that I have never seen any other bird do they hold themselves up and down and look flat against the sky.

A very famous French inventor of things that have to do with stabilization in aviation told me that what I told him magpies did could not be done by any bird but anyway whether the magpies at Avila do do it or do not at least they look as if they do do it. They look exactly like the birds in the Annunciation pictures the bird which is the Holy Ghost and rests flat against the side sky very high.

There were magpies in my landscape and there were scarecrows.

The scarecrows on the ground are the same thing as the magpies in the sky, they are a part of the landscape.

They the magpies may tell their story if they and you like or even if I like but stories are only stories but that they stay in the air is not a story but a landscape. That scarecrows stay on the ground is the same thing it could be a story but it is a piece of the landscape.

Then as I said streets and windows are also landscape and they added to my Spanish landscape.

8. ibid., p. 365.

While I was writing the *Four Saints* I wanted one always does want the saints to be actually saints before them as well as inside them, I had to see them as well as feel them. As it happened there is on the Boulevard Raspail a place where they make photographs that have always held my attention. They take a photograph of a young girl dressed in the costume of her ordinary life and little by little in successive photographs they change it into a nun. These photographs are small and the thing takes four or five changes but at the end it is a nun and this is done for the family when the nun is dead and in memoriam. For years I had stood and looked at these when I was walking and finally when I was writing Saint Therese in looking at these photographs I saw how Saint Therese existed from the life of an ordinary young lady to that of the nun. And so everything was actual and I went on writing.

Then in another window this time on the rue de Rennes there was a rather large porcelain group and it was of a young soldier giving alms to a beggar and taking off his helmet and his armour and leaving them in the charge of another.

It was somehow just what the young Saint Ignatius did and anyway it looked like him as I had known about him and so he too became actual not as actual as Saint Therese in the photographs but still actual and so the *Four Saints* got written.

All these things might have been a story but as a landscape they were just there and a play is just there. That is at least the way I feel about it.

Anyway I did write *Four Saints* an Opera to be Sung and I think it did almost what I wanted, it made a landscape and the movement in it was like a movement in and out with which anybody looking on can keep in time. I also wanted it to have the movement of nuns very busy and in continuous movement but placid as a landscape has to be because after all the life in a convent is the life of a landscape, it may look excited a landscape does sometimes look excited but its quality is that a landscape if it ever did go away would have to go away to stay.

Anyway the play as I see it is exciting and it moves but it also stays and that is as I said in the beginning might be what a play should do.

Anyway I am pleased. People write me that they are having a

good time while the opera is going on a thing which they say does not very often happen to them at the theatre.⁹

So you do see what I have after all meant.

And so this is just at present all I know about the theatre.

9. Gertrude Stein refers here to her opera *Four Saints In Three Acts*, music by Vergil Thomson, choreography by Frederick Ashton. It had its first public performance in Hartford, Connecticut, on 8 February 1934 and opened in New York on 20 February. It was being performed at the time when Gertrude Stein was still in France writing this lecture. She saw the opera later in Chicago during her lecture tour.

4

THE GRADUAL MAKING OF
THE MAKING OF AMERICANS

I AM going to read what I have written to read, because in a general way it is easier even if it is not better and in a general way it is better even if it is not easier to read what has been written than to say what has not been written. Any way that is one way to feel about it.

And I want to tell you about the gradual way of making *The Making of Americans*.[1] I made it gradually and it took me almost three years to make it, but that is not what I mean by gradual. What I mean by gradual is the way the preparation was made inside of me. Although as I tell it it will sound historical, it really is not historical as I still very much remember it. I do remember it. That is I can remember it. And if you can remember, it may be history but it is not historical.

To begin with, I seem always to be doing the talking when I am anywhere but in spite of that I do listen. I always listen. I always have listened. I always have listened to the way everybody has to tell what they have to say. In other words I always have listened in my way of listening until they have told me and told me until I really know it, that is know what they are.

I always as I admit seem to be talking but talking can be a way of listening that is if one has the profound need of hearing and seeing what every one is telling.

And I began very early in life to talk all the time and to listen all the time. At least that is the way I feel about it.

I cannot remember not talking all the time and all the same feeling that while I was talking while I was seeing that I was not only hearing but seeing while I was talking and that at the same time the relation between myself knowing I was talking and those

1. For publication details see Bibliography, p. 443.

to whom I was talking and incidentally to whom I was listening were coming to tell me and tell me in their way everything that made them.

Those of you who have read *The Making of Americans* I think will very certainly understand.

When I was young and I am talking of a period even before I went to college part of this talking consisted in a desire not only to hear what each one was saying in every way everybody has of saying it but also then of helping to change them and to help them change themselves.

I was very full of convictions in those days and I at that time thought that the passion I had for finding out by talking and listening just how everybody was always telling everything that was inside them that made them that one, that this passion for knowing the basis of existence in each one was in me to help them change themselves to become what they should become. The changing should of course be dependent upon my ideas and theirs theirs as much as mine at that time.

And so in those early days I wanted to know what was inside each one which made them that one and I was deeply convinced that I needed this to help them change something.

Then I went to college and there for a little while I was tremendously occupied with finding out what was inside myself to make me what I was. I think that does happen to one at that time. It had been happening before going to college but going to college made it more lively. And being so occupied with what made me myself inside me, made me perhaps not stop talking but for awhile it made me stop listening.

At any rate that is the way it seems to me now looking back at it.

While I was at college and doing philosophy and psychology I became more and more interested in my own mental and physical processes and less in that of others and all I then was learning of what made people what they were came to me by experience and not by talking and listening.

Then as I say I became more interested in psychology, and one of the things I did was testing reactions of the average college student in a state of normal activity and in the state of fatigue induced by their examinations. I was supposed to be interested in their reactions but soon I found that I was not but instead that I was enormously interested in the types of their characters that is what I even then thought of as the bottom nature of them, and when in May 1898 I wrote my half of the report of these experiments I expressed these results as follows:

In these descriptions it will be readily observed that habits of attention are reflexes of the complete character of the individual.

Then that was over and I went to the medical school where I was bored and where once more myself and my experiences were more actively interesting me than the life inside of others.

But then after that once more I began to listen, I had left the medical school and I had for the moment nothing to do but talk and look and listen, and I did this tremendously.

I then began again to think about the bottom nature in people, I began to get enormously interested in hearing how everybody said the same thing over and over again with infinite variations but over and over again until finally if you listened with great intensity you could hear it rise and fall and tell all that that there was inside them, not so much by the actual words they said or the thoughts they had but the movement of their thoughts and words endlessly the same and endlessly different.

Many things then come out in the repeating that make a history of each one for any one who always listens to them. Many things come out of each one and as one listens to them listens to all the repeating in them, always this comes to be clear about them, the history of them of the bottom nature in them, the nature or natures mixed up in them to make the whole of them in anyway it mixes up in them. Sometime then there will be a history of every one.

When you come to feel the whole of anyone from the beginning to the ending, all the kind of repeating there is in them, the different ways at different times repeating comes out of them, all the kinds of things and mixtures in each one, anyone can see then by looking hard at any one living near them that a history of every one must be a long one. A history of any one must be a long one, slowly it comes out from them from their beginning to their ending, slowly you can see it in them the nature and the mixtures in them, slowly everything comes out from each one in the kind of repeating each one does in the different parts and kinds of living they have in them, slowly then the history of them comes out from them, slowly then any one who looks well at any one will have the history of the whole of that one. Slowly the history of each one comes out of each one. Sometime then there will be a history of every one. Mostly every history will be a long one. Slowly it comes out of each one, slowly any one who looks at them gets the history of each part of the living of any one in the history of the whole of each one that sometime there will be of every one.[2]

Repeating then is in every one, in every one their being and their feeling and their way of realizing everything and every one comes out of them in repeating. More and more then every one comes to be clear to some one.

Slowly every one in continuous repeating, to their minutest variation, comes to be clearer to some one. Every one who ever was or is or will be living sometimes will be clearly realized by some one. Sometime there will be an ordered history of every one. Slowly every kind of one comes into ordered recognition. More and more then it is wonderful in living the subtle variations coming clear into ordered recognition, coming to make every one a part of some kind of them, some kind of men and women. Repeating then is in every one, every one then comes sometime to be clearer to some one, sometime there will be then an orderly history of every one who ever was or is or will be living.[3]

Then I became very interested in resemblances, in resemblances and slight differences between people. I began to make charts of all the people I had ever known or seen, or met or remembered.

Every one is always busy with it, no one of them then ever want to know it that every one looks like some one else and they see it mostly every one dislikes to hear it. It is very important to me to always know it, to always see it which one looks like others and to tell it. I write for myself and strangers, I do this for my own sake and for the sake of those who know I know it that they look like other ones, that they are separate and yet always repeated. There are some who like it that I know they are like many others and repeat it, there are many who never can really like it.

Every one is one inside them, every one reminds some one of some other one who is or was or will be living. Every one has it to say of each one he is like such a one I see it in him, every one has it to say of each one she is like some one else I can tell by remembering. So it goes on always in living, every one is always remembering some one who is

2. *The Making of Americans*, Harcourt, Brace, p. 128.
3. ibid.

resembling to the one at whom they are then looking. So they go on repeating, every one is themselves inside them and every one is resembling to others and that is always interesting.[4]

I began to see that as I saw when I saw so many students at college that all this was gradually taking form. I began to get very excited about it. I began to be sure that if I could only go on long enough and talk and hear and look and see and feel enough and long enough I could finally describe really describe every kind of human being that ever was or is or would be living.

I got very wrapped up in all this. And I began writing *The Making of Americans*.

Let me read you some passages to show you how passionately and how desperately I felt about all this.

I am altogether a discouraged one. I am just now altogether a discouraged one. I am going on describing men and women.[5]

I have been very glad to have been wrong. It is sometimes a very hard thing to win myself to having been wrong about something. I do a great deal of suffering.[6]

I was sure that in a kind of a way the enigma of the universe could in this way be solved. That after all description is explanation, and if I went on and on and on enough I could describe every individual human being that could possibly exist. I did proceed to do as much as I could.

Some time then there will be every kind of a history of every one who ever can or is or was or will be living. Some time then there will be a history of every one from their beginning to their ending. Sometime then there will be a history of all of them, of every kind of them, of every one, of every bit of living they ever have in them, of them when there is never more than a beginning to them, of every kind of them, of every one when there is very little beginning and then there is an ending, there will then sometime be a history of every one there will be a history of everything that ever was or is or will be them of everything that was or is or will be all of any one or all of all of them. Sometime then there will be a history of every one, of everything or anything that is all them or

4. *The Making of Americans*, pp. 211–12.
5. ibid., p. 308.
6. ibid., p. 310.

any part of them and sometime then there will be a history of how anything or everything comes out from everyone, comes out from every one or any one from the beginning to the ending of the being in them. Sometime then there must be a history of every one who ever was or is or will be living. As one sees every one in their living, in their loving, sitting, eating, drinking, sleeping, walking, working, thinking, laughing, as any one sees all of them from their beginning to their ending, sees them when they are little babies or children or young grown men and women or growing older men and women or old men and women then one knows it in them that sometime there will be a history of all of them, that sometime all of them will have the last touch of being, a history of them can give to them, sometime then there will be a history of each one, of all the kinds of them, of all the ways any one can know them, of all the ways each one is inside her or inside him, of all the ways anything of them comes out from them. Sometime then there will be a history of every one and so then every one will have in them the last touch of being a history of any one can give to them.[7]

This is then a beginning of the way of knowing everything in every one, of knowing the complete history of each one who ever is or was or will be living. This is then a little description of the winning of so much wisdom.[8]

Of course all the time things were happening that is in respect to my hearing and seeing and feeling. I found that as often as I thought and had every reason to be certain that I had included everything in my knowledge of any one something else would turn up that had to be included. I did not with this get at all discouraged I only became more and more interested. And I may say that I am still more and more interested I find as many things to be added now as ever and that does make it eternally interesting. So I found myself getting deeper and deeper into the idea of describing really describing every individual that could exist.

While I was doing all this all unconsciously at the same time a matter of tenses and sentences came to fascinate me.

While I was listening and hearing and feeling the rhythm of each human being I gradually began to feel the difficulty of putting it down. Types of people I could put down but a whole human being felt at one and the same time, in other words while in the act of feeling that person was very difficult to put into words.

7. ibid., p. 124.   8. ibid., p. 217.

And so about the middle of *The Making of Americans* I became very consciously obsessed by this very definite problem.

It happens very often that a man has it in him, that a man does something, that he does it very often that he does many things, when he is a young man when he is an old man, when he is an older man. One of such of these kind of them had a little boy and this one, the little son wanted to make a collection of Butterflies and beetles and it was all exciting to him and it was all arranged then and then the father said to the son you are certain this is not a cruel thing that you are wanting to be doing, killing things to make collections of them, and the son was very disturbed then and they talked about it together the two of them and more and more they talked about it then and then at last the boy was convinced it was a cruel thing and he said he would not do it and his father said the little boy was a noble boy to give up pleasure when it was a cruel one. The boy went to bed then and then the father when he got up in the early morning saw a wonderfully beautiful moth in the room and he caught him and he killed him and he pinned him and he woke up his son then and showed it to him and he said to him see what a good father I am to have caught and killed this one, the boy was all mixed up inside him and then he said he would go on with his collecting and that was all there was then of discussing and this is a little description of something that happened once and it is very interesting.[9]

And this brings us to the question of grammar. So let me talk a little about that.

You know by this time that although I do listen I do see I do hear I do feel that I do talk.

English grammar is interesting because it is so simple. Once you really know how to diagram a sentence really know it, you know practically all you have to know about English grammar. In short any child thirteen years old properly taught can by that time have learned everything there is to learn about English grammar. So why make a fuss about it. However one does.

It is this that makes the English language such a vital language that the grammar of it is so simple and that one does make a fuss about it.

When I was up against the difficulty of putting down the complete conception that I had of an individual, the complete rhythm of a personality that I had gradually acquired by listening seeing feel-

9. *The Making of Americans*, p. 284.

ing and experience, I was faced by the trouble that I had acquired all this knowledge gradually but when I had it I had it completely at one time. Now that may never have been a trouble to you but it was a terrible trouble to me. And a great deal of *The Making of Americans* was a struggle to do this thing, to make a whole present of something that it had taken a great deal of time to find out, but it was a whole there then within me and as such it had to be said.

That then and ever since has been a great deal of my work and it is that which has made me try so many ways to tell my story.

In *The Making of Americans* I tried it in a variety of ways. And my sentences grew longer and longer, my imaginary dependent clauses were constantly being dropped out, I struggled with relations between they them and then, I began with a relation between tenses that sometimes almost seemed to do it. And I went on and on and then one day after I had written a thousand pages, this was in 1908 I just did not go on any more.

I did however immediately begin again. I began *A Long Gay Book*, that was going to be even longer than *The Making of Americans* and was going to be even more complicated, but then something happened in me and I said in *Composition as Explanation*, so then naturally it was natural that one thing an enormously long thing was not everything an enormously short thing was also not everything nor was it all of it a continuous present thing nor was it always and always beginning again.

And so this is *The Making of Americans*. A book one thousand pages long, and I worked over it three years, and I hope this makes it a little more understandable to you.

As I say I began *A Long Gay Book* and it was to be even longer than *The Making of Americans* and it was to describe not only every possible kind of a human being, but every possible kind of pairs of human beings and every possible threes and fours and fives of human beings and every possible kind of crowds of human beings. And I was going to do it as *A Long Gay Book* and at the same time I began several shorter books which were to illustrate the *Long Gay Book*, one called *Many Many Women* another *Five*, another *Two* and another *G. M. P., Matisse, Picasso and Gertrude Stein*, but the chief book was to be the *Long Gay Book* and that was in a kind of way to go on and to keep going on and to go on before and it began in this way.

When they are very little just only a baby you can never tell which one is to be a lady.

There are some when they feel it inside them that it has been with them that there was once so very little of them, that they were a baby, helpless and no conscious feeling in them, that they knew nothing then when they were kissed and dandled and fixed by others who knew them when they could know nothing inside them or around them, some get from all this that once surely happened to them to that which was then every bit that was then them, there are some when they feel it later inside them that they were such once and that was all that there was then of them, there are some who have from such a knowing an uncertain curious kind of feeling in them that their having been so little once and knowing nothing makes it all a broken world for them that they have inside them, kills for them the everlasting feeling: and they spend their life in many ways, and always they are trying to make for themselves a new everlasting feeling.

One way perhaps of winning is to make a little one to come through them, little like the baby that once was all them and lost them their everlasting feeling. Some can win from just the feeling, the little one need not come, to give it to them.

And so always there is beginning and to some then a losing of the everlasting feeling. Then they make a baby to make for themselves a new beginning and so win for themselves a new everlasting feeling.[10]

I knew while I was writing *The Making of Americans* that it was possible to describe every kind there is of men and women.

I began to wonder if it was possible to describe the way every possible kind of human being acted and felt in relation with any other kind of human being and I thought if this could be done it would make *A Long Gay Book*. It is naturally gayer describing what any one feels acts and does in relation to any other one than to describe what they just are what they are inside them.

And as I naturally found it livelier, I myself was becoming livelier just then. One does you know, when one has come to the conclusion that what is inside every one is not all there is of any one. I was, there is no doubt about it, I was coming to be livelier in rela-

10. *A Long Gay Book*, included in *Matisse, Picasso and Gertrude Stein*, Plain Edition, Random House, p. 13.

tion to myself inside me and in relation to any one inside in them. This being livelier inside me, kept on increasing and so you see it was a natural thing that as the *Long Gay Book* began, it did not go on. If it were to be really lively would it go on. Does one if one is really lively and I was really very lively then does one go on and does one if one is really very lively does one content oneself with describing what is going on inside in one and going on inside in every one in any one.

At any rate what happened is this and every one reading these things, *A Long Gay Book, Many Many Women* and *G. M. P.* will see, that it changed, it kept on changing, until at last it led to something entirely different something very short and lively to the *Portrait of Mabel Dodge* and the little book called *Tender Buttons* but all that I will talk about later. To go back to *The Making of Americans* and *A Long Gay Book*.

One must not forget that although life seems long it is very short, that although civilization seems long it is not so very long. If you think about how many generations, granting that your grandfather to you make a hundred years, if you think about that, it is extraordinary how very short is the history of the world in which we live, the world which is the world where there is a world for us. It is like the generations in the Bible, they really do not take so very long. Now when you are beginning realizing everything, this is a thing that is not confusing but is a thing that as you might say is at one time very long and at the same time not at all long. Twenty-five years roll around so quickly and in writing they can do one of two things, they can either roll around more or they can roll around less quickly.

In writing *The Making of Americans* they rolled around less quickly. In writing *A Long Gay Book*, they did not roll around at all, and therefore it did not go on it led to *Tender Buttons* and many other things. It may even have led to war but that is of no importance.

The Making of Americans rolled around very slowly, it was only three years but they rolled around slowly and that is inevitable when one conceives everything as being there inside in one. Of course everything is always inside in one, that anybody knows but the kind of a one that one is is all inside in one or it is partly not all inside in one. When one is beginning to know everything, and that happens as it does happen, you all know that, when one is beginning to know everything inside in one description strengthens it being all inside in one. That was for me the whole of *The Making of Americans*, it was the strengthening the prolonging of the existing of everything being inside in one. You may call that being younger you may not just as you feel about it but what is important about it is, that if everything is all inside in one then it takes longer to know it than when it is not so completely inside in one.

Therefore it takes longer to know everything when everything is all inside one than when it is not. Call it being young if you like, or call it not including anything that is not everything. It does not make any difference whether you are young or younger or older or very much older. That does not make any difference because after all as I say civilization is not very old if you think about it by hundreds of years and realize that your grandfather to you can very much more than make a hundred years if it happens right.

And so I say and I saw that a complete description of every kind of human being that ever could or would be living is not such a very extensive thing because after all it can be all contained inside in any one and finally it can be done.

So then in writing *The Making of Americans* it was to me an enormously long thing to do to describe every one and slowly it was not an enormously long thing to do to describe every one. Because after all as I say civilization is not a very long thing, twenty-five years roll around so quickly and four times twenty-five years make a hundred years and that makes a grandfather to a granddaughter. Everybody is interested when that happens to any one, because it makes it long and it makes it short. And so and this is the thing that made the change a necessary change from *The Making of Americans* to *A Long Gay Book* and then to *Tender Buttons*.

I will read you some few little things that will show this thing. A few things out of *A Long Gay Book* that show how it changed, changed from *Making of Americans* to *Tender Buttons*.

It is a simple thing to be quite certain that there are kinds in men and women. It is a simple thing and then not any one has any worrying to be doing about any one being any one. It is a simple thing to be quite certain that each one is one being a kind of them and in being that kind

of a one is one being, doing, thinking, feeling, remembering and for-
getting, loving, disliking, being angry, laughing, eating, drinking, talking, sleeping, waking like all of them of that kind of them. There are
enough kinds in men and women so that any one can be interested in
that thing that there are kinds in men and women.[11]

Vrais says good good, excellent. Vrais listens and when he listens he
says good good, excellent. Vrais listens and he being Vrais when he has
listened he says good good, excellent.

Vrais listens, he being Vrais, he listens.

Anything is two things. Vrais was nicely faithful. He had been nicely
faithful. Anything is two things.

He had been nicely faithful. In being one he was one who had he been
one continuing would not have been one continuing being nicely faithful. He was one continuing, he was not continuing to be nicely faithful.
In continuing he was being one being the one who was saying good
good, excellent but in continuing he was needing that he was believing
that he was aspiring to be one continuing to be able to be saying good
good, excellent. He had been one saying good good, excellent. He had
been that one.[12]

If the accumulation of inexpediency produces the withdrawing of the
afternoon greeting then in the evening there is more preparation and
this will take away the paper that has been lying where it could be seen.
All the way that has the aging of a younger generation is part of the way
that resembles anything that is not disappearing. It is not alright as
colors are existing in being accommodating. They have a way that is
identical.[13]

Pardon the fretful autocrat who voices discontent. Pardon the colored
water-color which is burnt. Pardon the intoning of the heavy way.
Pardon the aristocrat who has not come to stay. Pardon the abuse which
was begun. Pardon the yellow egg which has run. Pardon nothing yet,
pardon what is wet, forget the opening now, and close the door again.[14]

A private life is the long thick tree and the private life is the life for
me. A tree which is thick is a tree which is thick. A life which is private
is not what there is. All the times that come are the times I sing, all the
singing I sing are the tunes I sing. I sing and I sing and the tunes I sing
are what are tunes if they come and I sing. I sing I sing.[15]

Suppose it did, suppose it did with a sheet and a shadow and a silver
set of water, suppose it did.[16]

11. *A Long Gay Book*, p. 23.   12. ibid., p. 53.   13. ibid., p. 86.
14. ibid., p. 100.   15. ibid., p. 107.   16. ibid., p. 114.

When I was working with William James I completely learned one thing, that science is continuously busy with the complete description of something, with ultimately the complete description of anything with ultimately the complete description of everything. If this can really be done the complete description of everything then what else is there to do. We may well say nothing, but and this is the thing that makes everything continue to be anything, that after all what does happen is that as relatively few people spend all their time describing anything and they stop and so in the meantime as everything goes on somebody else can always commence and go on. And so description is really unending. When I began *The Making of Americans* I knew I really did know that a complete description was a possible thing, and certainly a complete description is a possible thing. But as it is a possible thing one can stop continuing to describe this everything. That is where philosophy comes in, it begins when one stops continuing describing everything.

And so this was the history of the writing of *The Making of Americans* and why I began *A Long Gay Book*. I said I would go on describing everything in *A Long Gay Book*, but as inevitably indeed really one does stop describing everything being at last really convinced that a description of everything is possible it was inevitable that I gradually stopped describing everything in *A Long Gay Book*.

Nevertheless it would be nice to really have described every kind there is of men and women, and it really would not be very hard to do but it would inevitably not be a *Long Gay Book*, but it would be a *Making of Americans*.

But I do not want to begin again or go on with what was begun because after all I know I really do know that it can be done and if it can be done why do it, particularly as I say one does know that civilization has after all not existed such a very long time if you count it by a hundred years, and each time there has been civilization it has not lasted such a long time if you count it by a hundred years, which makes a period that can connect you with some other one.

I hope you like what I say.

And so *The Making of Americans* has been done. It must be remembered that whether they are Chinamen or Americans there are the same kinds in men and women and one can describe all the kinds of them. This I might have done.

And so then I began the *Long Gay Book*. As soon as I began the *Long Gay Book* I knew inevitably it would not go on to continue what *The Making of Americans* had begun. And why not. Because as my life was my life inside me but I was realizing beginning realizing that everything described would not do any more than tell all I knew about anything why should I tell all I knew about anything since after all I did know all I knew about anything.

So then I said I would begin again. I would not know what I knew about everything what I knew about anything.

And so the *Long Gay Book* little by little changed from a description of any one of any one and everything there was to be known about any one, to what if not was not not to be not known about any one about anything. And so it was necessary to let come what would happen to come because after all knowledge is what you know but what is happening is inevitably what is happening to come.

And so this brings us to other things.

In describing English literature I have explained that the twentieth century was the century not of sentences as was the eighteenth not of phrases as was the nineteenth but of paragraphs. And as I explained paragraphs were inevitable because as the nineteenth century came to its ending, phrases were no longer full of any meaning and the time had come when a whole thing was all there was of anything. Series immediately before and after made everybody clearly understand this thing. And so it was natural that in writing *The Making of Americans* I had proceeded to enlarge my paragraphs so as to include everything. What else could I do. In fact inevitably I made my sentences and my paragraphs do the same thing, made them be one and the same thing. This was inevitably because the nineteenth century having lived by phrases really had lost the feeling of sentences, and before this in English literature paragraphs had never been an end in themselves and now in the beginning of the twentieth century a whole thing, being what was assembled from its parts was a whole thing and so it was a paragraph. You will see that in *The Making of Americans* I did this thing, I made a paragraph so much a whole thing that it included in itself as a whole thing a whole sentence. That makes something clear to you does it not.

And this is what *The Making of Americans* was. Slowly it was not enough to satisfy myself with a whole thing as a paragraph as a whole thing and I will tell very much more about how that came about but *The Making of Americans* really carried it as far as it could be carried so I think the making a whole paragraph a whole thing.

Then at the same time is the question of time. The assembling of a thing to make a whole thing and each one of these whole things is one of a series, but beside this there is the important thing and the very American thing that everybody knows who is an American just how many seconds minutes or hours it is going to take to do a whole thing. It is singularly a sense for combination within a conception of the existence of a given space of time that makes the American thing the American thing, and the sense of this space of time must be within the whole thing as well as in the completed whole thing.

I felt this thing, I am an American and I felt this thing, and I made a continuous effort to create this thing in every paragraph that I made in *The Making of Americans*. And that is why after all this book is an American book an essentially American book, because this thing is an essentially American thing this sense of a space of time and what is to be done within this space of time not in any way excepting in the way that it is inevitable that there is this space of time and anybody who is an American feels what is inside this space of time and so well they do what they do within this space of time, and so ultimately it is a thing contained within. I wonder if I at all convey to you what I mean by this thing. I will try to tell it in every way I can as I have in all the writing that I have ever done. I am always trying to tell this thing that a space of time is a natural thing for an American to always have inside them as something in which they are continuously moving. Think of anything, of cowboys, of movies, of detective stories, of anybody who goes anywhere or stays at home and is an American and you will realize that it is something strictly American to conceive a space that is filled with moving, a space of time that is filled always filled with moving and my first real effort to express this thing which is an American thing began in writing *The Making of Americans*.

*portraits felt diff. in every gen.
generation; any per-og time, 2 to 100 yrs
a generation shews that moving is
existing.*

5

PORTRAITS AND REPETITION

IN *Composition as Explanation* I said nothing changes from generation to generation except the composition in which we live and the composition in which we live makes the art which we see and hear. I said in *Lucy Church Amiably*[1] that women and children change, I said if men have not changed women and children have. But it really is of no importance even if this is true. The thing that is important is the way that portraits of men and women and children are written, by written I mean made. And by made I mean felt. Portraits of men and women and children are differently felt in every generation and by a generation one means any period of time. One does mean any period of time by a generation. A generation can be anywhere from two years to a hundred years. What was it somebody said that the only thing God could not do was to make a two year old mule in a minute. But the strange thing about the realization of existence is that like a train moving there is no real realization of it moving if it does not move against something and so that is what a generation does it shows that moving is existing. So then there are generations and in a way that too is not important because, and this thing is a thing to know, if and we in America have tried to make this thing a real thing, if the movement, that is any movement, is lively enough, perhaps it is possible to know that it is moving even if it is not moving against anything. And so in a way the American way has been not to need that generations are existing. If this were really true and perhaps it is really true then really and truly there is a new way of making portraits of men and women and children. And I, I in my way have tried to do this thing.

It is true that generations are not of necessity existing that is to say if the actual movement within a thing is alive enough. A motor goes inside of an automobile and the car goes. In short this generation has conceived an intensity of movement so great that it has not

1. Plain Edition, Paris, 1930.

to be seen against something else to be known, and therefore, this generation does not connect itself with anything, that is what makes this generation what it is and that is why it is American, and this is very important in connection with portraits of anything. I say portraits and not description and I will gradually explain why. Then also there is the important question of repetition and is there any such thing. Is there repetition or is there insistence. I am inclined to believe there is no such thing as repetition. And really how can there be. This is a thing about which I want you to think before I go on telling about portraits of anything. Think about all the detective stories everybody reads. The kind of crime is the same, and the idea of the story is very often the same, take for example a man like Wallace, he always has the same theme, take a man like Fletcher he always has the same theme, take any American ones, they too always have the scene, the same scene, the kind of invention that is necessary to make a general scheme is very limited in everybody's experience, every time one of the hundreds of times a newspaper man makes fun of my writing and of my repetition he always has the same theme, always having the same theme, that is, if you like, repetition, that is if you like the repeating that is the same thing, but once started expressing this thing, expressing any thing there can be no repetition because the essence of that expression is insistence, and if you insist you must each time use emphasis and if you use emphasis it is not possible while anybody is alive that they should use exactly the same emphasis. And so let us think seriously of the difference between repetition and insistence.

Anybody can be interested in a story of a crime because no matter how often the witnesses tell the same story the insistence is different. That is what makes life that the insistence is different, no matter how often you tell the same story if there is anything alive in the telling the emphasis is different. It has to be, anybody can know that.

It is very like a frog hopping he cannot ever hop exactly the same distance or the same way of hopping at every hop. A bird's singing is perhaps the nearest thing to repetition but if you listen they too vary their insistence. That is the human expression saying the same thing and in insisting and we all insist varying the emphasizing.

I remember very well first beginning to be conscious of this thing.

I became conscious of these things, I suppose anybody does when they first really know that the stars are worlds and that everything is moving, that is the first conscious feeling of necessary repetition, and it comes to one and it is very disconcerting. Then the second thing is when you first realize the history of various civilizations, that have been on this earth, that too makes one realize repetition and at the same time the difference of insistence. Each civilization insisted in its own way before it went away. I remember the first time I really realized this in this way was from reading a book we had at home of the excavations of Nineveh, but these emotions although they tell one so much and one really never forgets them, after all are not in one's daily living, they are like the books of Jules Verne terribly real terribly near but still not here. When I first really realized the inevitable repetition in human expression that was not repetition but insistence when I first began to be really conscious of it was when at about seventeen years of age, I left the more or less internal and solitary and concentrated life I led in California and came to Baltimore and lived with a lot of my relations and principally with a whole group of very lively little aunts who had to know anything.

If they had to know anything and anybody does they naturally had to say and hear it often, anybody does, and as there were ten and eleven of them they did have to say and hear said whatever was said and any one not hearing what it was they said had to come in to hear what had been said. That inevitably made everything said often. I began then to consciously listen to what anybody was saying and what they did say while they were saying what they were saying. This was not yet the beginning of writing but it was the beginning of knowing what there was that made there be no repetition. No matter how often what happened had happened any time any one told anything there was no repetition. This is what William James calls the Will to Live. If not nobody would live.

And so I began to find out then by listening the difference between repetition and insisting and it is a very important thing to know. You listen as you know.

Then there is another thing that also has something to do with repeating.

When all these eleven little aunts were listening as they were talking gradually some one of them was no longer listening. When this happened it might be that the time had come that any one or one of them was beginning repeating, that it was ceasing to be insisting or else perhaps it might be that the attention of one of some one of them had been worn out by adding something. What is the difference. Nothing makes any difference as long as some one is listening while they are talking.

That is what I gradually began to know.

Nothing makes any difference as long as some one is listening while they are talking. If the same person does the talking and the listening why so much the better there is just by so much the greater concentration. One may really indeed say that that is the essence of genius, of being most intensely alive, that is being one who is at the same time talking and listening. It is really that that makes one a genius. And it is necessary if you are to be really and truly alive it is necessary to be at once talking and listening, doing both things, not as if there were one thing, not as if they were two things, but doing them, well if you like, like the motor going inside and the car moving, they are part of the same thing.

I said in the beginning of saying this thing that if it were possible that a movement were lively enough it would exist so completely that it would not be necessary to see it moving against anything to know that it is moving. This is what we mean by life and in my way I have tried to make portraits of this thing always have tried always may try to make portraits of this thing.

If this existence is this thing is actually existing there can be no repetition. There is only repetition when there are descriptions being given of these things not when the things themselves are actually existing and this is therefore how my portrait writing began.

So we have now, a movement lively enough to be a thing in itself moving, it does not have to move against anything to know that it is moving, it does not need that there are generations existing.

Then we have insistence insistence that in its emphasis can never be repeating, because insistence is always alive and if it is alive it is never saying anything in the same way because emphasis can never be the same not even when it is most the same that is when it has been taught.

How do you like what you have.

This is a question that anybody can ask anybody. Ask it.

In asking it I began to make portraits of anybody.

How do you like what you have is one way of having an important thing to ask of any one.

That is essentially the portrait of any one, one portrait of any one.

I began to think about portraits of any one.

If they are themselves inside them what are they and what has it to do with what they do.

And does it make any difference what they do or how they do it, does it make any difference what they say or how they say it. Must they be in relation with any one or with anything in order to be one of whom one can make a portrait. I began to think a great deal about all these things.

Anybody can be interested in what anybody does but does that make any difference, is it all important.

Anybody can be interested in what anybody says, but does that make any difference, is it at all important.

I began to wonder about all that.

I began to wonder what it was that I wanted to have as a portrait, what there is that was to be the portrait.

I do not wonder so much now about that. I do not wonder about that at all any more. Now I wonder about other things, I wonder if what has been done makes any difference.

I wonder now if it is necessary to stand still to live if it is not necessary to stand still to live, and if it is if that is not perhaps to be a new way to write a novel. I wonder if you know what I mean. I do not quite know whether I do myself. I will not know until I have written that novel.

I have just tried to begin in writing *Four In America* because I am certain that what makes American success is American failure.

I am certain about that.

Some time I will explain that at great length but now I want to tell about how I wrote portraits. I wrote portraits knowing that each one is themselves inside them and something about them perhaps everything about them will tell some one all about that thing all about what is themselves inside them and I was then hoping completely hoping that I was that one the one who would tell that thing. Perhaps I was that one.

There is another thing that one has to think about, that is about thinking clearly and about confusion. That is something about which I have almost as much to say as I have about anything.

The difference between thinking clearly and confusion is the same difference that there is between repetition and insistence. A great many think that they know repetition when they see or hear it but do they. A great many think that they know confusion when they know or see it or hear it, but do they. A thing that seems very clear, seems very clear but is it. A thing that seems to be exactly the same thing may seem to be a repetition but is it. All this can be very exciting, and it had a great deal to do with portrait writing.

As I say a thing that is very clear may easily not be clear at all, a thing that may be confused may be very clear. But everybody knows that. Yes anybody knows that. It is like the necessity of knowing one's father and one's mother one's grandmothers and one's grandfathers, but is it necessary and if it is can it be no less easily forgotten.

As I say the American thing is the vitality of movement, so that there need be nothing against which the movement shows as movement. And if this vitality is lively enough is there in that clarity any confusion is there in that clarity any repetition. I myself do not think so. But I am inclined to believe that there is really no difference between clarity and confusion, just think of any life that is alive, is there really any difference between clarity and confusion. Now I am quite certain that there is really if anything is alive no difference between clarity and confusion. When I first began writing portraits of any one I was not so sure, not so certain of this thing that there is no difference between clarity and confusion. I was however almost certain then when I began writing portraits that if anything is alive there is no such thing as repetition. I do not know that I have ever changed my mind about that. At any rate I did then begin the writing of portraits and I will tell you now all there is to tell about all that. I had of course written about every kind of men and women in *The Making of Americans* but in writing portraits I wanted not to write about any one doing or even saying anything, I found this a difficult enough thing to begin.

I remember very well what happened. As I say I had the habit of conceiving myself as completely talking and listening, listening was talking and talking was listening and in so doing I conceived what I at that time called the rhythm of anybody's personality. If listening was talking and talking was listening then and at the same time any little movement any little expression was a resemblance, and a resemblance was something that presupposed remembering.

Listening and talking did not presuppose resemblance and as they do not presuppose resemblance, they do not necessitate remembering. Already then as you see there was a complication which was a bother to me in my conception of the rhythm of a personality. I have for so many years tried to get the better of that the better of this bother. The bother was simply that and one may say it is the bother that has always been a bother to anybody for anybody conceiving anything. Dillinger[2] is dead it was even a bother for him.

As I say as I felt the existence of anybody later as I felt the existence of anybody or anything, there was then the listening and talking which I was doing which anybody was doing and there were the little things that made of any one some one resembling some one.

And one does of course by any little thing by any little way by any little expression, any one does of course resemble some one, and any one can notice this thing notice this resemblance and in so doing they have to remember some one and this is a different thing from listening and talking. In other words the making of a portrait of any one is as they are existing and as they are existing has nothing to do with remembering any one or anything. Do you see my point, but of course yes you do. You do see that there are two things and not one and if one wants to make one portrait of some one and not two you can see that one can be bothered completely bothered by this thing. As I say it is something that has always bothered any one.

Funnily enough the cinema has offered a solution of this thing. By a continuously moving picture of any one there is no memory of any other thing and there is that thing existing, it is in a way if you like one portrait of anything not a number of them. There again you do see what I mean.

Now I in my way wanted to make portraits of any one later in *Tender Buttons* I also wanted to make portraits of anything as one thing as one portrait and although and that was my trouble in the

2. John Dillinger (1903–34), American gangster, shot dead in Chicago by F.B.I. agents, after escaping from gaol where he had been detained on a murder charge.

beginning I felt the thing the person as existing and as everything in that person entered in to make that person little ways and expressions that made resembling, it was necessary for me nevertheless not to realize these things as remembering but to realize the one thing as existing and there they were and I was noticing, well you do see that it was a bother and I was bothering very much bothering about this thing.

In the beginning and I will read you some portraits to show you this I continued to do what I was doing in *The Making of Americans*, I was doing what the cinema was doing, I was making a continuous succession of the statement of what that person was until I had not many things but one thing. As I read you some of the portraits of that period you will see what I mean.

I of course did not think of it in terms of the cinema, in fact I doubt whether at that time I had ever seen a cinema but, and I cannot repeat this too often any one is of one's period and this our period was undoubtedly the period of the cinema and series production. And each of us in our own way are bound to express what the world in which we are living is doing.

You see then what I was doing in my beginning portrait writing and you also understand what I mean when I say there was no repetition. In a cinema picture no two pictures are exactly alike each one is just that much different from the one before, and so in those early portraits there was as I am sure you will realize as I read them to you also as there was in *The Making of Americans* no repetition. Each time that I said the somebody whose portrait I was writing was something that something was just that much different from what I had just said that somebody was and little by little in this way a whole portrait came into being, a portrait that was not description and that was made by each time, and I did a great many times, say it, that somebody was something, each time there was a difference just a difference enough so that it could go on and be a present something. Oh yes you all do understand. You understand this. You see that in order to do this there must be no remembering, remembering is repetition, remembering is also confusion. And this too you will presently know all about.

Remembering is repetition anybody can know that. In doing a portrait of any one, the repetition consists in knowing that that one is a kind of a one, that the things he does have been done by others like him that the things he says have been said by others like him, but, and this is the important thing, there is no repetition in hearing and saying the things he hears and says when he is hearing and saying them. And so in doing a portrait of him if it were possible to make that portrait a portrait of him saying and hearing what he says and hears while he is saying and hearing it there is then in so doing neither memory nor repetition no matter how often that which he says and hears is heard and said. This was the discovery I made as I talked and listened more and more and this is what I did when I made portraits of every one I know. I said what I knew as they said and heard what they heard and said until I had completely emptied myself of all they were that is all that they were in being one hearing and saying what they heard and said in every way that they heard and said anything.

And this is the reason why that what I wrote was exciting although those that did not really see what it was thought it was repetition. If it had been repetition it would not have been exciting but it was exciting and it was not repetition. It never is. I never repeat that is while I am writing.

As I say what one repeats is the scene in which one is acting, the days in which one is living, the coming and going which one is doing, anything one is remembering is a repetition, but existing as a human being, that is being listening and hearing is never repetition. It is not repetition if it is that which you are actually doing because naturally each time the emphasis is different just as the cinema has each time a slightly different thing to make it all be moving. And each one of us has to do that, otherwise there is no existing. As Galileo remarked, it does move.

So you see what I mean about those early portraits and the middle part of *The Making of Americans*. I built them up little by little each time I said it it changed just a little and then when I was completely emptied of knowing that the one of whom I was making a portrait existed I had made a portrait of that one.

To go back to something I said that remembering was the only repetition, also that remembering was the only confusion. And I think you begin to see what I mean by that.

No matter how complicated anything is, if it is not mixed up with remembering there is no confusion, but and that is the trouble with a great many so called intelligent people they mix up remembering with talking and listening, and as a result they have theories about anything but as remembering is repetition and confusion, and being existing that is listening and talking is action and not repetition intelligent people although they talk as if they knew something are really confusing, because they are so to speak keeping two times going at once, the repetition time of remembering and the actual time of talking but, and as they are rarely talking and listening, that is the talking being listening and the listening being talking, although they are clearly saying something they are not clearly creating something, because they are because they always are remembering, they are not at the same time talking and listening. Do you understand. Do you any or all of you understand. Anyway that is the way it is. And you hear it even if you do not say it in the way I say it as I hear it and say it.

I say I never repeat while I am writing because while I am writing I am most completely, and that is if you like being a genius, I am most entirely and completely listening and talking, the two in one and the one in two and that is having completely its own time and it has in it no element of remembering. Therefore there is in it no element of confusion, therefore there is in it no element of repetition. Do you do you do you really understand.

And does it make any difference to you if you do understand. It makes an awful lot of difference to me. It is very exciting to have all this be.

Gradually then I began making portraits. And how did I begin.

When I first began writing although I felt very strongly that something that made that some one be some one was something that I must use as being them, I naturally began to describe them as they were doing anything. In short I wrote a story as a story, that is the way I began, and slowly I realized this confusion, a real confusion, that in writing a story one had to be remembering, and that novels are soothing because so many people one may say everybody can remember almost anything. It is this element of remembering that makes novels so soothing. But and that was the thing that I was gradually finding out listening and talking at the same time that is realizing the existence of living being actually existing did not have in it any element of remembering and so the time of existing was not the same as in the novels that were soothing. As I say all novels are soothing because they make anything happen as they can happen that is by remembering anything. But and I kept wondering as I talked and listened all at once, I wondered is there any way of making what I know come out as I know it, come out not as remembering. I found this very exciting. And I began to make portraits.

I kept on knowing people by resemblances, that was partly memory and it bothered me but I knew I had to do everything and I tried to do that so completely that I would lose it. I made charts and charts of everybody who looked like anybody until I got so that I hardly knew which one I knew on the street and which one looked like them. I did this until at last any one looking like any one else had no importance. It was not a thing that was any longer an important thing, I knew completely how any one looked like any other one and that became then only a practical matter, a thing one might know as what any one was liable to do, but this to me then was no longer interesting. And so I went on with portrait writing.

I cannot tell you although I think I can, that, as I can read any number of soothing novels in fact nothing else soothes me I found it not a thing that it was interesting to do. And I think now you know why it was not an interesting thing to do. We in this period have not lived in remembering, we have living in moving being necessarily so intense that existing is indeed something, is indeed that thing that we are doing. And so what does it really matter what anybody does. The newspapers are full of what anybody does and anybody knows what anybody does but the thing that is important is the intensity of anybody's existence. Once more I remind you of Dillinger. It was not what he did that was exciting but the excitement of what he was as being exciting that was exciting. There is a world of difference and in it there is essentially no remembering.

And so I am trying to tell you what doing portraits meant to me, I had to find out what it was inside any one, and by any one I mean every one I had to find out inside every one what was in them that was intrinsically exciting and I had to find out not by what they said not by what they did not by how much or how little they resembled any other one but I had to find it out by the intensity of

movement that there was inside in any one of them. And of course
do not forget, of course I was interested in any one. I am. Of course
I am interested in any one. And in any one I must or else I must
betake myself to some entirely different occupation and I do not
think I will, I must find out what is moving inside them that makes
them them, and I must find out how I by the thing moving excitedly
inside in me can make a portrait of them.

You can understand why I did it so often, why I did it in so many
ways why I say that there is no repetition because, and this is
absolutely true, that the exciting thing inside in any one if it is
really inside in them is not a remembered thing, if it is really inside
in them, it is not a confused thing, it is not a repeated thing. And
if I could in any way and I have done it in every way if I could make
a portrait of that inside them without any description of what they
are doing and what they are saying then I too was neither repeating,
nor remembering nor being in a confusion.

You see what I mean by what I say. But I know you do.

Will you see it as clearly when I read you some of the portraits
that I have written. Maybe you will but I doubt it. But if you do
well then if you do you will see what I have done and do do.

A thing you all know is that in the three novels written in this
generation that are the important things written in this generation,
there is, in none of them a story. There is none in Proust in *The
Making of Americans* or in *Ulysses*. And this is what you are now to
begin to realize in this description I am giving you of making portraits.

It is of course perfectly natural that autobiographies are being
well written and well read. You do see anybody can see that so much
happens every day and that anybody literally anybody can read or
hear about it told the day that it happens. A great deal happens
every day and any day and as I say anybody literally anybody can
hear or read everything or anything about anything or everything
that happens every day just as it has happened or is happening on
that day. You do see what that means. Novels then which tell a
story are really then more of the same much more of the same, and
of course anybody likes more of the same and so a great many
novels are written and a great many novels are read telling more of
these stories but you can see you do see that the important things

written in this generation do not tell a story. You can see that it is natural enough.

You begin definitely to feel that it had to be that I was to write portraits as I wrote them. I began to write them when I was about in the middle of *The Making of Americans*, and if you read *The Making of Americans* you will realize why this was inevitable.

I began writing the portraits of any one by saying what I knew of that one as I talked and listened that one, and each time that I talked and listened that one I said what I knew they were then. This made my early portraits and some that I finally did such as *Four Dishonest Ones Told by a Description of What They Do*, *Matisse* and *Picasso* and a lot of others, did as completely as I then could strictly did this thing. Every time I said what they were I said it so that they were this thing, and each time I said what they were as they were, as I was, naturally more or less but never the same thing each time that I said what they were I said what they were, not that they were different nor that I was different but as it was not the same moment which I said I said it with a difference. So finally I was emptied of saying this thing, and so no longer said what they were.

FOUR DISHONEST ONES

TOLD BY A DESCRIPTION OF WHAT THEY DO

They are what they are. They have not been changing. They are what they are.

Each one is what that one is. Each is what each is. They are not needing to be changing.

One is what she is. She does not need to be changing. She is what she is. She is not changing. She is what she is.

She is not changing. She is knowing nothing of not changing. She is not needing to be changing.

What is she doing. She is working. She is not needing to be changing. She is working very well, she is not needing to be changing. She has been working very hard. She has been suffering. She is not needing to be changing.

She has been living and working, she has been quiet and working, she has been suffering and working, she has been watching and working, she has been waiting, she has been working, she has been waiting and working, she is not needing to be changing.[3]

At this time also I wanted to make portraits of places, I did. I did make them of the Bon Marché, of the Galeries Lafayette, of a crowd at Mi-Careme, I have always liked what I did with that one. It was completely something. And there again in doing the portraits of these places and these crowds, I did Italians, and Americans too like that, I continued to do as I had done in *The Making of Americans*. I told exactly and completely each time of telling what that one is inside in them. As I told you in comparing it to a cinema picture one second was never the same as the second before or after.

MI-CAREME

There was a man who said one could recognize him when one saw him again by the scar on the end of his nose and under his eye but these scars were very little ones almost not anything and one would remember him because he was one who had been saying that he was a man tired of working tired of being one being working, and that he would be very amusing, he could be amusing by saying something that would make any one listening begin blushing but, he said, he would not do such a thing he would be politely amusing and he was amusing and some being amused by him were not frightened by him. He might have been amusing to some who were at the same time ones frightened by him. He might be very amusing to some who would never in any way think that he could frighten any one.[4]

At any rate I did these portraits and they were very exciting, they were exciting to me and they were exciting to others who read them.

Then slowly once more I got bothered, after all I listened and talked but that was not all I did in knowing at any present time when I was stating anything what anything was. I was also looking, and that could not be entirely left out.

The trouble with including looking, as I have already told you, was that in regard to human beings looking inevitably carried in its train realizing movements and expression and as such forced me

3. *Portraits and Prayers*, Random House, New York, 1934, p. 57.
4. ibid., p. 173.

into recognizing resemblances, and so forced remembering and in forcing remembering caused confusion of present with past and future time.

Do you see what I mean. But certainly you certainly do. And so I began again to do portraits but this time it was not portraits of men and women and children, it was portraits of anything and so I made portraits of rooms and food and everything because there I could avoid this difficulty of suggesting remembering more easily while including looking with listening and talking than if I were to describe human beings. I will go a little more into that.

This is the great difficulty that bothered anybody creating anything in this generation. The painters naturally were looking, that was their occupation and they had too to be certain that looking was not confusing itself with remembering. Remembering with them takes the form of suggesting in their painting in place of having actually created the thing in itself that they are painting.

In writing the thing that is the difficulty is the question of confusing time, and this is the thing that bothered and still bothers any one in this generation. Later on in another writing I will tell about how this thing that is time has to do with grammar vocabulary and tenses. But now I am keeping strictly to the matter of portraits and repetition.

I began to make portraits of things and enclosures that is rooms and places because I needed to completely face the difficulty of how to include what is seen with hearing and listening and at first if I were to include a complicated listening and talking it would be too difficult to do. That is why painters paint still lives. You do see why they do.

So I began to do this thing, I tried to include color and movement and what I did is what you have all either read or heard of, a volume called *Tender Buttons*.

I for a time did not make portraits because as I was trying to live in looking, and looking was not to mix itself up with remembering I wished to reduce to its minimum listening and talking. In *Tender Buttons*, I described anything, and I will read you a few things to show you what I did then.

A DOG

A little monkey goes like a donkey that means to say that means to say that more sighs last goes. Leave with it. A little monkey goes like a donkey.[5]

Cloudiness what is cloudiness, is it a lining, is it a roll, is it melting.[6]

A hurt mended stick, a hurt mended cup, a hurt mended article of exceptional relaxation and annoyance, a hurt mended, hurt and mended is so necessary that no mistake is intended.[7]

Abandon a garden and the house is bigger. This is not smiling. This is comfortable. There is the comforting of predilection. An open object is establishing the loss that there was when the vase was not inside the place. It was not wandering.[8]

You see what I mean, I did express what something was, a little by talking and listening to that thing, but a great deal by looking at that thing.

This as I say has been the great problem of our generation, so much happens and anybody at any moment knows everything that is happening that things happening although interesting are not really exciting. And an artist an artist inevitably has to do what is really exciting. That is what he is inside him, that is what an artist really is inside him, he is exciting, and if he is not there is nothing to any of it.

And so the excitement in me was then that I was to more and more include looking to make it a part of listening and talking and I did the portrait of Mabel Dodge and Susie Assado and Preciocilla and some others. But this was all after I had done *Tender Buttons*.

I began to wonder at at about this time just what one saw when one looked at anything really looked at anything. Did one see sound, and what was the relation between color and sound, did it make itself by description by a word that meant it or did it make itself by a word in itself. All this time I was of course not interested in emotion or that anything happened. I was less interested then in these things than I ever had been. I lived my life with emotion and

5. *Tender Buttons*, Claire-Marie, New York, 1914, p. 26.

6. ibid., p. 38.

7. ibid., p. 43.

8. 'Portrait of Mabel Dodge at the Villa Curonia', in *Portraits and Prayers*, Random House, New York, 1934, p. 101.

with things happening but I was creating in my writing by simply looking. I was as I say at that time reducing as far as it was possible for me to reduce them, talking and listening.

I became more and more excited about how words which were the words that made whatever I looked at look like itself were not the words that had in them any quality of description. This excited me very much at that time.

And the thing that excited me so very much at that time and still does is that the words or words that make what I looked at be itself were always words that to me very exactly related themselves to that thing the thing at which I was looking, but as often as not had as I say nothing whatever to do with what any words would do that described that thing.

Those of you that have seen *Four Saints in Three Acts* must know do know something of what I mean.

Of course by the time *Four Saints* was written I had mastered very much what I was doing then when I wrote *Tender Buttons*. By the time I wrote the *Four Saints* I had written a great a great many portraits and I had in hundreds of ways related words, then sentences then paragraphs to the thing at which I was looking and I had also come to have happening at the same time looking and listening and talking without any bother about resemblances and remembering.

One of the things as I said that made me most anxious at one time was the relation of color to the words that exactly meant that but had no element in it of description. One portrait I did I will read it to you of Lipschitz did this color thing better than I had ever before been able to do it.

LIPSCHITZ

Like and like likely and likely likely and likely like and like.

He had a dream. He dreamed he heard a pheasant calling and very likely a pheasant was calling.

To whom went.

He had a dream he dreamed he heard a pheasant calling and most likely a pheasant was calling.

In time.[9]

9. *Portraits and Prayers*, p. 63.

Thus for over a very considerable period of time sometimes a great many at a time and sometimes one at a time and sometimes several at a time I continued to do portraits. Around about this time I did a second one of Carl Van Vechten, one of Sherwood Anderson, one of Cocteau and a second one of Picasso. They were different from those that I had done in the beginning and very different from those I did just after doing *Tender Buttons*. These were less concentrated, they moved more although the movement was definitely connected with color and not so closely connected with talking and listening.

VAN OR TWENTY YEARS AFTER

A SECOND PORTRAIT OF CARL VAN VECHTEN

Twenty years after, as much as twenty years after in as much as twenty years after, after twenty years and so on. It is it is it is it is it is.

Keep it in sight all right.

Not to the future but to the fuchsia.

Tied and untied and that is all there is about it. And as tied and as beside, and as beside and tied. Tied and untied and beside and as beside and as untied and as tied and as untied and as beside.[10]

And then slowly it changed again, talking and listening came slowly again to be more important than that at which I was looking. Talking and listening became more important again but at the same time that it was talking and listening it had within itself an entirely different emotion of moving.

Let me tell you just what I did as I did this thing.

As always happens one commences again. However often it happens one does commence again and now in my way I did commence again.

I was again bothered about something and it had to do as my bother always has had to do with a thing being contained within itself.

I realized that granted looking and listening and talking being all happening at one time and that I had been finding the words that did create that thing did create the portrait that was the object of the looking listening and talking I had been doing nevertheless I

10. *Portraits and Prayers*, p. 157.

had been losing something, something I had had, in *The Making of Americans* and in *Tender Buttons*, that is a thing contained within itself.

As I say a motor goes inside and the car goes on, but my business my ultimate business as an artist was not with where the car goes as it goes but with the movement inside that is of the essence of its going. And had I in these rather beautiful portraits I had been writing had I a little lost this thing. Whether I had or whether I had not began a little to worry me not really worry but to be there inside me, had I lost a little the excitement of having this inside me. Had I. I did not think I really had but had I.

This brings me back once more to the subject of repetition.

The composition we live in changes but essentially what happens does not change. We inside us do not change but our emphasis and the moment in which we live changes. That is it is never the same moment it is never the same emphasis at any successive moment of existing. Then really what is repetition. It is very interesting to ask and it is a very interesting thing to know.

If you think anything over and over and eventually in connection with it you are going to succeed or fail, succeeding and failing is repetition because you are always either succeeding or failing but any two moments of thinking it over is not repetition. Now you see that is where I differ from a great many people who say I repeat and they do not. They do not think their succeeding or failing is what makes repetition, in other words they do not think that what happens makes repetition but that it is the moment to moment emphasizing that makes repetition. Now I think the succeeding and failing is what makes the repetition not the moment to moment emphasizing that makes repetition.

Instinctively as I say you all agree with me because really in these days you all like crime stories or have liked crime stories or if you have not you should have and at any rate you do like newspapers or radio or funny papers, and in all these it is the moment to moment emphasis in what is happening that is interesting, the succeeding and failing is really not the thing that is interesting.

In the portraits that I did in that period of which I have just been speaking the later period considerably after the war the strictness of not letting remembering mix itself with looking and listening and talking which began with *The Making of Americans* and went on all through *Tender Buttons* and what came immediately after, all the period of *Geography and Plays* this strictness perhaps weakened a little weakened a little because and that in a way was an astonishment to me, I found that I was for a little while very much taken with the beauty of the sounds as they came from me as I made them.

This is a thing that may be at any time a temptation. This temptation came to me a little after the Saint Remy period when I wrote *Saints in Seven, Four Religions, Capital Capitals*. The strict discipline that I had given myself, the absolute refusal of never using a word that was not an exact word all through the *Tender Buttons* and what I may call the early Spanish and *Geography and Plays* period finally resulted in things like *Susie Assado* and *Preciocilla* etc. in an extraordinary melody of words and a melody of excitement in knowing that I had done this thing.

Then in concentrating this melody I wrote in Saint Remy these things I have just mentioned *Four Religions, Capital Capitals, Saints in Seven* and a great many other things. In doing these I concentrated the internal melody of existence that I had learned in relation to things seen into the feeling I then had there in Saint Remy of light and air and air moving and being still. I worked at these things then with a great deal of concentration and as it was to me an entirely new way of doing it I had as a result a very greatly increased melody. This melody for a little while after rather got the better of me and it was at that time that I wrote these portraits of which I have just spoken, the second Picasso, the second Carl Van Vechten, the Jean Cocteau, Lipschitz, the Sitwells, Edith Sitwell, Joe Davidson, quantities of portraits. Portraits after my concentrated effort at Saint Remy to really completely and exactly find the word for the air and sky and light and existence down there was relatively a simple thing and I as you may say held these portraits in my hand and they came easily and beautifully and truly. But as I say I did begin to think that I was rather drunk with what I had done. And I am always one to prefer being sober. I must be sober. It is so much more exciting to be sober, to be exact and concentrated and sober. So then as I say I began again.

So here we have it. There was the period of *The Making of Americans* portraiture, when by listening and talking I conceived at every moment the existence of some one, and I put down each moment that I had the existence of that one inside in me until I had completely emptied myself of this that I had had as a portrait of that one. This as I say made what has been called repetition but, and you will see, each sentence is just the difference in emphasis that inevitably exists in the successive moment of my containing within me the existence of that other one achieved by talking and listening inside in me and inside in that one. These were the early portraits I did. Then this slowly changed to portraits of spaces inclosed with or without somebody in them but written in the same way in the successive moments of my realizing them. As I said it was if you like, it was like a cinema picture made up of succession and each moment having its own emphasis that is its own difference and so there was the moving and the existence of each moment as it was in me.

Then as I said I had the feeling that something should be included and that something was looking, and so concentrating on looking I did the *Tender Buttons* because it was easier to do objects than people if you were just looking. Then I began to do plays to make the looking have in it an element of moving and during this time I also did portraits that did the same thing. In doing these things I found that I created a melody of words that filled me with a melody that gradually made me do portraits easily by feeling the melody of any one. And this then began to bother me because perhaps I was getting drunk with melody and I do not like to be drunk I like to be sober and so I began again.

I began again not to let the looking be predominating not to have the listening and talking be predominating but to once more denude all this of anything in order to get back to the essence of the thing contained within itself. That led me to some very different writing that I am going to tell about in the next thing I write but it also led to some portraits that I do think did do what I was then hoping would be done that is at least by me, would be done in this way if it were to be done by me.

Of these there were quite a number but perhaps two that did it the most completely the thing I wanted to do were portraits of George Hugnet and Bernard Faÿ. I will read them to you and you will see what I mean. All the looking was there the talking and listening was there but instead of giving what I was realizing at any and every moment of them and of me until I was empty of them I made them contained within the thing I wrote that was them. The thing in itself folded itself up inside itself like you might fold a thing up to be another thing which is that thing inside in that thing.

Do you see what I mean.

If you think how you fold things or make a boat or anything else out of paper or getting anything to be inside anything, the hole in the doughnut or the apple in the dumpling perhaps you will see what I mean. I will try and tell a little more about this thing and how I felt about this thing and how it happened.

This time I do repeat; in going over this again, there was the portrait writing of *The Making of Americans* period. There was the portrait writing of the *Tender Buttons* period, Mabel Dodge came into that. There was the portrait writing of the *Geography and Plays* period, which ended up with *Capital Capitals*, and then there was the portrait writing of the *Useful Knowledge* period, including portraits of Sherwood Anderson and Carl Van Vechten. Of course in each one of these periods there were many many portraits written as I wrote portraits of almost any one and as at all times I write practically every day, to be sure not long but practically every day and if you write not long but practically every day you do get a great deal written. This is what I do and so I do do get a great deal written. I have written a great many portraits.

So then as I said at the end of all this I had come to know I had a melody and to be certain of my melody that melody carried me to be sure always by looking and listening and talking but melody did carry me and so as always I had once more to begin again and I began again.

Melody should always be a by-product it should never be an end in itself it should not be a thing by which you live if you really and truly are one who is to do anything and so as I say I very exactly began again.

I had begun again some time before in working at grammar and sentences and paragraphs and what they mean and at plays and how they disperse themselves in relation to anything seen. And soon I was so completely concerned with these things that melody, beauty if you like was once more as it should always be a by-product.

I did at the same time as I did plays and grammar at this time, I did do portraits in these portraits I felt an entirely different thing. How could a thing if it is a human being if it is anything be entirely contained within itself. Of course it is, but is it and how is it and how did I know that it is.

This was the thing that I found then to be completely interesting, this was the thing I found then to be completely exciting. How was anything contained within itself.

I felt that I began then to feel any one to be inside them very differently than I had ever found any one be themselves inside them. This was the time that I wrote *Lucy Church Amiably* which quite definitely as a conception of what is seen was contained by itself inside it, although there it was a conceiving of what I was looking at as a landscape was to be itself inside in it, it was I said to be like an engraving and I think it is. But the people in it were in it as contained within the whole of it. I wanted however to do portraits where there was more movement inside in the portrait and yet it was to be the whole portrait completely held within that inside.

I began to feel movement to be a different thing than I had felt it to be.

It was to me beginning to be a less detailed thing and at the same time a thing that existed so completely inside in it and it was it was so completely inside that really looking and listening and talking were not a way any longer needed for me to know about this thing about movement being existing.

And how could I have this happen, let me read you the short portrait of George Hugnet and perhaps you will see what I mean. It is all there.

It really does not make any difference who George Hugnet was or what he did or what I said, all that was necessary was that there was something completely contained within itself and being contained within itself was moving, not moving in relation to anything not moving in relation to itself but just moving, I think I almost at that time did this thing. Do you at all in this portrait of George Hugnet that I will now read to you do you really see what I mean and in this portrait of Bernard Faÿ.

GEORGE HUGNET

George Genevieve Geronimo straightened it out without their finding it out.

Grammar makes George in our ring which Grammar makes George in our ring.

Grammar is as disappointed not is as grammar is as disappointed.

Grammar is not as Grammar is as disappointed.

George is in our ring. Grammar is not is disappointed. In are ring.

George Genevieve in are ring.[11]

BERNARD FAŸ

Patience is amiable and amiably.
What is amiable and amiably.
Patience is amiable and amiably.
What is impatience.
Impatience is amiable and amiably.[12]

Anyway this was to me a tremendously important thing and why. Well it was an important thing in itself for me but it was also an important thing because it made me realize what poetry really is.

This has something to do with what Edgar Allan Poe is.

But now to make you understand, that although I was as usual looking listening and talking perhaps more than ever at that time and leading a very complicated and perhaps too exciting every day living, never the less it really did not matter what I saw or said or heard, or if you like felt, because now there was at last something that was more vibrant than any of all that and somehow some way I had isolated it and in a way had gotten it written. It was about that time that I wrote *Four Saints*.

This was all very exciting and it went on and I did not do a great many portraits at that time. I wrote a great deal of poetry a great many plays and operas and some novels in which I tried again to do this thing, in one or two I more or less did, one called *Brim Beauvais*, I very often did, that is I created something out of something without adding anything, do you see what I mean.

11. *Portraits and Prayers*, p. 66.
12. ibid., p. 42.

It does mean something I do assure you it does mean something although it is very difficult to say it in any way except in the way that I said it then.

And so as I say I did not write a great many portraits at that time.

Then slowly I got a little tired, all that had been tremendously exciting, and one day then I began to write the *Autobiography of Alice B. Toklas.* You all know the joke of that, and in doing it I did an entirely different something something that I had been thinking about for some time and that had come out of some poetry I had been writing, *Before the Flowers Of Friendship Faded Friendship Faded*,[13] but that is too long a story to begin now but it will be all told in 'Poetry and Grammar'.

However the important thing was that for the first time in writing, I felt something outside me while I was writing, hitherto I had always had nothing but what was inside me while I was writing. Beside that I had been going for the first time since my college days to lectures. I had been going to hear Bernard Faÿ lecture about Franco-American things and I had become interested in the relation of a lecturer to his audience. I had never thought about an audience before, not even when I wrote *Composition as Explanation* which was a lecture but now I suddenly began, to feel the outside inside and the inside outside and it was perhaps not so exciting but it was very interesting. Anyway it was quite exciting.

And so I wrote the *Autobiography of Alice B. Toklas* and told what happened as it had happened.

As I said way back, as now everybody at any moment can know what it is that happens while it happens, what happens is interesting but it is not really exciting. And I am not sure that I am not right about that. I hope you all think I am right about that. At any rate it is true there is something much more exciting than anything that happens and now and always I am writing the portrait of that.

I have been writing the portraits of *Four In America*,[14] trying to write Grant, and Wilbur Wright and Henry James and Washington do other things than they did do so as to try to find out just what it is that what happens has to do with what is.

I have finished that and now I am trying in these lectures to

13. See p. 274.
14. See p. 291.

tell what is by telling about how it happened that I told about what it is.

I hope you quite all see what I mean. Anyway I suppose inevitably I will go on doing it.

6

POETRY AND GRAMMAR

WHAT is poetry and if you know what poetry is what is prose.

There is no use in telling more than you know, no not even if you do not know it.

But do you do you know what prose is and do you know what poetry is.

I have said that the words in plays written in poetry are more lively than the same words written by the same poet in other kinds of poetry. It undoubtedly was true of Shakespeare, is it inevitably true of everybody. That is one thing to think about. I said that the words in a play written in prose are not as lively words as the words written in other prose by the same writer. This is true of Goldsmith and I imagine it is true of almost any writer.

There again there is something to know.

One of the things that is a very interesting thing to know is how you are feeling inside you to the words that are coming out to be outside of you.

Do you always have the same kind of feeling in relation to the sounds as the words come out of you or do you not. All this has so much to do with grammar and with poetry and with prose.

Words have to do everything in poetry and prose and some writers write more in articles and prepositions and some say you should write in nouns, and of course one has to think of everything.

A noun is a name of anything, why after a thing is named write about it. A name is adequate or it is not. If it is adequate then why go on calling it, if it is not then calling it by its name does no good.

People if you like to believe it can be made by their names. Call anybody Paul and they get to be a Paul call anybody Alice and they get to be an Alice perhaps yes perhaps no, there is something in that, but generally speaking, things once they are named the name does not go on doing anything to them and so why write in nouns. Nouns are the name of anything and just naming names is alright when you want to call a roll but is it any good for anything else. To be sure in many places in Europe as in America they do like to call rolls.

As I say a noun is a name of a thing, and therefore slowly if you feel what is inside that thing you do not call it by the name by which it is known. Everybody knows that by the way they do when they are in love and a writer should always have that intensity of emotion about whatever is the object about which he writes. And therefore and I say it again more and more one does not use nouns.

Now what other things are there beside nouns, there are a lot of other things beside nouns.

When you are at school and learn grammar grammar is very exciting. I really do not know that anything has ever been more exciting than diagraming sentences. I suppose other things may be more exciting to others when they are at school but to me undoubtedly when I was at school the really completely exciting thing was diagraming sentences and that has been to me ever since the one thing that has been completely exciting and completely completing. I like the feeling the everlasting feeling of sentences as they diagram themselves.

In that way one is completely possessing something and incidentally one's self. Now in that diagraming of the sentences of course there are articles and prepositions and as I say there are nouns but nouns as I say even by definition are completely not interesting, the same thing is true of adjectives. Adjectives are not really and truly interesting. In a way anybody can know always has known that, because after all adjectives effect nouns and as nouns are not really interesting the thing that effects a not too interesting thing is of necessity not interesting. In a way as I say anybody knows that because of course the first thing that anybody takes out of anybody's writing are the adjectives. You see of yourself how true it is that which I have just said.

Beside the nouns and the adjectives there are verbs and adverbs. Verbs and adverbs are more interesting. In the first place they have one very nice quality and that is that they can be so mistaken. It is wonderful the number of mistakes a verb can make and that is equally true of its adverb. Nouns and adjectives never can make mistakes can never be mistaken but verbs can be so endlessly, both as to what they do and how they agree or disagree with whatever they do. The same is true of adverbs.

In that way any one can see that verbs and adverbs are more interesting than nouns and adjectives.

Beside being able to be mistaken and to make mistakes verbs can change to look like themselves or to look like something else, they are, so to speak on the move and adverbs move with them and each of them find themselves not at all annoying but very often very much mistaken. That is the reason any one can like what verbs can do. Then comes the thing that can of all things be most mistaken and they are prepositions. Prepositions can live one long life being really being nothing but absolutely nothing but mistaken and that makes them irritating if you feel that way about mistakes but certainly something that you can be continuously using and everlastingly enjoying. I like prepositions the best of all, and pretty soon we will go more completely into that.

Then there are articles. Articles are interesting just as nouns and adjectives are not. And why are they interesting just as nouns and adjectives are not. They are interesting because they do what a noun might do if a noun was not so unfortunately so completely unfortunately the name of something. Articles please, a and an and the please as the name that follows cannot please. They the names that is the nouns cannot please, because after all you know well after all that is what Shakespeare meant when he talked about a rose by any other name.

I hope now no one can have any illusion about a noun or about the adjective that goes with the noun.

But an article an article remains as a delicate and a varied something and any one who wants to write with articles and knows how to use them will always have the pleasure that using something that is varied and alive can give. That is what articles are.

Beside that there are conjunctions, and a conjunction is not varied but it has a force that need not make any one feel that they are dull. Conjunctions have made themselves live by their work. They work and as they work they live and even when they do not work and in these days they do not always live by work still nevertheless they do live.

So you see why I like to write with prepositions and conjunctions and articles and verbs and adverbs but not with nouns and adjectives. If you read my writing you will you do see what I mean.

Of course then there are pronouns. Pronouns are not as bad as nouns because in the first place practically they cannot have adjectives go with them. That already makes them better than nouns.

Then beside not being able to have adjectives go with them, they of course are not really the name of anything. They represent some one but they are not its or his name. In not being his or its or her name they already have a greater possibility of being something than if they were as a noun is the name of anything. Now actual given names of people are more lively than nouns which are the name of anything and I suppose that this is because after all the name is only given to that person when they are born, there is at least the element of choice even the element of change and anybody can be pretty well able to do what they like, they may be born Walter and become Hub, in such a way they are not like a noun. A noun has been the name of something for such a very long time.

That is the reason that slang exists it is to change the nouns which have been names for so long. I say again. Verbs and adverbs and articles and conjunctions and prepositions are lively because they all do something and as long as anything does something it keeps alive.

One might have in one's list added interjections but really interjections have nothing to do with anything not even with themselves. There so much for that. And now to go into the question of punctuation.

There are some punctuations that are interesting and there are some punctuations that are not. Let us begin with the punctuations that are not. Of these the one but the first and the most the completely most uninteresting is the question mark. The question mark is alright when it is all alone when it is used as a brand on cattle or when it could be used in decoration but connected with writing it is completely entirely completely uninteresting. It is evident that if you ask a question you ask a question but anybody who can read at all knows when a question is a question as it is written in writing. Therefore I ask you therefore wherefore should one use it the question mark. Beside it does not in its form go with ordinary printing and so it pleases neither the eye nor the ear and it is therefore like a noun, just an unnecessary name of something. A question is a question, anybody can know that a question is a question and so why add to it the question mark when it is already there when the question is already there in the writing. Therefore I never could bring myself to use a question mark, I always found it positively revolting, and now very few do use it. Exclamation marks have the same difficulty and also quotation marks, they are unnecessary, they are ugly, they spoil the line of the writing or the printing and anyway what is the use, if you do not know that a question is a question what is the use of its being a question. The same thing is true of an exclamation. And the same thing is true of a quotation. When I first began writing I found it simply impossible to use question marks and quotation marks and exclamation points and now anybody sees it that way. Perhaps some day they will see it some other way but now at any rate anybody can and does see it that way.

So there are the uninteresting things in punctuation uninteresting in a way that is perfectly obvious, and so we do not have to go any farther into that. There are besides dashes and dots, and these might be interesting spaces might be interesting. They might if one felt that way about them.

One other little punctuation mark one can have feelings about and that is the apostrophe for possession. Well feel as you like about that, I can see and I do see that for many that for some the possessive case apostrophe has a gentle tender insinuation that makes it very difficult to definitely decide to do without it. One does do without it, I do, I mostly always do, but I cannot deny that from time to time I feel myself having regrets and from time to time I put it in to make the possessive case. I absolutely do not like it all alone when it is outside the word when the word is a plural, no then positively and definitely no, I do not like it and in leaving it out I feel no regret, there it is unnecessary and not ornamental but inside a word and its s well perhaps, perhaps it does appeal by its weakness to your weakness. At least at any rate from time to time I do find myself letting it alone if it has come in and sometimes it has come in. I cannot positively deny but that I do from time to time let it come in.

So now to come to the real question of punctuation, periods, commas, colons, semi-colons and capitals and small letters.

I have had a long and complicated life with all these.

Let us begin with these I use the least first and these are colons and semi-colons, one might add to these commas.

When I first began writing, I felt that writing should go on, I still do feel that it should go on but when I first began writing I was completely possessed by the necessity that writing should go on and if writing should go on what had colons and semi-colons to do with it, what had commas to do with it, what had periods to do with it what had small letters and capitals to do with it to do with writing going on which was at that time the most profound need I had in connection with writing. What had colons and semi-colons to do with it what had commas to do with it what had periods to do with it.

What had periods to do with it. Inevitably no matter how completely I had to have writing go on, physically one had to again and again stop sometime and if one had to again and again stop some time then periods had to exist. Beside I had always liked the look of periods and I liked what they did. Stopping sometime did not really keep one from going on, it was nothing that interfered, it was only something that happened, and as it happened as a perfectly natural happening, I did believe in periods and I used them. I really never stopped using them.

Beside that periods might later come to have a life of their own to commence breaking up things in arbitrary ways, that has happened lately with me in a poem I have written called *Winning His Way*, later I will read you a little of it. By the time I had written this poem about three years ago periods had come to have for me completely a life of their own. They could begin to act as they thought best and one might interrupt one's writing with them that is not really interrupt one's writing with them but one could come to stop arbitrarily stop at times in one's writing and so they could be used and you could use them. Periods could come to exist in this way and they could come in this way to have a life of their own. They did not serve you in any servile way as commas and colons and semi-colons do. Yes you do feel what I mean.

Periods have a life of their own a necessity of their own a feeling of their own a time of their own. And that feeling that life that necessity that time can express itself in an infinite variety that is the reason that I have always remained true to periods so much so that as I say recently I have felt that one could need them more than one had ever needed them.

You can see what an entirely different thing a period is from a comma, a colon or a semi-colon.

There are two different ways of thinking about colons and semi-colons you can think of them as commas and as such they are purely servile or you can think of them as periods and then using them can make you feel adventurous. I can see that one might feel about them as periods but I myself never have, I began unfortunately to feel them as a comma and commas are servile they have no life of their own they are dependent upon use and convenience and they are put there just for practical purposes. Semi-colons and colons had for me from the first completely this character the character that a comma has and not the character that a period has and therefore and definitely I have never used them. But now dimly and definitely I do see that they might well possibly they might have in them something of the character of the period and so it might have been an adventure to use them. I really do not think so. I think however lively they are or disguised they are they are definitely more comma than period and so really I cannot regret not having used them. They are more powerful more imposing more pretentious than a comma but they are a comma all the same. They really have within them deeply within them fundamentally within them the comma nature. And now what does a comma do and what has it to do and why do I feel as I do about them.

What does a comma do.

I have refused them so often and left them out so much and did without them so continually that I have come finally to be indifferent to them. I do not now care whether you put them in or not but for a long time I felt very definitely about them and would have nothing to do with them.

As I say commas are servile and they have no life of their own, and their use is not a use, it is a way of replacing one's own interest and I do decidedly like to like my own interest my own interest in what I am doing. A comma by helping you along holding your coat for you and putting on your shoes keeps you from living your life as actively as you should lead it and to me for many years and I still do feel that way about it only now I do not pay as much attention to them, the use of them was positively degrading. Let me tell you what I feel and what I mean and what I felt and what I meant.

When I was writing those long sentences of *The Making of Americans*, verbs active present verbs with long dependent adverbial clauses became a passion with me. I have told you that I recognize verbs and adverbs aided by prepositions and conjunctions with pronouns as possessing the whole of the active life of writing.

Complications make eventually for simplicity and therefore I have always liked dependent adverbial clauses. I have liked dependent adverbial clauses because of their variety of dependence and independence. You can see how loving the intensity of complication of these things that commas would be degrading. Why if you want the pleasure of concentrating on the final simplicity of excessive complication would you want any artificial aid to bring about that simplicity. Do you see now why I feel about the comma as I did and as I do.

Think about anything you really like to do and you will see what I mean.

When it gets really difficult you want to disentangle rather than to cut the knot, at least so anybody feels who is working with any thread, so anybody feels who is working with any tool so anybody feels who is writing any sentence or reading it after it has been written. And what does a comma do, a comma does nothing but make easy a thing that if you like it enough is easy enough without the comma. A long complicated sentence should force itself upon you, make you know yourself knowing it and the comma, well at the most a comma is a poor period that it lets you stop and take a breath but if you want to take a breath you ought to know yourself that you want to take a breath. It is not like stopping altogether which is what a period does stopping altogether has something to do with going on, but taking a breath well you are always taking a breath and why emphasize one breath rather than another breath. Anyway that is the way I felt about it and I felt that about it very very strongly. And so I almost never used a comma. The longer, the more complicated the sentence the greater the number of the same kinds of words I had following one after another, the more the very many more I had of them the more I felt the passionate need of their taking care of themselves by themselves and not helping them, and thereby enfeebling them by putting in a comma.

So that is the way I felt punctuation in prose, in poetry it is a little different but more so and later I will go into that. But that is the way I felt about punctuation in prose.

Another part of punctuation is capital letters and small letters. Anybody can really do as they please about that and in English printing one may say that they always have.

If you read older books you will see that they do pretty well what they please with capitals and small letters and I have always felt that one does do pretty well what one pleases with capitals and small letters. Sometimes one feels that Italians should be with a capital and sometimes with a small letter, one can feel like that about almost anything. I myself do not feel like that about proper names, I rather like to look at them with a capital on them but I can perfectly understand that a great many do not feel that way about it. In short in prose capitals and small letters have really nothing to do with the inner life of sentences and paragraphs as the other punctuation marks have as I have just been saying.

We still have capitals and small letters and probably for some time we will go on having them but actually the tendency is always toward diminishing capitals and quite rightly because the feeling that goes with them is less and less of a feeling and so slowly and inevitably just as with horses capitals will have gone away. They will come back from time to time but perhaps never really come back to stay.

Perhaps yes perhaps not but really and inevitably really it really does not really make any difference.

But and they will be with us as long as human beings continue to exist and have a vocabulary, sentences and paragraphs will be with us and therefore inevitably and really periods will be with us and it is of these things that will be always inevitably with us in prose and in poetry because prose and also poetry will also always always be with us that I will go on telling to you all I know.

Sentences and paragraphs. Sentences are not emotional but paragraphs are. I can say that as often as I like and it always remains as it is, something that is.

I said I found this out first in listening to Basket my dog drinking.

And anybody listening to any dog's drinking will see what I mean.

When I wrote *The Making of Americans* I tried to break down this essential combination by making enormously long sentences that would be as long as the longest paragraph and so to see if there was really and truly this essential difference between paragraphs and sentences, if one went far enough with this thing with making the sentences long enough to be as long as any paragraph and so producing in them the balance of a paragraph not a balance of a sentence, because of course the balance of a paragraph is not the same balance as the balance of a sentence.

It is only necessary to read anything in order to know that. I say if I succeeded in making my sentences so long that they held within themselves the balance of both both sentences and paragraphs, what was the result.

I did in some sentences in *The Making of Americans* succeed in doing this thing in creating a balance that was neither the balance of a sentence nor the balance of a paragraph and in doing so I felt dimly that I had done something that was not leading to anything because after all you should not lose two things in order to have one thing because in doing so you make writing just that much less varied.

That is one thing about what I did. There is also another thing and that was a very important thing, in doing this in achieving something that had neither the balance of a sentence nor the balance of a paragraph but a balance a new balance that had to do with a sense of movement of time included in a given space which as I have already said is a definitely American thing.

An American can fill up a space in having his movement of time by adding unexpectedly anything and yet getting within the included space everything he had intended getting.

A young french boy he is a red-haired descendant of the niece of Madame Recamier went to America for two weeks most unexpectedly and I said to him what did you notice most over there. Well he said at first they were not as different from us frenchmen as I expected them to be and then I did see that they were that they were different. And what, said I, well he said, when a train was going by at a terrific pace and we waved a hat the engine driver could make a bell quite carelessly go ting ting ting, the way anybody playing at a thing could do, it was not if you know what I mean professional he said. Perhaps you do see the connection with that and my sentences that had no longer the balance of sentences because they were not the parts of a paragraph nor were they a paragraph but they had made in so far as they had come to be so long and with the balance of their own that they had they had become something that was a whole thing and in so being they had a balance which was the balance of a space completely not filled but created by something moving as moving is not as moving should be. As I said Henry James in his later writing had had a dim feeling that this was what he knew he should do.

And so though as I say there must always be sentences and paragraphs the question can really be asked must there always be sentences and paragraphs is it not possible to achieve in itself and not by sentences and paragraphs the combination that sentences are not emotional and paragraphs are.

In a book called *How To Write* I worked a lot at this thing trying to find out just exactly what the balance the unemotional balance of a sentence is and what the emotional balance of a paragraph is and if it were possible to make even in a short sentence the two things come to be one. I think I did a few times succeed. Will you listen to one or two sentences where I did think I had done this thing.

He looks like a young man grown old.[1]

It looks like a garden but he had hurt himself by accident.[2]

A dog which you have never had before has sighed.[3]

Once when they were nearly ready they had ordered it to close.[4]

If a sound is made which grows louder and then stops how many times may it be repeated.[5]

Battles are named because there have been hills which have made a hill in a battle.[6]

[1]. *How To Write*, Plain Edition, Random House, 1931, p. 25.
[2]. ibid., p. 26.
[3]. ibid., p. 27.
[4]. ibid., p. 29.
[5]. ibid., p. 89.
[6]. ibid.

A bay and hills hills are surrounded by their having their distance very near.[7]

Poplars indeed will be and may be indeed will be cut down and will be sawn up and indeed will be used as wood and may be used for wood.[8]

The thing to remember is that if it is not if it is not what having left it to them makes it be very likely as likely as they would be after all after all choosing choosing to be here on time.[9]

In spite of my intending to write about grammar and poetry I am still writing about grammar and prose, but and of course it may or may not be true if you find out essentially what prose is and essentially what poetry is may you not have an exciting thing happening as I had it happen with sentences and paragraphs.

After all the natural way to count is not that one and one make two but to go on counting by one and one as chinamen do as anybody does as Spaniards do as my little aunts did. One and one and one and one and one. That is the natural way to go on counting.

Now what has this to do with poetry. It has a lot to do with poetry.

Everything has a lot to do with poetry everything has a lot to do with prose.

And has prose anything to do with poetry and has poetry anything to do with prose.

And what have nouns to do with poetry and periods and capital letters. The other punctuation marks we never have to mention again. People may do as they like with them but we never have to mention them. But nouns still have to be mentioned because in coming to avoid nouns a great deal happens and has happened. It was one of the things that happened in a book I called *Tender Buttons*.

In *The Making of Americans* a long a very long prose book made up of sentences and paragraphs and the new thing that was something neither the sentence or the paragraph each one alone or in combination had ever done, I said I had gotten rid of nouns and adjectives as much as possible by the method of living in adverbs in verbs in pronouns, in adverbial clauses written or implied and in conjunctions.

7. *How To Write*, p. 89.   8. ibid., p. 90.   9. ibid., p. 259.

But and after I had gone as far as I could in these long sentences and paragraphs that had come to do something else I then began very short things and in doing very short things I resolutely realized nouns and decided not to get around them but to meet them, to handle in short to refuse them by using them and in that way my real acquaintance with poetry was begun.

I will try to tell a little more clearly and in more detail just what happened and why it was if it was like natural counting, that is counting by one one one one one.

Nouns as you all know are the names of anything and as the names of anything of course one has had to use them. And what have they done. And what has any one done with them. That is something to know. It is as you may say as I may say a great deal to know.

Nouns are the name of anything and anything is named, that is what Adam and Eve did and if you like it is what anybody does, but do they go on just using the name until perhaps they do not know what the name is or if they do know what the name is they do not care about what the name is. This may happen of course it may. And what has poetry got to do with this and what has prose and if everything like a noun which is a name of anything is to be avoided what takes place. And what has that to do with poetry. A great deal I think and all this too has to do with other things with short and long lines and rhymes.

But first what is poetry and what is prose. I wonder if I can tell you.

We do know a little now what prose is. Prose is the balance the emotional balance that makes the reality of paragraphs and the unemotional balance that makes the reality of sentences and having realized completely realized that sentences are not emotional while paragraphs are, prose can be the essential balance that is made inside something that combines the sentence and the paragraph, examples of this I have been reading to you.

Now if that is what prose is and that undoubtedly is what prose is you can see that prose real prose really great written prose is bound to be made up more of verbs adverbs prepositions prepositional clauses and conjunctions than nouns. The vocabulary in prose of course is important if you like vocabulary is always important, in fact one of the things that you can find out and that I experimented with a great deal in *How To Write* vocabulary in itself and by itself can be interesting and can make sense. Anybody can know that by thinking of words. It is extraordinary how it is impossible that a vocabulary does not make sense. But that is natural indeed inevitable because a vocabulary is that by definition, and so because this is so the vocabulary in respect to prose is less important than the parts of speech, and the internal balance and the movement within a given space.

So then we understand we do know what prose is.

But what is poetry.

Is it more or is it less difficult to know what poetry is. I have sometimes thought it more difficult to know what poetry is but now that I do know what poetry is and if I do know what poetry is then it is not more difficult to know what it is than to know what prose is.

What is poetry.

Poetry has to do with vocabulary just as prose has not.

So you see prose and poetry are not at all alike. They are completely different.

Poetry is I say essentially a vocabulary just as prose is essentially not.

And what is the vocabulary of which poetry absolutely is. It is a vocabulary entirely based on the noun as prose is essentially and determinately and vigorously not based on the noun.

Poetry is concerned with using with abusing, with losing with wanting, with denying with avoiding with adoring with replacing the noun. It is doing that always doing that, doing that and doing nothing but that. Poetry is doing nothing but using losing refusing and pleasing and betraying and caressing nouns. That is what poetry does, that is what poetry has to do no matter what kind of poetry it is. And there are a great many kinds of poetry.

When I said.

A rose is a rose is a rose is a rose.

And then later made that into a ring I made poetry and what did I do I caressed completely caressed and addressed a noun.

Now let us think of poetry any poetry all poetry and let us see if this is not so. Of course it is so anybody can know that.

I have said that a noun is a name of anything by definition that is what it is and a name of anything is not interesting because once you know its name the enjoyment of naming it is over and therefore in writing prose names that is nouns are completely uninteresting. But and that is a thing to be remembered you can love a name and if you love a name then saying that name any number of times only makes you love it more, more violently more persistently more tormentedly. Anybody knows how anybody calls out the name of anybody one loves. And so that is poetry really loving the name of anything and that is not prose. Yes any of you can know that.

Poetry like prose has lived through a good deal. Anybody or anything lives through a good deal. Sometimes it included everything and sometimes it includes only itself and there can be any amount of less and more at any time of its existence.

Of course when poetry really began it practically included everything it included narrative and feelings and excitements and nouns so many nouns and all emotions. It included narrative but now it does not include narrative.

I often wonder how I am ever to come to know all that I am to know about narrative. Narrative is a problem to me. I worry about it a good deal these days and I will not write or lecture about it yet, because I am still too worried about it worried about knowing what it is and how it is and where it is and how it is and how it will be what it is. However as I say now and at this time I do not I will not go into that. Suffice it to say that for the purpose of poetry it has now for a long time not had anything to do with being there.

Perhaps it is a mistake perhaps not that it is no longer there.

I myself think that something else is going to happen about narrative and I work at it a great deal at this time not work but bother about it. Bother is perhaps the better word for what I am doing just now about narrative. But anyway to go back to poetry.

Poetry did then in beginning include everything and it was natural that it should because then everything including what was happening could be made real to anyone by just naming what was happening in other words by doing what poetry always must do by living in nouns.

Nouns are the name of anything. Think of all that early poetry, think of Homer, think of Chaucer, think of the Bible and you will see what I mean you will really realize that they were drunk with nouns, to name to know how to name earth sea and sky and all that was in them was enough to make them live and love in names, and that is what poetry is it is a state of knowing and feeling a name. I know that now but I have only come to that knowledge by long writing.

So then as I say that is what poetry was and slowly as everybody knew the names of everything poetry had less and less to do with everything. Poetry did not change, poetry never changed, from the beginning until now and always in the future poetry will concern itself with the names of things. The names may be repeated in different ways and very soon I will go into that matter but now and always poetry is created by naming names the names of something the names of somebody the names of anything. Nouns are the names of things and so nouns are the basis of poetry.

Before we go any further there is another matter. Why are the lines of poetry short, so much shorter than prose, why do they rhyme, why in order to complete themselves do they have to end with what they began, why are all these things the things that are in the essence of poetry even when the poetry was long even when now the poetry has changed its form.

Once more the answer is the same and that is that such a way to express oneself is the natural way when one expresses oneself in loving the name of anything. Think what you do when you do do that when you love the name of anything really love its name. Inevitably you express yourself in that way, in the way poetry expresses itself that is in short lines in repeating what you began in order to do it again. Think of how you talk to anything whose name is new to you a lover a baby or a dog or a new land or any part of it. Do you not inevitably repeat what you call out and is that calling out not of necessity in short lines. Think about it and you will see what I mean by what you feel.

So as I say poetry is essentially the discovery, the love, the passion for the name of anything.

Now to come back to how I know what I know about poetry.

I was writing *The Making of Americans*, I was completely obsessed by the inner life of everything including generations of everybody's living and I was writing prose, prose that had to do with the balancing the inner balancing of everything. I have already told you all about that.

And then, something happened and I began to discover the names of things, that is not discover the names but discover the things the things to see the things to look at and in so doing I had of course to name them not to give them new names but to see that I could find out how to know that they were there by their names or by replacing their names. And how was I to do so. They had their names and naturally I called them by the names they had and in doing so having begun looking at them I called them by their names with passion and that made poetry, I did not mean it to make poetry but it did, it made the *Tender Buttons*, and the *Tender Buttons* was very good poetry it made a lot more poetry, and I will now more and more tell about that and how it happened.

I discovered everything then and its name, discovered it and its name. I had always known it and its name but all the same I did discover it.

I remember very well when I was a little girl and I and my brother found as children will the love poems of their very very much older brother. This older brother had just written one and it said that he had often sat and looked at any little square of grass and it had been just a square of grass as grass is, but now he was in love and so the little square of grass was all filled with birds and bees and butterflies, the difference was what love was. The poem was funny we and he knew the poem was funny but he was right, being in love made him make poetry, and poetry made him feel the things and their names, and so I repeat nouns are poetry.

So then in *Tender Buttons* I was making poetry but and it seriously troubled me, dimly I knew that nouns made poetry but in prose I no longer needed the help of nouns and in poetry did I need the help of nouns. Was there not a way of naming things that would not invent names, but mean names without naming them.

I had always been very impressed from the time that I was very young by having had it told me and then afterwards feeling it myself that Shakespeare in the forest of Arden had created a forest without mentioning the things that make a forest. You feel it all but he does not name its names.

Now that was a thing that I too felt in me the need of making it be a thing that could be named without using its name. After all one had known its name anything's name for so long, and so the name was not new but the thing being alive was always new.

What was there to do.

I commenced trying to do something in *Tender Buttons* about this thing. I went on and on trying to do this thing. I remember in writing *An Acquaintance with Description* looking at anything until something that was not the name of that thing but was in a way that actual thing would come to be written.

Naturally, and one may say that is what made Walt Whitman naturally that made the change in the form of poetry, that we who had known the names so long did not get a thrill from just knowing them. We that is any human being living has inevitably to feel the thing anything being existing, but the name of that thing of that anything is no longer anything to thrill any one except children. So as everybody has to be a poet, what was there to do. This that I have just described, the creating it without naming it, was what broke the rigid form of the noun the simple noun poetry which now was broken.

Of course you all do know that when I speak of naming anything, I include emotions as well as things.

So then there we were and what were we to do about it. Go on, of course go on what else does anybody do, so I did, I went on.

Of course you might say why not invent new names new languages but that cannot be done. It takes a tremendous amount of inner necessity to invent even one word, one can invent imitating movements and emotions in sounds, and in the poetical language of some languages you have that, the german language as a language suffers from this what the words mean sound too much like what they do, and children do these things by one sort or another of invention but this has really nothing to do with language. Language as a real thing is not imitation either of sounds or colors or emotions it is an intellectual recreation and there is no possible doubt about it and it is going to go on being that as long as humanity is anything. So every one must stay with the language their language that has come to be spoken and written and which has in it all the history of its intellectual recreation.

And so for me the problem of poetry was and it began with

Tender Buttons to constantly realize the thing anything so that I could recreate that thing. I struggled I struggled desperately with the recreation and the avoidance of nouns as nouns and yet poetry being poetry nouns are nouns. Let me read you bits of the *Portrait of Sherwood Anderson* and *The Birthplace of Bonnes* to show you what I mean.

Can anybody tell by looking which was the towel used for cooking.[10]

A VERY VALENTINE

Very fine is my valentine.
Very fine and very mine.
Very mine is my valentine very mine and very fine.
Very fine is my valentine and mine, very fine very mine and mine is my valentine.[11]

BUNDLES FOR THEM

A HISTORY OF GIVING BUNDLES

We were able to notice that each one in a way carried a bundle, they were not a trouble to them nor were they all bundles as some of them were chickens some of them pheasants some of them sheep and some of them bundles, they were not a trouble to them and then indeed we learned that it was the principal recreation and they were so arranged that they were not given away, and today they were given away.

I will not look at them again.
They will not look for them again.
They have not seen them here again.
They are in there and we hear them again.
In which way are stars brighter than they are. When we have come to this decision. We mention many thousands of buds. And when I close my eyes I see them.
If you hear her snore
It is not before you love her
You love her so that to be her beau is very lovely

10. 'B.B. or The Birthplace of Bonnes' in *Portraits and Prayers*, p. 162.
11. 'A Valentine to Sherwood Anderson' in *Portraits and Prayers*, p. 152.

She is sweetly there and her curly hair is very lovely.

She is sweetly here and I am very near and that is very lovely.

She is my tender sweet and her little feet are stretched out well which is a treat and very lovely.

Her little tender nose is between her little eyes which close and are very lovely.

She is very lovely and mine which is very lovely.[12]

I found in longer things like Operas and Plays and Portraits and *Lucy Church Amiably* and *An Acquaintance with Description* that I could come nearer to avoiding names in recreating something.

That brings us to the question will poetry continue to be necessarily short as it has been as really good poetry has been for a very long time. Perhaps not and why not.

If enough is new to you to name or not name, and these two things come to the same thing, can you go on long enough. Yes I think so.

So then poetry up to the present time has been a poetry of nouns a poetry of naming something of really naming that thing passionately completely passionately naming that thing by its name.

Slowly and particularly during the nineteenth century the English nineteenth century everybody had come to know too well very much too well the name anything had when you called it by its name.

That is something that inevitably happened. And what else could they do. They had to go on doing what they did, that is calling anything by its name passionately but if as I say they really knew its name too well could they call it its name simply in that way. Slowly they could not.

And then Walt Whitman came. He wanted really wanted to express the thing and not call it by its name. He worked very hard at that, and he called it *Leaves of Grass* because he wanted it to be as little a well known name to be called upon passionately as possible. I do not at all know whether Whitman knew that he wanted to do this but there is no doubt at all but that is what he did want to do.

You have the complete other end of this thing in a poet like Longfellow, I cite him because a commonplace poet shows you

12. ibid., p. 154.

more readily and clearly just what the basis of poetry is than a better one. And Longfellow knew all about calling out names, he on the whole did it without passion but he did it very well.

Of course in the history of poetry there have been many who have also tried to name the thing without naming its names, but this is not a history of poets it is a telling what I know about poetry.

And so knowing all this about poetry I struggled more and more with this thing. I say I knew all this about poetry but I did not really know all this then about poetry, I was coming to know then then when I was writing commencing to know what I do now know about prose but I did not then know anything really to know it of what I now know about poetry.

And so in *Tender Buttons* and then on and on I struggled with the ridding myself of nouns, I knew nouns must go in poetry as they had gone in prose if anything that is everything was to go on meaning something.

And so I went on with this exceeding struggle of knowing really knowing what a thing was really knowing it knowing anything I was seeing anything I was feeling so that its name could be something, by its name coming to be a thing in itself as it was but would not be anything just and only as a name.

I wonder if you do see what I mean.

What I mean by what I have just said is this. I had to feel anything and everything that for me was existing so intensely that I could put it down in writing as a thing in itself without at all necessarily using its name. The name of a thing might be something in itself if it could come to be real enough but just as a name it was not enough something. At any rate that is the way I felt and still do feel about it.

And so I went through a very long struggle and in this struggle I began to be troubled about narrative a narrative of anything that was or might be happening.

The newspapers tell us about it but they tell it to us as nouns tell it to us that is they name it, and in naming it, it as a telling of it is no longer anything. That is what a newspaper is by definition just as a noun is a name by definition.

And so I was slowly beginning to know something about what poetry was. And here was the question if in poetry one could lose the noun as I had really and truly lost it in prose would there be any difference between poetry and prose. As this thing came once more to be a doubt inside me I began to work very hard at poetry.

At that time I wrote *Before the Flowers of Friendship Faded Friendship Faded*[13] and there I went back again to a more or less regular form to see whether inside that regular form I could do what I was sure needed to be done and also to find out if eventually prose and poetry were one or not one.

In writing this poem I found I could be very gay I could be very lively in poetry, I could use very few nouns in poetry and call out practically no names in poetry and yet make poetry really feel and sound as poetry, but was it what I wanted that should be done. But it did not decide anything for me but it did help me in my way.

XII

I am very hungry when I drink,
   I need to leave it when I have it held,
     They will be white with which they know they see, that darker makes it be a color white for me, white is not shown when I am dark indeed with red despair who comes who has to care that they will let me a little lie like now I like to lie I like to live I like to die I like to lie and live and die and live and die and by and by I like to live and die and by and by they need to sew the difference is that sewing makes it bleed and such with them in all the way of seed and seeding and repine and they will which is mine and not all mine who can be thought curious of this of all of that made it and come lead it and done weigh it and mourn and sit upon it know it for ripeness without deserting all of it of which without which it has not been born. Oh no not to be thirsty with the thirst of hunger not alone to know that they plainly and ate or wishes. Any little one will kill himself for milk.[14]

XIV

   It could be seen very nicely
    That doves have each a heart,

13. See p. 274.
14. *Before the Flowers of Friendship Faded Friendship Faded,* Plain Edition, Paris, p. 14.

Each one is always seeing that they could not be apart,
A little lake makes fountains
And fountains have no flow,
And a dove has need of flying
And water can be low,
Let me go.
Any week is what they seek
When they have to halve a beak.
I like a painting on a wall of doves
And what do they do,
They have hearts
They are apart
Little doves are winsome
But not when they are little and left.[15]

I decided and *Lucy Church Amiably* had been an attempt to do it, I decided that if one definitely completely replaced the noun by the thing in itself, it was eventually to be poetry and not prose which would have to deal with everything that was not movement in space. There could no longer be form to decide anything, narrative that is not newspaper narrative but real narrative must of necessity be told by any one having come to the realization that the noun must be replaced not by inner balance but by the thing in itself and that will eventually lead to everything. I am working at this thing and what will it do this I do not know but I hope that I will know. In the *Four In America* I have gone on beginning but I am sure that there is in this what there is that it is necessary to do if one is to do anything or everything. Do you see what I mean. Well anyway that is the way that I do now feel about it, and this is all that I do know, and I do believe in knowing all I do know, about prose and poetry. The rest will come considerably later.

15. ibid., p. 16.

Early in 1936 Gertrude Stein was again invited to England to lecture at Oxford and Cambridge. She prepared two lectures – this one and the other which she called 'An American and France'. They were both published in the book *What Are Master-pieces*, Conference Press, Los Angeles, 1940.

*DOING ome has NO
identity*

7

WHAT ARE MASTER-PIECES AND WHY ARE THERE SO FEW OF THEM

I WAS almost going to talk this lecture and not write and read it because all the lectures that I have written and read in America have been printed and although possibly for you they might even being read be as if they had not been printed still there is something about what has been written having been printed which makes it no longer the property of the one who wrote it and therefore there is no more reason why the writer should say it out loud than anybody else and therefore one does not.

Therefore I was going to talk to you but actually it is impossible to talk about master-pieces and what they are because talking essentially has nothing to do with creation. I talk a lot I like to talk and I talk even more than that I may say I talk most of the time and I listen a fair amount too and as I have said the essence of being a genius is to be able to talk and listen to listen while talking and talk while listening but and this is very important very important indeed talking has nothing to do with creation. What are master-pieces and why after all are there so few of them. You may say after all there are a good many of them but in any kind of proportion with everything that anybody who does anything is doing there are really very few of them. All this summer I meditated and wrote about this subject and it finally came to be a discussion of the relation of human nature and the human mind and identity. The thing one gradually comes to find out is that one has no identity that is when one is in the act of doing anything. Identity is recognition, you know who you are because you and others remember anything about yourself but essentially you are not that when you are doing anything. I am I because my little dog knows me but, creatively speaking the little dog knowing that you are you and your recognizing that he knows, that is what destroys creation. That is what makes school. Picasso once remarked I do not care who it is that has or does influence me as long as it is not myself.

It is very difficult so difficult that it always has been difficult but even more difficult now to know what is the relation of human nature to the human mind because one has to know what is the relation of the act of creation to the subject the creator uses to create that thing. There is a great deal of nonsense talked about the subject of anything. After all there is always the same subject there are the things you see and there are human beings and animal beings and everybody you might say since the beginning of time knows practically commencing at the beginning and going to the end everything about these things. After all any woman in any village or men either if you like or even children know as much of human psychology as any writer that ever lived. After all there are things you do know each one in his or her way knows all of them and it is not this knowledge that makes master-pieces. Not at all not at all at all. Those who recognize master-pieces say that is the reason but it is not. It is not the way Hamlet reacts to his father's ghost that makes the master-piece, he might have reacted according to Shakespeare in a dozen other ways and everybody would have been as much impressed by the psychology of it. But there is no psychology in it, that is not probably the way any young man would react to the ghost of his father and there is no particular reason why they should. If it were the way a young man could react to the ghost of his father then that would be something anybody in any village would know they could talk about it talk about it endlessly but that would not make a master-piece and that brings us once more back to the subject of identity. At any moment when you are you you are you without the memory of yourself because if you remember yourself while you are you you are not for purposes of creating you. This is so important because it has so much to do with the question of a writer to his audience. One of the things that I discovered in lecturing was that gradually one ceased to hear what one said one heard what the audience hears one say, that is the reason that oratory is practically never a master-piece very rarely and very rarely history, because history deals with people who are orators who hear not what they are not what they say but what their audience hears them say. It is very interesting that letter writing has the same difficulty, the letter writes what the other person is to hear and so entity does not exist there are two present instead of one and so once again creation breaks down. I once wrote in writing *The Making of Americans* I write for myself and strangers but that was merely a literary formalism for if I did write for myself and strangers if I did I would not really be writing because already then identity would take the place of entity. It is awfully difficult, action is direct and effective but after all action is necessary and anything that is necessary has to do with human nature and not with the human mind. Therefore a master-piece has essentially not to be necessary, it has to be that is it has to exist but it does not have to be necessary it is not in response to necessity as action is because the minute it is necessary it has in it no possibility of going on.

To come back to what a master-piece has as its subject. In writing about painting I said that a picture exists for and in itself and the painter has to use objects landscapes and people as a way the only way that he is able to get the picture to exist. That is every one's trouble and particularly the trouble just now when every one who writes or paints has gotten to be abnormally conscious of the things he uses that is the events the people the objects and the landscapes and fundamentally the minute one is conscious deeply conscious of these things as a subject the interest in them does not exist.

You can tell that so well in the difficulty of writing novels or poetry these days. The tradition has always been that you may more or less describe the things that happen you imagine them of course but you more or less describe the things that happen but nowadays everybody all day long knows what is happening and so what is happening is not really interesting, one knows it by radios cinemas newspapers biographies autobiographies until what is happening does not really thrill any one, it excites them a little but it does not really thrill them. The painter can no longer say that what he does is as the world looks to him because he cannot look at the world any more, it has been photographed too much and he has to say that he does something else. In former times a painter said he painted what he saw of course he didn't but anyway he could say it, now he does not want to say it because seeing it is not interesting. This has something to do with master-pieces and why there are so few of them but not everything.

So you see why talking has nothing to do with creation, talking is really human nature as it is and human nature has nothing to do with master-pieces. It is very curious but the detective story which is you might say the only really modern novel form that has come into existence gets rid of human nature by having the man dead to begin with the hero is dead to begin with and so you have so to speak got rid of the event before the book begins. There is another very curious thing about detective stories. In real life people are interested in the crime more than they are in detection, it is the crime that is the thing the shock the thrill the horror but in the story it is the detection that holds the interest and that is natural enough because the necessity as far as action is concerned is the dead man, it is another function that has very little to do with human nature that makes the detection interesting. And so always it is true that the master-piece has nothing to do with human nature or with identity, it has to do with the human mind and the entity that is with a thing in itself and not in relation. The moment it is in relation it is common knowledge and anybody can feel and know it and it is not a master-piece. At the same time every one in a curious way sooner or later does feel the reality of a master-piece. The thing in itself of which the human nature is only its clothing does hold the attention. I have meditated a great deal about that. Another curious thing about master-pieces is, nobody when it is created there is in the thing that we call the human mind something that makes it hold itself just the same. The manner and habits of Bible times or Greek or Chinese have nothing to do with ours today but the master-pieces exist just the same and they do not exist because of their identity, that is what any one remembering then remembered then, they do not exist by human nature because everybody always knows everything there is to know about human nature, they exist because they came to be as something that is an end in itself and in that respect it is opposed to the business of living which is relation and necessity. That is what a master-piece is not although it may easily be what a master-piece talks about. It is another one of the curious difficulties a master-piece has that is to begin and end, because actually a master-piece does not do that it does not begin and end if it did it would be of necessity and in relation and that is just what a master-piece is not. Everybody worries about that just now everybody that is what makes them talk about abstract and worry about punctuation and capitals and small letters and what a history is. Everybody worries about that not because everybody knows what a master-piece is but because a certain number have found out what a master-piece is not. Even the very master-pieces have always been very bothered about beginning and ending because essentially that is what a master-piece is not. And yet after all like the subject of human nature master-pieces have to use beginning and ending to become existing. Well anyway anybody who is trying to do anything today is desperately not having a beginning and an ending but nevertheless in some way one does have to stop. I stop.

I do not know whether I have made any of this very clear, it is clear, but unfortunately I have written it all down all summer and in spite of everything I am now remembering and when you remember it is never clear. This is what makes secondary writing, it is remembering, it is very curious you begin to write something and suddenly you remember something and if you continue to remember your writing gets very confused. If you do not remember while you are writing, it may seem confused to others but actually it is clear and eventually that clarity will be clear, that is what a master-piece is, but if you remember while you are writing it will seem clear at the time to any one but the clarity will go out of it that is what a master-piece is not.

All this sounds awfully complicated but it is not complicated at all, it is just what happens. Any of you when you write you try to remember what you are about to write and you will see immediately how lifeless the writing becomes that is why expository writing is so dull because it is all remembered, that is why illustration is so dull because you remember what somebody looked like and you make your illustration look like it. The minute your memory functions while you are doing anything it may be very popular but actually it is dull. And that is what a master-piece is not, it may be unwelcome but it is never dull.

And so then why are there so few of them. There are so few of them because mostly people live in identity and memory that is when they think. They know they are they because their little dog knows them, and so they are not an entity but an identity. And being so memory is necessary to make them exist and so they cannot create master-pieces. It has been said of geniuses that they are eternally young. I once said what is the use of being a boy if you are going to grow up to be a man, the boy and the man have nothing to do with each other, except in respect to memory and identity, and if they have anything to do with each other in respect to memory and identity then they will never produce a master-piece. Do you do you understand well it really does not make much difference because after all master-pieces are what they are and the reason why is that there are very few of them. The reason why is any of you try it just not to be you are you because your little dog knows you. The second you are you because your little dog knows you you cannot make a master-piece and that is all of that.

It is not extremely difficult not to have identity but it is extremely difficult the knowing not having identity. One might say it is impossible but that it is not impossible is proved by the existence of master-pieces which are just that. They are knowing that there is no identity and producing while identity is not.

That is what a master-piece is.

And so we do know what a master-piece is and we also know why there are so few of them. Everything is against them. Everything that makes life go on makes identity and everything that makes identity is of necessity a necessity. And the pleasures of life as well as the necessities help the necessity of identity. The pleasures that are soothing all have to do with identity and the pleasures that are exciting all have to do with identity and moreover there is all the pride and vanity which play about master-pieces as well as about every one and these too all have to do with identity, and so naturally it is natural that there is more identity that one knows about than anything else one knows about and the worst of all is that the only thing that anyone thinks about is identity and thinking is something that does so nearly need to be memory and if it is then of course it has nothing to do with a master-piece.

But what can a master-piece be about mostly it is about identity and all it does and in being so it must not have any. I was just thinking

trouble about time
women + men + what they say
154   *Lectures*

about anything and in thinking about anything I saw something. In seeing that thing shall we see it without it turning into identity, the moment is not a moment and the sight is not the thing seen and yet it is. Moments are not important because of course masterpieces have no more time than they have identity although time like identity is what they concern themselves about of course that is what they do concern themselves about.

Once when one has said what one says it is not true or too true. That is what is the trouble with time. That is what makes what women say truer than what men say. That is undoubtedly what is the trouble with time and always in its relation to master-pieces. I once said that nothing could bother me more than the way a thing goes dead once it has been said. And if it does it is because of there being this trouble about time.

Time is very important in connection with master-pieces, of course it makes identity time does make identity and identity does stop the creation of master-pieces. But time does something by itself to interfere with the creation of master-pieces as well as being part of what makes identity. If you do not keep remembering yourself you have no identity and if you have no time you do not keep remembering yourself and as you remember yourself you do not create anybody can and does know that.

Think about how you create if you do create you do not remember yourself as you do create. And yet time and identity is what you tell about as you create only while you create they do not exist. That is really what it is.

And do you create yes if you exist but time and identity do not exist. We live in time and identity but as we are we do not know time and identity everybody knows that quite simply. It is so simple that anybody does know that. But to know what one knows is frightening to live what one lives is soothing and though everybody likes to be frightened what they really have to have is soothing and so the master-pieces are so few not that the master-pieces themselves are frightening no of course not because if the creator of the masterpiece is frightened then he does not exist without the memory of time and identity, and insofar as he is that then he is frightened and insofar as he is frightened the master-piece does not exist, it looks like it and it feels like it, but the memory of the fright destroys it as a master-piece. Robinson Crusoe and the footstep of the man Friday is one of the most perfect examples of the non-existence of time and identity which makes a master-piece. I hope you do see what I mean but anyway everybody who knows about Robinson Crusoe and the footstep of Friday knows that that is true. There is no time and identity in the way it happened and that is why there is no fright.

And so there are very few master-pieces of course there are very few master-pieces because to be able to know that is not to have identity and time but not to mind talking as if there was because it does not interfere with anything and to go on being not as if there were no time and identity but as if there were and at the same time existing without time and identity is so very simple that it is difficult to have many who are that. And of course that is what a master-piece is and that is why there are so few of them and anybody really anybody can know that.

What is the use of being a boy if you are going to grow up to be a man. And what is the use there is no use from the standpoint of master-pieces there is no use. Anybody can really know that.

There is really no use in being a boy if you are going to grow up to be a man because then man and boy you can be certain that that is continuing and a master-piece does not continue it is as it is but it does not continue. It is very interesting that no one is content with being a man and boy but he must also be a son and a father and the fact that they all die has something to do with time but it has nothing to do with a master-piece. The word timely as used in our speech is very interesting but you can any one can see that it has nothing to do with master-pieces we all readily know that. The word timely tells that master-pieces have nothing to do with time.

It is very interesting to have it be inside one that never as you know yourself you know yourself without looking and feeling and looking and feeling make it be that you are some one you have seen. If you have seen any one you know them as you see them whether it is yourself or any other one and so the identity consists in recognition and in recognizing you lose identity because after all nobody looks as they look like, they do not look like that we all know that of ourselves and of any one. And therefore in every way it is a trouble and so you write anybody does write to confirm what any one is and the more one does the more one looks like what one was and in being so identity is made more so and that identity is not what any one can have as a thing to be but as a thing to see. And it being a thing to see no master-piece can see what it can see if it does then it is timely and as it is timely it is not a master-piece.

There are so many things to say. If there was no identity no one could be governed, but everybody is governed by everybody and that is why they make no master-pieces, and also why governing has nothing to do with master-pieces it has completely to do with identity but it has nothing to do with master-pieces. And that is why governing is occupying but not interesting, governments are occupying but not interesting because master-pieces are exactly what they are not.

There is another thing to say. When you are writing before there is an audience anything written is as important as any other thing and you cherish anything and everything that you have written. After the audience begins, naturally they create something that is they create you, and so not everything is so important, something is more important than another thing, which was not true when you were you that is when you were not you as your little dog knows you.

And so there we are and there is so much to say but anyway I do not say that there is no doubt that master-pieces are master-pieces in that way and there are very few of them.

PART TWO

WRITINGS

Portraits of Objects

The pieces which are included in *Tender Buttons* were written during the year 1911 and they were originally published as a book in 1914 by the publishing house Claire-Marie, New York.

For references to this work, see the lectures 'The Gradual Making of *The Making of Americans*', 'Portraits and Repetition' and 'Poetry and Grammar'.

8

TENDER BUTTONS

Objects

A CARAFE, THAT IS A BLIND GLASS

A KIND in glass and a cousin, a spectacle and nothing strange a single hurt color and an arrangement in a system to pointing. All this and not ordinary, not unordered in not resembling. The difference is spreading.

GLAZED GLITTER

Nickel, what is nickel, it is originally rid of a cover.

The change in that is that red weakens an hour. The change has come. There is no search. But there is, there is that hope and that interpretation and sometime, surely any is unwelcome, sometime there is breath and there will be a sinecure and charming very charming is that clean and cleansing. Certainly glittering is handsome and convincing.

There is no gratitude in mercy and in medicine. There can be breakages in Japanese. That is no programme. That is no color chosen. It was chosen yesterday, that showed spitting and perhaps washing and polishing. It certainly showed no obligation and perhaps if borrowing is not natural there is some use in giving.

A SUBSTANCE IN A CUSHION

The change of color is likely and a difference a very little difference
is prepared. Sugar is not a vegetable.

Callous is something that hardening leaves behind what will be
soft if there is a genuine interest in there being present as many girls
as men. Does this change. It shows that dirt is clean when there is a
volume.

A cushion has that cover. Supposing you do not like to change,
supposing it is very clean that there is no change in appearance,
supposing that there is regularity and a costume is that any the worse
than an oyster and an exchange. Come to season that is there any extreme use in feather and cotton. Is there not much more joy in a table
and more chairs and very likely roundness and a place to put them.

A circle of fine card board and a chance to see a tassel.

What is the use of a violent kind of delightfulness if there is no
pleasure in not getting tired of it. The question does not come before there is a quotation. In any kind of place there is a top to
covering and it is a pleasure at any rate there is some venturing in
refusing to believe nonsense. It shows what use there is in a whole
piece if one uses it and it is extreme and very likely the little things
could be dearer but in any case there is a bargain and if there is the
best thing to do is to take it away and wear it and then be reckless
be reckless and resolved on returning gratitude.

Light blue and the same red with purple makes a change. It
shows that there is no mistake. Any pink shows that and very likely
it is reasonable. Very likely there should not be a finer fancy present.
Some increase means a calamity and this is the best preparation for
three and more being together. A little calm is so ordinary and in
any case there is sweetness and some of that.

A seal and matches and a swan and ivy and a suit.

A closet, a closet does not connect under the bed. The band if it
is white and black, the band has a green string. A sight a whole sight
and a little groan grinding makes a trimming such a sweet singing
trimming and a red thing not a round thing but a white thing, a red
thing and a white thing.

The disgrace is not in carelessness nor even in sewing it comes
out of the way.

What is the sash like. The sash is not like anything mustard it is not like a same thing that has stripes, it is not even more hurt than that, it has a little top.

A BOX

Out of kindness comes redness and out of rudeness comes rapid same question, out of an eye comes research, out of selection comes painful cattle. So then the order is that a white way of being round is something suggesting a pin and is it disappointing, it is not, it is so rudimentary to be analysed and see a fine substance strangely, it is so earnest to have a green point not to red but to point again.

A PIECE OF COFFEE

More of double.

A place in no new table.

A single image is not splendor. Dirty is yellow. A sign of more in not mentioned. A piece of coffee is not a detainer. The resemblance to yellow is dirtier and distincter. The clean mixture is whiter and not coal color, never more coal color than altogether.

The sight of a reason, the same sight slighter, the sight of a simpler negative answer, the same sore sounder, the intention to wishing, the same splendor, the same furniture.

The time to show a message is when too late and later there is no hanging in a blight.

A not torn rose-wood color. If it is not dangerous then a pleasure and more than any other if it is cheap is not cheaper. The amusing side is that the sooner there are no fewer the more certain is the necessity dwindled. Supposing that the case contained rose-wood and a color. Supposing that there was no reason for a distress and more likely for a number, supposing that there was no astonishment, is it not necessary to mingle astonishment.

The settling of stationing cleaning is one way not to shatter scatter and scattering. The one way to use custom is to use soap and silk for cleaning. The one way to see cotton is to have a design concentrating the illusion and the illustration. The perfect way is to accustom the thing to have a lining and the shape of a ribbon and to be solid, quite solid in standing and to use heaviness in morning. It is light enough in that. It has that shape nicely. Very nicely may not be exaggerating. Very strongly may be sincerely fainting. May be strangely flattering. May not be strange in everything. May not be strange to.

DIRT AND NOT COPPER

Dirt and not copper makes a color darker. It makes the shape so heavy and makes no melody harder.

It makes mercy and relaxation and even a strength to spread a table fuller. There are more places not empty. They see cover.

NOTHING ELEGANT

A charm a single charm is doubtful. If the red is rose and there is a gate surrounding it, if inside is let in and there places change then certainly something is upright. It is earnest.

MILDRED'S UMBRELLA

A cause and no curve, a cause and loud enough, a cause and extra a loud clash and an extra wagon, a sign of extra, a sac a small sac and an established color and cunning, a slender grey and no ribbon, this means a loss a great loss a restitution.

A METHOD OF A CLOAK

A single climb to a line, a straight exchange to a cane, a desperate adventure and courage and a clock, all this which is a system, which has feeling, which has resignation and success, all makes an attractive black silver.

A RED STAMP

If lilies are lily white if they exhaust noise and distance and even dust, if they dusty will dirt a surface that has no extreme grace, if they do this and it is not necessary it is not at all necessary if they do this they need a catalogue.

A BOX

A large box is handily made of what is necessary to replace any substance. Suppose an example is necessary, the plainer it is made the more reason there is for some outward recognition that there is a result.

A box is made sometimes and them to see to see to it neatly and to have the holes stopped up makes it necessary to use paper.

A custom which is necessary when a box is used and taken is that a large part of the time there are three which have different connections. The one is on the table. The two are on the table. The three are on the table. The one, one is the same length as is shown by the cover being longer. The other is different there is more cover that shows it. The other is different and that makes the corners have the same shade the eight are in singular arrangement to make four necessary.

Lax, to have corners, to be lighter than some weight, to indicate a wedding journey, to last brown and not curious, to be wealthy, cigarettes are established by length and by doubling.

Left open, to be left pounded, to be left closed, to be circulating in summer and winter, and sick color that is grey that is not dusty and red shows, to be sure cigarettes do measure an empty length sooner than a choice in color.

Winged, to be winged means that white is yellow and pieces pieces that are brown are dust color if dust is washed off, then it is choice that is to say it is fitting cigarettes sooner than paper.

An increase why is an increase idle, why is silver cloister, why is the spark brighter, if it is brighter is there any result, hardly more than ever.

A PLATE

An occasion for a plate, an occasional resource is in buying and how soon does washing enable a selection of the same thing neater. If the party is small a clever song is in order.

Plates and a dinner set of colored china. Pack together a string and enough with it to protect the centre, cause a considerable haste and gather more as it is cooling, collect more trembling and not any even trembling, cause a whole thing to be a church.

A sad size a size that is not sad is blue as every bit of blue is precocious. A kind of green a game in green and nothing flat nothing quite flat and more round, nothing a particular color strangely, nothing breaking the losing of no little piece.

A splendid address a really splendid address is not shown by giving a flower freely, it is not shown by a mark or by wetting.

Cut cut in white, cut in white so lately. Cut more than any other and show it. Show it in the stem and in starting and in evening coming complication.

A lamp is not the only sign of glass. The lamp and the cake are not the only sign of stone. The lamp and the cake and the cover are not the only necessity altogether.

A plan a hearty plan, a compressed disease and no coffee, not even a card or a change to incline each way, a plan that has that excess and that break is the one that shows filling.

A SELTZER BOTTLE

Any neglect of many particles to a cracking, any neglect of this makes around it what is lead in color and certainly discolor in silver. The use of this is manifold. Supposing a certain time selected is assured, suppose it is even necessary, suppose no other extract is permitted and no more handling is needed, suppose the rest of the message is mixed with a very long slender needle and even if it could be any black border, supposing all this altogether made a dress and suppose it was actual, suppose the mean way to state it was occasional, if you suppose this in August and even more melodiously, if you suppose this even in the necessary incident of there certainly being no middle in summer and winter, suppose this and an elegant settlement a very elegant settlement is more than of consequence, it is not final and sufficient and substituted. This which was so kindly a present was constant.

A LONG DRESS

What is the current that makes machinery, that makes it crackle, what is the current that presents a long line and a necessary waist. What is this current.

What is the wind, what is it.

Where is the serene length, it is there and a dark place is not a dark place, only a white and red are black, only a yellow and green are blue, a pink is scarlet, a bow is every color. A line distinguishes it. A line just distinguishes it.

A RED HAT

A dark grey, a very dark grey, a quite dark grey is monstrous ordinarily, it is so monstrous because there is no red in it. If red is in everything it is not necessary. Is that not an argument for any use of it and even so is there any place that is better, is there any place that has so much stretched out.

A BLUE COAT

A blue coat is guided guided away, guided and guided away, that is the particular color that is used for that length and not any width not even more than a shadow.

A PIANO

If the speed is open, if the color is careless, if the selection of a strong scent is not awkward, if the button holder is held by all the waving color and there is no color, not any color. If there is no dirt in a pin and there can be none scarcely, if there is not then the place is the same as up standing.

This is no dark custom and it even is not acted in any such a way that a restraint is not spread. That is spread, it shuts and it lifts and awkwardly not awkwardly the centre is in standing.

A CHAIR

A window in a wise veil and more garments shows that shadows are even. It addresses no more, it shadows the stage and learning. A regular arrangement, the severest and the most preserved is that which has the arrangement not more than always authorized.

A suitable establishment, well housed, practical, patient and staring, a suitable bedding, very suitable and not more particularly than complaining, anything suitable is so necessary.

A fact is that when the direction is just like that, no more, longer, sudden and at the same time not any sofa, the main action is that without a blaming there is no custody.

Practice measurement, practice the sign that means that really means a necessary betrayal, in showing that there is wearing.

Hope, what is a spectacle, a spectacle is the resemblance between the circular side place and nothing else, nothing else.

To choose it is ended, it is actual and more and more than that it has it certainly has the same treat, and a seat all that is practiced and more easily much more easily ordinarily.

Pick a barn, a whole barn, and bend more slender accents than have ever been necessary, shine in the darkness necessarily.

Actually not aching, actually not aching, a stubborn bloom is so artificial and even more than that, it is a spectacle, it is a binding accident, it is animosity and accentuation.

If the chance to dirty diminishing is necessary, if it is why is there no complexion, why is there no rubbing, why is there no special protection.

A FRIGHTFUL RELEASE

A bag which was left and not only taken but turned away was not found. The place was shown to be very like the last time. A piece was not exchanged, not a bit of it, a piece was left over. The rest was mismanaged.

A PURSE

A purse was not green, it was not straw color, it was hardly seen and it had a use a long use and the chain, the chain was never missing, it was not misplaced, it showed that it was open, that is all that it showed.

A MOUNTED UMBRELLA

What was the use of not leaving it there where it would hang what was the use if there was no chance of ever seeing it come there and show that it was handsome and right in the way it showed it. The lesson is to learn that it does show it, that it shows it and that nothing, that there is nothing, that there is no more to do about it and just so much more is there plenty of reason for making an exchange.

A CLOTH

Enough cloth is plenty and more, more is almost enough for that and besides if there is no more spreading is there plenty of room for it. Any occasion shows the best way.

MORE

An elegant use of foliage and grace and a little piece of white cloth and oil.

Wondering so winningly in several kinds of oceans is the reason that makes red so regular and enthusiastic. The reason that there is more snips are the same shining very colored rid of no round color.

A NEW CUP AND SAUCER

Enthusiastically hurting a clouded yellow bud and saucer, enthusiastically so is the bite in the ribbon.

OBJECTS

Within, within the cut and slender joint alone, with sudden equals and no more than three, two in the centre make two one side.

If the elbow is long and it is filled so then the best example is all together.

The kind of show is made by squeezing.

EYE GLASSES

A color in shaving, a saloon is well placed in the centre of an alley.

A CUTLET

A blind agitation is manly and uttermost.

CARELESS WATER

No cup is broken in more places and mended, that is to say a plate is broken and mending does do that it shows that culture is Japanese. It shows the whole element of angels and orders. It does more to choosing and it does more to that ministering counting. It does, it does change in more water.

Supposing a single piece is a hair supposing more of them are orderly, does that show that strength, does that show that joint, does that show that balloon famously. Does it.

A PAPER

A courteous occasion makes a paper show no such occasion and this makes readiness and eyesight and likeness and a stool.

A DRAWING

The meaning of this is entirely and best to say the mark, best to say it best to shown sudden places, best to make bitter, best to make the length tall and nothing broader, anything between the half.

WATER RAINING

Water astonishing and difficult altogether makes a meadow and a stroke.

COLD CLIMATE

A season in yellow sold extra strings makes lying places.

MALACHITE

The sudden spoon is the same in no size. The sudden spoon is the wound in the decision.

AN UMBRELLA

Coloring high means that the strange reason is in front not more in front behind. Not more in front in peace of the dot.

A PETTICOAT

A light white, a disgrace, an ink spot, a rosy charm.

A WAIST

A star glide, a single frantic sullenness, a single financial grass greediness.

Object that is in wood. Hold the pine, hold the dark, hold in the rush, make the bottom.

A piece of crystal. A change, in a change that is remarkable there is no reason to say that there was a time.

A woolen object gilded. A country climb is the best disgrace, a couple of practices any of them in order is so left.

A TIME TO EAT

A pleasant simple habitual and tyrannical and authorized and educated and resumed and articulate separation. This is not tardy.

A LITTLE BIT OF A TUMBLER

A shining indication of yellow consists in there having been more of the same color than could have been expected when all four were bought. This was the hope which made the six and seven have no use for any more places and this necessarily spread into nothing. Spread into nothing.

A FIRE

What was the use of a whole time to send and not send if there was to be the kind of thing that made that come in. A letter was nicely sent.

A HANDKERCHIEF

A winning of all the blessings, a sample not a sample because there is no worry.

RED ROSES

A cool red rose and a pink cut pink, a collapse and a sold hole, a little less hot.

IN BETWEEN

In between a place and candy is a narrow foot-path that shows more mounting than anything, so much really that a calling meaning a bolster measured a whole thing with that. A virgin a whole virgin is judged made and so between curves and outlines and real seasons and more out glasses and a perfectly unprecedented arrangement between old ladies and mild colds there is no satin wood shining.

COLORED HATS

Colored hats are necessary to show that curls are worn by an addition of blank spaces, this makes the difference between single lines and broad stomachs, the least thing is lightening, the least thing means a little flower and a big delay a big delay that makes more nurses than little women really little women. So clean is a light that nearly all of it shows pearls and little ways. A large hat is tall and me and all custard whole.

A FEATHER

A feather is trimmed, it is trimmed by the light and the bug and the post, it is trimmed by little leaning and by all sorts of mounted reserves and loud volumes. It is surely cohesive.

A BROWN

A brown which is not liquid not more so is relaxed and yet there is a change, a news is pressing.

A LITTLE CALLED PAULINE

A little called anything shows shudders.

Come and say what prints all day. A whole few water-melon. There is no pope.

No cut in pennies and little dressing and choose wide soles and little spats really little spices.

A little lace makes boils. This is not true.

Gracious of gracious and a stamp a blue green white bow a blue green lean, lean on the top.

If it is absurd then it is leadish and nearly set in where there is a tight head.

A peaceful life to arise her, noon and moon and moon. A letter a cold sleeve a blanket a shaving house and nearly the best and regular window.

Nearer in fairy sea, nearer and farther, show white has lime in sight, show a stitch of ten. Count, count more so that thicker and thicker is leaning.

I hope she has her cow. Bidding a wedding, widening received treading, little leading mention nothing.

Cough out cough out in the leather and really feather it is not for.

Please could, please could, jam it not plus more sit in when.

A SOUND

Elephant beaten with candy and little pops and chews all bolts and reckless reckless rats, this is this.

A TABLE

A table means does it not my dear it means a whole steadiness. Is it likely that a change.

A table means more than a glass even a looking glass is tall. A table means necessary places and a revision a revision of a little thing it means it does mean that there has been a stand, a stand where it did shake.

SHOES

To be a wall with a damper a stream of pounding way and nearly enough choice makes a steady midnight. It is pus.

A shallow hole rose on red, a shallow hole in and in this makes ale less. It shows shine.

A DOG

A little monkey goes like a donkey that means to say that means to say that more sighs last goes. Leave with it. A little monkey goes like a donkey.

A WHITE HUNTER

A white hunter is nearly crazy.

A LEAVE

In the middle of a tiny spot and nearly bare there is a nice thing to say that wrist is leading. Wrist is leading.

SUPPOSE AN EYES

Suppose it is within a gate which open is open at the hour of closing summer that is to say it is so.

All the seats are needing blackening. A white dress is in sign. A soldier a real soldier has a worn lace a worn lace of different sizes that is to say if he can read, if he can read he is a size to show shutting up twenty-four.

Go red go red, laugh white.

Suppose a collapse in rubbed purr, in rubbed purr get.

Little sales ladies little sales ladies little saddles of mutton.

Little sales of leather and such beautiful beautiful, beautiful beautiful.

A SHAWL

A shawl is a hat and hurt and a red balloon and an under coat and a sizer a sizer of talks.

A shawl is a wedding, a piece of wax a little build. A shawl.

Pick a ticket, pick it in strange steps and with hollows. There is hollow hollow belt, a belt is a shawl.

A plate that has a little bobble, all of them, any so.

Please a round it is ticket.

It was a mistake to state that a laugh and a lip and a laid climb and a depot and a cultivator and little choosing is a point it.

BOOK

Book was there, it was there. Book was there. Stop it, stop it, it was a cleaner, a wet cleaner and it was not where it was wet, it was not high, it was directly placed back, not back again, back it was returned, it was needless, it put a bank, a bank when, a bank care.

Suppose a man a realistic expression of resolute reliability suggests pleasing itself white all white and no head does that mean soap. It does not so. It means kind wavers and little chance to beside beside rest. A plain.

Suppose ear rings that is one way to breed, breed that. Oh chance to say, oh nice old pole. Next best and nearest a pillar. Chest not valuable, be papered.

Cover up cover up the two with a little piece of string and hope rose and green, green.

Please a plate, put a match to the seam and really then really then, really then it is a remark that joins many many lead games. It is a sister and sister and a flower and a flower and a dog and a colored sky a sky colored grey and nearly that nearly that let.

PEELED PENCIL, CHOKE

Rub her coke.

IT WAS BLACK, BLACK TOOK

Black ink best wheel bale brown.

Excellent not a hull house, not a pea soup, no bill no care, no precise no past pearl pearl goat.

THIS IS THE DRESS, AIDER

Aider, why aider why whow, whow stop touch, aider whow, aider stop the muncher, muncher munchers.

A jack in kill her, a jack in, makes a meadowed king, makes a to let.

Food

ROASTBEEF; MUTTON; BREAKFAST; SUGAR; CRANBERRIES; MILK; EGGS; APPLE; TAILS; LUNCH; CUPS; RHUBARB; SINGLE FISH; CAKE; CUSTARD; POTATOES; ASPARAGUS; BUTTER; END OF SUMMER; SAUSAGES; CELERY; VEAL; VEGETABLE; COOKING; CHICKEN; PASTRY; CREAM; CUCUMBER; DINNER; DINING; EATING; SALAD; SAUCE; SALMON; ORANGE; COCOA; AND CLEAR SOUP AND ORANGES AND OAT-MEAL; SALAD DRESSING AND AN ARTICHOKE; A CENTRE IN A TABLE.

ROASTBEEF

In the inside there is sleeping, in the outside there is reddening, in the morning there is meaning, in the evening there is feeling. In the evening there is feeling. In feeling anything is resting, in feeling anything is mounting, in feeling there is resignation, in feeling there is recognition, in feeling there is recurrence and entirely mistaken there is pinching. All the standards have steamers and all the curtains have bed linen and all the yellow has discrimination and all the circle has circling. This makes sand.

Very well. Certainly the length is thinner and the rest, the round rest has a longer summer. To shine, why not shine, to shine, to station, to enlarge, to hurry the measure all this means nothing if there is singing, if there is singing then there is the resumption.

The change the dirt, not to change dirt means that there is no beefsteak and not to have that is no obstruction, it is so easy to exchange meaning, it is so easy to see the difference. The difference is that a plain resource is not entangled with thickness and it does not mean that thickness shows such cutting, it does mean that a meadow is useful and a cow absurd. It does not mean that there are tears, it does not mean that exudation is cumbersome, it means no more than a memory, a choice and a reëstablishment, it means more than any escape from a surrounding extra. All the time that there is use there is use and any time there is a surface there is a surface, and every time there is an exception there is an exception and every time there is a division there is a dividing. Any time there is a surface there is a surface and every time there is a suggestion there is a suggestion and every time there is silence there is silence and every time that is languid there is that there then and not oftener, not always, not particular, tender and changing and external and central and surrounded and singular and simple and the same and the surface and the circle and the shine and the succor and the white and the same and the better and the red and the same and the centre and the yellow and the tender and the better, and altogether.

Considering the circumstances there is no occasion for a reduction, considering that there is no pealing there is no occasion for an obligation, considering that there is no outrage there is no necessity for any reparation, considering that there is no particle sodden there is no occasion for deliberation. Considering everything and which way the turn is tending, considering everything why is there no restraint, considering everything what makes the place settle and the plate distinguish some specialities. The whole thing is not understood and this is not strange considering that there is no education, this is not strange because having that certainty does show the difference in cutting, it shows that when there is turning there is no distress.

In kind, in a control, in a period, in the alteration of pigeons, in kind cuts and thick and thin spaces, in kind ham and different colors, the length of leaning a strong thing outside not to make a sound but to suggest a crust, the principal taste is when there is a whole chance to be reasonable, this does not mean that there is overtaking, this means nothing precious, this means clearly that the chance to exercise is a social success. So then the sound is not obtrusive. Suppose it is obtrusive suppose it is. What is certainly the desertion is not a reduced description, a description is not a birthday.

Lovely snipe and tender turn, excellent vapor and slender butter, all the splinter and the trunk, all the poisonous darkening drunk, all the joy in weak success, all the joyful tenderness, all the section and the tea, all the stouter symmetry.

Around the size that is small, inside the stern that is the middle, besides the remains that are praying, inside the between that is turning, all the region is measuring and melting is exaggerating.

Rectangular ribbon does not mean that there is no eruption it means that if there is no place to hold there is no place to spread. Kindness is not earnest, it is not assiduous it is not revered.

Room to comb chickens and feathers and ripe purple, room to curve single plates and large sets and second silver, room to send everything away, room to save heat and distemper, room to search a light that is simpler, all room has no shadow.

There is no use there is no use at all in smell, in taste, in teeth, in toast, in anything, there is no use at all and the respect is mutual.

Why should that which is uneven, that which is resumed, that which is tolerable why should all this resemble a smell, a thing is there, it whistles, it is not narrower, why is there no obligation to stay away and yet courage, courage is everywhere and the best remains to stay.

If there could be that which is contained in that which is felt there would be a chair where there are chairs and there would be no more denial about a clatter. A clatter is not a smell. All this is good.

The Saturday evening which is Sunday is every week day. What choice is there when there is a difference. A regulation is not active. Thirstiness is not equal division.

Anyway, to be older and ageder is not a surfeit nor a suction, it is not dated and careful, it is not dirty. Any little thing is clean, rubbing is black. Why should ancient lambs be goats and young colts and never beef, why should they, they should because there is so much difference in age.

A sound, a whole sound is not separation, a whole sound is in an order.

Suppose there is a pigeon, suppose there is.

Looseness, why is there a shadow in a kitchen, there is a shadow in a kitchen because every little thing is bigger.

The time when there are four choices and there are four choices in a difference, the time when there are four choices there is a kind and there is a kind. There is a kind. There is a kind. Supposing there is a bone, there is a bone. Supposing there are bones. There are bones. When there are bones there is no supposing there are bones. There are bones and there is that consuming. The kindly way to feel separating is to have a space between. This shows a likeness.

Hope in gates, hope in spoons, hope in doors, hope in tables, no hope in daintiness and determination. Hope in dates.

Tin is not a can and a stove is hardly. Tin is not necessary and neither is a stretcher. Tin is never narrow and thick.

Color is in coal. Coal is outlasting roasting and a spoonful, a whole spoon that is full is not spilling. Coal any coal is copper.

Claiming nothing, not claiming anything, not a claim in everything, collecting claiming all this makes a harmony, it even makes a succession.

Sincerely gracious one morning, sincerely graciously trembling, sincere in gracious eloping, all this makes a furnace and a blanket. All this shows quantity.

Like an eye, not so much more, not any searching, no compliments.

Please be the beef, please beef, pleasure is not wailing. Please beef, please be carved clear, please be a case of consideration.

Search a neglect. A sale, any greatness is a stall and there is no memory, there is no clear collection.

A satin sight, what is a trick, no trick is mountainous and the color, all the rush is in the blood.

Bargaining for a little, bargain for a touch, a liberty, an estrangement, a characteristic turkey.

Please spice, please no name, place a whole weight, sink into a standard rising, raise a circle, choose a right around, make the resonance accounted and gather green any collar.

To bury a slender chicken, to raise an old feather, to surround a garland and to bake a pole splinter, to suggest a repose and to settle simply, to surrender one another, to succeed saving simpler, to satisfy a singularity and not to be blinder, to sugar nothing darker and to read redder, to have the color better, to sort our dinner, to remain together, to surprise no sinner, to curve nothing sweeter, to continue thinner, to increase in resting recreation to design string not dimmer.

Cloudiness what is cloudiness, is it a lining, is it a roll, is it melting.

The sooner there is jerking, the sooner freshness is tender, the sooner the round it is not round the sooner it is withdrawn in cutting, the sooner the measure means service, the sooner there is chinking, the sooner there is sadder than salad, the sooner there is none do her, the sooner there is no choice, the sooner there is a gloom freer, the same sooner and more sooner, this is no error in hurry and in pressure and in opposition to consideration.

A recital, what is a recital, it is an organ and use does not strengthen valor, it soothes medicine.

A transfer, a large transfer, a little transfer, some transfer, clouds and tracks do transfer, a transfer is not neglected.

Pride, when is there perfect pretence, there is no more than yesterday and ordinary.

A sentence of a vagueness that is violence is authority and a mission and stumbling and also certainly also a prison. Calmness, calm is beside the plate and in way in. There is no turn in terror. There is no volume in sound.

Tnere is coagulation in cold and there is none in prudence. Something is preserved and the evening is long and the colder spring has sudden shadows in a sun. All the stain is tender and lilacs really lilacs are disturbed. Why is the perfect reëstablishment practiced and prized, why is it composed. The result the pure result is juice and size and baking and exhibition and nonchalance and sacrifice and volume and a section in division and the surrounding recognition and horticulture and no murmur. This is a result. There is no superposition and circumstance, there is hardness and a reason and the rest and remainder. There is no delight and no mathematics.

MUTTON

A letter which can wither, a learning which can suffer and an outrage which is simultaneous is principal.

Students, students are merciful and recognized they chew something.

Hates rests that is solid and sparse and all in a shape and largely very largely. Interleaved and successive and a sample of smell all this makes a certainty a shade.

Light curls very light curls have no more curliness than soup. This is not a subject.

Change a single stream of denting and change it hurriedly, what does it express, it expresses nausea. Like a very strange likeness and pink, like that and not more like that than the same resemblance and not more like that than no middle space in cutting.

An eye glass, what is an eye glass, it is water. A splendid specimen, what is it when it is little and tender so that there are parts. A centre can place and four are no more and two and two are not middle.

Melting and not minding, safety and powder, a particular recollection and a sincere solitude all this makes a shunning so thorough and so unrepeated and surely if there is anything left it is a bone. It is not solitary.

Any space is not quiet it is so likely to be shiny. Darkness very dark darkness is sectional. There is a way to see in onion and surely very surely rhubarb and a tomato, surely very surely there is that seeding. A little thing in is a little thing.

Mud and water were not present and not any more of either. Silk and stockings were not present and not any more of either. A receptacle and a symbol and no monster were present and no more. This made a piece show and was it a kindness, it can be asked was it a kindness to have it warmer, was it a kindness and does gliding mean more. Does it.

Does it dirty a ceiling. It does not. Is it dainty, it is if prices are sweet. Is it lamentable, it is not if there is no undertaker. Is it curious, it is not when there is youth. All this makes a line, it even makes makes no more. All this makes cherries. The reason that there is a suggestion in vanity is due to this that there is a burst of mixed music.

A temptation any temptation is an exclamation if there are misdeeds and little bones. It is not astonishing that bones mingle as they vary not at all and in any case why is a bone outstanding, it is so because the circumstance that does not make a cake and character is so easily churned and cherished.

Mouse and mountain and a quiver, a quaint statue and pain in an exterior and silence more silence louder shows salmon a mischief intender. A cake, a real salve made of mutton and liquor, a specially retained rinsing and an established cork and blazing, this which resignation influences and restrains, restrains more altogether. A sign is the specimen spoken.

A meal in mutton, mutton, why is lamb cheaper, it is cheaper because so little is more. Lecture, lecture and repeat instruction.

BREAKFAST

A change, a final change includes potatoes. This is no authority for the abuse of cheese. What language can instruct any fellow.

A shining breakfast, a breakfast shining, no dispute, no practice, nothing, nothing at all.

A sudden slice changes the whole plate, it does so suddenly.

An imitation, more imitation, imitation succeed imitations.

Anything that is decent, anything that is present, a calm and a cook and more singularly still a shelter, all these show the need of clamor. What is the custom, the custom is in the centre.

What is a loving tongue and pepper and more fish than there is when tears many tears are necessary. The tongue and the salmon, there is not salmon when brown is a color, there is salmon when there is no meaning to an early morning being pleasanter. There is no salmon, there are no tea-cups, there are the same kind of mushes as are used as stomachers by the eating hopes that makes eggs delicious. Drink is likely to stir a certain respect for an egg cup and more water melon than was ever eaten yesterday. Beer is neglected and cocoa-nut is famous. Coffee all coffee and a sample of soup all soup these are the choice of a baker. A white cup means a wedding. A wet cup means a vacation. A strong cup means an especial regulation. A single cup means a capital arrangement between the drawer and the place that is open.

Price a price is not in language, it is not in custom, it is not in praise.

A colored loss, why is there no leisure. If the persecution is so outrageous that nothing is solemn is there any occasion for persuasion.

A grey turn to a top and bottom, a silent pocketful of much heating, all the pliable succession of surrendering makes an ingenious joy.

A breeze in a jar and even then silence, a special anticipation in a rack, a gurgle a whole gurgle and more cheese than almost anything, is this an astonishment, does this incline more than the original division between a tray and a talking arrangement and even then a calling into another room gently with some chicken in any way.

A bent way that is a way to declare that the best is all together, a bent way shows no result, it shows a slight restraint, it shows a necessity for retraction.

Suspect a single buttered flower, suspect it certainly, suspect it and then glide, does that not alter a counting.

A hurt mended stick, a hurt mended cup, a hurt mended article of exceptional relaxation and annoyance, a hurt mended, hurt and mended is so necessary that no mistake is intended.

What is more likely than a roast, nothing really and yet it is never disappointed singularly.

A steady cake, any steady cake is perfect and not plain, any steady cake has a mounting reason and more than that it has singular crusts. A season of more is a season that is instead. A season of many is not more a season than most.

Take no remedy lightly, take no urging intently, take no separation leniently, beware of no lake and no larder.

Burden the cracked wet soaking sack heavily, burden it so that it is an institution in fright and in climate and in the best plan that there can be.

An ordinary color, a color is that strange mixture which makes, which does make which does not make a ripe juice, which does not make a mat.

A work which is a winding a real winding of the cloaking of a relaxing rescue. This which is so cool is not dusting, it is not dirtying in smelling, it could use white water, it could use more extraordinarily and in no solitude altogether. This which is so not winsome and not widened and really not so dipped as dainty and really dainty, very dainty, ordinarily, dainty, a dainty, not in that dainty and dainty. If the time is determined, if it is determined and there is reunion there is reunion with that then outline, then there is in that a piercing shutter, all of a piercing shouter, all of a quite weather, all of a withered exterior, all of that in most violent likely.

An excuse is not dreariness, a single plate is not butter, a single weight is not excitement, a solitary crumbling is not only martial.

A mixed protection, very mixed with the same actual intentional unstrangeness and riding, a single action caused necessarily is not more a sign than a minister.

Seat a knife near a cage and very near a decision and more nearly a timely working cat and scissors. Do this temporarily and make no more mistake in standing. Spread it all and arrange the white place, does this show in the house, does it not show in the green that is not necessary for that color, does it not even show in the explanation and singularly not at all stationary.

SUGAR

A violent luck and a whole sample and even then quiet.

Water is squeezing, water is almost squeezing on lard. Water, water is a mountain and it is selected and it is so practical that there is no use in money. A mind under is exact and so it is necessary to have a mouth and eye glasses.

A question of sudden rises and more time than awfulness is so easy and shady. There is precisely that noise.

A peck a small piece not privately overseen, not at all not a slice, not at all crestfallen and open, not at all mounting and chaining and evenly surpassing, all the bidding comes to tea.

A separation is not tightly in worsted and sauce, it is so kept well and sectionally.

Put it in the stew, put it to shame. A little slight shadow and a solid fine furnace.

The teasing is tender and trying and thoughtful.

The line which sets sprinkling to be a remedy is beside the best cold.

A puzzle, a monster puzzle, a heavy choking, a neglected Tuesday.

Wet crossing and a likeness, any likeness, a likeness has blisters, it has that and teeth, it has the staggering blindly and a little green, any little green is ordinary.

One, two and one, two, nine, second and five and that.

A blaze, a search in between, a cow, only any wet place, only this tune.

Cut a gas jet uglier and then pierce pierce in between the next and negligence. Choose the rate to pay and pet pet very much. A collection of all around, a signal poison, a lack of languor and more hurts at ease.

A white bird, a colored mine, a mixed orange, a dog.

Cuddling comes in continuing a change.

A piece of separate outstanding rushing is so blind with open delicacy.

A canoe is orderly. A period is solemn. A cow is accepted.

A nice old chain is widening, it is absent, it is laid by.

CRANBERRIES

Could there not be a sudden date, could there not be in the present settlement of old age pensions, could there not be by a witness, could there be.

Count the chain, cut the grass, silence the noon and murder flies. See the basting undip the chart, see the way the kinds are best seen from the rest, from that and untidy.

Cut the whole space into twenty-four spaces and then and then is there a yellow color, there is but it is smelled, it is then put where it is and nothing stolen.

A remarkable degree of red means that, a remarkable exchange is made.

Climbing altogether in when there is a solid chance of soiling no more than a dirty thing, coloring all of it in steadying is jelly.

Just as it is suffering, just as it is succeeded, just as it is moist so is there no countering.

MILK

A white egg and a colored pan and a cabbage showing settlement, a constant increase.

A cold in a nose, a single cold nose makes an excuse. Two are more necessary.

All the goods are stolen, all the blisters are in the cup.

Cooking, cooking is the recognition between sudden and nearly sudden very little and all large holes.

A real pint, one that is open and closed and in the middle is so bad.

Tender colds, seen eye holders, all work, the best of change, the meaning, the dark red, all this and bitten, really bitten.

Guessing again and golfing again and the best men, the very best men.

MILK

Climb up in sight climb in the whole utter needles and a guess a whole guess is hanging. Hanging hanging.

EGGS

Kind height, kind in the right stomach with a little sudden mill.

Cunning shawl, cunning shawl to be steady.

In white in white handkerchiefs with little dots in a white belt all shadows are singular they are singular and procured and relieved.

No that is not the cows shame and a precocious sound, it is a bite.

Cut up alone the paved way which is harm. Harm is old boat and a likely dash.

APPLE

Apple plum, carpet steak, seed clam, colored wine, calm seen, cold cream, best shake, potato, potato and no no gold work with pet, a green seen is called bake and change sweet is bready, a little piece a little piece please.

A little piece please. Cane again to the presupposed and ready eucalyptus tree, count out sherry and ripe plates and little corners of a kind of ham. This is use.

TAILS

Cold pails, cold with joy no joy.

A tiny seat that means meadows and a lapse of cuddles with cheese and nearly bats, all this went messed. The post placed a loud loose sprain. A rest is no better. It is better yet. All the time.

LUNCH

Luck in loose plaster makes holy gauge and nearly that, nearly more states, more states come in town light kite, blight not white.

A little lunch is a break in skate a little lunch so slimy, a west end of a board line is that which shows a little beneath so that necessity is a silk under wear. That is best wet. It is so natural, and why is there flake, there is flake to explain exhaust.

A real cold hen is nervous is nervous with a towel with a spool with real beads. It is mostly an extra sole nearly all that shaved, shaved with an old mountain, more than that bees more than that dinner and a bunch of likes that is to say the hearts of onions aim less.

Cold coffee with a corn a corn yellow and green mass is a gem.

CUPS

A single example of excellence is in the meat. A bent stick is surging and might all might is mental. A grand clothes is searching out a candle not that wheatly not that by more than an owl and a path. A ham is proud of cocoanut.

A cup is neglected by being all in size. It is a handle and meadows and sugar any sugar.

A cup is neglected by being full of size. It shows no shade, in come little wood cuts and blessing and nearly not that not with a wild bought in, not at all so polite, not nearly so behind.

Cups crane in. They need a pet oyster, they need it so hoary and nearly choice. The best slam is utter. Nearly be freeze.

Why is a cup a stir and a behave. Why is it so seen.

A cup is readily shaded, it has in between no sense that is to say music, memory, musical memory.

Peanuts blame, a half sand is holey and nearly.

RHUBARB

Rhubarb is susan not susan not seat in bunch toys not wild and laughable not in little places not in neglect and vegetable not in fold coal age not please.

SINGLE FISH

Single fish single fish single fish egg-plant single fish sight.

A sweet win and not less noisy than saddle and more ploughing and nearly well painted by little things so.

Please shade it a play. It is necessary and beside the large sort is puff.

Every way oakly, please prune it near. It is so found.

It is not the same.

CAKE

Cake cast in went to be and needles wine needles are such.

This is to-day. A can experiment is that which makes a town, makes a town dirty, it is little please. We came back. Two bore, bore what, a mussed ash, ash when there is tin. This meant cake. It was a sign.

Another time there was extra a hat pin sought long and this dark made a display. The result was yellow. A caution, not a caution to be.

It is no use to cause a foolish number. A blanket stretch a cloud, a shame, all that bakery can tease, all that is beginning and yesterday yesterday we had it met. It means some change. No some day.

A little leaf upon a scene an ocean any where there, a bland and likely in the stream a recollection green land. Why white.

CUSTARD

Custard is this. It has aches, aches when. Not to be. Not to be narrowly. This makes a whole little hill.

It is better than a little thing that has mellow real mellow. It is better than lakes whole lakes, it is better than seeding.

POTATOES

Real potatoes cut in between.

POTATOES

In the preparation of cheese, in the preparation of crackers, in the preparation of butter, in it.

ROAST POTATOES

Roast potatoes for.

ASPARAGUS

Asparagus in a lean in a lean to hot. This makes it art and it is wet wet weather wet weather wet.

BUTTER

Boom in boom in, butter. Leave a grain and show it, show it. I spy.

It is a need it is a need that a flower a state flower. It is a need that a state rubber. It is a need that a state rubber is sweet and sight and a swelled stretch. It is a need. It is a need that state rubber.

Wood a supply. Clean little keep a strange, estrange on it.

Make a little white, no and not with pit, pit on in within.

END OF SUMMER

Little eyelets that have hammer and a check with stripes between a lounge, in wit, in a rested development.

SAUSAGES

Sausages in between a glass.

There is read butter. A loaf of it is managed. Wake a question. Eat an instant, answer.

A reason for bed is this, that a decline, any decline is poison, poison is a toe a toe extractor, this means a solemn change. Hanging.

No evil is wide, any extra in leaf is so strange and singular a red breast.

CELERY

Celery tastes tastes where in curled lashes and little bits and mostly in remains.

A green acre is so selfish and so pure and so enlivened.

VEAL

Very well very well, washing is old, washing is washing.

Cold soup, cold soup clear and particular and a principal a principal question to put into.

VEGETABLE

What is cut. What is cut by it. What is cut by it in.

It was a cress a crescent a cross and an unequal scream, it was upslanting, it was radiant and reasonable with little ins and red.

News. News capable of glees, cut in shoes, belike under plump of wide chalk, all this combing.

WAY LAY VEGETABLE

Leaves in grass and mow potatoes, have a skip, hurry you up flutter.

Suppose it is ex a cake suppose it is new mercy and leave charlotte and nervous bed rows. Suppose it is meal. Suppose it is sam.

COOKING

Alas, alas the pull alas the bell alas the coach in china, alas the little put in leaf alas the wedding butter meat, alas the receptacle, alas the back shape of mussle, mussle and soda.

CHICKEN

Pheasant and chicken, chicken is a peculiar bird.

CHICKEN

Alas a dirty word, alas a dirty third alas a dirty third, alas a dirty bird.

CHICKEN

Alas a doubt in case of more go to say what it is cress. What is it.
Mean. Potato. Loaves.

CHICKEN

Stick stick call then, stick stick sticking, sticking with a chicken.
Sticking in a extra succession, sticking in.

CHAIN-BOATS

Chain-boats are merry, are merry blew, blew west, carpet.

PASTRY

Cutting shade, cool spades and little last beds, make violet, violet
when.

CREAM

In a plank, in a play sole, in a heated red left tree there is shut in
specs with salt be where. This makes an eddy. Necessary.

CREAM

Cream cut. Any where crumb. Left hop chambers.

CUCUMBER

Not a razor less, not a razor, ridiculous pudding, red and relet
put in, rest in a slender go in selecting, rest in, rest in in white
widening.

DINNER

Not a little fit, not a little fit sun sat in shed more mentally.

Let us why, let us why weight, let us why winter chess, let us why why.

Only a moon to soup her, only that in the sell never never be the cocups nice be, shatter it they lay.

Egg ear nuts, look a bout. Shoulder. Let is strange, sold in bell next herds.

It was a time when in the acres in late there was a wheel that shot a burst of land and needless are niggers and a sample sample set of old eaten butterflies with spoons, all of it to be are fled and measure make it, make it, yet all the one in that we see where shall not it set with a left and more so, yes there add when the longer not it shall the best in the way when all be with when shall not for there with see and chest how for another excellent and excellent and easy easy excellent and easy express e c, all to be nice all to be no so. All to be no so no so. All to be not a white old chat churner. Not to be any example of an edible apple in.

DINING

Dining is west.

EATING

Eat ting, eating a grand old man said roof and never never re soluble burst, not a near ring not a bewildered neck, not really any such bay.

Is it so a noise to be is it a least remain to rest, is it a so old say to be, is it a leading are been. Is it so, is it so, is it so, is it so is it so is it so.

Eel us eel us with no no pea no pea cool, no pea cool cooler, no pea cooler with a land a land cost in, with a land cost in stretches.

Eating he heat eating he heat it eating, he heat it heat eating. He heat eating.

A little piece of pay of pay owls owls such as pie, bolsters.

Will leap beat, willie well all. The rest rest oxen occasion occasion to be so purred, so purred how.

It was a ham it was a square come well it was a square remain, a square remain not it a bundle, not it a bundle so is a grip, a grip to shed bay leave bay leave draught, bay leave draw cider in low, cider in low and george. George is a mass.

EATING

It was a shame it was a shame to stare to stare and double and relieve relieve be cut up show as by the elevation of it and out out more in the steady where the come and on and the all the shed and that.

It was a garden and belows belows straight. It was a pea, a pea pour it in its not a succession, not it a simple, not it a so election, election with.

SALAD

It is a winning cake.

SAUCE

What is bay labored what is all be section, what is no much. Sauce sam in.

SALMON

It was a peculiar bin a bin fond in beside.

ORANGE

Why is a feel oyster an egg stir. Why is it orange centre.

A show at tick and loosen loosen it so to speak sat.

It was an extra leaker with a see spoon, it was an extra licker with a see spoon.

ORANGE

A type oh oh new new not no not knealer knealer of old show beef-steak, neither neither.

ORANGES

Build is all right.

ORANGE IN

Go lack go lack use to her.

Cocoa and clear soup and oranges and oat-meal.

Whist bottom whist close, whist clothes, woodling.

Cocoa and clear soup and oranges and oat-meal.

Pain soup, suppose it is question, suppose it is butter, real is, real is only, only excreate, only excreate a no since.

A no, a no since, a no since when, a no since when since, a no since when since a no since when since, a no since, a no since when since, a no since, a no, a no since a no since, a no since, a no since.

SALAD DRESSING AND AN ARTICHOKE

Please pale hot, please cover rose, please acre in the red stranger, please butter all the beef-steak with regular feel faces.

SALAD DRESSING AND AN ARTICHOKE

It was please it was please carriage cup in an ice-cream, in an ice-cream it was too bended bended with scissors and all this time. A whole is inside a part, a part does go away, a hole is red leaf. No choice was where there was and a second and a second.

A CENTRE IN A TABLE

It was a way a day, this made some sum. Suppose a cod liver a cod liver is an oil, suppose a cod liver oil is tunny, suppose a cod liver oil tunny is pressed suppose a cod liver oil tunny pressed is china and secret with a bestow a bestow reed, a reed to be a reed to be, in a reed to be.

Next to me next to a folder, next to a folder some waiter, next to a foldsome waiter and re letter and read her. Read her with her for less.

Rooms

Act so that there is no use in a centre. A wide action is not a width. A preparation is given to the ones preparing. They do not eat who mention silver and sweet. There was an occupation.

A whole centre and a border make hanging a way of dressing. This which is not why there is a voice is the remains of an offering. There was no rental.

So the tune which is there has a little piece to play, and the exercise is all there is of a fast. Then tender and true that makes no width to hew is the time that there is question to adopt.

To begin the placing there is no wagon. There is no change lighter. It was done. And then the spreading, that was not accomplishing that needed standing and yet the time was not so difficult as they were not all in place. They had no change. They were not respected. They were that, they did it so much in the matter and this showed that that settlement was not condensed. It was spread there. Any change was in the ends of the centre. A heap was heavy. There was no change.

Burnt and behind and lifting a temporary stone and lifting more than a drawer.

The instance of there being more is an instance of more. The shadow is not shining in the way there is a black line. The truth has come. There is a disturbance. Trusting to a baker's boy meant that there would be very much exchanging and anyway what is the use of a covering to a door. There is a use, they are double.

If the centre has the place then there is distribution. That is natural. There is a contradiction and naturally returning there comes to be both sides and the centre. That can be seen from the description.

The author of all that is in there behind the door and that is entering in the morning. Explaining darkening and expecting relating is all of a piece. The stove is bigger. It was of a shape that made no audience bigger if the opening is assumed why should there not be kneeling. Any force which is bestowed on a floor shows rubbing. This is so nice and sweet and yet there comes the change, there comes the time to press more air. This does not mean the same as disappearance.

A little lingering lion and a Chinese chair, all the handsome cheese which is stone, all of it and a choice, a choice of a blotter. If it is difficult to do it one way there is no place of similar trouble. None. The whole arrangement is established. The end of which is that there is a suggestion, a suggestion that tnere can be a different whiteness to a wall. This was thought.

A page to a corner means that the shame is no greater when the table is longer. A glass is of any height, it is higher, it is simpler and if it were placed there would not be any doubt.

Something that is an erection is that which stands and feeds and silences a tin which is swelling. This makes no diversion that is to say what can please exaltation, that which is cooking.

A shine is that which when covered changes permission. An enclosure blends with the same that is to say there is blending. A blend is that which holds no mice and this is not because of a floor it is because of nothing, it is not in a vision.

A fact is that when the place was replaced all was left that was stored and all was retained that would not satisfy more than another. The question is this, is it possible to suggest more to replace that thing. This question and this perfect denial does make the time change all the time.

The sister was not a mister. Was this a surprise. It was. The conclusion came when there was no arrangement. All the time that there was a question there was a decision. Replacing a casual acquaintance with an ordinary daughter does not make a son.

It happened in a way that the time was perfect and there was a growth of a whole dividing time so that where formerly there was no mistake there was no mistake now. For instance before when there was a separation there was waiting, now when there is separation there is the division between intending and departing. This made no more mixture than there would be if there had been no change.

A little sign of an entrance is the one that made it alike. If it were smaller it was not alike and it was so much smaller that a table was bigger. A table was much bigger, very much bigger. Changing that made nothing bigger, it did not make anything bigger littler, it did not hinder wood from not being used as leather. And this was so charming. Harmony is so essential. Is there pleasure when there is a passage, there is when every room is open. Every room is open when there are not four, there were there and surely there were four, there were two together. There is no resemblance.

A single speed, the reception of table linen, all the wonder of six little spoons, there is no exercise.

The time came when there was a birthday. Every day was no excitement and a birthday was added, it was added on Monday, this made the memory clear, this which was a speech showed the chair in the middle where there was copper.

Alike and a snail, this means Chinamen, it does there is no doubt that to be right is more than perfect there is no doubt and glass is confusing it confuses the substance which was of a color. Then came the time for discrimination, it came then and it was never mentioned it was so triumphant, it showed the whole head that had a hole and should have a hole it showed the resemblance between silver.

Startling a starving husband is not disagreeable. The reason that nothing is hidden is that there is no suggestion of silence. No song is sad. A lesson is of consequence.

Blind and weak and organized and worried and betrothed and resumed and also asked to a fast and always asked to consider and never startled and not at all bloated, this which is no rarer than frequently is not so astonishing when hair brushing is added. There is quiet, there certainly is.

No eye-glasses are rotten, no window is useless and yet if air will not come in there is a speech ready, there always is and there is no dimness, not a bit of it.

All along the tendency to deplore the absence of more has not been authorized. It comes to mean that with burning there is that pleasant state of stupefication. Then there is a way of earning a living. Who is a man.

A silence is not indicated by any motion, less is indicated by a motion, more is not indicated it is enthralled. So sullen and so low, so much resignation, so much refusal and so much place for a lower and an upper, so much and yet more silence, why is not sleeping a feat why is it not and when is there some discharge when. There never is.

If comparing a piece that is a size that is recognized as not a size but a piece, comparing a piece with what is not recognized but what is used as it is held by holding, comparing these two comes to be repeated. Suppose they are put together, suppose that there is an interruption, supposing that beginning again they are not changed as to position, suppose all this and suppose that any five two of whom are not separating suppose that the five are not consumed. Is there an exchange, is there a resemblance to the sky which is admitted to be there and the stars which can be seen. Is there. That was a question. There was no certainty. Fitting a failing meant that any two were indifferent and yet they were all connecting that, they were all connecting that consideration. This did not determine rejoining a letter. This did not make letters smaller. It did.

The stamp that is not only torn but also fitting is not any symbol. It suggests nothing. A sack that has no opening suggests more and the loss is not commensurate. The season gliding and the torn hangings receiving mending all this shows an example, it shows the force of sacrifice and likeness and disaster and a reason.

The time when there is not the question is only seen when there is a shower. Any little thing is water.

There was a whole collection made. A damp cloth, an oyster, a single mirror, a mannikin, a student, a silent star, a single spark, a little movement and the bed is made. This shows the disorder, it does, it shows more likeness than anything else, it shows the single mind that directs an apple. All the coats have a different shape, that does not mean that they differ in color, it means a union between use and exercise and a horse.

A plain hill, one is not that which is not white and red and green, a plain hill makes no sunshine, it shows that without a disturber. So the shape is there and the color and the outline and the miserable centre, it is not very likely that there is a centre, a hill is a hill and no hill is contained in a pink tender descender.

A can containing a curtain is a solid sentimental usage. The trouble in both eyes does not come from the same symmetrical carpet, it comes from there being no more disturbance than in little paper. This does show the teeth, it shows color.

A measure is that which put up so that it shows the length has a steel construction. Tidiness is not delicacy, it does not destroy the whole piece, certainly not it has been measured and nothing has been cut off and even if that has been lost there is a name, no name is signed and left over, not any space is fitted so that moving about is plentiful. Why is there so much resignation in a package, why is there rain, all the same the chance has come, there is no bell to ring.

A package and a filter and even a funnel, all this together makes a scene and supposing the question arises is hair curly, is it dark and dusty, supposing that question arises, is brushing necessary, is it, the whole special suddenness commences then, there is no delusion.

A cape is a cover, a cape is not a cover in summer, a cape is a cover and the regulation is that there is no such weather. A cape is not always a cover, a cape is not a cover when there is another, there is always something in that thing in establishing a disposition to put wetting where it will not do more harm. There is always that disposition and in a way there is some use in not mentioning changing and in establishing the temperature, there is some use in it as establishing all that lives dimmer freer and there is no dinner in the middle of anything. There is no such thing.

Why is a pale white not paler than blue, why is a connection made by a stove, why is the example which is mentioned not shown to be the same, why is there no adjustment between the place and the separate attention. Why is there a choice in gamboling. Why is there no necessary dull stable, why is there a single piece of any color, why is there that sensible silence. Why is there the resistance in a mixture, why is there no poster, why is there that in the window, why is there no suggester, why is there no window, why is there no oyster closer. Why is there a circular diminisher, why is there a bather, why is there no scraper, why is there a dinner, why is there a bell ringer, why is there a duster, why is there a section of a similar resemblance, why is there that scissor.

South, south which is a wind is not rain, does silence choke speech or does it not.

Lying in a conundrum, lying so makes the springs restless, lying so is a reduction, not lying so is arrangeable.

Releasing the oldest caution that is the pleasing some still renewing.

Giving it away, not giving it away, is there any difference. Giving it away. Not giving it away.

Almost very likely there is no seduction, almost very likely there is no stream, certainly very likely the height is penetrated, certainly certainly the target is cleaned. Come to sit, come to refuse, come to surround, come slowly and age is not lessening. The time which showed that was when there was no eclipse. All the time that resenting was removal all that time there was breadth. No breath is shadowed, no breath is painstaking and yet certainly what could be the use of paper, paper shows no disorder, it shows no desertion.

Why is there a difference between one window and another, why is there a difference, because the curtain is shorter There is no distaste in beefsteak or in plums or in gallons of milk water, there is no defiance in original piling up over a roof, there is no daylight in the evening, there is none there empty.

A tribune, a tribune does not mean paper, it means nothing more than cake, it means more sugar, it shows the state of lengthening any nose. The last spice is that which shows the whole evening spent in that sleep, it shows so that walking is an alleviation, and yet this astonishes everybody the distance is so sprightly. In all the time there are three days, those are not passed uselessly. Any little thing is a change that is if nothing is wasted in that cellar. All the rest of the chairs are established.

A success, a success is alright when there are there rooms and no vacancies, a success is alright when there is a package, success is alright anyway and any curtain is wholesale. A curtain diminishes and an ample space shows varnish.

One taste one tack, one taste one bottle, one taste one fish, one taste one barometer. This shows no distinguishing sign when there is a store.

Any smile is stern and any coat is a sample. Is there any use in changing more doors than there are committees. This question is so often asked that squares show that they are blotters. It is so very agreeable to hear a voice and to see all the signs of that expression.

Cadences, real cadences, real cadences and a quiet color. Careful and curved, cake and sober, all accounts and mixture, a guess at anything is righteous, should there be a call there would be a voice.

A line in life, a single line and a stairway, a rigid cook, no cook and no equator, all the same there is higher than that another evasion. Did that mean shame, it meant memory. Looking into a place that was hanging and was visible looking into this place and seeing a chair did that mean relief, it did, it certainly did not cause constipation and yet there is a melody that has white for a tune when there is straw color. This shows no face.

Star-light, what is star-light, star-light is a little light that is not always mentioned with the sun, it is mentioned with the moon and the sun, it is mixed up with the rest of the time.

Why is the name changed. The name is changed because in the little space there is a tree, in some space there are no trees, in every space there is a hint of more, all this causes the decision.

Why is there education, there is education because the two tables which are folding are not tied together with a ribbon, string is used and string being used there is a necessity for another one and another one not being used to hearing shows no ordinary use of any evening and yet there is no disgrace in looking, none at all. This came to separate when there was simple selection of an entire pre-occupation.

A curtain, a curtain which is fastened discloses mourning, this does not mean sparrows or elocution or even a whole preparation, it means that there are ears and very often much more altogether.

Climate, climate is not southern, a little glass, a bright winter, a strange supper an elastic tumbler, all this shows that the back is furnished and red which is red is a dark color. An example of this is fifteen years and a separation of regret.

China is not down when there are plates, lights are not ponderous and incalculable.

Currents, currents are not in the air and on the floor and in the door and behind it first. Currents do not show it plainer. This which is mastered has so thin a space to build it all that there is plenty of room and yet is it quarreling, it is not and the insistence is marked. A change is in a current and there is no habitable exercise.

A religion, almost a religion, any religion, a quintal in religion, a relying and a surface and a service in indecision and a creature and a question and a syllable in answer and more counting and no quarrel and a single scientific statement and no darkness and no question and an earned administration and a single set of sisters and an outline and no blisters and the section seeing yellow and the centre having spelling and no solitude and no quaintness and yet solid quite so solid and the single surface centred and the question in the placard and the singularity, is there a singularity, and the singularity, why is there a question and the singularity why is the surface outrageous, why is it beautiful why is it not when there is no doubt, why is anything vacant, why is not disturbing a centre no virtue, why is it when it is and why is it when it is and there is no doubt, there is no doubt that the singularity shows.

A climate, a single climate, all the time there is a single climate, any time there is a doubt, any time there is music that is to question more and more and there is no politeness, there is hardly any ordeal and certainly there is no table-cloth.

This is a sound and obligingness more obligingness leads to a harmony in hesitation.

A lake a single lake which is a pond and a little water any water which is an ant and no burning, not any burning, all this is sudden.

A canister that is the remains of furniture and a looking-glass and a bed-room and a larger size, all the stand is shouted and what is ancient is practical. Should the resemblance be so that any little cover is copied, should it be so that yards are measured, should it be so and there be a sin, should it be so then certainly a room is big enough when it is so empty and the corners are gathered together.

The change is mercenary that settles whitening the coloring and serving dishes where there is metal and making yellow any yellow every color in a shade which is expressed in a tray. This is a monster and awkward quite awkward and the little design which is flowered which is not strange and yet has visible writing, this is not shown all the time but at once, after that it rests where it is and where it is in place. No change is not needed. That does show design.

Excellent, more excellence is borrowing and slanting very slanting is light and secret and a recitation and emigration. Certainly shoals are shallow and nonsense more nonsense is sullen. Very little cake is water, very little cake has that escape.

Sugar any sugar, anger every anger, lover sermon lover, centre no distractor, all order is in a measure.

Left over to be a lamp light, left over in victory, left over in saving, all this and negligence and bent wood and more even much more is not so exact as a pen and a turtle and even, certainly, and even a piece of the same experience as more.

To consider a lecture, to consider it well is so anxious and so much a charity and really supposing there is grain and if a stubble every stubble is urgent, will there not be a chance of legality. The sound is sickened and the price is purchased and golden wheat is golden, a clergyman, a single tax, a currency and an inner chamber.

Checking an emigration, checking it by smiling and certainly by the same satisfactory stretch of hands that have more use for it than nothing, and mildly not mildly a correction, not mildly even a circumstance and a sweetness and a serenity. Powder, that has no color, if it did have would it be white.

A whole soldier any whole soldier has no more detail than any case of measles.

A bridge a very small bridge in a location and thunder, any thunder, this is the capture of reversible sizing and more indeed more can be cautious. This which makes monotony careless makes it likely that there is an exchange in principle and more than that, change in organization.

This cloud does change with the movements of the moon and the narrow the quite narrow suggestion of the building. It does and then when it is settled and no sounds differ then comes the moment when cheerfulness is so assured that there is an occasion.

A plain lap, any plain lap shows that sign, it shows that there is not so much extension as there would be if there were more choice in everything. And why complain of more, why complain of very much more. Why complain at all when it is all arranged that as there is no more opportunity and no more appeal and not even any more clinching that certainly now some time has come.

A window has another spelling, it has 'f' all together, it lacks no more then and this is rain, this may even be something else, at any rate there is no dedication in splendor. There is a turn of the stranger.

Catholic to be turned is to venture on youth and a section of debate, it even means that no class where each one over fifty is regular is so stationary that there are invitations.

A curving example makes righteous finger-nails. This is the only object in secretion and speech.

To being the same four are no more than were taller. The rest had a big chair and surveyance a cold accumulation of nausea, and even more than that, they had a disappointment.

Nothing aiming is a flower, if flowers are abundant then they are lilac, if they are not they are white in the centre.

Dance a clean dream and an extravagant turn up, secure the steady rights and translate more than translate the authority, show the choice and make no more mistakes than yesterday.

This means clearness it means a regular notion of exercise, it means more than that, it means liking counting, it means more than that, it does not mean exchanging a line.

Why is there more craving than there is in a mountain. This does not seem strange to one, it does not seem strange to an echo and more surely is in there not being a habit. Why is there so much useless suffering. Why is there.

Any wet weather means an open window, what is attaching eating, anything that is violent and cooking and shows weather is the same in the end and why is there more use in something than in all that.

The cases are made and books, back books are used to secure tears and church. They are even used to exchange black slippers. They can not be mended with wax. They show no need of any such occasion.

A willow and no window, a wide place stranger, a wideness makes an active center.

The sight of no pussy cat is so different that a tobacco zone is white and cream.

A lilac, all a lilac and no mention of butter, not even bread and butter, no butter and no occasion, not even a silent resemblance, not more care than just enough haughty.

A safe weight is that which when it pleases is hanging. A safer weight is one more naughty in a spectacle. The best game is that which is shiny and scratching. Please a pease and a cracker and a wretched use of summer.

Surprise, the only surprise has no occasion. It is an ingredient and the section the whole section is one season.

A pecking which is petting and no worse than in the same morning is not the only way to be continuous often.

A light in the moon the only light is on Sunday. What was the sensible decision. The sensible decision was that notwithstanding many declarations and more music, not even notwithstanding the choice and a torch and a collection, notwithstanding the celebrating hat and a vacation and even more noise than cutting, notwithstanding Europe and Asia and being overbearing, not even notwithstanding an elephant and a strict occasion, not even withstanding more cultivation and some seasoning, not even with drowning and with the ocean being encircling, not even with more likeness and any cloud, not even with terrific sacrifice of pedestrianism and a special resolution, not even more likely to be pleasing. The care with which the rain is wrong and the green is wrong and the white is wrong, the care with which there is a chair and plenty of breathing. The care with which there is incredible justice and likeness, all this makes a magnificent asparagus, and also a fountain.

Portraits of People

In her lecture 'Portraits and Repetitions' Gertrude Stein describes how she came to think about portrait writing and how the writing of them gradually changed. The selection of portraits which follows is based on this lecture. The dates given refer to the time they were written.

The following portraits are read by Gertrude Stein on the record Caedmon TC 1050, recorded in New York 1934–5: 'Matisse', 'A Valentine to Sherwood Anderson', 'If I Told Him: A Completed Portrait of Picasso', and also 'Madame Recamier' (see her lecture 'Plays') and excerpts from *The Making of Americans*.

9

MATISSE

ONE was quite certain that for a long part of his being one being living he had been trying to be certain that he was wrong in doing what he was doing and then when he could not come to be certain that he had been wrong in doing what he had been doing, when he had completely convinced himself that he would not come to be certain that he had been wrong in doing what he had been doing he was really certain then that he was a great one and he certainly was a great one. Certainly every one could be certain of this thing that this one is a great one.

Some said of him, when anybody believed in him they did not then believe in any other one. Certainly some said this of him.

He certainly very clearly expressed something. Some said that he did not clearly express anything. Some were certain that he expressed something very clearly and some of such of them said that he would have been a greater one if he had not been one so clearly expressing what he was expressing. Some said he was not clearly expressing what he was expressing and some of such of them said that the greatness of struggling which was not clear expression made of him one being a completely great one.

Some said of him that he was greatly expressing something struggling. Some said of him that he was not greatly expressing something struggling.

He certainly was clearly expressing something, certainly some-time any one might come to know that of him. Very many did come to know it of him that he was clearly expressing what he was ex-pressing. He was a great one. Any one might come to know that of him. Very many did come to know that of him. Some who came to know that of him, that he was a great one, that he was clearly ex-pressing something, came then to be certain that he was not greatly expressing something being struggling. Certainly he was expressing something being struggling. Any one could be certain that he was expressing something being struggling. Some were certain that he was greatly expressing this thing. Some were certain that he was not greatly expressing this thing. Every one could come to be certain that he was a great man. Any one could come to be certain that he was clearly expressing something.

Some certainly were wanting to be needing to be doing what he was doing, that is clearly expressing something. Certainly they were willing to be wanting to be a great one. They were, that is some of them, were not wanting to be needing expressing anything being struggling. And certainly he was one not greatly expressing some-thing being struggling, he was a great one, he was clearly expressing something. Some were wanting to be doing what he was doing that is clearly expressing something. Very many were doing what he was doing, not greatly expressing something being struggling. Very many were wanting to be doing what he was doing were not want-ing to be expressing anything being struggling.

There were very many wanting to be doing what he was doing that is to be one clearly expressing something. He was certainly a great man, any one could be really certain of this thing, every one could be certain of this thing. There were very many who were wanting to be ones doing what he was doing that is to be ones clearly expressing something and then very many of them were not wanting to be being ones doing that thing, that is clearly expressing something, they wanted to be ones expressing something being struggling, something being going to be some other thing, some-thing being going to be something some one sometime would be clearly expressing and that would be something that would be a thing then that would then be greatly expressing some other thing then that thing, certainly very many were then not wanting to be doing what this one was doing clearly expressing something and some of them had been ones wanting to be doing that thing wanting to be ones clearly expressing something. Some were wanting to be ones doing what this one was doing wanted to be ones clearly expressing something. Some of such of them were ones certainly clearly expressing something, that was in them a thing not really interesting then any other one. Some of such of them went on being all their living ones wanting to be clearly expressing something and some of them were clearly expressing something.

This one was one very many were knowing some and very many were glad to meet him, very many sometimes listened to him, some listened to him very often, there were some who listened to him, and he talked then and he told them then that certainly he had been one suffering and he was then being one trying to be certain that he was wrong in doing what he was doing and he had come then to be certain that he never would be certain that he was doing what it was wrong for him to be doing then and he was suffering then and he was certain that he would be one doing what he was doing and he was certain that he should be one doing what he was doing and he was certain that he would always be one suffering and this then made him certain this, that he would always be one being suffering, this made him certain that he was expressing something being struggling and certainly very many were quite certain that he was greatly expressing something being struggling. This one was knowing some who were listening to him and he was telling very often about being one suffering and this was not a dreary thing to any one hearing that then, it was not a saddening thing to any one hearing it again and again, to some it was quite an interesting thing hearing it again and again, to some it was an exciting thing hearing it again and again, some knowing this one and being certain that this one was a great man and was one clearly expressing something were ones hearing this one telling about being one being living were hearing this one telling this thing again and again. Some who were ones knowing this one and were ones certain that this one was one who was clearly telling something, was a great man, were not listening very often to this one telling again and again about being one being living. Certainly some who were certain that this one was a great man and one clearly expressing something and greatly expressing something being struggling were listening to this one telling about being living telling about this again and again and again. Certainly very many knowing this one and being certain that this one was a great man and that this one was clearly telling something were not listening to this one telling about being living, were not listening to this one telling this again and again.

This one was certainly a great man, this one was certainly clearly expressing something. Some were certain that this one was clearly expressing something being struggling, some were certain that this one was not greatly expressing something being struggling.

Very many were not listening again and again to this one telling about being one being living. Some were listening again and again to this one telling about this one being one being in living.

Some were certainly wanting to be doing what this one was doing that is were wanting to be ones clearly expressing something. Some of such of them did not go on in being ones wanting to be doing what this one was doing that is in being ones clearly expressing something. Some went on being ones wanting to be doing what this one was doing that is, being ones clearly expressing something. Certainly this one was one who was a great man. Any one could be certain of this thing. Every one would come to be certain of this thing. This one was one certainly clearly expressing something. Any one could come to be certain of this thing. Every one would come to be certain of this thing. This one was one, some were quite certain, one greatly expressing something being struggling. This one was one, some were quite certain, one not greatly expressing something being struggling.

(1909)

device of the
"continuous present"
"the isolation of
present internal
time"
(D. Sutherland)

10

PICASSO

ONE whom some were certainly following was one who was completely charming. One whom some were certainly following was one who was charming. One whom some were following was one who was completely charming. One whom some were following was one who was certainly completely charming.

Some were certainly following and were certain that the one they were then following was one working and was one bringing out of himself then something. Some were certainly following and were certain that the one they were then following was one bringing out of himself then something that was coming to be a heavy thing, a solid thing and a complete thing.

One whom some were certainly following was one working and certainly was one bringing something out of himself then and was one who had been all his living had been one having something coming out of him.

Something had been coming out of him, certainly it had been coming out of him, certainly it was something, certainly it had been coming out of him and it had meaning, a charming meaning, a solid meaning, a struggling meaning, a clear meaning.

One whom some were certainly following and some were certainly following him, one whom some were certainly following was one certainly working.

One whom some were certainly following was one having something coming out of him something having meaning and this one was certainly working then.

This one was working and something was coming then, something was coming out of this one then. This one was one and always there was something coming out of this one and always there had been something coming out of this one. This one had never been one not having something coming out of this one. This one was one having something coming out of this one. This one had been one whom some were following. This one was one whom some were following. This one was being one whom some were following. This one was one who was working.

This one was one who was working. This one was one being one having something being coming out of him. This one was one going on having something come out of him. This one was one going on working. This one was one whom some were following. This one was one who was working.

This one always had something being coming out of this one. This one was working. This one always had been working. This one was always having something that was coming out of this one that was a solid thing, a charming thing, a lovely thing, a perplexing thing, a disconcerting thing, a simple thing, a clear thing, a complicated thing, an interesting thing, a disturbing thing, a repellant thing, a very pretty thing. This one was one certainly being one having something coming out of him. This one was one whom some were following. This one was one who was working.

This one was one who was working and certainly this one was needing to be working so as to be one being working. This one was one having something coming out of him. This one would be one all his living having something coming out of him. This one was working and then this one was working and this one was needing to be working, not to be one having something coming out of him something having meaning, but was needing to be working so as to be one working.

This one was certainly working and working was something this one was certain this one would be doing and this one was doing that thing, this one was working. This one was not one completely working. This one was not ever completely working. This one certainly was not completely working.

This one was one having always something being coming out of him, something having completely a real meaning. This one was one whom some were following. This one was one who was working. This one was one who was working and he was one needing this thing needing to be working so as to be one having some way of being one having some way of working. This one was one who was working. This one was one having something come out of him something having meaning. This one was one always having something come out of him and this thing the thing coming out of him always had real meaning. This one was one who was working. This one was one who was almost always working. This one was not one completely working. This one was one not ever completely working. This one was not one working to have anything come out of him. This one did have something having meaning that did come out of him. He always did have something come out of him. He was working, he was not ever completely working. He did have some following. They were always following him. Some were certainly following him. He was one who was working. He was one having something coming out of him something having meaning. He was not ever completely working.

(1909)

II

FOUR DISHONEST ONES

Told by a description of what they do

THEY are what they are. They have not been changing. They are what they are.

Each one is what that one is. Each is what each is. They are not needing to be changing.

One is what she is. She does not need to be changing. She is what she is. She is not changing. She is what she is.

She is not changing. She is knowing nothing of not changing. She is not needing to be changing.

What is she doing. She is working. She is not needing to be changing. She is working very well, she is not needing to be changing. She has been working very hard. She has been suffering. She is not needing to be changing.

She has been living and working, she has been quiet and working, she has been suffering and working, she has been watching and working, she has been waiting, she has been working, she has been waiting and working, she is not needing to be changing.

She has been working, she is not needing to be changing. She has been one working and every one was knowing that she was not needing to be changing. She is what she is, she is not needing to be changing.

She is one working. She is one not needing to be changing. She is one working. She is one earning this thing earning not needing to be changing. She is one not needing to be changing. She is one being the one she is being. She is not needing to be changing.

She is earning being one working. She is going on earning being one working. She is working. She is not needing being changing.

She is completely earning being one working. She is helping in this thing, helping completing earning being one working. She is not needing to be changing.

She is working. She is not needing to be changing. She is working and is earning being paid for that thing being paid for working. She is not needing being changing.

She is working. She is paid for that thing, for working. She is working. She is not needing to be changing.

She has been earning being paid for working. She has earned being paid for working. She has been working. She has been paid for working. She is working. She is paid for working. She is not needing to be changing.

She has come to be one being paid for working. She is not needing to be changing. She is helping being paid for working. She is helping in this thing, she is helping to paying her for working. She is helping to pay her for working. She is beginning completing this thing. She is completing helping to pay her for working.

She is not needing to be changing. She is working. She has been earning being one working. She has been going on earning this thing earning being working.

She has earned working. She has gone on earning working. She has not been changing. She has come to be helping paying her for working. She has been working. She is working. She has been completely earning being working. She has been beginning helping paying her. She has not been changing. She is not needing being changing. She has been working. She is working.

She is not needing being changing. She is working. She is going on working. She has been earning being working. She has been earning being paid, almost completely paid for working. She has been beginning helping paying herself. She is not needing to be changing. She has been completely earning working.

Some have not been needing to be changing. Some one is not needing to be changing. That one is what that one is, she is not one needing to be changing.

He is one working. He has been working a long time. He has been completely patient, completely obliging, he has been completely working, he is one working, he is one working and is one going on working. He is one doing that thing, doing going on working.

He naturally is one working. He has been one working. He is one working. He is one some one is paying something. He is one some pay something. He is one who has been working and any one knowing that he is working is knowing that it is a natural thing that he is regularly working and that some one is paying him and that some are paying him something.

He is a steady one, he has been working a long time in the way he is working. Another one is working with him and is knowing that he has been working a very long time.

He is working, he is one being such a one. He is one working a long time where he is working. He is such a one. He is one some one working with him is knowing a long time in being one working with him. He is one some one is paying. He is one some are paying.

He is one some one is paying. He is one some are paying. He is one being one working and the work he is doing is being one working so that some are paying him something. He is honestly such a one one whom some is paying, one whom some are paying. He is such a one.

He is such a one. He is not needing being changing. He is helping a little helping some to be paying him. He is a good deal helping some to be paying him. He is helping some to pay him and helping then a good deal in their being ones being paying him. He is one some one is paying. He is not helping that one. He is one who is not needing to be changing.

Some are what they are. Some are not needing to be changing. Each one is what that one is.

One is what he is, he is not needing to be changing. He is what he is. He is working. He is delicately doing this thing. He is not needing to be changing. He is steadily, he is delicately working, he is not needing to be changing.

He was one wanting something. He was given that thing, the thing he was wanting.

He was going to be going on delicately working. He went on delicately working.

He was one wanting to be owning this thing, wanting to be owning being delicately working. He was needing something to buy this thing to buy being one owning being one delicately working. He was asking some to be helping him. He saw some one. He asked that one.

He got what he was needing. He bought selling his work then, he bought being one delicately working.

He was earning then something. He was not paying then some one. He was not denying anything. He had bought something. He was one having bought being delicately working. He was then not denying anything. He did not then pay some one.

He did not pay that one. He saw that one again and again. That one did that thing, he did having the one who had not paid him see him again and again and again and again.

The one went on working. He was delicately working. He had bought that thing. He went on buying that thing and selling the things he was delicately making. He was one who was not denying anything. He did not deny anything.

He was not needing to be changing. He was delicately working, he had bought that thing, he was selling things. He did not deny anything. He was not needing to be changing.

Each one is as that one is. Some are as they are, they are not needing to be changing. One, who is one not needing to be changing, is one who has not been changing.

She is one and she has not been changing. She has not been changing and she has not been completely mentioning this thing but she has been one of whom some have been saying this thing. She has not been changing.

She is not needing to be changing. She is working some. She has been paid, she is paid for this thing. She is not needing to be changing.

She is working some. She is paid for this thing, for working some. She has not been changing.

She has not been changing. She is not really mentioning this thing.

She is not needing to be changing. She has been feeling this thing. She has been feeling that she is not needing to be changing. She is not needing to be changing.

(1911)

12

MI-CAREME

THERE was a man who said one could recognize him when one saw him again by the scar on the end of his nose and under his eye but these scars were very little ones almost not anything and one would remember him because he was one who had been saying that he was a man tired of working tired of being one being working, and that he would be very amusing, he could be amusing by saying something that would make any one listening begin blushing but, he said, he would not do such a thing he would be politely amusing and he was amusing and some being amused by him were not frightened by him. He might have been amusing to some who were at the same time ones frightened by him. He might be very amusing to some who would never in any way think that he could frighten any one.

There was a man who did not frighten some one because that one did not know that any one might be frightened by such a one. He did not frighten another one because that one was not going to be one being frightened just then. He did not frighten another one because that one was never frightened by any such a kind of one. He did not frighten another one because that one did not notice that he was being there then. He did not frighten another one because that one was certain that he would not be staying there long enough to be frightening any one if he was one who could frighten any one. He did not then frighten any one this one and in a way that was a strange thing as he was one who might frighten any one.

There were some who are ones who are very frightened and these were not frightened by some doing things that sometimes completely frighten them when any one is doing any such thing. These then were not frightened and not any one really was frightened then and yet certainly these have been frightened by just some such thing. There were very many then who were not frightened then and some of such of them are ones always being frightened when they are where any one could be frightening any one.

It was quite pleasant to some to know then that any one can be somewhere and doing something and not be at all frightened by the thing they are doing then. It is quite pleasant to some to be certain that each one, that they themselves then can be doing something and not be frightened when some one else is doing something and certainly some of such of them can be very often frightened when they are doing a thing and when some one else is then doing something.

Certainly it is very difficult to be certain just how completely one is frightened in being living. Certainly it is very difficult to be really certain just how much one is not frightened in being one being living.

One is frightened in being one being living. One is not frightened in being one being living. One is frightened again and again. One is again and again not frightened. One is almost completely frightened. One is completely not frightened. Certainly one can and one cannot be frightened in being one being living. One can be certain that one is going to be frightened and one can be frightened then and one is frightened then and one is not frightened then. One can be certain that one is not going to be frightened and one can and one cannot then be frightened. Certainly very many are frightened when very many are being ones being living. Certainly very many are frightened when there are not very many being ones being. Certainly very many are in being living frightened again and again. Certainly very many in being living are completely frightened, are almost completely frightened, are quite completely not frightened, are not frightened, are pretty nearly frightened, are being ones who might be completely frightened, are being ones coming near enough to being completely frightened, are being one coming sometimes quite near to being completely not frightened.

Very often very many are together. Some of them are then working, some of them are then looking, some are not looking. Very often there are very many together. Each of them is certain that being living is something they are needing being ones being doing.

Very often very many are together. Very many are together and each one of them is certain that they are ones needing being ones being living and each one of them is not certain that they are ones needing being ones being living.

Very often very many are together. Very many are together and each one of them could be one showing needing being one being living. Very many are together and each one of them could be one not showing needing being one being living.

Very many are together, it is very often happening that very many are together and some of them are looking and some of them are waiting and some of them are working and some of them are being taught to be polite in answering and some of them are hoping to be ones being ones not being at all polite to any one and some of them are remembering something.

Very many are together, very often very many are together and some of them are completely politely answering some one and some of them might be not politely answering some one and some are certain that some one will not be completely politely answering them and some are certain that some one will be teaching every one to be completely politely answering them.

Very many are together, very often a very great many are together, certainly some are quite certain that each one of them, that each one of all of them might be doing something certainly showing that each one is needing being one being living. Some are quite certain that each one is doing this thing is completely showing that each one is needing being living, some then are quite certain that each one that each one of all of them, very many are together then, are showing that each one is one needing to be living.

Perhaps each one is one needing to be living each one of all of them, very many being together then. If each one of all of them is one needing being living then certainly each one of all of them, very many being together then are ones needing being living. Each one being ones needing being living is then one in a way showing this thing showing being one needing being living. Each one being living is one in a way not showing being one needing being living. If one is one being one needing being living one is in any way showing this thing. In a way each one is not needing being living, perhaps each one, each one of all of them, very many being together then, are ones not needing being living. If they are in a way ones not needing being living, if each one of them is in a way each one of all of them is one being one not needing being living, in a way not needing being living then each one of them is showing this thing.

Some are certain that each one, very many being together then, some are certain that each one of all of them, very many being together then, are showing that they are ones needing being living. Some are certain that each one showing this thing could be politely showing this thing, showing being one needing to be living. Some are certain that each one cannot be politely showing this thing showing that they are ones needing being living.

Certainly some are needing to be ones not showing that they are ones needing being living some who are ones certain they are ones needing being living. Certainly some are ones not showing this thing, very many being together then, are ones not showing then that they are ones being ones needing being living, some of such of them are ones completely not showing this thing not showing that they are ones needing being living. Perhaps some of such of them are not ones needing being living. Perhaps all of such of them are ones needing being living. Perhaps all of such of them are ones not needing being living.

Very often very many are together. Very many are together and some of them are showing then in some way that they are ones needing being living. Some are very politely showing this thing, some are not very politely showing this thing. Some are ones showing this thing showing they are ones needing being living and some of such of them are not then completely certain that they are ones needing being living.

Very many are together, very often very many are together. Some are liking being ones needing being living. Some are not liking being ones needing being living. Some are liking making some other one certain completely that that one is one needing being living. Some are liking making some one come to be completely certain that that one is one needing being living. Some certainly are ones who can come to be again and again completely certain that they are ones needing being living. Some certainly are ones who can be made certain completely certain again and again that they are ones needing being living.

(1912)

13

A VALENTINE TO SHERWOOD ANDERSON

Idem the Same

I KNEW too that through them I knew too that he was through, I knew too that he threw them. I knew too that they were through, I knew too I knew too, I knew I knew them.

I knew to them.

If they tear a hunter through, if they tear through a hunter, if they tear through a hunt and a hunter, if they tear through the different sizes of the six, the different sizes of the six which are these, a woman with a white package under one arm and a black package under the other arm and dressed in brown with a white blouse, the second Saint Joseph the third a hunter in a blue coat and black garters and a plaid cap, a fourth a knife grinder who is full faced and a very little woman with black hair and a yellow hat and an excellently smiling appropriate soldier. All these as you please.

In the meantime examples of the same lily. In this way please have you rung.

WHAT DO I SEE

A very little snail.
A medium sized turkey.
A small band of sheep.
A fair orange tree.
All nice wives are like that.
Listen to them from here.
Oh.
You did not have an answer.
Here.
Yes.

A VERY VALENTINE

Very fine is my valentine.

Very fine and very mine.

Very mine is my valentine very mine and very fine.

Very fine is my valentine and mine, very fine very mine and mine is my valentine.

WHY DO YOU FEEL DIFFERENTLY

Why do you feel differently about a very little snail and a big one.

Why do you feel differently about a medium sized turkey and a very large one.

Why do you feel differently about a small band of sheep and several sheep that are riding.

Why do you feel differently about a fair orange tree and one that has blossoms as well.

Oh very well.

All nice wives are like that.

To Be.

No Please.

To Be

They can please

Not to be

Do they please.

Not to be

Do they not please

Yes please.

Do they please

No please.

Do they not please

No please.

Do they please.

Please.

If you please.

And if you please.

And if they please

And they please.
To be pleased.
Not to be pleased.
Not to be displeased.
To be pleased and to please.

KNEELING

One two three four five six seven eight nine and ten.

The tenth is a little one kneeling and giving away a rooster with this feeling.

I have mentioned one, four five seven eight and nine.

Two is also giving away an animal.

Three is changed as to disposition.

Six is in question if we mean mother and daughter, black and black caught her, and she offers to be three she offers it to me.

That is very right and should come out below and just so.

BUNDLES FOR THEM

A HISTORY OF GIVING BUNDLES

We were able to notice that each one in a way carried a bundle, they were not a trouble to them nor were they all bundles as some of them were chickens some of them pheasants some of them sheep and some of them bundles, they were not a trouble to them and then indeed we learned that it was the principal recreation and they were so arranged that they were not given away, and to-day they were given away.

I will not look at them again.

They will not look for them again.

They have not seen them here again.

They are in there and we hear them again.

In which way are stars brighter than they are. When we have come to this decision. We mention many thousands of buds. And when I close my eyes I see them.

If you hear her snore
It is not before you love her
You love her so that to be her beau is very lovely

She is sweetly there and her curly hair is very lovely
She is sweetly here and I am very near and that is very lovely.

She is my tender sweet and her little feet are stretched out well which is a treat and very lovely

Her little tender nose is between her little eyes which close and are very lovely.

She is very lovely and mine which is very lovely.

ON HER WAY

If you can see why she feels that she kneels if you can see why he knows that he shows what he bestows, if you can see why they share what they share, need we question that there is no doubt that by this time if they had intended to come they would have sent some notice of such intention. She and they and indeed the decision itself is not early dissatisfaction.

IN THIS WAY

Keys please, it is useless to alarm any one it is useless to alarm some one it is useless to be alarming and to get fertility in gardens in salads in heliotrope and in dishes. Dishes and wishes are mentioned and dishes and wishes are not capable of darkness. We like sheep. And so does he.

LET US DESCRIBE

Let us describe how they went. It was a very windy night and the road although in excellent condition and extremely well graded has many turnings and although the curves are not sharp the rise is considerable. It was a very windy night and some of the larger vehicles found it more prudent not to venture. In consequence some of those who had planned to go were unable to do so. Many others did go and there was a sacrifice, of what shall we, a sheep, a hen, a cock, a village, a ruin, and all that and then that having been blessed let us bless it.

(1922)

14

VAN OR TWENTY YEARS AFTER

A Second Portrait of Carl Van Vechten

TWENTY years after, as much as twenty years after in as much as twenty years after, after twenty years and so on. It is it is it is it is it is.

If it and as if it, if it or as if it, if it is as if it, and it is as if it and as if it. Or as if it. More as if it. As more As more. as if it. And if it. And for and as if it.

If it was to be a prize a surprise if it was to be a surprise to realize, if it was to be if it were to be, was it to be. What was it to be. It was to be what it was. And it was. So it was. As it was. As it is. Is it as it as. It is and as it is and as it is. And so and so as it was.

Keep it in sight all right.

Not to the future but to the fuchsia.

Tied and untied and that is all there is about it. And as tied and as beside, and as beside and tied. Tied and untied and beside and as beside and as untied and as tied and as untied and as beside. As beside as by and as beside. As by as by the day. By their day and as it may, may be they will may be they may. Has it been reestablished as not to weigh. Weigh how. How to weigh. Or weigh. Weight, state, await, state, late state rate state, state await weight state, in state rate at any rate state weight state as stated. In this way as stated. Only as if when the six sat at the table they all looked for those places together. And each one in that direction so as to speak look down and see the same as weight. As weight for weight as state to state as wait to wait as not so. Beside.

For arm absolutely for arm.

They reinstate the act of birth.

Bewildering is a nice word but it is not suitable at present.

They meant to be left as they meant to be left, as they meant to be left left and their center, as they meant to be left and and their center. So that in their and do, so that in their and to do. So suddenly and at his request. Get up and give it to him and so suddenly and as his request. Request to request in request, as request, for a request by request, requested, as requested as they requested, or so have it to be nearly there. Why are the three waiting, there are more than three. One two three four five six seven.

As seven.

Seating, regard it as the rapidly increased February.

Seating regard it as the very regard it as their very nearly regard as their very nearly or as the very regard it as the very settled, seating regard it as the very as their very regard it as their very nearly regard it as the very nice, seating regard as their very nearly regard it as the very nice, known and seated seating regard it, seating and regard it, regard it as the very nearly center left and in the center, regard it as the very left and in the center. And so I say so. So and so. That. For. For that. And for that. So and so and for that. And for that and so and so. And so I say so.

Now to fairly see it have, now to fairly see it have and now to fairly see it have. Have and to have. Now to fairly see it have and to have. Naturally.

As naturally, naturally as, as naturally as. As naturally.

Now to fairly see it have as naturally.

(1923)

15

IF I TOLD HIM

A Completed Portrait of Picasso

IF I told him would he like it. Would he like it if I told him.

Would he like it would Napoleon would Napoleon would would he like it.

If Napoleon if I told him if I told him if Napoleon. Would he like it if I told him if I told him if Napoleon. Would he like it if Napoleon if Napoleon if I told him. If I told him if Napoleon if Napoleon if I told him. If I told him would he like it would he like it if I told him.

Now.

Not now.

And now.

Now.

Exactly as as kings.

Feeling full for it.

Exactitude as kings.

So to beseech you as full as for it.

Exactly or as kings.

Shutters shut and open so do queens. Shutters shut and shutters and so shutters shut and shutters and so and so shutters and so shutters shut and so shutters shut and shutters and so. And so shutters shut and so and also. And also and so and so and also.

Exact resemblance to exact resemblance the exact resemblance as exact as a resemblance, exactly as resembling, exactly resembling, exactly in resemblance exactly a resemblance, exactly and resemblance. For this is so. Because.

Now actively repeat at all, now actively repeat at all, now actively repeat at all.

Have hold and hear, actively repeat at all.

I judge judge.

As a resemblance to him.

Who comes first. Napoleon the first.

Who comes too coming coming too, who goes there, as they go they share, who shares all, all is as all as as yet or as yet.

Now to date now to date. Now and now and date and the date.

Who came first Napoleon at first. Who came first Napoleon the first. Who came first, Napoleon first.

Presently.

Exactly do they do.

First exactly.

Exactly do they do too.

First exactly.

And first exactly.

Exactly do they do.

And first exactly and exactly.

And do they do.

At first exactly and first exactly and do they do.

The first exactly.

And do they do.

The first exactly.

At first exactly.

First as exactly.

At first as exactly.

Presently.

As presently.

As as presently.

He he he he and he and he and and he and he and he and and as and as he and as he and he. He is and as he is, and as he is and he is, he is and as he and he and as he is and he and he and and he and he.

Can curls rob can curls quote, quotable.

As presently.

As exactitude.

As trains.

Has trains.

Has trains.

As trains.

As trains.

Presently.

Proportions.

Presently.

As proportions as presently.

Father and farther.

Was the king or room.

Farther and whether.

Was there was there was there what was there was there what was there was there there was there.

Whether and in there.

As even say so.

One.

I land.

Two.

I land'

Three.

The land.

Three.

The land.

Three.

The land.

Two.

I land.

Two.

I land.

One.

I land.

Two.

I land.

As a so.

They cannot.

A note.

They cannot.

A float

They cannot.

They dote.

They cannot.

They as denote.

Miracles play.
Play fairly.
Play fairly well.
A well.
As well.
As or as presently.
Let me recite what history teaches. History teaches.

(1923)

16

LIPSCHITZ

LIKE and like likely and likely likely and likely like and like.

He had a dream. He dreamed he heard a pheasant calling and very likely a pheasant was calling.

To whom went.

He had a dream he dreamed he heard a pheasant calling and most likely a pheasant was calling.

In time.

This and twenty and forty-two makes every time a hundred and two thirty.

Any time two and too say.

When I knew him first he was looking looking through the glass and the chicken. When I knew him then he was looking looking at the looking at the looking. When I knew him then he was so tenderly then standing. When I knew him then he was then after then to then by then and when I knew him then he was then we then and then for then. When I knew him then he was for then by then as then so then to then in then and so.

He never needs to know.

He never needs he never seeds but so so can they sink settle and rise and apprise and tries. Can at length be long. No indeed and a song. A song of so much so.

When I know him I look at him for him and I look at him for him and I look at him for him when I know him.

I like you very much.

(1926)

17

GEORGE HUGNET

GEORGE and Genevieve.

Geronimo with a with whether they thought they were with whether.

Without their finding it out. Without. Their finding it out. With whether.

George whether they were about. With their finding their whether it finding it out whether with their finding about it out.

George with their finding it with out.

George whether their with their it whether.

Redoubt out with about.

With out whether it their whether with out doubt.

Azure can with out about.

It is welcome welcome thing.

George in are ring.

Lain away awake.

George in our ring.

George Genevieve Geronimo straightened it out without their finding it out.

Grammar makes George in our ring which Grammar make George in our ring.

Grammar is as disappointed not is as grammar is as disappointed.

Grammar is not as Grammar is as disappointed.

George is in our ring. Grammar is not is disappointed. In are ring.

George Genevieve in are ring.

(1928)

BERNARD FAŸ

A is an article.

They are usable. They are found and able and edible. And so they are predetermined and trimmed.

The which is an article. With them they have that. That which. They have the point in which it is close to the purpose.

The in articles.

In inclusion.

A fine finely.

A is an advice.

If a is an advice an is and temptation ridden. If a is an advice and is a temptation redden.

An article is when of them they leak without their wishes.

A an article. A an article.

A the same.

A and the. A and the.

The this that and an and end in deed indeed intend in end and lend and send and tend intended.

An article is when they have wishes.

A is an article.

The is an article.

A and the. Thank you.

Chapter One.

A preliminary survey of them they day of two a day.

When this as a tree when this with this a tree.

Night with articles.

Alight with articles.

A is an article. The is an article.

A and the.

There is hope with a. There is hope with the. A and the

Articles are a an and the.

When this you see remember me.

An article is an and the

A man and the man.

A man and a man and the.

An a man and the.

Part three

The Human race, the races of mankind and impatience, the race of man and patience and impatience.

What is patience.

One two three and after unity.

Unify and try, recast and asked.

What is patience.

Patience is amiable and amiably.

What is amiable and amiably.

Patience is amiable and amiably.

What is impatience.

Impatience is amiable and amiably.

What is a fact. A fact is alone and display their zeal. Display their zeal is hour by hour. Hour by hour is every half an hour. Every half an hour is often once in a while. Once in a while is a chain of their beauty. A chain of their beauty is ordinary with a chalk. With a chalk is their in radiance. Their with radiance is left when they will. When they will is all as they can. All as they can they delight. They delight. They delight. Deliberation. They delight. Deliberation they way delight. Deliberation they way they way they they delight.

To refuse to stop to end. That is however just.

Partly four.

We call partly for. We call partly for it we call it partly for we call for it partly we for call for part let partly call part a part call part let for eight for let partly for four forfeit for it.

No part in parted as part let part three partly.

Part three.

A noun is the name of anything.

Who has held him that a noun is the name. A noun is a name. Who has held him for a thing that a noun is a name of a thing.

A dislike.

A noun is a name of everything.

A king a wing. A thing a wing.

Noun a dislike.

He said sense.

To go and uneasy.

He said sense

A noun means he said sense.

He said sense. What is sense.

Sense is their origin in relieve.

Relieve is not abominable.

Relieve is not abominable.

They relieve which is sense. They relieve as in the sense. Relieve is a sense. A noun is a sense. What is a noun. A noun is the name of anything.

A noun can be best.

What is best. A noun can be best. What is a noun. Favored. A noun can be best. Why does he like it as he does. Because of a grown noun. A noun is grown. Thanking for the noun.

Never made dolls. Dolls should be seen. They should be gathered. They should be. With all my heart.

That is a noun. That they use winces. What is a noun.

There is no strength in their calling for a noun. What is a noun.

A noun made with his care.

Carefree a noun made with his care.

Forget the heart of their weeding.

A long interval of carefulness.

If they know in threes.

He will play to by and by and by.

He will play and why and my and by and by and by.

He has seriously asked them to sit.

It is not that they think, in a hurry, with their mass, of their offering, the reunion, of naming, as a process, without about a crowd, with name of a herd, which can fatter than an instance, in may day with a scream, left in a joining, that is relative, with their announcement, our with stretches, shell and well joined, mainly in a cover, with out a plundering, if in ribbon ribbons ribboned are in are there, all of which, is very precious, without their detail, with with their detail, made of their silk or, in as if stretches, it is all or all of their, give or given or gave or gave of, made in that case, that it is pour in planted, which makes it leave their as less, follow in occupy action, that they were merry, made as less, then than which calls fell where they with as well bell, that they in as most much, for in as can resemble such, with as with welcome call, called to be sure, to be sure is an action in their leaving it to him. Being sure is in an after in action in an leaving it with in him.

Partly a the

An article is a and an and the.

Thank you for all three.

The making of never stop. Or the making of stop or stopped.

The own owned own owner.

This is a sentence. Or either.

(1929)

Plays

Gertrude Stein read extracts from both the following plays in her lecture 'Plays' and they are given here in full. *A List* was written in 1923 and *Say It with Flowers* in 1931. Both were published in *Operas and Plays*, Plain Edition, Paris, 1932.

Because of the difficulty Gertrude Stein experienced in getting some of her work published, Alice Toklas decided to become her publisher. Gertrude Stein provided the capital by selling one of her Picasso paintings – *Girl with a Fan*. The name of the Alice Toklas 'publishing house' was Plain Edition. Apart from *Operas and Plays*, she published: *Lucy Church Amiably* (1930), *How To Write* (1931), *Before the Flowers of Friendship Faded Friendship Faded* (1931) and *Matisse, Picasso and Gertrude Stein*, which also includes *A Long Gay Book* and *Many Many Women* (1933).

19

A LIST

MARTHA: not interesting.

MARYAS: Precluded.

MARTHA: Not interesting.

MARIUS: challenged.

MARTHA AND MARYAS: Included.

MARYAS: If we take Marius.

MABEL: And an old window and still.

MABEL, MARTHA AND MARYAS: Various re-agents make me see victoriously.

MARYAS: In as we thrust them trust them trust them thrust them in. In as we brush them, we do not brush them in. In as we trust them in.

MABEL, MARTHA AND MABEL AND MARTHA: Susan Mabel Martha and Susan, Mabel and Martha and a father. There was no sinking there, there where there was no placid carrier.

MARTHA: not interesting.

MARYAS: Not included.

MABEL: And an old window and still.

MARIUS: Exchange challenges.

MARYAS: If added to this speeches are made are speeches played, speeches are included and thrust in and they trust in and they trust in speeches and they brush them in.

MARTHA: Smiles.

MABEL: And still she did mean to sing-song. We know how to very nearly please her.

MARIUS: Exchange challenges for challenges and by and by defy, and define by and by Battling Siki and so high. He is higher than they say. You know why beads are broader, in order to be in order to be an order to be strung together.

MARYAS AND MARTHA: Yes indeed.

MARYAS: Can intend to seize her objects seize the objects place the objects, place the objects.

MARTHA: A list.

MARYAS: A list.

MARIUS: A list.

MARTHA

MARYAS: A list.

MARTHA

MARYAS: A list lost.

MARTHA: A list lost reminds her of a fire lost. Smoke is not black nor if you turn your back is a fire burned if you are near woods which abundantly supply wood.

MARYAS: A list lost does not account for the list which has been lost nor for the inequality of cushions shawls and awls. Nowadays we rarely mention awls and shawls and yet an awl is still used commercially and a shawl is still used is still used and also used commercially. Shawls it may be mentioned depend upon their variety. There is a great variety in calculation and in earning.

MARIUS: A list.

MABEL: A list.

MARTHA: A list.

MARTHA: There is a great variety in the settlement of claims. We claim and you claim and I claim the same.

MARTHA: A list.

MARYAS: And a list.

MABEL: I have also had great pleasure from a capital letter.

MARTHA: And forget her.

MARYAS: And respect him.

MARIUS: And neglect them.

MABEL: And they collect them as lilies of the valley in this country.

MARTHA: A list.

MARYAS: Sixteen if sixteen carry four, four more, if five more carry four for more if four more carry four, if four carry fifty more, if four more five hundred and four and for more than that, and four more than eighty four. Four more can carry sixteen if you please if it is acceptable.

MARTHA: She knows very well that if five are sitting at a table and one leaning upon it, that it makes no difference.

MARYAS AND MARTHA: Nearly all of it has made nearly all of it. Nearly all of it has made nearly all of it.

MARYAS AND MARTHA: Nearly all of it has made nearly all of it has made nearly all of it has made nearly all of it.

MARTHA AND MARYAS: Nearly all of it has made nearly all of it.

MARTHA: Plenty of time as the pansy is a bird as well as a flower rice is a bird as well as a plant, cuckoo is a flower as well as a bird.

MARTHA AND MARIUS: A single instance of able to pay any day and as you say we exchange ribbons for ribbons and pictures for pictures successfully.

MARIUS: Is spelled in this way.

MARYAS: They saved it why did they save it they saved it as wire. In this way did you hear me say did they save it in this way, did they save it and will they use it in this way.

MARYAS AND MARTHA: Maryas and Martha.

MARYAS AND MARTHA: Did you hear me say cloudlessly.

MARYAS: Yes.

MARYAS AND MARTHA: Yes.

MARYAS: May be I do but I doubt it.

MARTHA: I do but I do doubt it.

MARTHA AND MARYAS: May be I do but I doubt. I do but I do doubt it.

MARIUS AND MABEL: Please to please. Pleasure to give pleasure.

MARIUS: To please and to give pleasure.

MARIUS AND MABEL: To please and please and to give pleasure and to give pleasure.

MARIUS: To please and to give pleasure.

MARIUS AND MABEL: If you please if you please and if you give pleasure.

MARIUS: If you give pleasure and if you please.

MARIUS AND MABEL: Please please and pleasure.

MARIUS: I am very pleased I am indeed very pleased that it is a great pleasure.

MARTHA: If four are sitting at a table and one of them is lying upon it it does not make any difference. If bread and pomegranates are on a table and four are sitting at the table and one of them is leaning upon it it does not make any difference.

MARTHA: It does not make any difference if four are seated at a table and one is leaning upon it.

MARYAS: If five are seated at a table and there is bread on it and there are pomegranates on it and one of the five is leaning on the table it does not make any difference.

MARTHA: If on a day that comes again and if we consider a day a week day it does come again if on a day that comes again and we consider every day to be a day that comes again it comes again then when accidentally when very accidentally every other day and every other day every other day and every other day that comes again and every day comes again when accidentally every other day comes again, every other day comes again and every other and every day comes again and accidentally and every day and it comes again, a day comes again and a day in that way comes again.

MARYAS: Accidentally in the morning and after that every evening and accidentally every evening and after that every morning and after that accidentally every morning and after that accidentally and after that every morning.

MARYAS: After that accidentally. Accidentally after that.

MARYAS: Accidentally after that. After that accidentally.

MARYAS AND MARTHA: More Maryas and more Martha.

MARYAS AND MARTHA: More Martha and more Maryas.

MARTHA AND MARYAS: More and more and more Martha and more Maryas.

MARIUS: It is spoken of in that way.

MABEL: It is spoken of in that way.

MARIUS AND MABEL: It is spoken in that way and it is spoken of in that way.

MARIUS AND MABEL: It is spoken of in that way.

MABEL: I speak of it in that way.

MARIUS: I have spoken of it in that way and I speak it in that way. I have spoken of it in that way.

MABEL: I speak of it in that way.

MABEL: Spelled in this way.

MARIUS: Spelled in that way.

MABEL: Spelled in this way and spelled in that way and spoken of in this way and spoken of in that way and spoken in this way.

MARTHA: In this way. If in a family where some member is devoutly religious another member of the family is ill, other members are not at home and other members have been killed in war, a ball is given for whose benefit is the ball given. For the benefit of the three young ladies who have not as yet left their home.

MARTHA AND MARYAS: It was unexpected but intended, it was intended and expected, it was intended.

MARYAS: It was intended and in a reasonable degree and not unreasonably she valued it as she was intended to value it as she was expected to value as she expected to value as she intended to value. She did intend to remain. Remember she did intend to remain. She did intend to remain.

MARTHA: Not too merrily for me. She had thirty three thirds. Safely. In this way she has a standard, she keeps to it and although she may be although she may be although she will be changed, she will change.

MARYAS: Not too long.

MARYAS AND MARTHA: Not too long.

MARYAS: To long and to long.

MARTHA: To long.

MARYAS: Able to long able to be and to be safely to be safely able to be safely to be safely to be seen to be seen able to long to be safely to safely be here and there to be there. Able to be there. To long. Who is longing now.

MARTHA: Change songs for safety, change their songs for their safety. Safely change their songs.

MARYAS: Change songs and change singing and change singing songs and change singing songs for singing songs.

MARTHA: Not how do you do.

MARYAS: Not yet.

MARYAS AND MARTHA: And not yet and not who are you and how are you not how are you.

MARTHA AND MARYAS: And not yet not how are you and where are you and how are you and not yet how and where are you and we are here.

MARYAS AND MARTHA: Where are you.

MARYAS AND MARTHA: How are you.

MARTHA AND MARYAS: How do you do and how are you.

MARIUS: As a change from this.

MARIUS: In a way to change in that way to change this.

MARIUS: In this way.

MARIUS: To change in this way.

MARIUS: And if they were in various ways differently decided, and if they were delighted, no not delighted, and if they were accidentally relieved and repeatedly received and reservedly deceived, if they were separately announced and deposed and respectfully recalled and regularly preceded, indeed they were there indeed they were there and in the way of it all and why did they ask what do they mean when they say that hay is no more fruitful than fruit and birds no more plentiful than battles. Battles are arranged here and there. Battles are arranged for here and there. Streets have been named so they have, a street might be named Battle Street.

MABEL: And if they were to be here and there and they are very often here, will I be pleased.

MARIUS AND MABEL: If they are very often here and there and they are very often here and they are very often here.

MABEL AND MARIUS: They are here very often.

MARTHA: Yes and know.

MARYAS: Yes.

MARTHA: Every day by the by every day has a connection between what happened when she kneeled and what she left when she came back to kneel.

MARYAS: Every day has a connection by the by every day has a connection between when she went and when she was separately sent.

MARTHA: Every day has a connection between six and seven in the morning and the disturbances of certainly causing and the disturbance of certainly calling and the disturbance of certainly returning and the disturbance of certainly telling that no address was given. That is a strange story of the address that was found and turned out to be given by her and it was her habit to give her address. Written down to be written down. We do not color her for that, this does not color her, this does not make lilacs white, they mostly are when they are made in winter.

MARYAS: Made in winter, when they are made in winter.

MARYAS AND MARTHA: This is not an instance of being polite and perfect.

MARYAS: Eighty and eighty pages.

MARTHA: Eight and eight pages.

MARTHA AND MARYAS: Eight pages and eighty pages.

MARTHA: An instance and for instance, for instance did she leave her key and for instance were we pleased to see that she came to be carefully pleased to be that she came to be carefully that she came to be careful.

MARYAS: Contents and intend. I intend to be careful of ashes Tuesdays kneeling and prizes. I intend to be careful of kneeling Tuesdays ashes and prizes.

MARTHA: We have allowed for it.

MARYAS: You do prepare it for me.

MARTHA AND MARYAS: We do we will and not forever.

MARIUS: How do you spell Marius.

MABEL: How do you spell Mabel.

MABEL AND MARIUS: We spell them both correctly.

LIST A

Maryas Martha Marius Mabel.

MARYAS MARTHA MARIUS MABEL: A list may be taken care of.

MARYAS MARTHA MARIUS MABEL: If a list is taken care of by five, if five are sitting at a table if four are seated at a table and one is leaning upon it it does not make any difference.

MARIUS MARTHA MARYAS MABEL: If five are seated at a table and one is leaning upon it it does not make any difference.

MARIUS MARTHA MARYAS: And if there are four seated at a table and one is leaning upon it it does not make any difference.

MARYAS: An instance of this is when we have all meant to be well dressed.

MARYAS: An instance of this is when we have all meant to be well dressed.

MARYAS: Dress well.

MARTHA: I know.

MARYAS AND MARTHA: We know how.

MARYAS MABEL MARTHA AND MARYAS: We know how now.

MARTHA AND MARYAS: A sector is a piece cut out, a fragment is a piece broken off and an article is all of one piece.

MARYAS: Stems and pleasantness.

MARYAS: I see I see how creditably and when they stand and she stands and there are stands.

MARTHA: And how creditably they prepare and she prepares and there are there as there are.

MARYAS: And how creditably if they care.

MARTHA: Very creditable as who can share their thanks for that. Yes that is it and we are not excited.

MARTHA AND MARYAS: If you can only tell him so.

MARTHA AND MARYAS: If they do and plenty of them would.

MARTHA: If we do.

MARYAS: Can you procure a place for a pillar.

MARTHA: And he thought of it and saw it.

MARTHA AND MARYAS: He thought of it and saw to it.

MARTHA: That which is lost becomes first comes first to be sent.

MARYAS: And might it be predicted by me.

MARTHA: Extravagantly very extravagantly.

MARTHA AND MARYAS: We translate this into that and Mary is so gracious and Mary.

MARTHA: A second list makes one day, a second list makes some day, a second list makes Monday, a second list makes Sunday, a second list makes more than one day a second list makes one day and makes one day.

MARYAS: We never kissed, we have never kissed.

MARTHA: A second list.

MARTHA AND MARYAS: A second list makes a second list.

MARIUS: If you do prepare to carry olives away from olive trees and rain away from rain and you are necessarily in that case pleased with me are you in earnest when you say that there are plenty of pleasures left.

MABEL: One hundred and one make a second list as naturally one hundred finishes one, probably the first one.

MARIUS AND MABEL: We could be married.

MARYAS: One authority.

MARTHA: No monotony is necessary since I do visit. You do visit, yes I do wisely to visit where my visits are appreciated.

MARYAS: Is wisdom perfect.

MARTHA: And festive.

MARIUS AND MABEL: A Sunday is marked as a Sunday.

MARYAS: In this way perfectly.

MARTHA: In this way not so carefully.

MARIUS AND MABEL: In this way they are allowed to retaliate.

THIRD LIST

MARYAS: Texas.

MARTHA: Mary.

MARYAS AND MARTHA. Texas berry.

MARYAS: To meet to meet me here.

MARTHA: To meet me here.

MARTHA AND MARYAS: To meet me here.

MARYAS: Examples of wool.
Samples of wool.
Samples of silk and wool. Sheep and wool.
Lions and wool.
Lions and sheep and wool. Lions and sheep and wool and silk. Silk and sheep and wool and silk. Silk and sheep, silk and wool, silk and sheep and silk and wool and silk. Sheep and silk and wool and silk and sheep.

MARTHA: If a feather meant a feather and if a feather meant a feather, we would gather together and it would not matter. What would not matter. My dear it would not matter.

MARTHA: In a minute.

MARIUS MARYAS MABEL: And a third.

MARY: A third of it.

A fourth.

A fourth of it.

A fourth.

A fourth of it.

MARTHA: In a minute and a third a third of it.

MARIUS: A third of it and in a minute a fourth of it.

MABEL: In a minute and a fourth of it in a minute and a fourth of it.

MARY: In a minute and a fourth of it, a third of it and in a minute and a third and a fourth of it.

MARYAS: We calm.

MARTHA: We can call silver silver.

MARIUS: We can mix silver with silver.

MABEL: We can mix more silver with silver.

MARY: We can mix more than silver with more than silver.

MARYAS MARTHA MARIUS MABEL AND MARY: If there are four seated at a table and one of them is leaning upon it it does not make any difference.

FOURTH LIST

MARTHA: If I am displeased.

MARTHA: One may say that one may say that a brother tardily marries.

MARYAS: In this way.

MARYAS AND MARTHA: Make it selected.

MARYAS: We are not confused by separation.

MARTHA AND MARIUS: If you confuse if you are separated by confusion, if you exchange standing for standing, I often think about exchanging standing for standing.

MARTHA: Anybody can anybody settle it for me.

MARTHA: We have met, to be safely arrived. To exchange kneeling for kneeling.

MARTHA AND MARYAS: And thoughtful.

MARTHA: In no great merriment.

MARTHA AND MARYAS: I have exactly they have exactly they have called them all in.

MARTHA: Equally so.

MARYAS: It is very well to know this.

MARTHA: I have no longer any actual reason for this as well.

MARYAS: Very evenly.

MARTHA AND MARYAS: Can we say we do not.

MARTHA AND MARYAS: Fourteen and more are inconsistent.

MARTHA: Fourteen and more and they are one may believe, they are one may believe liable to abuse.

MARTHA: Indeed for them and differently preserved pears.

MARTHA AND MARYAS: Indeed for them.

MARTHA AND MARYAS: In a minute or very nervously or very nervously or in a minute.

MARTHA: Next to their end.

MARTHA AND MARYAS: They left it a half an hour later.

MARTHA AND MARYAS: Return it to me.

MARTHA AND MARYAS: Two at half past one. Three at half past two.

MARTHA AND MARYAS: Three at half past three.

MARTHA: I present well.

MARYAS: I represent well.

MARTHA AND MARYAS: We are pleased to be represented by them for them.

MARTHA: What was it that was said.

MARYAS: No secrets.

MARTHA AND MARYAS: No secrets and no secrecy.

MARTHA MARIUS MARYAS AND MABEL: To see and to see.

MARTHA MARIUS MARYAS MABEL AND MARY: To see and to see and to see.

MARTHA: We are not to see.

MARYAS: I am to see where I am to go and what I am to do.

MARTHA: You do and I do.

MARYAS: You do too.

MARTHA AND MARYAS: They do believe that no secrets and not secretly will make investigation easy.

LIST FIVE

MARTHA: This is the way a play fades away.

MARTHA: You praise me as you say.

MARYAS: Ordinarily in this way.

MARTHA AND MARYAS: Ordinarily you praise me as you say you say you praise me.

MARTHA: And a measure. To measure exactly how often six and one, how very often six and one how often is there to be reasonable certainty. How often are they reasonably certain. Six and one and not another more than one.

MARYAS: I smile for certainty.

MARTHA: Martin too was certain to be known.

MARYAS MABEL AND MARTIN: How are you known you are known by your name and your share. Share and share alike.

MABEL MARTHA AND MARYAS: Rain mingles with water and a tree can be sweet and can you mingle water with rain and suck at a tree.

MARTHA: Mentions the place.

MARYAS: Yields abundant resemblance.

MABEL: Needs only adequate calls.

MARIUS: Needs only division of birth.

MARTIN: Only needs mentioning here.

MARY. Only needs mentioning here.

MARTHA AND MARYAS: If they ask me to leave them and they ask them to leave me if they ask me to leave them and they ask them to leave if they ask them to leave and they ask me if they ask me and if they ask them, if they ask them and if they ask them, and if they ask them and if they ask me if they ask I say yes that is it.

MARYAS: They said he said, he said, two centers, two centers, two surroundings, two surroundings, two centers, and two centers, and they centre, and their center, they centre, they do not centre here.

MABEL: Mabel little Mabel with her face against the pane and it may as can say wistfulness may no wistfulness may, they come again today and tomorrow they go to America.

MARTIN: Exactly Martin, and may useful and preliminary off-shoots.

MARIUS: Recognize it by the name in the way of deliberation and baskets. A great many baskets are made here and there and with some care, that is to say one may give an order to them and indeed they may fulfil. They may even learn to weave and braid officially and not fancifully and in this way they have many certainties and many mountains and a cow, I doubt if they will have a cow. I say they advisedly and speaking entirely in a different sense. You do understand me.

MARY: Mary may no I may say may Mary. So that season is anonymous and indeed easily as they own land in town and country.

A LAST LIST

MARIUS: Choose to choose you cannot expect me to choose you.

MARTHA: Carrots and artichokes marguerites and roses. If you can repeat it and somebody chose it, somebody shows it, somebody knows it. If you can repeat and somebody knows it.

MARYAS: Half of the marriages, valentines and half of the marriages. I did the valentines and half of the marriages.

MABEL: A little girl is very nearly the same size as she was she was very nearly the same prize and we may say excited.

MAY: And Mary.

MARTHA MABEL MARYAS AND MARY: We may marry.

20

SAY IT WITH FLOWERS

A Play

George Henry, Henry Henry and Elisabeth Henry.
Subsidiary characters.
Elizabeth and William Long.

Time Louis XI.

Place Gisors.
Action in a cake shop and the sea shore.
Other interests.

The welcoming of a man and his dog and the wish that they would come back sooner.

George Henry and Elizabeth Henry and Henry Henry ruminating.
Elizabeth and William Long.

Waiting.

Who has asked them to be amiable to me.

She said she was waiting.

George Henry and Elizabeth Henry and Henry Henry.

Who might be asleep if they were not waiting for me.

She.

Elizabeth Henry and Henry Henry and George Henry.

She might be waiting with me.

Henry Henry absolutely ready to be here with me.

Scenery.

The home where they were waiting for William Long to ask them to come along and ask them not to be waiting for them.

Will they be asleep while they are waiting.

They will be pleased with everything.

What is everything.

A hyacinth is everything.

Will they be sleeping while they are waiting for everything.

William Long and Elizabeth Long were so silent you might have heard an egg shell breaking. They were busy all day long with everything.

Elizabeth and William Long were very busy waiting for him to come and bring his dog alone.

Why did they not go with him.

Because they were busy waiting.

ACT I

Formerly they were married women.

They were having dinner as married women.

The cake shop in Gisors.

They did not open the door before.

Elizabeth Ernest and William Long.

Who makes threads pay.

Butter is used as much as hay.

So they will shoulder it in every way

To ask did they expect to come in the month of May.

Ernest and William Long and Elizabeth Long were not happy.

They will meet them and recover with them the afternoon which they were losing.

Elizabeth Long and Ernest Long.

They happen to like it themselves.

William Long.

I go to see if it is best left alone and after a little while they will like it it will not bother them they will not be careful to do it they will think as well as they can about it which is after all what they wish.

Ernest Long and Elizabeth Long are nervous when they hear about Louis the eleventh. They knew that they live in Gisors. They knew that they will not come home any more they know that William Long has gone to the sea shore.

Henry Henry and Elizabeth Henry come in and wish every one a merry Christmas they sing for money.

Who has been invited not to sell but to give away violets with a complaint.

George Henry walks away and in the distance he sees William Long. They need no one to like it noisily.

William Long.

They will be able to have it a hope that it will not rain.

George Henry. Rain is not happily what is to cloud our relation we are thoughtful we prepare to be often more than they disturb and finally it is no way more than their arrangement everybody can wait the arrival of a man and a dog.

Or whether they are serviceable.

William Long follows George Henry and they are thought to be very quiet.

George Henry.

If he heard if I heard mainly for that that if I heard often of it.

William Long.

They may be laying it where they will it is by the time that they are there for as often.

George Henry.

A noise is a pleasure if they come and go.

William Long.

It is never selfish of me to think easily.

Back to Gisors in the cake shop there is Elizabeth Henry and Henry Henry they are seated and the door can be open.

It is very likely that they make it matter. To them. That they are likely to go away. Farther. Than they went before. Because they like it as we have very well heard. Which they mean by what they say.

Elizabeth Long comes in and leaves them to think very well of it.

Elizabeth and Henry Henry.

Every one knows that Louis the eleventh is ill.

Elizabeth Long.

May be they do but I doubt it.

Henry Henry.

No advice is better than this come home easily and bring a hyacinth to your wife and make her happy by giving her this gift and she will be pleased with you and will say so and you will be pleased with her and equally will say so.

ACT II

The sea shore where they are near Gisors.

George Henry and William Long come in and see a ship in the distance they sing in unison.

I will be believed.

They make no mistake in their attachment.

George Henry and William Long save themselves for their pleasure. They may be thought to be welcome.

Elizabeth Long and Elizabeth Henry come to the seashore and gather roses. They say they will share their mother. All four of them look longingly and they see the ship and they know it is Louis the eleventh and they are slightly aware of the distances.

George Henry and Elizabeth Long.

Think they are waiting for the approach of their hope that they will be welcome welcomed by a dog and the hope that they will be very welcome when they come. They will be very welcome when they come. They do delight in being very welcome.

George Henry William Long and Christian William have many instances that they mention.

Will William come and will he be welcome.

Will he come and will Louis the Eleventh be willing to have been welcome when he has come.

Will Christian William be welcome.

Will Elizabeth Long be thought to be welcome. Will Elizabeth Henry come. Will George Henry be welcome.

They all stand and cover the happiness they feel as best they can.

It is a preparation for their hearing the preparation.

They all go away.

William Long and Elizabeth Long are waiting they have been discussing waiting.

Will we wait any longer for Henry Henry and Christian William. Will we wait for Elizabeth Henry. Will we wait for George Henry and Christian William. Will we wait for Henry Henry and Christian Henry and Elizabeth Henry and Christian William.

They wait patiently and they see Louis the Eleventh announced as coming and they go away disturbed and laughing.

Who has mentioned Christian William.

SCENE II

Gisors and the baker's shop.

William Long and Elizabeth Long and Elizabeth Henry are sitting and they say they are waiting for Christian William and Henry Henry to come with him.

Who is pleased to see something. This is what they are saying.

George Henry and Christian William and Henry Henry come in they all like one another they are pleased that they are all helped by everything. Who can be seen as they are all leaving.

Elizabeth Long and William Long have been waiting.

She likes it.

ACT III

Ernest Long at Gisors.

Narrowly arrayed.
They have adjusted felt to names
They will be at last
With them.
Who does better it.
It is called careless
To think more than they are willing
Close at hand.

Ernest Long waits and Henry and George Henry come and ask him to wait.

They will be often present particularly if they think well of them.

All three of them are waiting and they they go away.

Who is called by the time they come they are called and they will wait for it themselves.

Elizabeth Long and William Long are seen covering the cakes with tissue paper they have to have the door closed at last.

Who may be always known as coming here.

They will be often able to save that.
They will think that Elizabeth is a name and also William.
They will wait while they are careful
They will hope that he is not nervous
They will delight in Louis the Eleventh so they say.
He has been heard to wait three times.
They will be careful to hear them preach
They need to be.

    William Long and Elizabeth Long add to it.
    George Henry and Elizabeth Henry are frequently seen together.
        George Henry and William Long.
Who likes to be near here.

SCENE II

The sea shore
They all sit down as is natural.
They may wait for the dog to swim.
They may also go away.

SCENE II

    William Long and Elizabeth Long have asked will they differ as to the matter of saying how do you do.
Be able to be careful.
They think very well of these things.

    George Henry is relieved that is to say he is waiting for a decision.
    Louis the Eleventh is expected at Gisors.
They will not allow them to interfere.
They will not allow them to interfere.

    William Long and Elizabeth Long may well not be a disappointment.
To them.
With them
In them.
They may then.
Will they hope to have her finish it.
Keep away from that door

SCENE III

Why is milk good.

    Louis the Eleventh has come to Gisors.

They will ask him to be ready to marry.

SCENE IV

George Henry and William Long.

It is better.

To be most

Most and best

Finally

As it does happen

To matter enough to be that.

They will hope to eat slowly.

Always on account.

If they go

They will seem

To be mine.

In a way

All of it

Very well.

   Elizabeth Henry and Elizabeth Long see each other.

Do not be very often thought to be held as they were equal to having it be felt.

A hyacinth is not awkward even in two.

All four meet and do not speak of whether they were there.

They will long to say more than they believe as if they were selfish.

     Who made them leave me.

   They all go away without Henry Henry and Ernest Long.

Better be with them.

It is better to be with them

And come with them

Because they will need to go there

As they have been waiting for it.

And it is not only that they will but they can be hurt by asking if they were waiting.

They will not come anxiously.

SCENE V

In pleasures they receive
Who has heard them believe

William Long and Elizabeth Henry think of these things.
George Henry and Elizabeth Long.

Follow fairly
They do better than without it
They think it of themselves
They will not be selfish
William Long and Elizabeth Henry and Henry Henry think well of
it very carefully
Who has been heard to give them names for themselves.
They will be very much more than they were with them.
It is most of all a carriage.
Louis the Eleventh is exactly welcome.
Elizabeth Long and Ernest Long come alone to say how do you do
singly.
They might be mistaken.
George Henry and Elizabeth Henry are not made for them.
They will welcome women and then men.
Louis the Eleventh is not patiently waiting.
At Gisors Louis the Eleventh is to make his entry.
Ernest Long and Genevieve Taylor are married.
They have meant to be gracious.

ACT IV

The Scene at Gisors.

Four men come in and two women.

They are not waiting to hear them say when they are coming they
will not presently go away they will be anxious to think this of them.
George Henry and Ernest Long are waiting. They will be think-
ing presently of leaving.
Genevieve Taylor and Elizabeth Long know that they are leaving.
This is made pleasantly.

As if they were having
That they were without.
In its having been
Not carried further.

SCENE II

Sixty-five is not seventy then.
They make it different then
When they come to wish them
To think of them
  Henry Henry and Elizabeth and William Long add to it.
They may be careful
Themselves and like to be
Mentioned separately.
  Elizabeth Long thinks that she will accompany William Long and
Henry Henry.
  Elizabeth Henry comes with George Henry and they have to
have rested.
They were not standing.
                    Henry Henry.
Think well after carefully.
                    George Henry.
Be very well told affectionately.
                    Elizabeth Long.
They may be careful of treasure.
                    Elizabeth Henry.
They may not be long.
                    Ernest Long.
Away. They have meant more than they come to attach pleasures
in amount.
Who is curious as to why they attended.

        Louix XI has hopes for France.

SCENE III

There is no silence in their attention.
To please them.
They will be careful

To please them.
They will ask them
If it pleases them
That they like to know of it
As it is in a measure
A means of doing good.

Elizabeth Long and William Long stay away while Elizabeth Henry and George Henry put everything where they will be pleased to find that they may place it.

There is an opening of a door and most of the time they are very satisfied.

George Henry and Henry Henry have liked Louis the Eleventh.

ACT V

Elizabeth Long asks them not to be made to have them ask them. She is obliged to them for having meant them.
They will be thought to think that they will give them what they would like to have in having had more than they had of them.

Genevieve Henry asks any one what they can do to think well of asking it of them.

George Henry.

Might they not be asked to have been having more than they had with them and so they will ask them to see them with them some of them as they have all of them with all of them as they will give it for them.
They will have if made by them.
They will without be asking it for them.

Elizabeth Henry thinking as she is walking.
They will then be having it for them.

George Henry adding something for nothing.
Thank you very much for asking for everything.

SCENE II

Elizabeth Henry having been left to the encouragement of George Henry who said they are following they may be left to have it been heard or borne.

Elizabeth Long hears Elizabeth Henry repeating that she will be told that they were hearing it themselves.

George Henry and Elizabeth Long made it a part of their arrangement that they would wait for Monday.

The sea shore and they wished to remember that it had had a name as well as afterwards.

Who came to be left to have it helped as they were preparing to accustom them to their arrangement.

SCENE III

Does dust make feathers they do and does give pleasure.

Leave Genevieve Long to never have pleasure in giving and gaining theirs as mine.

A mine makes a sea shore have a wealth of knowledge of better which they may be in aground.

Elizabeth Long and William Long.

They ought to be noisily in along.

Elizabeth and George Henry make it a return of a present of a melon. Which they have received. As well as chinese nuts. Which they have not. Undertaken to divide.

The tragedy of Louis the Eleventh and Louis the twelfth is that they will have the habit of hurrying.

SCENE IV

They will please or they will not.

Which is why they are to originally distinguish between partly and why they have it.

The time that they were able to please is what reminded them of it at first.

Elizabeth Long and Elizabeth Henry come and see that they are without the habit of a purse in the middle. They will be advantageous mutually.

They think of it together.

William Long and Ernest Long and George Henry satisfy themselves as to their wonder.

Ernest Long saying that he has been without wishes.

William Long fairly well as puzzled.

Ernest Long.

They seize aloud in place of which they must they will be had around more than they caught. They will be joined in hurts and places which makes it for them whether they are felt to know now. In placing theirs around.

George Henry and Genevieve come in and please themselves.

Louis the eleventh is a king.

And he looks at anything.

They will think that they have explained this thing.

SCENE

The inside of the cake shop.

Elizabeth Long and William Long are waiting and they are ready to sell to those who come in and wish to buy something.

All come in and give them what they are asking for everything that they are selling.

Elizabeth Henry and Ernest Long have made no difference in paying.

George Henry and Henry Henry have not hesitated about paying.

Scene on the sea shore.

Elizabeth Long and Ernest Long and Henry Henry and George Henry come along. They like to leave them as they were too exciting. Who makes it do for them.

They will be having wealth of bettering which they may with enjoyment.

They all wait and as they wait they must be thought to like to have him be more to them than they were as they were coming.

Louis the eleventh might be reminded that everything is with them.

A scene in the place where they were standing.

How often do they mean to add more to add more to have theirs leave them with that.

William Long.

He was deceived.

He liked him because he was added before.

Before what.

Before they came.

And will willows have their leaves as they do.

They will have their leaves as they do.

They make for them.

They make it for them.

They will have theirs have their insistence that they will prepare theirs with them, which in allowance where theirs in theirs as in which they have in there not in with by the time with in their had with in their resting within the allowance.

She made changes in churches.

He made more than they combine with in a change.

They must be thought for them. They will be welcomed with them.

It is in spite of quiet.

That they engage them.

In fortunate allowance.

For them.

They meant that they are taking the same as they mean as interruption.

Thank them in eddying.

SCENE

Louis the Eleventh had been thought to be pleasant as a witness. They will arrange more as they follow.

SCENE

The sea shore.
William Long.

In welcome and they might.

Might remains as must they leave us.

They will go.

They will prepare whether.

It is falsely an alliance.

They manage to be used to it.

They kindle all of it.

For them shortly.

It is in amusement.

They may be prepared easily.

It is in their manner that they think.

They think that they thought them.

Very gracious.

To be not at all bothered.

In coming together.

To allow further
That they will
Have more of it.
Which is usual.
In the partly shown.
They will quit in hand.
By them By this.
They meant to be at once
Nicely.
Without them.
Could they do it.
Strangely
Not at all thank you.

FINIS

Poetry

Before the Flowers of Friendship Faded Friendship Faded. This was written about 1930 and published by Alice Toklas in the Plain Edition, Paris, 1931. Gertrude Stein often referred to the poem, because she herself learned something from doing it (see *Henry James* page 291 and also the lecture 'Poetry and Grammar') and also because it caused a break in her friendship with the French poet Georges Hugnet, facts which are borne out in the following extracts:

'Georges Hugnet wrote a poem called *Enfance*. Gertrude Stein offered to translate it for him but instead she wrote a poem about it. This at first pleased Georges Hugnet too much and then did not please him at all. Gertrude Stein then called the poem *Before the Flowers of Friendship Faded Friendship Faded.* Everybody mixed themselves up in all of this. The group broke up. Gertrude Stein was very upset and then consoled herself by telling all about it in a delightful short story called 'From Left To Right' and which was printed in the London *Harper's Bazaar*.'[1]

'I had a funny experience once, this was a long time after I had been writing anything and everything as you all more or less have come to know it, it was about five years ago and I said I would translate the poems of a young french poet.

'I did this not because of the poetry but because of the poet he had been very nice to me and I was grateful for it and so I wanted to make him happy and the way to show it was to translate the poetry of the young french poet.

'So I began to translate and before I knew it a very strange thing had happened.

'Hitherto I had always been writing, with a concentration of recognition of *292* the thing that was to be existing as my writing as it was being written. And now, the recognition was prepared beforehand there it was it was already recognition a thing I could recognize because it had been recognized before I began my writing, and a very queer thing was happening.

'The words as they came out had a different relation than any words I had hitherto been writing, as they came out they had a certain smoothness they went one into the other in a different kind of a fashion than any words ever had done before any words that I had ever written and I was perplexed at what was happening and I finished the whole thing not translating but carrying out an idea which was already existing and then suddenly I realized something I realized that words come out differently if there is no recognition as the words are forming because recognition had already taken place.'[2]

1. *Harper's Bazaar*, London, September 1931. From *The Autobiography of Alice B. Toklas* by Gertrude Stein, first published Harcourt, Brace, New York, 1933, Penguin 1967.

2. After lecturing at the University of Chicago in November 1934, Gertrude Stein was invited to return the following March. At that time she gave four lectures which she called *Narration* and which were published by the University of Chicago Press, Chicago, December 1935. The quotation is from the fourth lecture, p. 51.

BEFORE THE FLOWERS OF FRIENDSHIP
FADED FRIENDSHIP FADED

Written on a poem by Georges Hugnet

In the one hundred small places of myself my youth,
And myself in if it is the use of passion,
In this in it and in the nights alone
If in the next to night which is indeed not well
I follow you without it having slept and went.
Without the pressure of a place with which to come unfolded folds
    are a pressure and an abusive stain
A head if uncovered can be as hot, as heated,
to please to take a distance to make life,
And if resisting, little, they have no thought,
a little one which was a little which was as all as still,
Or with or without fear or with it all,
And if in feeling all it will be placed alone beside
And it is with with which and not beside not beside may,
Outside with much which is without with me, and not an Indian
    shawl, which could it be but with my blood.

II

A little a little one all wooly or in wool
As if within or not in any week or as for weeks
A little one which makes a street no name
without it having come and went farewell
And not with laughing playing
Where they went they would or work
it is not that they look alike with which in up and down as chickens
    without dogs,

Coming to have no liking for a thief which is not left to have away,
To live like when
And very many things
Being with me with them with which with me whoever with and
    born and went as well
Meant,
Five which are seen
And with it five more lent,
As much as not mixed up,
With love

III

I often live with many months with years of which I think
And they as naturally think well of those
My littlest shoes which were not very much without that care left
    there
where I would like the heat
and very nearly find that trees have many little places that make
    shade
Which never went away when there was sun
In a way there were cries and it was felt to be the cruelest yet
I am very happy in my play
and I am very thirsty in hunger
Which is not what is always there with love
And after all when was I born.
I can touch wood and think
I can also see girls who were in finding
and they will laugh and say
And yes say so as yes as yes with woe
And now they with me think and love love that they hold with hide
    and even
It is as if all fields would grow what do they grow, tobacco even
    so,
And they will not delight in having had,
Because after no fear and not afraid,
they have been having that they join as well,
And always it is pretty to see dogs.

It is no double to have more with when they met and in began who
  can.
There is very little to hide,
When there is everything beside
And there is a well inside
In hands untied.

IV

I follow as I can and this to do
With never vaguely that they went away
I have been left to bargain with myself
And I have come not to be pleased to see
They wish to watch the little bird
Who flew at which they look
They never mentioned me to it,
I stopped to listen well it is a pleasure to see a fire which does not
  inspire them to see me
I wish to look at dogs
Because they will be having with they wish
To have it look alike as when it does.

V

Everything is best of all for you which is for me,
I like a half of which it is as much
Which never in alone is more than most
Because I easily can be repaid in difficulty of the hurry left
Between now not at all and after which began
It could be morning which it was at night
And little things do feed a little more than all
What was it that was meant by things as said
There is a difference between yet and well
And very well and when there was as much which is as well as more
And it is very likely made away again
Very nearly as much as not before
Which is as better than to have it now
Which it is taken to make my blood thin.

VI

It is very likely counting it as well
Named not alas but they must lend it for
In welcome doubt which they need for deceit
They face a little more than most and made it.
They will be born in better than at least with not at all relieved and
    left away a little said
Which is not with made not unless.
Unless is used with where liked what.

VII

A very long a little way
They have to have
In which array
They make it wring
Their tendering them this.
It is whatever originally read read can be two words smoke can be
    all three
And very much there were.
It is larger than around to think them a little amiably
What is it said to incline learnt and places it as place
As which were more than the two made it do.
Remember not a color
Every little boy has his own desk.

VIII

Who leaves it to be left to like it less
which is to leave alone what they have left
They made it act as if to shout
Is when they make it come away and sit.
Nobody need say no nor yes.
They who had known or which was pressed as press
They might with thought come yet to think without
With which it is to like it with its shell,
A shell has hold of what is not with held

It is just as well not to be well as well
Nevertheless
As when it is in short and long and pleasure
It is a little thing to ask to wait
It is in any kind of many chances
They like it best with all its under weight
And will they miss it when they meet its frame,
A frame is such that hours are made by sitting
Rest it in little pieces
They like it to be held to have and hold
Believe me it is not for pleasure that I do it.

IX

Look at me now and here I am
And with it all it is not preparation,
They make it never breathless without breath
And sometimes in a little while they wait.
Without its leaving.
It is mine to sit and carefully to be thought thorough
Let it be that it is said let me alone,
You alone have a way to think and swim,
Leave it as well
And noises have no other.
It is in their refrain that they sing me
It just can happen so

X

Did he hear it when it was as said
And did he sing it when he sang a song
And did he like it when it was not said
And did he make it when he went along
There is a little doubt without which meant
That he did go that he went that he was not sent,
Who could send whom
Which went which way where
It is alike that they say that this is so

In any little while more may be most
Most may be most and best may be most best
It is at once a very little while
that they eat more when many are more there
Like it alike
Every little while they twitch and snore
It is a hope of eating all alike
That makes them grow
And so say so.

XI

Here once in a while she says he says
When it is well it is not more than ill
He says we say she says
When it is very well it is not more than still it is not more than ill
And all he says it is and all and very well and very much that was of
    very ill.
And anyway who was as strong as very strong with all and come
    along,
It is a height which makes it best to come to be a matter that they had
Alike in not no end of very well and in divide with better than the
    most,
And very well who knows of very well and best and most and not as
    well as ill.
It could be made as curly as they lie which when they think with
    me.
Who is with me that is not why they went to be just now.
Just now can be well said.
In imitation there is no more sign than if I had not been without
    my filling it with absence made in choosing extra bright.
I do mind him, I do mind them I do mind her,
Which was the same as made it best for me for her for them.
Any leaf is more annoying than a tree when this you see see me she
    said of me of three of two of me.
And then I went to think of me of which of one of two of one of
    three of which of me I went to be away of three of two of one
    of me.

Any pleasure leads to me and I lead them away away from pleasure
and from me.

XII

I am very hungry when I drink
I need to leave it when I have it held,
   They will be white with which they know they see, that darker
makes it be a color white for me, white is not shown when I am dark
indeed with red despair who comes who has to care that they will
let me a little lie like now I like to lie I like to live I like to die I like
to lie and live and die and live and die and by and by I like to live
and die and by and by they need to sew, the difference is that
sewing makes it bleed and such with them in all the way of seed and
seeding and repine and they will which is mine and not all mine
who can be thought curious of this of all of that made it and come
lead it and done weigh it and mourn and sit upon it know it for
ripeness without deserting all of it of which without which it has
not been born. Oh no not to be thirsty with the thirst of hunger not
alone to know that they plainly and ate or wishes. Any little one
will kill himself for milk.

XIII

Known or not known to follow or not follow or not lead.
It is all oak when known as not a tree,
It is all best of all as well as always gone when always sent
In all a lent for all when grass is dried and grass can dry when all
   have gone away and come back then to stay.
Who might it be that they can see that candied is a brush that
   bothers me.
Any way come any way go any way stay any way show any way
   show me.
They ask are peas in one beets in another one beans in another one,
They follow yes beets are in one peas are in one beans are in one.
They hear without a letter which they love, they love above they
   sit and when they sit they stare.
So when a little one has more and any one has more and who has

more who has more when there can be heard enough and not
enough of where.
Who has more where.

XIV

It could be seen very nicely
That doves have each a heart,
Each one is always seeing that they could not be apart,
A little lake makes fountains
And fountains have no flow,
And a dove has need of flying
And water can be low,
Let me go.
Any week is what they seek
When they have to halve a beak.
I like a painting on a wall of doves
And what do they do,
They have hearts
They are apart
Little doves are winsome
But not when they are little and left.

XV

It is always just as well
That there is a better bell
Than that with which a half is a whole
Than that with which a south is a pole
Than that with which they went away to stay
Than that with which after any way,
Needed to be gay to-day.

XVI

Any little while is longer any little while is shorter any little while
is better any little while for me when this you see then think of me.

It is very sad that it is very bad that badly and sadly and mourn

and shorn and torn and thorn and best and most and at least and
all and better than to call if you call you sleep and if you sleep you
must and if you must you shall and if you shall when then when is it
then that Angelina she can see it make it be that it is all that it can
have it color color white white is for black what green which is a
hope is for a yellow which can be very sweet and it is likely that a
long tender not as much as most need names to make a cake or dance
or loss or next or sweetening without sugar in a cell or most unlikely
with it privately who makes it be called practice that they came.
They come thank you they come. Any little grass is famous to be
grass grass green and red blue and all out but you.

XVII

He is the exact age he tells you
He is not twenty two, he is twenty three and when this you see
    remember me,
And yet what is it that he can see,
He can see veritably three, all three which is to be certainly
And then.
    He tells of oceans which are there and little lakes as well he sings
it lightly with his voice and thinks he had to shout and not at all
with oceans near and not at all at all, he thinks he is he will he does
he knows he was he knows he was he will he has he is he does and
now and when is it to be to settle without sillily to be without without with doubt let me. So he says. It is easy to put heads together
really. Head to head it is easily done and easily said head to head
in bed.

XVIII

When I sleep I sleep and do not dream because it is as well that I
    am what I seem when I am in my bed and dream.

XIX

It was with him that he was little tall and old and just as young
as when begun by seeming soldiers young and hold and with a little

change in place who hopes that women are a race will they be thin will they like fat does milk does hope does age does that no one can think when all have thought that they will think but have not bought no without oceans who hears wheat do they like fish think well of meat it is without without a change that they like this they have it here it is with much that left by him he is within within within actually how many hear actually what age is here actually they are with hope actually they might be bespoke believe me it is not for pleasure that I do it. They often have too much rain as well as too much sun.

They will not be won.

One might be one.

Might one be one.

XX

A little house is always held
By a little ball which is always held,
By a little hay which is always held
By a little house which is always held,
A house and a tree a little house and a large tree,
And a little house not for them and a large tree.
And after all fifteen are older than one two three.

It is useful that no one is barred from looking out of a house to see a tree even when there is a tree to see. She made it mentioned when she was not there and so was he.

XXI

He likes that felt is made of beaver and cotton made of trees and feathers made of birds and red as well. He likes it.

XXII

He likes to be with her so he says does he like to be with her so he says.

XXIII

Every one which is why they will they will be will he will he be for her for her to come with him with when he went he went and came and any little name is shame as such tattoo. Any little ball is made a net and any little net is made for mine and any little mine that any have will always violate the hope of this which they wore as they lose. It is a welcome, nobody knows a circumstance is with whatever water wishes now. It is pleasant that without a hose no water is drawn. No water is drawn pleasantly without a hose. Doublet and hose not at all water and hose not at all any not at all. Not at all. Either not at all by not at all with me. When this you do not hear and do not see believe me.

XXIV

They were easily left alone they were as easily left alone they were as easily left alone with them. Which makes mistakes mistakes which are mistakes who mistakes mistakes let them see the seal what is the difference between seal and school what is the difference between school and singing school and seeing school and leaving school and sitting in a school. They know the difference when they see the screen which is why leaves are dry when rain is thin and appetising which can be when they win. They win a little exercise in win. Win and win. Perhaps with happens to be thin. It is not easy to be led by them. Not easy to be led and led and led to no brim. In doubt not with them. Not in doubt not with them. Leave it to me to know three from three and they did leave it to him.

XXV

It is easy to mingle sails with steam oil with coal water with air, it is easy to mingle everywhere and to leave single everywhere water and air oil and coal butter and a share it is a share to ask them where and in a little they will have it there they like it there they had it to prepare and to be a comfort to them without care. It is a need to see without a glare of having it come in does it come in and where. They like a little dog to be afraid to have a nightingale be told a chicken is afraid and it is true he is she is and where whenever there is a hawk up in the air. Like that. It makes anybody think of sail-boats.

XXVI

Little by little two go if two go three go if three go four go if four go they go. It is known as does he go he goes if they go they go and they know they know best and most of whether he will go. He is to go. They will not have vanilla and say so. To go Jenny go, Ivy go Gaby go any come and go is go and come and go and leave to go. Who has to hold it while they go who has to who has had it held and have them come to go. He went and came and had to go. No one has had to say he had to go come here to go go there to go go go to come to come to go to go and come and go.

XXVII

In a little while they smile in a little while and one two three they smile they smile a while in a little while a little smile with which to smile a while and when they like to be as once in a while it is about the time with which in which to smile. He can smile and any smile is when as when to smile. It is to show that now that he can know and if to smile it is to smile and smile that he can know and any making it be ready there for them to see to change a smile to change a smile into a stare and very likely more than if they care he can care does and will and not to have to care and this is made with and without a need to carry horses horses without sails sails have an ocean sometimes just the land but to believe to have relief in them who can share horses sails and little less a very little less and they like them. It does it hope. They come they see they sew and always with it a hope is for more not more than yesterday but more today more today more to say more today. A little long and birds can drink with beaks and chickens do and horses drink and sails and even all.

XXVIII

A clock in the eye ticks in the eye a clock ticks in the eye.
A number with that and large as a hat which makes rims think
    quicker than I.
A clock in the eye ticks in the eye a clock ticks ticks in the eye.

XXIX

I love my love with a v
Because it is like that
I love myself with a b
Because I am beside that
A king.
I love my love with an a
Because she is a queen
I love my love and a a is the best of then
Think well and be a king,
Think more and think again
I love my love with a dress and a hat
I love my love and not with this or with that
I love my love with a y because she is my bride
I love her with a d because she is my love beside
Thank you for being there
Nobody has to care
Thank you for being here
Because you are not there.

   And with and without me which is and without she she can be
late and then and how and all around we think and found that it is
time to cry she and I.

XXX

There are a few here now and the rest can follow a cow,
The rest can follow now there are a few here now,
They are all all here now the rest can follow a cow
And mushrooms on a hill and anything else until
They can see and sink and swim with now and then a brim,

A brim to a hat
What is that,
Anyway in the house they say
Anyway every day
Anyway outside as they may
Think and swim with hearing him,
Love and sing not any song a song is always then too long to just sit
  there and sing
Sing song is a song
When sing and sung
Is just the same as now among
Among them,
They are very well placed to be seated and sought
They are very well placed to be cheated and bought
And a bouquet makes a woods
A hat makes a man
And any little more is better than
The one.
And so a boat a goat and wood
And so a loaf which is not said to be just bread
Who can be made to think and die
And any one can come and cry and sing.
Which made butter look yellow
And a hope be relieved
By all of it in case
Of my name.
What is my name.
That is the game
Georges Hugnet
By Gertrude Stein.

Later Works

This 'portrait' is from *Four In America*. The book was written between 1932 and 1933 and it begins in the following way:

'If Ulysses S. Grant had been a religious leader who was to become a saint what would he have done.

'If the Wright brothers had been artists that is painters what would they have done.

'If Henry James had been a general what would he have had to do.

'If General Washington had been a writer that is a novelist what would he do.'

Henry James is the third 'portrait' in the book and in this piece Gertrude 273 Stein reveals what she has learned in the writing of *Before the Flowers of Friendship Faded Friendship Faded*.

Four In America was published by the Yale University Press, New Haven, 1947.

22

HENRY JAMES

WHAT is the difference between Shakespeare's plays and Shakespeare's sonnets.

I have found out the difference between Shakespeare's plays and Shakespeare's sonnets. One might say I have found out the difference by accident, or one might say I have found out the difference by coincidence.

What is the difference between accident and coincidence.

An accident is when a thing happens. A coincidence is when a thing is going to happen and does.

DUET

And so it is not an accident but a coincidence that there is a difference between Shakespeare's sonnets and Shakespeare's plays. The coincidence is with *Before the Flowers of Friendship Faded Friendship Faded*.

Who knew that the answer was going to be like that. Had I told that the answer was going to be like that.

The answer is not like that. The answer is that.

I am I not any longer when I see.

This sentence is at the bottom of all creative activity. It is just the exact opposite of I am I because my little dog knows me.

Of course I have always known Shakespeare's plays. In a way I have always known Shakespeare's sonnets. They have not been the same. Their not being the same is not due to their being different in their form or in their substance. It is due to something else. That something else I now know all about. I know it now but how did I come to know it.

These things never bothered me because I knew them, anybody who knows how to read and write knows them.

It is funny about reading and writing. The word funny is here used in the double sense of amusing and peculiar.

Some people of course read and write. One may say everybody reads and writes and it is very important that everybody should.

Now think everybody think with me, how does reading and writing agree, that is with you. With almost everybody it agrees either pretty well or very well.

Now let me tell a little story. Once upon a time there were a great many people living and they all knew how to read and write. They learnt this in school, they also learnt it when anybody taught it. This made them not at all anxious to learn more. But yet they were as ready to learn more as they ever had been.

There were some who knew that it was very like them, they might have said, very like themselves, to know how to read and write, and they knew too that not everybody could do it.

Do you see what I mean.

Everybody can read and write because they learn how and it is a natural thing to do. But there are others who learn how, they learn how to read and write, but they read and write as if they knew how.

Now one of these who had just come to read and write as if he knew how, said, oh yes, I knew them, I knew them before they knew how to read and write.

I could if I liked mention the names of all of these people. I could mention the name of the one who said he had known them before they knew how to read and write. I could mention the names of the ones he knew before they knew how to read and write.

Shakespeare's plays were written, the sonnets too were written.

Plays and Shakespeare's sonnets. Shakespeare's sonnets and *Before the Flowers of Friendship Faded Friendship Faded*. Now the point is this. In both cases these were not as if they were being written but as if they were going to be written. That is the difference between Shakespeare's plays and Shakespeare's sonnets. Shakespeare's plays were written as they were written. Shakespeare's sonnets were written as they were going to be written.

I now wish to speak very seriously, that is to say, I wish to converse, I did so, that is I did converse after I had made my discovery. I conversed very seriously about it.

In reading and writing, you may either be, without doubt, attached to what you are saying, or you may not. Attached in the sense of being connected to it.

Supposing you know exactly what you say and you continue to say it. Supposing instead you have decided not to continue to say what you say and you neither do nor do not continue to say it. Does it or does it not make any difference to you whether you do continue to say it.

That is what you have to know in order to know which way you may or may not do it, might or might not do it, can or cannot do it. In short which way you come or do not come to say what you say. Certainly in some way you say what you say. But how. And what does it do, not to you, but what does it do. That is the question.

Shakespeare's plays were written. The sonnets too were written.

Anything anybody writes is written.

Anything anybody reads has been written.

But if anything that anybody writes is written why is it that anybody writing writes and if anybody writing writes, in whom is the writing that is written written.

That is the question.

This brings me to the question of audience of an audience.

What is an audience.

Everybody listen.

That is not an audience because will everybody listen. Is it an audience because will anybody listen.

When you are writing who hears what you are writing.

That is the question.

Do you know who hears or who is to hear what you are writing and how does that affect you or does it affect you.

That is another question.

If when you are writing you are writing what some one has written without writing does that make any difference.

Is that another question.

Are there, is there many another question. Is there.

On the other hand if you who are writing know what you are writing, does that change you or does it not change you.

That is that might be an important question.

If you who are writing know what it is that is coming in writing, does that make you make you keep on writing or does it not.

Which guess is the right guess or is there not a guess yes.

That too is very important.

Perhaps you may say they had it written, they thought they had it written and you thought so more than that you know so, and so in writing that you write is as they thought so, or perhaps as they know so.

Does that make it like that.

Perhaps yes perhaps no.

There are so many ways of writing and yet after all there are perhaps only two ways of writing.

Perhaps so.

Perhaps no.

Perhaps so.

There is one way the common way of writing that is writing what you are writing. That is the one way of writing, oh yes that is one way of writing.

The other way is an equally common way. It is writing, that is writing what you are going to be writing. Of course this is a common way a common way of writing. Now do you or how do you make a choice. And how do you or do you know that there are two common ways of writing and that there is a difference between.

It is true that there is a difference between the one way and the other way. There is a difference between writing the way you are writing and writing the way you are going to be writing. And there is also choosing. There may be a choosing of one way or of the other way.

Now how do you make a choice if you make a choice. Or do you make a choice or do you not make a choice. Or do some do. Or is it true that some do. Or is it true that some do not do so. That some make a choice that some do not do so.

Now if you do how do you make a choice and if you do do make a choice what do you do.

It is true that any one writing and making a choice does choose to write in one of these two ways. They either write as they write or they write as they are going to write and they may and they may not choose to do what they are going to do.

If not why not. And if so do they know what they do or do they not.

I am sure you do not understand yet what I mean by the two ways.

I said once when I was seriously conversing, I not only say it but I think it. By this I mean that I did not choose to use either one of two ways but two ways as one way.

I mean I do mean that there are two ways of writing.

Once you know that you have written you go on writing. This explains nothing.

But quite naturally it does not explain because what is it that it does not explain. Indeed what is it that it does not explain. You can refuse to explain, when you have written, but what is it that you can refuse to explain. Oh dear what is it.

You can refuse if you refuse you can refuse to explain when you have written.

You can explain before and you can explain after and you can even explain while you are writing. But does that make the two kinds of writing. No at once I can say not it does not. But and this is or it may be very exciting or may be not, but in this way you can be and become interesting. And may be not.

But what is the use of being interesting.

Of course everybody who writes is interesting other wise why would everybody read everybody's letters.

Do you begin to see does everybody begin to see what this has to do with Shakespeare's plays and Shakespeare's sonnets. Or do they not. And if they do begin to see why do they and where do they and how do they and if they do not do not begin to see why do they not begin to see. If not why not.

Two ways two ways of writing are not more than one way. They are two ways and that has nothing to do with being more than one way. Yes you all begin to see that. There can not be any one who can not begin to see that. So now there is no use in saying if not why not. No indeed indeed not.

I hope no one has forgotten the coincidence of Shakespeare's sonnets and *Before the Flowers of Friendship Faded Friendship Faded*. I hope nobody has. At any rate by the time I am all through and everybody knows not only everything I will tell but everything I can tell and everything I can know then no one not any one will forget will not remember to remember if any one asks any one do they remember, the coincidence between Shakespeare's sonnets and *Before the Flowers of Friendship Faded Friendship Faded*.

Ordinarily in writing one writes.

Suppose one is writing. It is to be presumed that one knows what it is to be that which one has written.

Suppose one is writing. It is to be presumed that one does not know what it is to be that which they have written.

But in any case one does write it if one is the person who is writing it.

Supposing you are writing anything, you write it.

That is one way of writing and the common way.

There is another way of writing. You write what you intend to write.

That is one way. You write what you intended to write.

There is one way. Is it another way.

You write what has always been intended, by any one, to be written.

Is there another way to write.

You write what some one has intended to write.

This is not an uncommon way of writing.

No one way of writing no way of any of these ways is an uncommon way of writing.

Presumably a great many people write that way.

Now when the same person writes in two different ways that is to say writes as they write, writes as they intended to write, writes as any one intended to write, writes as some one intended to write why does it sound different why does each writing sound different although written by the same person writing. Now why does it sound different. Does it sound different if the words used are the same or are the words used different when the emotion of writing, the intention in writing is different.

That is the funny part of it. That all this is the thing to know. Funny is again used in the sense of diverting and disturbing.

There are then really there are then two different ways of writing.

There is the writing which is being written because the writing and the writer look alike. In this case the words next to each other make a sound. When the same writer writes and the writing and the writer look alike but they do not look alike because they are writing what is going to be written or what has been written then the words next to each other sound different than they did when the writer writes when the writer is writing what he is writing.

The words next to each other actually sound different to the ear that sees them. Make it either sees or hears them. Make it the eyes hear them. Make it either hears or sees them. I say this not to explain but to make it plain.

Anybody knows the difference between explain and make it plain. They sound the same if anybody says they do but they are not the same.

Now another thing. The words next to each other that sound different to the eye that hears them or the ear that sees them, remember this is just to make it plain, do not necessarily sound different to the writer seeing them as he writes them.

We had a motto. This is it.

I am I, not any longer when I see.

There are two different ways in which writing is done is easily done. They are both easy in the same as well as in the different way.

All this begins to make it clear that Shakespeare's plays and Shakespeare's sonnets even when they are all here are different to the eye and ear. Words next to each other are different to the eye and ear and the reason of it is clear. It not only is clear but it will be clear. Words next to each other make a sound to the eye and the ear. With which you hear.

Oh yes with which you do hear.

All this seems simple but it takes a great deal of coincidence to make it plain. A coincidence is necessary all the same to make it plain.

The coincidence happened and then it was plain.

That makes me say that the *Before the Flowers of Friendship Faded Friendship Faded* had to be written by me before it made it plain, it was for me a coincidence and this coincidence I will explain, I will also tell it to make it plain. I will also tell it so I do tell it just the same.

When I was very young I knew that there was a way of winning by being winsome. Listen to me nevertheless.

Anybody who is a baby or has been one knows this way.

Then later one knows that there is a way of winning by having been winsome.

Perhaps yes nevertheless.

Later one knows there is a way of winning by being intriguing.

Later one knows that there is a way of winning by having been intriguing.

Later every one knows there is a way of winning by simply being able to have them know that you can be displeased by their being displeasing.

Then later there is a way of winning by having been winning.

What has this to do with writing, something and nothing, considerable and everything, a little and very little. But it is useful. It is useful to think of everything if one wishes to reduce anything to two ways. Two ways of any one thing is enough for a beginning and for an ending.

None of these knowledges are knowledges in one way of writing. Any one of these knowledges are knowledges in the other way of writing.

That is to say and this is where everybody who can write and think will say that it is their way, that is to say if you know these things and you can know these things then you can write as if you knew or as if you had known or as if you were going to know these things.

This is an ordinary way of writing and when ordinary writing is written in this way anybody can say that they can read what anybody can say. And if they do do they do it again. Of course they do and that makes them certain of that thing that as they can do it again they have not done it before. Oh yes we all know what to say if we say it that way. Yes yes yes. No one has any need not to guess yes. Or if you like no. What is the difference between no and yes. Think.

On the other hand if you do not know these things although the time will or will not come that you will know these things, then you write as one who has been allowed to know these things without knowing them.

What things. Have you forgotten, because if you have not may be I have. May be I have but I doubt it. May be you have.

The knowledge is that you write what you intend to write because you do or do not win the way you intend to win. Even if you do not win. Or even if nothing. Not even if it is nothing not to be pleasing even if it is nothing to be or not be pleased or to be or not be displeasing. It is not only used as such but it is also only not used as such.

And that makes it all clear just why in the one case and in the other case the words next to each other sound different or not the same.

Is it all clear. Is it all plain.

Or is it why they do not have to say it is not all clear it is not all plain. Forgive no one and partly forgive no one because there is nothing to forgive.

But it is true that there are two ways of writing.

There is the way when you write what you are writing and there is the way when you write what you are going to be writing or what some other one would have written if they had been writing. And in a way this can be a caress. It can not be tenderness. Well well. Of course you can understand and imagine.

And this brings it all to two words next to each other and how when the same person writes what he writes and the same person as that person writes what he is going to write the sound of the words next to each other are different.

The words next to each other can sound different or not the same.

What is a sound.

A sound is two things heard at one and the same time but not together. Let us take any two words.

That is a sound heard by the eyes, that is a sound.

Let us take any two words.

Perhaps he is right even if he seems wrong.

It is all very difficult not to explain nor to know but to do without.

Mr Owen Young made a mistake, he said the only thing he wished his son to have was the power of clearly expressing his ideas. Not at all. It is not clarity that is desirable but force.

Clarity is of no importance because nobody listens and nobody knows what you mean no matter what you mean, nor how clearly you mean what you mean. But if you have vitality enough of knowing enough of what you mean, somebody and sometime and sometimes a great many will have to realize that you know what you mean and so they will agree that you mean what you know, what you know you mean, which is as near as anybody can come to understanding any one.

Why yes of course, it is needless to say why yes of course when anybody who can say why yes of course can say so.

Now nobody can think nobody can, that this has nothing to do with Shakespeare's sonnets and Shakespeare's plays, nobody who can, because in no instance is there not a lack of what they have in either one of one.

But they have not the same thing and there is a reason why and a reason why is sound and sense. Oh please be pleased with that. Pleased with what. With very much whatever they have which of course they do have.

Shakespeare's sonnets are not Shakespeare's plays and there is a reason why and they sound different. You all know the reason why and they sound different.

Henry James nobody has forgotten Henry James even if I have but I have not. If Henry James was a general who perhaps would win an army to win a battle he might not know the difference but if he could he would and if he would he might win an army to win not a war but a battle not a battle but an army.

There is no use in denying that there could be a difference can be a difference.

Perhaps, he, make he what you like. If you like or if you do not like whichever you like.

Perhaps he is right even if he seems wrong.

But there is no doubt about seems wrong. There is no occupation in where he went or how he came or whichever or whatever more of which it was like.

Think how you can change your mind concerning this matter. Think how carefully you can say this.

If you can say this carefully, you can either not change your mind concerning this matter, or you can act entirely differently, that is, you can change your mind concerning this matter.

Remember how Henry James was or was not a general.

And think what there is to express.

All who wish do express what they have to express.

Do you know how every one feels in this world just now. If you do leave it to me to say it again.

I return to the question of the difference between Shakespeare's plays and Shakespeare's sonnets and you do too.

Like it or not if I do you do too and if you do not do it too, you do not do it too.

Do you begin to realize what it is that makes sound.

Think of your ears as eyes. You can even think of your eyes as ears but not so readily perhaps.

Shakespeare wrote plays and in these plays there is prose and poetry and very likely every time one word that makes two words, is next to each other, it makes three sounds, each word makes a sound, that is two words make two sounds and the words next to each other make not only a sound but nearly a sound. This makes it readily that any two words next each other written by any one man make the same sound although all the words and their meaning are different.

That is they do if he feels alike. But there we are that is what it is all about. And what is feeling alike. It is that that makes it important if I say so.

It all depends now here is where it all not commences but is, it all depends upon the two ways to write.

One way is to write as you write, the other way is to write the way you are going to write. And then some can some do once in a while write the way some one would write if they write only they do not that is to say they say they would if they could. That is different than if you think they do that is if you write as if they think they do.

This sounds mixed but it is not and it is so important. Oh dear it is so important.

Before I say which I do say that when Shakespeare wrote his sonnets the words next to each other too but this time they did not make three sounds they made one sound.

There is a reason and this is the reason. I will try you will try. Oh yes you will try, I will try, we will try, if we can we will try to make it all apply. Oh yes we can oh yes we can try, to do this as we do. Yes one of two. One of two ways to write. There are many more but about this no one can or does care because if it makes a difference it does not make a difference too.

So yes. Very well now.

There are two ways to write, listen while I tell it right. So you can know I know.

Two ways to write.

If two ways are two ways which is the only way. Remember how to say a coincidence may occur any day.

And what is a coincidence.

A coincidence is having done so.

Shakespeare he wrote sonnets and Shakespeare he wrote plays but there is no coincidence about that. Not at all. That is an example. Listen. That is an example of the fact that there are two ways of writing. There is the way of writing as it is written those are the plays, and there is the way of writing as it was going to be written and those are the sonnets. Does it make any difference whether the way it was going to be written is his way or some way of somebody's. In this case it does not. That is if you are only interested and just now I am only interested in one of two ways.

But there is a coincidence and that is *Before the Flowers of Friendship Faded Friendship Faded*. By coincidence I mean just this, this which is that.

The coincidence is simply that. That *Before the Flowers* was written too in the second way that is as it was going to be written whether as the writer was going or somebody else having been the writer was going to write it. And this makes it be what there is of excitement.

I found out by doing so that when that happened the words next to each other had a different sound and having a different sound they did not have a different sense but they had a different intensity and having a different intensity they did not feel so real and not feeling so real they sounded more smooth and sounding more smooth they sounded not so loud and not sounding so loud they sounded pretty well and sounding pretty well they made everybody tell, just why they like them sounding so well. Oh yes not oh tell. Yes sounding as they sound or sounded very well.

And so I found out that Shakespeare's sonnets were like that and so yes you see it was important to me.

When Shakespeare wrote his sonnets there were words next to each other too but this time they did not make three sounds they made one sound.

And this is why they are different this is why the sonnets are different from the plays and the plays different from the sonnets.

And by a coincidence I found out all about it.

The coincidence was *Before the Flowers of Friendship Faded Friendship Faded.*

There is no use in hesitating before a coincidence.

Shakespeare's plays and Shakespeare's sonnets are not a coincidence.

They are different.

Now it is very entertaining that all this comes out so well between the sonnets because the plays you might say the plays are about what other people did could and would have said, but not at all, not at all at all, they were written while writing not as they were going to be written.

No sound really makes any difference because really a sound is not heard but seen and anything seen is successful.

A thing heard is not necessarily successful.

A thing seen is necessarily successful.

By the time Shakespeare's sonnets have been seen Shakespeare's plays have been heard.

But really this is not true.

Shakespeare's plays have been seen, and any sound seen is successful.

Shakespeare's sonnets have been heard. Any sound heard well any sound heard is heard. Any sound heard if it is heard is successful.

Supposing everybody gets well into their head the difference between the sound seen and heard of Shakespeare's plays and the sound seen and heard of Shakespeare's sonnets and that there is a difference.

Any one can by remembering hear how a thing looks. This sounds foolish but really it is not foolish, it is as easy as anything else.

All natural people say I have heard it burning, I have seen it called, I have heard it shown. They say these things and they are right. One sees much better than one hears sounds.

That is true of all beauty.

You hear the beauty you see the sound.

And so Shakespeare goes on.

And now everybody has a gift for making one sound follow another even when they hesitate.

If they really hesitate then as one word does not follow another there is no such result.

But do they really hesitate. Does any one really hesitate. Or do they really not do this, really and truly not hesitate.

But if they do not hesitate and most people who have a gift of making one word follow another naturally do not hesitate, there is as I have said two ways of writing.

You do understand that about hesitating, there is a waltz called Hesitation, but you do understand that sooner or later than this will then be then about Henry James and his having been a general then and winning a battle then and a war then if there is to be a war then.

But to begin again.

And perhaps again to begin again.

Most people or if they do most people who have a gift of making one word follow another naturally do not hesitate, there is as I have said two ways of writing.

And the two ways are two ways that everybody writes. Some do not ever write the one way or the other way.

Shakespeare did. He wrote both ways.

He wrote as he wrote and he wrote as he was going to write.

One way is the way Shakespeare wrote when he wrote his plays, the other way is the way he wrote when he wrote his sonnets, and the words one after the other next to each other are different in the two different ways.

And now to tell the story of the coincidence.

To have always written in the one way, that is to write so that the writing and the writer not only look alike but are alike, is what has been done by any one, of which one is one.

Remember I wish to say later what Henry James did but that has nothing whatever to do with coincidences, nothing whatever, nothing whatever to do with coincidences.

Those who run can read, I remember as a child being very puzzled by that.

There was a moment many years ago when I had a meaning for it but now I have forgotten that and now I have none.

Supposing it does mean something these words, he who runs can read.

It makes one feel that very likely to feel is to feel well.

If to feel well makes one feel that perhaps it makes one not feel to feel well.

Very likely that is not what they meant, did mean by he who runs can read.

Feel well and add well to feel.

And so he who runs can read.

And that makes partly what they have be theirs.

Oh yes.

If they have partly what they have.

To have written always so that what is it, that what or is written is like that which is doing the writing. If not exactly why not.

To have written always so that which is written is like that that which, who is doing the writing, only, that is, that it not only sounds alike and looks alike but that it is alike.

He who runs can read. I do not know who wrote this line nor what it means but it used to be used in copy books when I went to school.

And this brings us all to Shakespeare's plays and Shakespeare's sonnets and it also brings us to coincidences, and it also brings us to *Before the Flowers of Friendship Faded Friendship Faded*.

And I often think how Henry James saw.

He saw he could write both ways at once which he did and if he did he did. And there is nothing alike in heard and saw. Not now or ever by itself, not now.

Owen Young said that everything should be clear and everything is now clear.

Or one may say now everything is clear. So much at any rate is clear.

There are the plays and there are the sonnets of Shakespeare and they were written by the same man but they were not written in the same way.

Each lot was written in one of the two ways and the two ways are not the same way.

Henry James and therefore I tell you about Henry James and perhaps being a general and perhaps winning a battle and if perhaps knowing if perhaps winning a war.

The way to find this out all this out is to do likewise, not to do it alike but to do it likewise. Do you see what I mean, how the difference is not the same no not the same which it is not.

The way to find this out find it find it out is to do likewise. That is not to write Shakespeare's plays and Shakespeare's sonnets but to write, write plays and sonnets, and if you do that and I have done that, I have written what I have written and I have written *Before the Flowers of Friendship Faded Friendship Faded*. Then it comes over you all of a sudden or very slowly or a little at a time why it is all as it is.

You make a diagram or a discovery, which is to discover by a coincidence. Oh yes a diagram I say a diagram to discover by coincidence, that is not what a diagram is but let it be. I say let it be.

You make a discovery, it is a coincidence, of course yes a coincidence, not an accent but an access, yes a coincidence which tells you yes. Yes it makes it possible to make the discovery.

And after that, yes after that, a great deal that has perplexed you about sound in connection with sense is suddenly clear.

Also what the relation of a writer is to his audience, oh yes an audience that is suddenly clear, whether one and one and one makes one or three and just as often one and two, all this all this is clear.

But most of all oh most of all just why two words next to each other make a different sound one way than they do the other way and why oh yes and why.

There is nothing means more than oh yes and why.

I will now patiently tell all about everything.

I had always written myself out in relation to something.

Think everybody think.

Is not that the way all who can run can read.

Perhaps that is what that means. Perhaps there is more to it, there is perhaps the concentration upon the reading as well as upon the running. That is the thing that makes writing.

I have said who has said what has been said which ever I have said or indeed, as it might or might not or even may be left to be said that. And now in or as their fashion.

I have said that there are two ways of writing, writing as it is written writing as it is going to be written whether as the one writing has written or as some one as intended made it for which it is written. If this is so and indeed it is so, then in that case there are the two ways of writing.

Perhaps it is surprising after all after all that I have said that it is the plays of Shakespeare that were written as they were written and the sonnets that were written as they were going to be written.

And in each case I tell you and in each case the words next to each other make a different sound. In one case a smooth sound without which need they mean what they said. In the other case a real sound which need not mean what they said as they just do. Of course they just do.

The sonnets in the sonnets the words next to each other make the smooth sound without which they need to mean what they said.

In the plays they make the lively sound and if they mean what they said they mean it because a lively sound can as it will or if it does mean what is said.

Do you begin to see or do you begin just as well not begin to see.

It is all very interesting curious if one had not found it out by a coincidence but one that is I having found it out by a coincidence it is not curious.

The coincidence as I have said was the writing of *Before the Flowers of Friendship Faded Friendship Faded*. There too like the Shakespeare sonnets the words next to each other made a smooth sound and the meaning had to be meant as something had been learnt. If not why not.

And in all the other things oh yes in all the other things the words next to each other make a lively sound and they mean which they mean as they mean can they mean as indeed must they mean, I mean. Indeed yes.

And so now anybody can know because I tell them so that the coincidence was so and so and so it was.

Listen to me. And so it was.

Now what has all this to do with Henry James and if he was a general and if he won a battle and if he would be if he would win a war. If he would win a war.

Now Henry James had two ways in one. He had not begun oh dear no he had not begun, he had indeed dear no, not had he begun.

That is one thing.

The other thing is that mostly there are one of two sometimes one of three that do not listen but they hear.

That is what most writing is. Sometimes two of three do listen and do hear.

Perhaps they do if they do it is not queer, it is not queer of them so to do.

Now in the case of Henry James listen in the case of Henry James all of them all three of them listened as if they did or indeed as if they did not hear. Indeed not, indeed they listened as if they did or as if they did listen and not hear or if they all three did listen and did hear. And all of this was not queer not at all not at all queer.

That made it be that Henry James all the same Henry James if he had been a general what would he have done.

I ask you if he had been a general what would he have done.

Let us think carefully about all this.

Then everybody will know that it was not begun.

All that was important to know. For me to know now.

I am carefully going into the question of Henry James.

Before I go any further let everybody think of generals and what they do.

What do generals do.

Of course generals do do something. That is something is done when there are generals. And one general if he is a general does do something. To think of this as Henry James. A general who does do something. What did he do when he did something when Henry James was a general what did he do as he did something which he certainly did.

Henry James is a combination of the two ways of writing and that makes him a general a general who does something. Listen to it.

Does a general or does a general not win a war. Does a general or does a general not win a battle and if he does how does he do it.

Well he does it because not right away or even after a little while nothing happens together and then all of a sudden it all happens together or if not then why not.

Now Henry James if he could not have been otherwise would have had that it was like that. Sometimes not of course sometimes not.

A general can not have it come all at once as often as not if he did then there would be nothing that would happen or if it did nothing would be amiss.

For instance if Henry James had been a general and had not anything to do but this. Of course not he would not then have done have had anything to do but this.

Everything that could happen or not happen would have had a preparation. Oh yes you know you know very well how Henry James had had to do this.

So then if Henry James had been a general what would he have had to have done. This which he did do. Oh yes he would have had to do that which he has done, had done, did do, to do this.

Think anybody think.

How did or does Henry James do this.

He came not to begin but to have begun.

Any general who can win or can not have won a battle has come to do this.

He came not to begin but to have begun.

Henry James came not one by one and not to have won but to have begun.

He came to do this.

Let us think a little how he was this.

He knew why he knew how it would have been begun. Not as beginning but as begun. He knew this not as having been won, not why he knew this and did not know this, never knew this as one, one, one.

Numbers never came or came amiss but it was not whether or not numbers were begun that made him know this.

I like to think of begun. Not as beginning or having begun but as being begun oh yes he could and did with this as this.

Think how Henry James knew which one, which one won. He knew this. That is how a general can win or not win being a general and having or not having won a battle or a war, as this.

It is the same thing.

And Henry James was not the same thing. A general is not the same thing. He was a general, he was the same thing, not the same thing as a general but really one.

Would he lose a battle a battle that was begun. Perhaps yes.

A general which he was could do this.

I like to think how he looked as this which he was when he was one.

I like to think how everything can make one, he was begun, as one.

It is not necessary to know the life history of a general. As I say a battle, as I say a war, a war, a battle is begun, that is what is always happening about it about any one who has been a general and had one had a war had a battle had either one or both of either one.

Let it not make any difference what happened to either one of one.

What did Henry James do, neither he nor I knew. Which is which. It is not necessary to be plainly helped or not. Not at all necessary.

I wish to say that I know that any day it will happen to be the way he knew how Henry James came not to stay not to have gone away but to have begun, oh yes to have begun, that is what I say to have begun, it is necessary, if you are a general, it is necessary, to have begun and Henry James is a general, it is necessary to have begun, which is what has been done.

I like very well what I have said.

Remember that there are two ways of writing and Henry James being a general has selected both, any general has selected both otherwise he is not a general and Henry James is a general and he has selected both. Neither either or or nor.

It was a glorious victory oh yes it was, for which it was, for which oh yes it was.

I can recognize coming to heat hands in winter and plans in summer. But this is not here nor there.

Can you see that any day was no part of his life.

It meant very likely it meant just that, just that is different, as different from only that. In every case they meant as much more as they did.

Oh how can I not recognize that Americans recognize roofs recognize doors recognize theirs recognize cares. Of course they can go where they can go if they go but do they go. If he did.

Henry James was an American, but not as a general as a general he was a European as a general, which he was as he was a European general.

But this may go to make an American if an American which they do can say so.

Henry James never said he never made everything more or nothing more of that. No he did not.

In this way in a little while you will see and really you will see what is American. You will see what is American. If you will see what is American.

If Henry James had been a general which he was what would he have had to do. He would have to do what a general has to do. He would have had to have it begun a battle or a war, if a general is to be a general any more and Henry James was one.

Do not forget that there are two ways to write, you remember two ways to write and that Henry James chose both. Also you must remember that in a battle or a war everything has been prepared which is what has been called begun and then everything happens at once which is what is called done and then a battle or a war is either not or won. Which is as frequently as one, one, one.

You can see that he chose both Henry James, you can see that he was a general Henry James, you can see that a war or a battle may or may not be won or both or one, one, one.

I like Henry James as that.

VOLUME II

All three Jameses sat together. This they naturally would do. Would there be any other Jameses.

In accord with the way that they use what they had and in

accord with the hope that they will use what they have all Jameses get together.

After a while all and any James remains or stays apart.

And this cannot be told as they never become old, not any James.

Do generals become old. Yes if they continue to be generals.

So there is a difference between a James and a general, and in a way we come to that.

It makes no difference that they never remember either General or a James.

Nor what they remember that is what they do not remember or rather do not remember. Do you wish a James to remember. Do you wish a general to remember.

Well anyway neither a General nor a James will remember.

And so Henry James is a general.

He has not so many things to do things which he does do but he does do the things which he has to do. Oh yes Henry James does. And that makes it interesting. What he has to do makes it interesting.

That is just like a general is it not just like a general that the thing which he has to do makes it interesting.

All that they have told, no matter whether which it is I wish to refuse that it is told and again refuse that that which it is is told. Oh yes refuse as much as any wish as any anybody which is a wish. Do you see by what I mean that Henry James is not a queen but a general. Oh yes you do you understand that.

Henry James made no one care for plans. Do you see that he is a general. He made nobody care for plans and after all they were fairly able of course they were fairly able.

None of this is what to wish.

Henry James had no wishes and if he were a general he would have no wishes and he was a general and he had no wishes.

In the meantime and there is no intermediate in the mean time Henry James cannot be said to come prepared. Oh yes it seems like that but is it true.

If he had been a general and had to win a war or a battle or even a part of a battle what would he have had to do. He would have done it. In a way he would have done it. Oh yes in a way he would have won it.

I have often thought what he would do if he had been a enlarge.

VOLUME III

I like to think what would he do if he had been a general.

VOLUME IV

Little by little he would have been a general but would he have been a general little by little. Not at all. He would not have been a general little by little. He would have been begun as a general. That is what he would have been begun, he would have been begun a general.

And after a little while the three Jameses would again have sat together. Just as they did. Having sat together. And would there have been any other Jameses. Just as well any other Jameses as there often are. Even to be said habitually are.

And when any three Jameses sat together you might say they sat in a circle as they sat together as three Jameses sat together any of them would have been what they were. Would Henry James have been a general. Why not. I see no reason why not.

I can again think how they sat if they sat.

But they did sit.

Henry James did sit and as he sat the way he sat was the way he would have sat if he had been a general and so there we are, or at least yes there we are.

Now do you understand what I mean by what I say and what he was and what he was in what there is to be what he was. He was a general because a general is begun. He was a general because he sat as one who had been and was still the general he had been.

Three Jameses sat together but that did not make any difference. That might happen or might have happened or indeed did happen does happen to any general who has and still has been a general.

I wish to disclose everything I know.

I wish to disclose why I feel a general so.

He felt a general can feel that he need never kneel.

What do I mean to say. That he was not married in any way. And is that true as a general or is it true in general. No it is not true in general but he as a general of him it is true as a general.

And why not.

Once more if not why not.

Because if alike allowed alike, he would catch it all as they say.

This to him was not more important than if he wished either not to be there or to be alone.

Now I wish to say generously why he was never married either as a general or as a man.

How can a man be a general too. Not if no one knew.

But he knew.

He knew that he was a general too.

And now yes so you do.

How was he a general.

Not by not being married or yes is it as nice.

He was a general by the circumstance that he had begun and if a general has been married it is of no importance.

How when Henry James was a general did he conduct his war. There is no difference between conduct and how did he conduct his war.

Did he win his battle or did he win his part of his battle if he was not the full general or the only general in his battle. If he did not, but he did, why not.

There are two things to be said. He was not married, to be said and he was a general, to be said.

He was not married not only for this reason but of which he did not take part.

He took part in the battle, which is the battle in which he as a general did take his part. And if the battle which was the battle in which he did take his part was won then as a general he did take part in winning the battle which was won. Also the war.

Thank you, also the war.

How can you state what you wish to say. That is the question. What you wish. That is the question. To say. That is the question.

By being called to kindle.

What do you wish to say.

When Henry James was this general which he was and they made the most of that, by the time they did, and he was not married, which he undoubtedly was not, and placed beside, where they had the right, whenever it happened, and they on their account, made mention of their violence by any failure, no more than of course told in toiling, so they could undoubtedly in time, face themselves here, where.

It is not only in this and in this way that a battle is fought.

It is of great importance that Henry James never was married.

That might make theirs be mine.

VOLUME V

For which they spare neither one of themselves. No general that is a general as a general has won one at a time.

Believe me if you like.

VOLUME VI

I think easily of three who sat and one who did that.

VOLUME VII

I, he, it may not be set in place of stated.

I state that it may not be settled in place of stated.

He may not be seated to settle in place of stating what there is to be stated.

It may not be of advantage to have no settlement in place of not stating what is to be settled in place of settling.

In this way he could adventure to wander away from being a general. But in every little while more may be there.

This is the way it was with Henry James.

And so what is there to say.

If he had been a general what would he have had to do, he would have had to take part in a battle if there was a battle in a war if there were a war if not then why not.

But no questions can be asked to which no questions can have as an answer.

And so they make an occasion of this.

This makes you see how lightly or heavily a general can take place.

May they recognize being married as yes and no in marriage.

Henry James had no marriage as he was not married. They were obliged to give this answer. Not when they heard him. Or even after they had him.

So often do generals but generals are not more than are more.

That makes a general no hazard.

A general begun.

Why can marriage be made away.

Henry James was not married. By this they mean what they say.

I wish to tell you all who wish to hear why marriage married if they can name him here.

They do name him.

They name him Henry James.

A little still a little by that they all grew.

For which I ask you, how do you do.

VOLUME VIII

To come back to that he never was married would he be very likely to live alone and if he was very likely to live alone would he be as if he were alone. Now think of any general any regular general and how it would be.

If he were not married and lived alone he would live as if he were not married and lived alone but really not he would live as if he were not married. If they are not married do they live as if they live alone. Think about this a Henry James and think about this a general and then think about this as this.

What did he make him do when he wrote what did it make him do when he had it to do to help with a battle or help with a war or help with whatever he ordered that he should help. He would of course never help himself. Any one who is not married and who lives as if he is not married does not help himself. He can not help himself. And this makes him write as he does, does or was.

In many instances marriages are arranged in many instances of generals. Was Henry James one of such a one. In a way not because he was not married and if he was not married it was not because he was ever married. No not for instance not one.

A great deal has to do with everything. And marrying.

Well will they lightly go away.

For which they knew who likes a crowd. Or who will please when they lower or do not lower a boat.

He was or was not prepared for as much as he had.

This has nothing or something to do with either not married or not.

Believe those who do not rather not have to leave it as that.

He never felt awkward as married but he should recite only really who could or did recite or not quite.

I tell you and it is a fact if you are not married why are you married or not. Henry James or a general were never like that.

And that after all is not all or everything they have to say.

The thing to wonder is did he not have to say what he did not have to say.

That can happen to any general who is regularly a general.

Any general.

VOLUME IX

Now who has or wills to have that they have or have to have and whether, whether will they have or rather.

I could count many times as many wives and Henry James or a general could not count as many times as many wives and what difference does that make if they venture or do not place a general before or after. A general is placed before or after and so is Henry James. He is placed before or after.

And no doubt a married no doubt a married man is not no doubt a married man is doubt.

Henry James or a general are never in tears about a married man and so they are not.

What could they feel if they live.

They could if they could feel if they live they could feel or they could live or they could do both or they could not and if not if they did not is did not the same as could not or if indeed if could not is not the same who will change the same.

Henry James meant and met and if he was a general and he was if he was a general and if is not necessary because he was he was not ready but being not ready was of no importance because he was.

I wish to say he was.

Rather I wish to say he was.

I wish rather to say he was.

I wish now to give the life history of Henry James who was a general. And yes. Whether no or yes whether yes or no or to tell it so.

I wish not wish but do do tell it so.

There is no hope of either or oh no.

VOLUME X

Henry James may be, not a place he could not be a place a general cannot be a place, he or it can not.

Henry James then can not be a place and in so much as he is not a place and can not be a place and a general can not be a place and is not a place insomuch Henry James is a general and a general is Henry James.

Oh yes they say there can be others but oh yes there are not.

Henry James begins to be as he is. Indeed if not why not. But there is never any if not as Henry James is as he is. He controls nothing by only that but a general a general controls nothing oh no oh yes a general controls something, and so triumphantly I say triumphantly and so triumphantly so does Henry James he controls something he does control something. And so when and why not is not Henry James a general and a general Henry James. They are that. Henry James is a general and he controls something even though and it can be said that Henry James does not control anything and even then it can be said a general does not control anything.

Who has a general at heart or Henry James. They have that with that wish.

Pray pray pray prepare to wish.

Henry James comes for them for them and them

Was a general known to wish.

No no general not as a general a general was not known to wish. Neither was Henry James.

VOLUME XI

There is no use always beginning before before what. I wished to say wish to say that there is no use there is no use in my beginning in my having been beginning before. Once more I have it to do before what. Before he was Henry James. Before he was a general. Some one might they be some one. Not before. Not before Henry James. Might he be some one before Henry James. Not if he was to have been Henry James which he was and a blessing even if not everything a blessing something not to be arranging to be Henry James. A general is in any and all of any way or ways the same.

But to begin. Having begun there is no refusal in to begin but there might be. In this case there might only be as there more than just there there might have been.

Think of an American thing a poetic American thing there might have been.

This may not refer to a general. Not may but also not might, might not refer to a general. May or might not refer to Henry James. All of which connects with not to begin. In a new continent and is any new continent, no not new, in a new continent they might not begin not might not have been begun. That makes a new continent not any fun.

Why do you say so if you know so.

Henry James might not have begun. Neither a general too.

I wish to think a little of a difference in age and why nobody says so. And is there any hope of sitting there or any where. Or is there any hope of using any hope.

I wish to see that you know Henry James.

I may be acquainted with him by and by.

Who says it is easily said. Who says or said that it was easily said.

Forget who said what was easily said and come back to remember Henry James.

One at a time is of no use as just as often there is more than not one at a time. In place of that who is in place of that.

This makes partly an understanding of Henry James and I am not as pleased as not relieved that it is so.

One should always think well of how to spell.

All who have have it to do so.

As newly as not wed Henry James.

For this and made for this as in and for a use a use for this.

Of and for are always different and never no never different as not one at a time.

I begin to see how I can quiver and not quiver at like and alike.

A great deal can be felt so.

VOLUME XII

Henry James one.

VOLUME XIII

The young James a young James was a young James a James. He might be and he might be even might be Henry James.

VOLUME XIV

Once upon a time there was no dog if there had been a dog nobody wept.

Once upon a time there was no name and if any one had a name nobody could cover a name with a name. But nobody except somebody who had not that name wept.

Once upon a time there was a place for a name and when that name was the same no one and why not if no one, no one wept. Once upon a time if once upon a time a name was not to blame not to blame not if as a name, if once upon a time a name was the same and if not no one had any one to blame then no one not this time no one had to weep and so this time and no one at this time had been having it as a blame that no one was weeping as if no one had wept.

Once upon a time no one not any one wept that there was a name which was the same as the same name. And so no one wept.

VOLUME XV

Once upon a time if you wonder once upon a time what was his name, his name Henry James was a name, and weeping he wept.

If he wept was it his name.

Oh yes it was his name, all the same yes all the same it was his name.

He wept.

VOLUME XVI

Any time Henry James wept it was his name.

VOLUME XVII

To return but nobody can, if they can may they if they began, to return to Henry James.

Not to say this slowly is not to say this not at all. To say this not at all slowly is not not to say this at all.

And so all.

All can return slowly.

Nobody can return slowly if they do not move. And did they move.

If they did not better than if they did which they did move.

Henry James cannot return slowly. Or have it as a pleasant and a pleasure. Pleasant in time.

How can all who have arranged to remain where or when or wherever may they may they be alike.

Nobody is alike Henry James.

Better prepare enough.

Nobody is alike Henry James.

Is it is that it, is it because Henry and James are both first names.

Believe this if this is true.

Does it mean that you are you or who are you.

Henry James and names.

He neither now or either how invented names.

May be by a character. Or may be or may be not.

Nobody could make a mistake.

If for instance nobody could make a mistake.

I wish I was used to think of a difference between won and young.

Which made around around.

He heard nobody care.

But this was this or is it.

He he who heard nobody care.

Or is or is it.

He or he and he was prepared to remain there.

Not exactly not.

He was not not prepared not to remain where, there where.

In his care.

In its care.

Where.

It is delightful to know who can go home if they go and if they do not if they do not go.

I have to say here here I very well know what it is that has happened.

He will not begin again because he has it is has been begun.

I have said it for me there.

Which will undertake that care.

I understand you undertake to overthrow my undertaking.

Henry James when he was young.

We discussed we said we discussed did or was he young.

She said he was fresh that is fresher but he was not young and I said he was young quite young that is what I said.

And he was not young but fresher then or was he young and not fresher then.

Which one went on, one not before the other one.

If they were not the same.

If he were young that is to say had been he would have been read to been a young or younger one. I think this is a thing.

Not only by a wish but by not watches or wishes.

He had both both watches and wishes Henry James when he was fresher or Henry James when he was young.

There is no use hanging on to some one wishes and watches but some have some hung when that is young that one.

Decline may make or makes one at a time.

There is no decline when they are not sickly when they are young.

That is one thing.

Henry James one thing.

Henry James for one thing.

He never pursued one at a time no not one thing a thing.

That was not one thing a young thing but he was a he was a young thing. Henry James was was was a young thing. If he was fresher then fresher and add her. But not by him. Not any one thing.

I wish to add that I knew I know one thing.

One thing one thing.

That Henry James was young one thing.

Prepare for flight.

Henry James did not prepare for flight.

Hours what. What are hours for. Hours are not for one thing.

Anything makes nothing and nothing makes anything not a young thing.

Any one is easily equal to that.

Forgive wishes with watches nor watches with wishes.

Forget one thing.

This makes it feel reasonable not to read but indeed this one thing that Henry James was young with one thing.

For them for names for days.

Not which had been. He had not been. That makes him a young then a middle aged thing not so fresh a thing that he had not been. Which he had not been.

But all the same it is true he had been a young thing.

It is not difficult not very difficult to remember what he had been, any one can any day in walking see anything. Anything is any one and any one is a young one. Oh yes you do. He did too.

When this was true where were they. They were here. He was here. This that was so. He was here where he would have been to have been told that it was so.

Henry James you see Henry James was young. Not necessarily but nicely young. Is there any difference between necessarily and nicely. Not when one had been begun.

And then he went on as if he had been young. Oh yes he did go on as if he had been young. No doubt about it yes this was the way it was when he had been begun.

Henry James never came amiss. He did not come slowly nor did he come to kiss.

Which may be there which may be there which may be there.

Did no one not run.

Added bliss to miss and miss to kiss and kiss to remember remember any one.

This made him be have been young.

So I say it is not only not that he was freshened and had been begun but that he had been young.

There now add nothing whatsoever as to how it never meant more than allow.

I wish every one knew exactly how to feel, about Henry James.

VOLUME XVIII

I may remember how to walk up and down.

VOLUME XIX

They felt as well as very well and in no sort and at no time, well very nearly addedly as well.

This makes that they fell which and where they kneel.

Henry James had well you might say he had no time.

VOLUME XX

But just as much as it might be that he was uneasy not uneasy not afraid.

They might be caught alone. Who might be caught alone.

VOLUME XXI

There might not only be left as it.

As it is a chance to bequeathe.

He felt as if they met with which they met not to bequeathe which in their change they met.

How could Henry James fancy that with his name it was not a similar name to that of his brother. Was his brother another.

There now you see. It is not necessary never to mention never to have a brother.

Fortunately many foil an instance of that.

She bowed to her brother.

That is coming in here.

VOLUME XXII

I wish to make it perfectly clear that this is neither there nor here.

Henry James is adamant if you say so.

VOLUME XXIII

By which he may and did mean if you say so.

VOLUME XXIV

Let me tell the history of Henry James simply tell the history of Henry James which brings me and us back to names.

I still have nothing to say about names even if I make a mistake.

VOLUME XXV

A name is a name by which some one reads something or if not then why does he does she not.

And if he does if she does, does it make a moon.

A moon is no name.

James is no name
Henry is no name.
Why is no name.
Shares is no name.
Blinded is no name
Predicate is no name.
This is no name.
Henry James if you say so Henry James was a name.

You can think of a name as a name or not a name. It is very easy to think of Henry James as not a name.

When a boy is a general that is to be is going to be a general being the son and the grandson of one and another one and either of them have been a general they may say to him you cannot be afraid. And he may say but I am I am afraid, I am often afraid, I am afraid when I see something and it turns out to be a horse then I am afraid. But then how can you come to be a general. But a general is on a horse and on a horse it is not on a horse that there is any way to be afraid. And beside that any general is not where it is any danger to be a general in any danger as a general oh no not indeed not for a general. So that is it.

Henry James if he was to be a boy was then to be a general oh yes if not then if not why not a general. But he is and was to be a general.

Come often to see me is not said by a general.

But any one can see a general indeed yes any one.

Henry James was a general.

In general.

The general likes his coffee cold.

In general.

He does not take coffee or milk. Not in general. Not at all. Not a general.

That may be a general.

But Henry James is a general.

And now read what he says.

What does a general say when they read what he says.

In general.

To come back to having been a boy.

Is there a difference between having been a boy and being begun. Not at once and at the same time.

But it is true.

Henry James has been a boy, and he has been begun.

He was never so otherwise.

No never so otherwise.

And this is what is painful that when in tears he was never so otherwise.

But when in tears was he so otherwise.

A general was a general so.

If the little boy was afraid there were no tears because if he was to be a general it would be so otherwise.

When once when twice when once when twice there were no tears otherwise than no tears not twice not once not otherwise.

And so after all anybody can see after all that Henry James was after all a general.

VOLUME XXVI

Play to remember everything that happened within to him.

But which was otherwise when they were not happening.

Play be otherwise.

Can a general be otherwise.

Can he play be otherwise.

Can he play happened to him.

When they happened to him did they happen within.

Did they happen otherwise than it happened for him.

Not otherwise.

Henry James was very ready to have it happen for him.

VOLUME XXVII

A narrative of Henry James told by one who listened to some one else telling about some one entirely different from Henry James.

To some one entirely different from Henry James is a woman who might have killed somebody else another woman only very probably she did not. She was not really under any suspicion of having killed her or any other woman or any other man but really she was entirely a different kind of human being from Henry James entirely a different kind of human being and one who had led and did lead an entirely different kind of life. She lived alone and in the country and so did Henry James. She was heavy set and seductive and so was Henry James. She was slow in movement and light in speech and could change her speech without changing her words so that at one time her speech was delicate and witty and at another time slow and troubling and so was that of Henry James. She was not at all at all at all resembling to Henry James and never knew him and never heard of him and was of another nationality and lived in another country. And that is all there is to it.

So one has quite frequently told different people about her. Because it is a matter that remains to be told about her that something is what any one can tell about her.

Indeed very often as often as ever and yet again find once more as often.

So that is why I like to listen to her to the one that tells any story that she tells about what happens to any one and something did happen at least it happened near that one.

This one the one telling the story had always admired Henry James.

So there you are. That is the connection.

VOLUME XXVIII
Henry James fairly well Henry James.

VOLUME XXIX
It makes no difference what you say when you read.

It makes no difference what you say if you read.

Neither does it make any difference what you say because you read.

None of this makes any difference.

Now think about what does or does not make any difference.

Think about it and do not cry although tears do come easily at least they seem to come easily if they come or if they do not come.

Now when what you say does not make any difference and tears do or do not come and if they do come or if they do not come they could come easily or not easily in coming or not coming this is what it is when Henry James gradually one can not say gradually because by that time it was there but gradually what it was that was said came to rise not like cries but like tears and no one can say that they did or did not come easily but one might say indeed and could say that they did or did not come at all and this made it all there.

Now do you see what I mean when I read.

Even if I do not read do you see what I mean if I do read.

That is what Henry James did, any one does but all the same he did it like that.

Shall I tell you again all about tears and how they rise and how they come and how they will and how they can or not be full. Full is a word so well-known.

Who knows who is well-known.

Henry James is well-known.

But of course he is Henry James is well-known.

Sometimes I wonder about a name like James when it is not a first name but when it is a last name.

David James.

Henry James could not have been named David James.

There was a wicked family named James, and their names make James a very different name and no one needs to feel that tears could come to mean that as a name.

Henry James. A very different name from David James or William James or Robin James or Winslow James. Or even a very different name from Ethel James although that is not so far away, Ethel James and Henry James. Thomas James can never harden any one to the name James. But nevertheless in no distress Henry James is well-known.

VOLUME XXX

To commence to cover the ground.

VOLUME XXXI

It will soon be thought that anybody can be bought.

It will not soon be thought that anybody can be taught.

What can anybody buy.

Anybody can buy, that anybody can cry.

Henry James moved as he bought.

There are other words that no one need use, caught, fought, taught.

Henry James was meant by all.

Has any country forgot any country.

That is what they try to say.
But what do they say.
That is what there is. What do they say.
For which five mean as six.

VOLUME XXXII

I am going to tell it very well.

VOLUME XXXIII

He knew what was in a name all the same.

VOLUME XXXIV

It has been remarked and it is very curious that in opening a page you know it is that page not by its age not by the words upon the page not by the number upon the page but because on that page there are three names and those three names are not together upon any other of any page.

Now this has been told to me and is it true. If it has been told to me it certainly is true.

Further more it has been told to me that very likely nothing is said upon that page about any one whose name is upon that page. This has been told to me and it is true it is true that it has been told to me.

And in this way you see that everything that has been told to me is true if it has been told to me.

Henry James is well-known as that oh yes as that.

And now consider fortune and misfortune failure and success, butter and water, ham and water cress.

First then fortune and misfortune. He had no fortune and misfortune and nevertheless he had no distress and no relief from any pang. Any pang. Oh yes any pang.

And failure and success. He had no failure and no success and he had no relief from any failure and he had no relief from any distress. Nevertheless. He had no relief not as having had a relief from any other pleasure and anxiety and in that place any removal and any surprise.

This what has been arranged to say has not been said but all that I have heard has been said. Which they may say. Has been said.

Once upon a time nobody managed to be useful and nobody managed to be there.

Once upon a time and tears will flow once upon a time nobody has arranged to be useful and nobody has arranged as yet and further yet not anybody need have been placed to arrange that anybody wept. In place is not the same as in spite of all. And yet well-known is not more easily arranged. In place of that not well-known is not more than more easily arranged.

I wish to help myself to as much as they had more.

That is what they said not to me but not that is not not to me.

And so it happened I wish you to know to know it as often as well as not very-well that is is not not to me.

What they said to me they said as if it were true and what is there to say.

Some do some do tell some do say so, as if it were so. Some some do. Some do do so.

Some do.

Some do not.

But some who do not say so do not say so. They say some do say that some some one does or do. Do what there is or is not to do. Some do.

Gertrude Stein never earned any money from her writing until she was almost sixty years old, when the *Autobiography of Alice B. Toklas* was published in America and became a best-seller. In her book *Everybody's Autobiography* she wrote: 'I had never made any money before in my life and I was most excited. When I was a child I used to be fascinated with the stories of how everybody had earned their first dollar. I always wanted to have earned my first dollar but I never had. I know a lot about money just because I never had earned my first dollar and now I have. We were all amused during the war there was an American over here and he once said he had just made five hundred thousand dollars and he added all honestly earned. Well, that is the way I felt there it was and all honestly earned. I have been writing a lot about money lately, it is a fascinating subject, it is really the difference between men and animals, most of the things men feel animals feel and vice versa, but animals do not know about money, money is purely a human conception and that is very important to know very very important. . . . Anyway the *Saturday Evening Post* printed the little articles I wrote about money then and the young ones said I was reactionary and they said how could I be I who had always been so well ahead of every one and I myself was not and am not certain that I am not again well ahead as ahead as I ever have been.'

These short articles were written in 1936 and printed in the *Saturday Evening Post* between June and October of that year.

23

MONEY

EVERYBODY now just has to make up their mind. Is money money or isn't money money. Everybody who earns it and spends it every day in order to live knows that money is money, anybody who votes it to be gathered in as taxes knows money is not money. That is what makes everybody go crazy.

Once upon a time there was a king and he was called Louis the fifteenth. He spent money as they are spending it now. He just spent it and spent it and one day somebody dared say something to the king about it. Oh, he said, after me the deluge, it would last out his time, and so what was the difference. When this king had begun his reign he was known as Louis the Well-beloved, when he died, nobody even stayed around to close his eyes.

But all the trouble really comes from this question is money

money. Everybody who lives on it every day knows that money is money but the people who vote money, presidents and congress, do not think about money that way when they vote it. I remember when my nephew was a little boy he was out walking somewhere and he saw a lot of horses; he came home and he said, oh papa, I have just seen a million horses. A million, said his father, well anyway, said my nephew, I saw three. That came to be what we all used to say when anybody used numbers that they could not count well anyway a million or three. That is the whole point. When you earn money and spend money every day anybody can know the difference between a million and three. But when you vote money away there really is not any difference between a million and three. And so everybody has to make up their mind is money money for everybody or is it not.

That is what everybody has to think about a lot or everybody is going to be awfully unhappy, because the time does come when the money voted comes suddenly to be money just like the money everybody earns every day and spends every day to live and when that time comes it makes everybody very unhappy. I do wish everybody would make up their mind about money being money.

It is awfully hard for anybody to think money is money when there is more of it than they can count. That is why there ought to be some kind of system that money should not be voted right away. When you spend money that you earn every day you naturally think several times before you spend more than you have, and you mostly do not. Now if there was some arrangement made that when one lot voted to spend money, that they would have to wait a long time, and another lot have to vote, before they vote again to have that money, in short, if there was any way to make a government handle money the way a father of a family has to handle money if there only was. The natural feeling of a father of a family is that when anybody asks him for money he says no. Any father of a family, any member of a family, knows all about that.

So until everybody who votes public money remembers how he feels as a father of a family, when he says no, when anybody in the family wants money, until that time comes, there is going to be a lot of trouble and some years later everybody is going to be very unhappy.

In Russia they tried to decide that money was not money, but now slowly and surely they are coming back to know that money is money.

Whether you like it or whether you do not money is money and that is all there is about it. Everybody knows it. When they earn it and spend what they earn they know it they really know that money is money and when they vote it they do not know it as money.

That is the trouble with everybody, it is awfully hard to really know what you know. When you earn it and spend it you do know the difference between three dollars and a million dollars, but when you say it and vote it, it all sounds the same. Of course it does, it would to anybody, and that is the reason they vote it and keep on voting it. So, now please, everybody, everybody everybody, please, is money money, and if it is, it ought to be the same whether it is what a father of a family earns and spends or a government, if it isn't sooner or later there is disaster.

24

ALL ABOUT MONEY

IT is very funny about money. The thing that differentiates man from animals is money. All animals have the same emotions and the same ways as men. Anybody who has lots of animals around knows that. But the thing no animal can do is count, and the thing no animal can know is money.

Men can count, and they do, and that is what makes them have money.

And so, as long as the earth turns around there will be men on it, and as long as there are men on it, they will count, and they will count money.

Everybody is always counting money.

The queen was in the parlor eating bread and honey the king was in his counting house counting out his money.

That is the way it is and the only trouble comes when they count money without counting it as money.

Counting is funny.

When you see a big store and see so many of each kind of anything that is in it, and on the counters. it is hard to believe that one more or less makes any difference to any one. When you see a cashier in a bank with drawers filled with money, it is hard to realize that one more or less makes any difference. But it does, if you buy it, or if you take it away, or if you sell it, or if you make a mistake in giving it out. Of course it does. But a government, well a government does just that, it does not really believe that when there is such a lot that one more or less does make any difference. It is funny, if you buy anything well it may cost four dollars and fifty-five cents or four hundred and eighty-nine dollars or any other sum, but when government votes money it is always even money. One or five or fifteen or thirty-six more or less does not make any difference. The minute it gets to be billions it does not make any difference, fifteen or twenty-five or thirty-six more or less. Well, everybody has to think about that, because when it is made up it has to be made up by all sorts of odd numbers, everybody who pays taxes knows that, and it does make a difference.

All these odd pieces of money have to go to make that even money that is voted, but does it. It is voted even but it is collected odd. Everybody has to think about it.

25

MORE ABOUT MONEY

WHEN the parliament was invented by England long ago it was mostly done to keep the king from spending too much money.

Since then every country has a parliament but who is there to stop the parliaments from spending too much money. If anybody starts spending money they never stop themselves. If they stop, it is because somebody stops them. And who is to stop congress from spending too much money. Everybody has to think about that now.

In France the chamber has been doing the same thing spending too much money and so everybody voted for the communists hoping that the communists would stop them. Now everybody thinks that the chamber under the communists will just go on spending the money and so a great many frenchmen are thinking of getting back a king, and that the king will stop the french parliament from spending money.

That is funny. Parliament was invented to stop a king spending money and now the french are thinking of getting back a king to stop the parliament from spending all their money.

In America where, ever since George Washington, nobody really can imagine a king, who is to stop congress from spending too much money. They will not stop themselves, that is certain. Everybody has to think about that now. Who is to stop them.

26

STILL MORE ABOUT MONEY

ONE of the funny things is that when there is a great deal of unemployment you can never get any one to do any work. It was true in England it is true in America and it is now true in France. Once unemployment is recognized as unemployment and organized as unemployment nobody starts to work. If you are out of work and you find some work then you go to work. But if you are part of the unemployed then you are part of that, and if work comes you have to change your position from the unemployed to the employed, and then perhaps you will have to change back again, so perhaps you had better just stay where you are.

That is what happens.

We have given up trying to employ french people, those who were not working were unemployed and that was no way of changing them back to work, so we took to Indo-Chinamen. Indo-Chinamen are after all frenchmen, so finally they too became part of the unemployed. I asked one of them, his name is Trac, and why don't any of you stay in a job when you get it. Why he said it's like this. They get ten francs a day as unemployed. Now a

Chinaman can live on five francs a day and that gives him five
francs to gamble. The rest of the time he puts on his hat and goes
out. He takes a temporary job, which still leaves him unemployed,
and buys a new suit of clothes. Then by and by he catches cold,
he goes to a hospital, free, and then he dies, and has a free coffin.
All the Indo-Chinamen in Indo-China want to come to Paris to
live like that. They call that living like frenchmen.

Everybody has to think about the unemployed getting to be that
and is there any way to stop them. Everybody has to think about
that.

27

MY LAST ABOUT MONEY

GETTING rid of the rich does end up very funnily. It is easy to get
rid of the rich but it is not easy to get rid of the poor. Wherever
they have tried it they have got rid of the rich all right and so then
everybody is poor and also there are there more than ever there
of ever so much poorer. And that is natural enough. When there
are the rich you can always take from the rich to give to the poor
but when everybody is poor then you cannot take from the poor
to give to the ever so much poorer and there they are.

That is the inevitable end of too much organization. That
organization business is a funny story.

The beginning of the eighteenth century, after everything had
been completely under feudal and religious domination, was full
of a desire for individual liberty and they went at it until they
thought they had it, which ended up with first the English and then
the American and then the French revolution, so there they were
and everybody was free and then that went on to Lincoln. Then
they began inventing machinery and at the same time they found
virgin lands that could be worked with machinery and so they
began organization, they began factory organization and laborers
organization, and the more they began organization the more
everybody wanted to be organized and the more they were or-

ganized the more everybody liked the slavery of being in an organization.

Just the other day I was reading a Footner detective story and the crooks who were being held together under orders under awful conditions said when somebody tried to free them sure you got to be organized these days you got to have somebody do your thinking for you. And also the other day a very able young man, you would not have expected he would feel that way about it, wrote to me and said after all we are all glad to have Roosevelt do our thinking for us.

That is the logical end of organization and that is where the world is to-day, the beginning of the eighteenth century went in for freedom and ended with the beginning of the nineteenth century that went in for organization.

Now organization is getting kind of used up.

The virgin lands are getting kind of used up, the whole surface of the world is known now and also the air, and everywhere you see organization killing itself by just ending in organization. The more backward countries are still excited about it because they have just heard of it but in their hearts the rest of them know the poor are always there and the very much poorer are always there and what are you going to do about it.

Organization is a failure and everywhere the world over everybody has to begin again.

What are they going to try next, what does the twenty-first century want to do about it? They certainly will not want to be organized, the twentieth century is seeing the end of that, perhaps as the virgin lands will by that time be pretty well used up, and also by that time everybody will have been as quickly everywhere as anybody can be, perhaps they will begin looking for liberty again and individually amusing themselves again and old-fashioned or dirt farming.

One thing is sure until there are rich again everybody will be poor and there will be more than ever of everybody who is even poorer.

That is sure and certain.

Since *Ida* is no ordinary narrative story, it is relevant to quote Gertrude Stein on the subject of narrative. In the third lecture in *Narration* before posing the question 'What do you tell and how do you tell it' she says: 'Narrative has been the telling of anything because there has been always has been a feeling that something followed another thing that there was succession in happening. In a kind of a way what has made the Old Testament such permanently good reading is that really in a way in the Old Testament writing there really was not any such thing there was not really any succession of anything . . . in the Old Testament writing there is really no actual conclusion that anything is progressing that one thing is succeeding another thing, that anything in that sense in the sense of succeeding happening is a narrative of anything, but most writing is based on this thing most writing has been a real narrative writing a telling of the story of anything in the way that thing has been happening and now everything is not that thing there is at present not a sense of anything being successively happening, moving is in every direction beginning and ending is not really exciting, anything is anything, anything is happening. . . . And this has come to be a natural thing in a perfectly natural way that the narrative of to-day is not a narrative of succession as all the writing for a good many hundreds of years has been.'[1]

Ida was written in 1940 and published by Random House, New York, 1941.

28

IDA

First Half

PART ONE

THERE was a baby born named Ida. Its mother held it with her hands to keep Ida from being born but when the time came Ida came. And as Ida came, with her came her twin, so there she was Ida-Ida.

The mother was sweet and gentle and so was the father. The whole family was sweet and gentle except the great-aunt. She was the only exception.

An old woman who was no relation and who had known the great-aunt when she was young was always telling that the great-aunt had had something happen to her oh many years ago, it was a

[1]. *Narration*, University of Chicago Press, 1935. (See footnote 2 on p. 273.)

soldier, and then the great-aunt had had little twins born to her and then she had quietly, the twins were dead then, born so, she had buried them under a pear tree and nobody knew.

Nobody believed the old woman perhaps it was true but nobody believed it, but all the family always looked at every pear tree and had a funny feeling.

The grandfather was sweet and gentle too. He liked to say that in a little while a cherry tree does not look like a pear tree.

It was a nice family but they did easily lose each other.

So Ida was born and a very little while after her parents went off on a trip and never came back. That was the first funny thing that happened to Ida.

The days were long and there was nothing to do.

She saw the moon and she saw the sun and she saw the grass and she saw the streets.

The first time she saw anything it frightened her. She saw a little boy and when he waved to her she would not look his way.

She liked to talk and to sing songs and she liked to change places. Wherever she was she always liked to change places. Otherwise there was nothing to do all day. Of course she went to bed early but even so she always could say, what shall I do now, now what shall I do.

Some one told her to say no matter what the day is it always ends the same day, no matter what happens in the year the year always ends one day.

Ida was not idle but the days were always long even in winter and there was nothing to do.

Ida lived with her great-aunt not in the city but just outside.

She was very young and as she had nothing to do she walked as if she was tall as tall as any one. Once she was lost that is to say a man followed her and that frightened her so that she was crying just as if she had been lost. In a little while that is some time after it was a comfort to her that this had happened to her.

She did not have anything to do and so she had time to think about each day as it came. She was very careful about Tuesday. She always just had to have Tuesday. Tuesday was Tuesday to her.

They always had plenty to eat. Ida always hesitated before eating. That was Ida.

One day it was not Tuesday, two people came to see her great-aunt. They came in very carefully. They did not come in together. First one came and then the other one. One of them had some orange blossoms in her hand. That made Ida feel funny. Who were they? She did not know and she did not like to follow them in. A third one came along, this one was a man and he had orange blossoms in his hat brim. He took off his hat and he said to himself here I am, I wish to speak to myself. Here I am. Then he went on into the house.

Ida remembered that an old woman had once told her that she Ida would come to be so much older that not anybody could be older, although, said the old woman, there was one who was older.

Ida began to wonder if that was what was now happening to her. She wondered if she ought to go into the house to see whether there was really any one with her great-aunt, and then she thought she would act as if she was not living there but was somebody just coming to visit and so she went up to the door and she asked herself is any one at home and when they that is she herself said to herself no there is nobody at home she decided not to go in.

That was just as well because orange blossoms were funny things to her great-aunt just as pear trees were funny things to Ida.

And so Ida went on growing older and then she was almost sixteen and a great many funny things happened to her. Her great-aunt went away so she lost her great-aunt who never really felt content since the orange blossoms had come to visit her. And now Ida lived with her grandfather. She had a dog, he was almost blind not from age but from having been born so and Ida called him Love, she liked to call him naturally she and he liked to come even without her calling him.

It was dark in the morning any morning but since her dog Love was blind it did not make any difference to him.

It is true he was born blind nice dogs often are. Though he was blind naturally she could always talk to him.

One day she said. Listen Love, but listen to everything and listen while I tell you something.

Yes Love she said to him, you have always had me and now you are going to have two, I am going to have a twin yes I am Love, I am tired of being just one and when I am a twin one of us can go out and one of us can stay in, yes Love yes I am yes I am going to have a twin. You know Love I am like that when I have to have it I have to have it. And I have to have a twin, yes Love.

The house that Ida lived in was a little on top of a hill, it was not a very pretty house but it was quite a nice one and there was a big field next to it and trees at either end of the field and a path at one side of it and not very many flowers ever because the trees and the grass took up so very much room but there was a good deal of space to fill with Ida and her dog Love and anybody could understand that she really did have to have a twin.

She began to sing about her twin and this is the way she sang.

Oh dear oh dear Love, that was her dog, if I had a twin well nobody would know which one I was and which one she was and so if anything happened nobody could tell anything and lots of things are going to happen and oh Love I felt it yes I know it I have a twin.

And then she said Love later on they will call me a suicide blonde because my twin will have dyed her hair. And then they will call me a murderess because there will come the time when I will have killed my twin which I first made come. If you make her can you kill her. Tell me Love my dog tell me and tell her.

Like everybody Ida had lived not everywhere but she had lived in quite a number of houses and in a good many hotels. It was always natural to live anywhere she lived and she soon forgot the other addresses. Anybody does. There was nothing funny about Ida but funny things did happen to her.

Ida had never really met a man but she did have a plan.

That was while she was still living with her great-aunt. It was not near the water that is unless you call a little stream water or quite a way off a little lake water, and hills beyond it water. If you do not call all these things water then there where Ida was living was not at all near water but it was near a church.

It was March and very cold. Not in the church that was warm. Ida did not often go to church, she did not know anybody and if you do not know anybody you do not often go to church not to a church that is only open when something is going on.

And then she began to know a family of little aunts. There were five of them, they were nobody's aunts but they felt like aunts and

Ida went to church with them. Somebody was going to preach. Was it about life or politics or love? It certainly was not about death, anyway, they asked Ida to go and they all went. It was crowded inside the church cold outside and hot inside. Ida was separated from the aunts, they were little and she could not see them, she was tall as tall as any one and so they could see her.

There was nothing funny about Ida but funny things did happen to her. There she was there was a crowd it was not very light, and she was close against so many, and then she stayed close against one or two, there might have been more room around her but she did not feel that way about it, anyway it was warm being so close to them and she did not know any of them, she did not see any of them, she looked far away, but she felt something, all right she felt something, and then the lecture or whatever it was was over.

She went out, everybody did, and soon she met the five little aunts, they did not seem to be liking her very much but they all went on together, it was cold it was in March and there was almost snow. There were trees of course there was a sidewalk but nobody was on it except themselves, and then all of a sudden some one a man of course jumped out from behind the trees and there was another with him. Ida said to the aunts go on go on quickly I will walk back of you to protect you, the aunts hurried on, Ida hurried a little less quickly, she turned toward the men but they were gone. The five aunts and Ida went on, they said good night to her but she never saw them again. These were the first and last friends she ever had, and she really never went to church again not really.

When she got home her dog Love met her and she began to sing about her twin and this is the way she sang.

Oh dear oh dear Love (that was her dog), if I had a twin well nobody would know which one I was and which one she was and so if anything happened nobody could tell anything and lots of things are going to happen and oh Love I feel it yes I know I have a twin.

And then she began to look far away and she began to think about her parents. She remembered them when she grew a little older but there were plenty to take care of her and they did. (Think of all the refugees there are in the world just think.) And then one day she looked and she saw some one, she saw two of them but they

were not her parents. She was learning to read and write then and
the first thing she learned was that there were miracles and so she
asked any one to give her one. Then one day, she said she had one.
She sat alone and it was summer and suddenly it was snowing and
as it snowed she saw two dogs a black and a white one both little
and as she looked they both both the little dogs ran away and they
ran away together. Ida said this was a miracle and it was.

Ida gradually was a little older and every time she was a little
older some one else took care of her. She liked the change of address
because in that way she never had to remember what her address
was and she did not like having to remember. It was so easy to
forget the last address and she really forgot to guess what the next
address was.

Little by little she knew how to read and write and really she said
and she was right it was not necessary for her to know anything
else. And so quite gradually little by little she grew older.

She always had a dog, at every address she had a dog and the
dog always had a name and once she had one and its name was
Iris. Just at this time Ida was living up in the mountains. She liked
it up there. But then Ida liked living anywhere. She had lived in
so many places and she liked any where.

Her dog Iris was not afraid of thunder and lightning but he was
afraid of the rain and when it began to rain he ran away from Ida
and then he ran back to her because after all he could not run away
from the rain because the rain followed him. And so he ran back
again to Ida.

And then Ida left there and went to live in a city. She lived with
her old grandfather. He was so old and weak you wondered how he
could walk any farther but he always could. Ida paid no attention
to her grandfather.

While she was in the city funny things happened to her.

It was the month of August. August is a month when if it is hot
weather it is really very hot.

Some funny things happened then. Ida was out, she was always
out or in, both being exciting.

She was out it was towards evening it was time when public
parks were closed and Ida was looking in through the railing, and
she saw right across the corner that some one else was looking

and looking at her. It was a policeman. He was bending down and looking at her. She was not worrying but she did wonder why he was getting down to look at her across the corner. And then she saw next to her a very old woman, well was it or was it not a woman, she had so much clothing on and so many things hanging from her and she was carrying so many things she might have been anything.

Ida went away it was time for her to be at home.

Finally August was over and then it was September.

Sometimes in a public park she saw an old woman making over an old brown dress that is pieces of it to make herself another dress. She had it all on all she owned in the way of clothes and she was very busy. Ida never spoke to her.

Ida was getting to be older. Sometimes she thought about a husband but she knew that a husband meant marriage and marriage meant changes and changes meant names and after all she had so many changes but she did have just that one name Ida and she liked it to stay with her. And then another funny thing happened to her.

It was winter and Ida never wondered because thunder rumbled in winter, that lightning struck and thunder rumbled in winter. It just did.

Ida paid no attention to that but she did one day see a man carrying an advertisement on his back, a sandwich man, that was all right but what was funny was that he stopped and he was talking as if he knew him to a big well dressed rich man.

Ida very quickly went off home.

Then she went to live with another great-aunt outside of the city and there she decided and she told her dog Love about it, she decided that she would be a twin.

She had not yet decided to be a twin when another funny thing happened to her.

She was walking with her dog Love, they were walking and suddenly he left her to bark at something, that something was a man stretched out by the side of the road, not sleeping, because his legs were kicking, not dead, because he was rolling, not happy, because he just was not, and he was dressed in soldier's clothing. Love the dog went up to him, not to sniff, not to bark, he just went up to him and when Ida came near she saw he was not a white man, he was an

Arab, and of course the dog Love did not bark at him. How could he when an Arab smells of herbs and fields and not of anything human? Ida was not frightened, he got up the Arab and he began to make motions of drinking. Ida might have been frightened if it had been toward evening, which it was, and she had been all alone, which she was, but she motioned back that she had nothing, and the Arab got up, and stood, and then suddenly, he went away. Ida instead of going on the way she was going went back the way she had come.

She heard about religion but she never really did happen to have any. One day, it was summer, she was in another place and she saw a lot of people under the trees and she went too. They were there and some one was moving around among them, they were all sitting and kneeling, not all of them but most of them and in the middle there was one slowly walking and her arms were slowly moving and everybody was following and some when their arms were started moving could not stop their arms from going on moving. Ida stayed as long as she could and then she went away. She always stayed as long as she could.

One day, it was before or after she made up her mind to be a twin, she joined a walking marathon. She kept on moving, sleeping or walking, she kept on slowly moving. This was one of the funny things that happened to her. Then she lived outside of a city, she was eighteen then, she decided that she had had enough of only being one and she told her dog Love that she was going to be two she was going to be a twin. And this did then happen.

Ida often wrote letters to herself that is to say she wrote to her twin.

Dear Ida my twin

Here I am sitting not alone because I have dear Love with me, and I speak to him and he speaks to me, but here I am all alone and I am thinking of you Ida my dear twin. Are you beautiful as beautiful as I am dear twin Ida, are you, and if you are perhaps I am not. I can not go away Ida, I am here always, if not here then somewhere, but just now I am here, I am like that, but you dear Ida you are not, you are not here, if you were I could not write to you. Do you know what I think Ida, I think that you could be a queen of beauty, one of the ones they elect when everybody has a vote. They are elected and they go everywhere and everybody looks at them and everybody sees them. Dear Ida oh dear Ida do do be one. Do not let them know you have any name but Ida and I know Ida will win, Ida Ida Ida,

from your twin
Ida

Ida sat silently looking at her dog Love and playing the piano softly until the light was dim. Ida went out first locking the door she went out and as she went out she knew she was a beauty and that they would all vote for her. First she had to find the place where they were going to vote, but that did not make any difference anywhere would do they would vote for her just anywhere, she was such a beauty.

As she went she saw a nicely dressed little girl with a broken arm who threw a stone at a window. It was the little girl's right arm that was broken. This was a sign.

So when Ida arrived they voted that she was a great beauty and the most beautiful and the completest beauty and she was for that year the winner of the beauty prize for all the world. Just like that. It did happen. Ida was her name and she had won.

Nobody knew anything about her except that she was Ida but that was enough because she was Ida the beauty Ida.

PART TWO

There was an older man who happened to go in where they were voting. He did not know they were voting for the prize beauty but once there he voted too. And naturally he voted for her. Anybody would. And so she won. The only thing for her to do then was to go home which she did. She had to go a long way round otherwise they would have known where she lived of course she had to give an address and she did, and she went there and then she went back outside of the city where she was living.

On the way, just at the end of the city she saw a woman carrying a large bundle of wash. This woman stopped and she was looking at a photograph, Ida stopped too and it was astonishing, the woman was looking at the photograph, she had it in her hand, of Ida's dog Love. This was astonishing.

Ida was so surprised she tried to snatch the photograph and just then an automobile came along, there were two women in it, and the automobile stopped and they stepped out to see what was happening. Ida snatched the photograph from the woman who was busy looking at the automobile and Ida jumped into the automobile and tried to start it, the two women jumped into the automobile threw Ida out and went on in the automobile with the photograph. Ida and the woman with a big bundle of wash were left there. The two of them stood and did not say a word.

Ida went away, she was a beauty, she had won the prize she was judged to be the most beautiful but she was bewildered and then she saw a package on the ground. One of the women in the automobile must have dropped it. Ida picked it up and then she went away.

So then Ida did everything an elected beauty does but every now and then she was lost.

One day she saw a man he looked as if he had just come off a farm and with him was a very little woman and behind him was an ordinary-sized woman. Ida wondered about them. One day she saw again the woman with a big bundle of wash. She was talking to a man, he was a young man. Ida came up near them. Just then an automobile with two women came past and in the automobile was Ida's dog Love, Ida was sure it was Love, of course it was Love and in its mouth it had a package, the same package Ida had picked up. There it all was and the woman with the bundle of wash and the young man and Ida, they all stood and looked and they did not any one of them say anything.

Ida went on living with her great-aunt, there where they lived just outside of the city, she and her dog Love and her piano. She did write letters very often to her twin Ida.

Dear Ida, she said.

Dear Ida

So pleased so very pleased that you are winning, I might even call you Winnie because you are winning. You have won being a beautiful one the most beautiful one. One day I was walking with my dog Love and a man came up to him, held out his hand to him and said how do you do you the most beautiful one. I thought he was a very funny man and now they have decided that you are the one the most beautiful one.

And one day the day you won, I saw a funny thing, I saw my dog Love belonging to some one. He did not belong to me he did belong to them. That made me feel very funny, but really it is not true he is here he belongs to me and you and now I will call you Winnie because you are winning everything and I am so happy that you are my twin.

Your twin, Ida-Ida

And so Winnie was coming to be known to be Winnie.

Winnie Winnie is what they said when they saw her and they were beginning to see her.

They said it different ways. They said Winnie. And then they said Winnie.

She knew.

It is easy to make everybody say Winnie, yes Winnie. Sure I know Winnie. Everybody knows who Winnie is. It is not so easy, but there it is, everybody did begin to notice that Winnie is Winnie.

This quite excited Ida and she wrote more letters to Winnie.

Dear Winnie

Everybody knows who you are, and I know who you are. Dear Winnie we are twins and your name is Winnie. Never again will I not be a twin,

Your twin
Ida

So many things happened to Winnie. Why not when everybody knew her name.

Once there were two people who met together. They said. What shall we do? So what did they do. They went to see Winnie. That is they went to look at Winnie.

When they looked at her they almost began to cry. One said. What if I did not look at her did not look at Winnie. And the other said. Well that is just the way I feel about it.

After a while they began to think that they had done it, that they had seen Winnie, that they had looked at her. It made them nervous because perhaps really had they.

One said to the other. Say have we and the other answered back, say have we.

Did you see her said one of them. Sure I saw her did you. Sure he said sure I saw her.

They went back to where they came from.

One day Ida went to buy some shoes. She liked to look at yellow shoes when she was going to buy red ones. She liked to look at black shoes when she was not going to buy any shoes at all.

It was crowded in the shoe store. It was the day before Easter.

There were a great many places but each one had some one, it is hard to try on shoes standing, hard, almost impossible and so she waited for her turn, a man was sitting next to his wife who was trying on shoes, he was not, and so not Ida but the saleswoman told him to get up, he did, and he did not look at Ida. Ida was used to that.

The place was full, nobody looked at Ida. Some of them were talking about Winnie. They said. But really, is Winnie so interesting? They just talked and talked about that.

So that is the way life went on.

There was Winnie.

Once in a while a man is a man and he comes from Omaha, where they catch all they can. He almost caught Ida. It happened like this.

He went out one night and he saw Winnie. Winnie was always there. She went everywhere.

He followed Winnie.

He did it very well.

The next day he went and rang the bell.

He asked for Winnie.

Of course there was no Winnie.

That was not surprising and did not surprise him.

He could not ask for Ida because he did not know Ida. He almost asked for Ida. Well in a way he did ask for Ida.

Ida came.

Ida was not the same as Winnie. Not at all.

Ida and he, the man from Omaha said. How do you do. And then they said. Good-bye.

The Omaha man went away. He did follow Winnie again but he never rang the bell again. He knew better.

Ida lived alone. She tried to make her dog Iris notice birds but he never did. If he had she would have had more to do because she would have had to notice them too.

It is funny the kind of life Ida led but all the same it kept her going day after day.

But all the same something did happen.

One day she was there doing nothing and suddenly she felt very funny. She knew she had lost something. She looked everywhere and she could not find out what it was that she had lost but she knew she had lost something. All of a sudden she felt or rather she heard somebody call to her. She stopped, she really had not been walking but anyway she stopped and she turned and she heard them say, Ida is that you Ida. She saw somebody coming toward her. She had never seen them before. There were three of them, three women. But soon there was only one. That one came right along. It is funny isn't it. She said. Yes said Ida. There, said the woman, I told them I knew it was.

That was all that happened.

They all three went away.

Ida did not go on looking for what she had lost, she was too excited.

She remembered that one day in front of the house a man with a hat a cane and a bottle stopped. He put down the cane but then he did not know what to do with his hat, so he began again. He put his cane into a window so that stuck out, and he hung his hat on the cane and then with the bottle he stood up. This, he said, is a bottle and in it there is wine, and I who am drunk am going to drink this wine. He did.

And then he said.

It might be like having a handkerchief in a drawer and never taking it out but always knowing it was there. It would always be new and nobody ever would be through with having it there.

What is peace what is war said the man, what is beauty what is ice, said the man. Where is my hat, said the man, where is my wine said the man. I have a cane, he said, I have a hat, he said, I have a bottle full of wine. Good-bye, he said, but Ida had gone away.

She had certain habits. When she counted ten she always counted them on her fingers to make ten times ten. It was very hard to remember how many times she had counted ten when once she had counted them because she had to remember twice and then when she had counted a hundred then what happened. Really nothing.

Ida just sat down. Living alone as she did counting was an occupation.

She was walking and she saw a woman and three children, two little girls and a little boy. The boy was carrying a black coat on his arms, a large one.

A woman said to Ida, I only like a white skin. If when I die I come back again and I find I have any other kind of skin then I will be sure that I was very wicked before.

This made Ida think about talking.

She commenced to talk. She liked to see people eat, in restaurants and wherever they eat, and she liked to talk. You can always talk with army officers. She did.

Army officers do not wear their uniforms in the cities, soldiers do but officers do not. This makes conversation with them easier and more difficult.

If an officer met Ida he said, how do you do and she answered very well I thank you. They were as polite as that.

He said to her. Thank you for answering me so pleasingly, and she said. You are very welcome.

The officer would then go on conversing.

What is it that you like better than anything else, he asked and she said. I like being where I am. Oh said he excitedly, and where are you. I am not here, she said, I am very careful about that. No I am not here, she said, it is very pleasant, she added and she turned slightly away, very pleasant indeed not to be here.

The officer smiled. I know he said I know what you mean. Winnie is your name and that is what you mean by your not being here.

She suddenly felt very faint. Her name was not Winnie it was Ida, there was no Winnie. She turned toward the officer and she said to him. I am afraid very much afraid that you are mistaken. And she went away very slowly. The officer looked after her but he did not follow her. Nobody could know in looking at him that he was an officer because he did not wear a uniform and he did not know whether she knew it or not.

Perhaps she did and perhaps she did not.

Every day after that Ida talked to some officer.

If I am an officer, said an officer to Ida, and I am an officer. I am an officer and I give orders. Would you, he said looking at Ida.

Would you like to see me giving orders. Ida looked at him and did not answer. If I were to give orders and everybody obeyed me and they do, said the officer, would that impress you. Ida looked at him, she looked at him and the officer felt that she must like him, otherwise she would not look at him and so he said to her, you do like me or else you would not look at me. But Ida sighed. She said, yes and no. You see, said Ida, I do look at you but that is not enough. I look at you and you look at me but we neither of us say more than how do you do and very well I thank you, if we do then there is always the question. What is your name. And really, said Ida, if I knew your name I would not be interested in you, no, I would not, and if I do not know your name. I could not be interested, certainly I could not. Good-bye, said Ida, and she went away.

Ida not only said good-bye but she went away to live somewhere else.

Once upon a time way back there were always gates, gates that opened so that you could go in and then little by little there were no fences no walls anywhere. For a little time they had a gate even when there was no fence. It was there just to look elegant and it was nice to have a gate that would click even if there was no fence. By and by there was no gate.

Ida when she had a dog had often stood by a gate and she would hold the dog by the hand and in this way they would stand.

But that was long ago and Ida did not think of anything except now. Why indeed was she always alone if there could be anything to remember. Why indeed.

And so nothing happened to her yet. Not yet.

One day Ida saw a moth that was flying and it worried her. It was one of the very few things that ever worried Ida. She said to an officer. This was another officer. There is an army and there is a navy and there are always lots of officers. Ida said to this one. When you put your uniform away for the summer you are afraid of moths. Yes said the officer. I understand that, said Ida, and she slowly drifted away, very thoughtfully, because she knew of this. Alone and she was alone and she was afraid of moths and of mothballs. The two go together.

Ida rarely coughed. She had that kind of health.

In New England there are six states, Maine, Massachusetts,

Vermont, New Hampshire, Connecticut and Rhode Island.

Ida turned up in Connecticut. She was living there quite naturally, quietly living there. She had a friend who was tall and thin
and her eyes were gray and her hair was messed and she dressed in
black and she was thin and her legs were long and she wore a large
hat. She did not mind the sun but she did wear a wide-brimmed hat.
Yes she did. She was like that. Yes she was.

This friend did not interest Ida. She saw her, yes, but she did not
interest her.

Except this one woman nobody knew Ida in Connecticut. For a
while she did not talk to anybody there. She spent the day sitting
and then that was a day. On that day she heard somebody say
something. They said who is Winnie. The next day Ida left
Connecticut.

She began to think about what would happen if she were married.

As she was leaving Connecticut she began to listen to a man. He
was an officer in the army. His name was Sam Hamlin. He was a
lively Sam Hamlin. He said if he had a wife he could divorce her.
He came originally from Connecticut and he was still in Connecticut. He said the only way to leave Connecticut was to go out of it.
But he never would. If he had left Connecticut he might have
gotten to Washington, perhaps to Utah and Idaho, and if he had
he might have gotten lost. That is the way he felt about Connecticut.

Little by little very little by little he said it all to Ida. He said I
know, and he said when I say I know I mean it is just like that.
I like, he said to Ida, I like everything I say to be said out loud.

He said I know. He said I know you, and he not only said it to
Ida but he said it to everybody, he knew Ida he said hell yes he
knew Ida. He said one day to Ida it is so sweet to have soft music it
is so sweet.

He told her how once upon a time he had been married and he
said to her. Now listen. Once upon a time I was married, by the
time you came to Connecticut I wasn't. Now you say you are leaving Connecticut. The only way to leave Connecticut is to go out,
and I am not going out of Connecticut. Listen to me, he said, I am
not going out of Connecticut. I am an officer in the army and of
course perhaps they will send me out of Connecticut there is
Massachusetts and Rhode Island and New Hampshire and Vermont

and Maine but I am going to stay in Connecticut, believe it or not I am.

Ida left Connecticut and that was the first time Ida thought about getting married and it was the last time anybody said Winnie anywhere near her.

There was a woman in California her name was Eleanor Angel and she had a property and on that property she found gold and silver and she found platinum and radium. She did not find oil. She wrote to everybody about it and they were all excited, anybody would be, and they did believe it, and they said it was interesting if it was true and they were sure it was true.

Ida went out to stay with her.

Ida was never discouraged and she was always going out walking.

As she walked along, she thought about men and she thought about presidents. She thought about how some men are more presidents than other men when they happen to be born that way and she said to herself. Which one is mine. She knew that there must be one that could be hers one who would be a president. And so she sat down and was very satisfied to do nothing.

Sit down, somebody said to her, and she sat.

Well it was not that one. He sat too and then that was that.

Ida always looked again to see if it was that one or another one, the one she had seen or not, and sometimes it was not.

Then she would sit down not exactly to cry and not exactly to sit down but she did sit down and she felt very funny, she felt as if it was all being something and that was what always led her on.

Ida saw herself come, then she saw a man come, then she saw a man go away, then she saw herself go away.

And all the time well all the time she said something, she said nice little things, she said all right, she said I do.

Was she on a train or an automobile, an airplane or just walking.

Which was it.

Well she was on any of them and everywhere she was just talking. She was saying, yes yes I like to be sitting. Yes I like to be moving. Yes I have been here before. Yes it is very pleasant here. Yes I will come here again. Yes I do wish to have them meet, I meet them and they meet me and it is very nice.

Ida never sighed, she just rested. When she rested she turned a little and she said, yes dear. She said that very pleasantly.

This was all of Ida's life just then.

She said. I do not like birds.

She liked mechanical birds but not natural birds. Natural birds always sang.

She sat with her friend and they talked together. Ida said, I am never tired and I am never very fresh. I change all the time. I say to myself, Ida, and that startles me and then I sit still.

Her friend said, I will come again.

Do said Ida.

It was very quiet all day long but Ida was ready for that.

Ida married Frank Arthur.

Arthur had been born right in the middle of a big country.

He knew when he was a tiny boy that the earth was round so it was never a surprise to him. He knew that trees had green leaves and that there was snow when time for snow came and rain when time for rain came. He knew a lot.

When Arthur was little he knew a handsome boy who had a club-foot and was tall and thin and worked for a farmer.

The boy with the club-foot rode a bicycle and he would stand and lean on his bicycle and tell Arthur everything.

He told him all about dogs.

He told him how a little dog, once he had found out about it, would just go on making love to anything, the hind leg of a big dog, a leg of a table, anything, he told him how a young hunting dog's voice changed, it cracked just like boys' voices did and then it went up and down and then finally it settled down. He told him about shepherds' dogs, how shepherds only could work their dogs eight years that when the dog was nine years old the shepherd had to hang him, that often the shepherd was awfully sad and cried like anything when he had to hang his dog to kill him but he could not keep him after the dog was eight years old, they did not really care anything for sheep after that and how could you feed a dog if he did not care about sheep any more and so the shepherds sometimes cried a lot but when the dog was eight years old they did hang him. Then he told Arthur about another dog and a girl. She always used to give that dog a lump of sugar whenever she saw him. She was a girl in a store where they sold sugar, and then one day she saw the man come in who had the dog, and when he came she said where is the dog and he said the dog is dead. She had the piece of sugar in her hand and when he said that she put the piece of sugar in her mouth and ate it and then she burst out crying.

He told Arthur about sheep, he told him that sheep were curious about everything but mostly about dogs, they always were looking for a dog who looked like a sheep and sometimes they found one and when they did they the young ones the baby sheep were pleased, but the older ones were frightened, as soon as they saw a dog who really looked like a sheep, and they ran at him and tried to butt him.

He also told Arthur about cows, he said cows were not always willing, he said some cows hated everything. He also told him about bulls. He said bulls were not very interesting.

He used to stand, the boy with a club-foot, leaning on his bicycle and telling Arthur everything.

When Arthur was a little bigger he came to know a man, not a tall man. He was a fairly little man and he was a good climber. He could climb not only in and out of a window but out of the top of a door if the door was closed. He was very remarkable. Arthur asked him and he then heard him say that he never thought about anything else than climbing. Why should he when he could climb anything.

Arthur was not very good at climbing. All he could do was to listen to the little man. He told about how he climbed to the top of a gate, to the top of a door, to the top of a pole. The little man's name was Bernard. He said it was the same name as that of a saint. Then well naturally then he went away. He finally did go away alone.

Arthur was almost old enough to go away. Pretty soon he did go away.

He tried several ways of going away and finally he went away on a boat and got shipwrecked and had his ear frozen.

He liked that so much that he tried to get shipwrecked again but he never did. He tried it again and again, he tried it on every kind of boat but they never were wrecked again. Finally he said, Once and not again.

He did lots of things before he went back to the middle of the big country where he had been born.

Finally he became an officer in the army and he married Ida but
before that he lived around.

One of the things he did was to sleep in a bed under a bridge.
The bed was made of cardboard. He was not the first to make it.
Somebody else made it but when Arthur had no place to go because
he had used up all his money he used to go to sleep there. Some one
always was asleep there. Day and night there was always somebody
sleeping there. Arthur was one who when he woke up shaved and
washed himself in the river, he always carried the things with him.

It was a nice time then. Instead of working or having his money
Arthur just listened to anybody. It made him sleepy and he was
never more than half awake and in his sleep he had a way of talking
about sugar and cooking. He also used to talk about medicine glasses.

Arthur never fished in a river. He had slept too often under a
bridge to care anything about going fishing. One evening he met a
man who had been fishing. They talked a little and the man said
that he was not much good at fishing, he saw the fish but he never
could catch them. Finally he said to Arthur, do you know who I am.
No said Arthur. Well said the man taking off his hat, I am chief of
police. Well why can't you catch fish, said Arthur. Well I caught a
trout the other day and he got away from me. Why didn't you take
his number said Arthur. Because fish can't talk was the answer.

Arthur often wished on a star, he said star bright, star light, I
wish I may I wish I might have the wish I wish tonight.

The wish was that he would be a king or rich.

There is no reason why a king should be rich or a rich man should
be a king, no reason at all.

Arthur had not yet come to decide which one was the one for
him. It was easy enough to be either the one or the other one. He
just had to make up his mind, be rich or be a king and then it would
just happen. Arthur knew that much.

Well anyway he went back to where he came from, he was in the
middle of his country which was a big one and he commenced to
cry. He was so nervous when he found himself crying that he lay
full length on the ground turned on his stomach and dug his palms
into the ground.

He decided to enter the army and he became an officer and some
few years after he met Ida.

He met her on the road one day and he began to walk next to her and they managed to make their feet keep step. It was just like a walking marathon.

He began to talk. He said. All the world is crying crying about it all. They all want a king.

She looked at him and then she did not. Everybody might want a king but anybody did not want a queen.

It looks, said Arthur, as if it was sudden but really it took me some time, some months even a couple of years, to understand how everybody wants a king.

He said. Do you know the last time I was anywhere I was with my mother and everybody was good enough to tell me to come again. That was all long ago. Everybody was crying because I went away, but I was not crying. That is what makes anybody a king that everybody cries but he does not.

Philip was the kind that said everything out loud.

I knew her, he said and he said he knew Ida, hell he said, yes I know Ida. He said it to every one, he said it to her. He said he knew her.

Ida never saw Arthur again.

She just did not.

She went somewhere and there she just sat, she did not even have a dog, she did not have a town, she lived alone and just sat.

She went out once in a while, she listened to anybody talking about how they were waiting for a fall in prices.

She saw a sign up that said please pay the unemployed and a lot of people were gathered around and were looking.

It did not interest her. She was not unemployed. She just sat and she always had enough. Anybody could.

Somebody came and asked her where Arthur was. She said, Arthur was gone.

Pretty soon she was gone and when she was gone nobody knew what to say.

They did not know she was gone but she was.

They wanted to read about her but as there was nothing written about her they could not read about her. So they just waited.

Ida went to live with a cousin of her uncle.

He was an old man and he could gild picture frames so that they looked as if they had always had gold on them. He was a good man that old man and he had a son, he sometimes thought that he had two sons but anyway he had one and that one had a garage and he made a lot of money. He had a partner and they stole from one another. One day the son of the old man was so angry because the partner was most successful in getting the most that he up and shot him. They arrested him. They put him in jail. They condemned him to twenty years hard labor because the partner whom he had killed had a wife and three children. The man who killed the other one had no children that is to say his wife had one but it was not his. Anyway there it was. His mother spent all her time in church praying that her son's soul should be saved. The wife of their doctor said it was all the father and mother's fault, they had brought up their son always to think of money, always of money, had not they the old man and his wife got the cousin of the doctor's wife always to give them presents of course they had.

Ida did not stay there very long. She went to live with the cousin of the doctor's wife and there she walked every day and had her dog. The name of this dog was Claudine. Ida did not keep her. She gave her away.

She began to say to herself Ida dear Ida do you want to have two sisters or do you want to be one.

There were five sisters once and Ida might have been one.

Anybody likes to know about then and now, Ida was one and it is easy to have one sister and be a twin too and be a triplet three and be a quartet and four and be a quintuplet it is easy to have four but that just about does shut the door.

Ida began to be known.

As she walked along people began to be bewildered as they saw her and they did not call out to her but some did begin to notice her. Was she a twin well was she.

She went away again. Going away again was not monotonous although it seemed so. Ida ate no fruit. It was the end of the week and she had gone away and she did not come back there.

Pretty soon she said to herself Now listen to me, I am here and I know it, if I go away I will not like it because I am so used to my being here. I would not know what has happened, now just listen to me, she said to herself, listen to me, I am going to stop talking and I will.

Of course she had gone away and she was living with a friend.

How many of those who are yoked together have ever seen oxen.

This is what Ida said and she cried. Her eyes were full of tears and she waited and then she went over everything that had ever happened and in the middle of it she went to sleep.

When she awoke she was talking.

How do you do she said.

First she was alone and then soon everybody was standing listening. She did not talk to them.

Of course she did think about marrying. She had not married yet but she was going to marry.

She said if I was married I'd have children and if I had children then I'd be a mother and if I was a mother I'd tell them what to do.

She decided that she was not going to marry and was not going to have children and was not going to be a mother.

Ida decided that she was just going to talk to herself. Anybody could stand around and listen but as for her she was just going to talk to herself.

She no longer even needed a twin.

Somebody tried to interrupt her, he was an officer of course but how could he interrupt her if she was not talking to him but just talking to herself.

She said how do you do and people around answered her and said how do you do. The officer said how do you do, here I am, do you like peaches and grapes in winter, do you like chickens and bread and asparagus in summer. Ida did not answer, of course not.

It was funny the way Ida could go to sleep and the way she could cry and the way she could be alone and the way she could lie down and the way anybody knew what she did and what she did not do.

Ida thought she would go somewhere else but then she knew that she would look at everybody and everything and she knew it would not be interesting.

She was interesting.

She remembered everything and she remembered everybody but she never talked to any of them, she was always talking to herself.

She said to herself. How old are you, and that made her cry.

Then she went to sleep and oh it was so hard not to cry. So hard.

So Ida decided to earn a living. She did not have to, she never had to but she decided to do it.

There are so many ways of earning a living and most of them are failures. She thought it was best to begin with one way which would be most easy to leave. So she tried photography and then she tried just talking.

It is wonderful how easy it is to earn a living that way. To be sure sometimes everybody thinks you are starving but you never are. Ida never starved.

Once she stayed a week in a hotel by herself. She said when she saw the man who ran it, how often do you have your hotel full. Quite often he answered. Well, said Ida, wait awhile and I will leave and then everybody will come, but while I am here nobody will come. Why not said the hotel keeper. Because said Ida, I want to be in the hotel all alone. I only want you and your wife and your three boys and your girl and your father and your mother and your sister in it while I am here. Nobody else. But do not worry, you will not have to keep the others out, they will not come while I am here.

Ida was right. The week she was there nobody came to eat or sleep in the hotel. It just did happen that way.

Ida was very much interested in the wife of the hotel keeper who was sweet-voiced and managed everything because Ida said that sooner or later she would kill herself, she would go out of a window, and the hotel would go to pieces.

Ida knew just what was going to happen. This did not bother her at all. Mostly before it happened she had gone away.

Once she was caught.

It was in a hilly country.

She knew two young men there, one painted in water colors and the other was an engineer. They were brothers. They did not look alike.

Ida sat down on a hillside. A brother was on each side of her.

The three sat together and nothing was said.

Then one brother said. I like to sit here where nothing is ever said. The other brother said. I I like bread, I like to sit here and eat bread. I like to sit here and look about me. I like to sit here and watch the trees grow. I like to sit here.

Ida said nothing. She did not hear what they said. Ida liked sitting. They all three did.

One brother said, It pleases me very much that I have discovered how prettily green looks next to blue and how water looks so well rushing down hill. I am going away for a little while. He said this to his brother. He got up and he went away.

His brother who was very polite did not go away as long as Ida stayed. He sat on and Ida sat on. They did not go to sleep but they almost stopped breathing. The brother said out loud. I am talking to myself. I am not disturbing any one. I feel it is better that everybody is dangerous than that they are not and if they are everybody will either die or be killed.

He waited a minute to listen to himself and then he went on.

I feel that it is easy to expect that we all wish to do good but do we. I know that I will follow any one who asks me to do anything. I myself am strong and I will help myself to anything I need.

Ida paid no attention.

Slowly this other brother went away.

Ida sat on. She said to herself. If a great many people were here and they all said hello Ida, I would not stand up, they would all stand up. If everybody offered me everything I would not refuse anything because everything is mine without my asking for it or refusing it.

Ida understood what she was saying, she knew who she was and she knew it was better that nobody came there. If they did she would not be there, not just yet.

It is not easy to forget all that. Ida did not say that but it is true it is not easy to forget all that.

It was very quiet all day long but Ida was ready for that.

And then she went away.

She went away on a train in an automobile by airplane and walking.

When she answered she looked around for water she looked around for a bay, for a plowed field and then she saw a man standing and she said to him, do you live here. The man said no.

Ida was always ready to wait but there was nothing to wait for here and she went away.

When she came to the next place she had better luck. She saw two men standing and she said to them, do you live here. They both said, they did. That did seem a good place to begin and Ida began.

This time she did not talk to herself she talked to them.

She sat down and the two men sat down. Ida began. She said. Do you know that I have just come. Yes said one of the men because we have never seen you before.

The other man said, Perhaps you are not going to stay.

I am not answered Ida.

Well then said one of the men it is not interesting and I am not listening.

Ida got very angry.

You are not listening to me, she said, you do not know what you are saying, if I talk you have to listen to what I say, there is nothing else you can do.

Then she added.

I never talk much anyway so if you like both of you can go away.

They both did go away.

Ida sat down. She was very satisfied to be sitting.

Sit again she said to some one and they sat, they just sat.

I do not think that Ida could like Benjamin Williams.

He did get up again and he did walk on.

Ida was not careful about whom she met, how could she be if she was always walking or sitting and she very often was.

She saw anybody who was on her way. That was her way. A nice way.

Ida went back again not to Connecticut but to New Hampshire. She sighed when she said New Hampshire.

New Hampshire, she said, is near Vermont and when did I say Vermont and New Hampshire.

Very often, she whispered, very often.

That was her answer.

This time she was married.

PART THREE

Ida did not get married so that never again would she be alone. As a matter of fact until the third time she was married she would not be married long. This first time she was married her husband came

from Montana. He was the kind that when he was not alone he
would look thoughtful. He was the kind that knew that in Montana
there are mountains and that mountains have snow on them. He
was not born in Montana. He had not lived very long in Montana,
he would leave Montana, he had to to marry Ida and he was very
thoughtful.

Ida, he said and then he sighed.

Oh Ida, he said.

How often, he said, how often have I said, Oh Ida.

He was careful. He began to count. He counted the number of
times he said, Oh Ida.

It is not easy to count, said he to himself because when I count, I
lose count.

Oh dear he said, it is lovely in Montana, there are mountains in
Montana and the mountains are very high and just then he looked
up and he saw them and he decided, it was not very sudden, he
decided he would never see Montana again and he never did.

He went away from Montana and he went to Virginia. There he
saw trees and he was so pleased. He said I wonder if Ida has ever
seen these trees. Of course she had. It was not she who was blind,
it was her dog Iris.

Funnily enough even if Ida did see trees she always looked on the
ground to see what had fallen from the trees. Leaves might and nuts
and even feathers and flowers. Even water could fall from a tree.
When it did well there was her umbrella. She had a very pretty
short umbrella. She had lost two and now she had the third. Her
husband said, Oh Ida.

Ida's husband did not love his father more than he did his mother
or his mother more than he did his father.

Ida and he settled down together and one night she dreamed of
a field of orchids, white orchids each on their stalk in a field. Such a
pretty girl to have dreamed of white orchids each on its stalk in a
field. That is what she dreamed.

And she dreamed that now she was married, she was not Ida she
was Virginia. She dreamed that Virginia was her name and that she
had been born in Wyoming not in Montana. She dreamed that
she often longed for water. She dreamed that she said. When I close
my eyes I see water and when I close my eyes I do see water.

What is water, said Virginia.

And then suddenly she said. Ida.

Ida was married and they went to live in Ohio. She did not love anybody in Ohio.

She liked apples. She was disappointed but she did not sigh. She got sunburned and she had a smile on her face. They asked her did she like it. She smiled gently and left it alone. When they asked her again she said not at all. Later on when they asked her did she like it she said. Perhaps only not yet.

Ida left Ohio.

As she left they asked her can you come again. Of course that is what she said, she said she could come again. Somebody called out, who is Ida, but she did not hear him, she did not know that they were asking about her, she really did not.

Ida did not go directly anywhere. She went all around the world. It did not take her long and everything she saw interested her.

She remembered all the countries there were but she did not count them.

First they asked her, how long before you have to go back to Washington.

Second they said, how soon after you get back to Washington will you go back to Ohio.

Thirdly they asked her. How do you go back to Washington from Ohio.

She always answered them.

She did not pay much attention to weather. She had that kind of money to spend that made it not make any difference about weather.

Ida had not been in love very much and if she were there she was.

Some said, Please like her.

They said regularly. Of course we like her.

Ida began to travel again.

She went from Washington to Wyoming, from Wyoming to Virginia and then she had a kind of feeling that she had never been in Washington although of course she had and she went there again.

She said she was going there just to see why they cry.

That is what they do do there.

She knew just how far away one state is from another. She said to herself. Yes it is all whole.

And so there she was in Washington and her life was going to begin. She was not a twin.

Once upon a time a man had happened to begin walking. He lived in Alabama and walking made it seem awfully far away. While he was walking all of a sudden he saw a tree and on that tree was a bird and the bird had its mouth open. The bird said Ida, anyway it sounded like Ida, and the man, his name was Frederick, Frederick saw the bird and he heard him and he said, that kind of a bird is a mocking bird. Frederick went on walking and once every once in a while he saw another tree and he remembered that a bird had said Ida or something like Ida. That was happening in Alabama.

Frederick went into the army became an officer and came to Washington. There he fell in love with a woman, was she older was she younger or was she the same age. She was not older perhaps she was younger, very likely she was not the same age as his age.

Her name was not Ida.

Ida was in Washington.

If there are two little dogs little black dogs and one of them is a female and the other a male, the female does not look as foolish as the male, no not.

So Ida did not look foolish and neither she was.

She might have been foolish.

Saddest of all words are these, she might have been.

Ida felt very well.

PART FOUR

So Ida settled down in Washington. This is what happened every day.

Ida woke up. After a while she got up. Then she stood up. Then she ate something. After that she sat down.

That was Ida.

And Ida began her life in Washington. In a little while there were more of them there who sat down and stood up and leaned. Then they came in and went out. This made it useful to them and to Ida.

Ida said. I am not careful. I do not win him to come away. If he goes away I will not have him. Ida said I can count any one up to ten. When I count up to ten I stop counting. When she said that

they listened to her. They were taken with her beginning counting
and she counted from one to ten. Of course they listened to her.

Ida knew that. She knew that it is not easy to count while anybody listens to them, but it is easy to listen to them while they are
counting.

More and more came to see Ida. Frederick came to see Ida.

Little by little Frederick fell in love with Ida. Ida did not stop
him. He did not say that he was in love with her. He did not say
that, not that.

And then he was and then they were all there together.

He married her and she married him.

Then suddenly not at all suddenly, they were sent there, he was
in the army, they got up and had decided to leave for Ohio.
Yesterday or today they would leave for Ohio.

When they got to Ohio, Ohio is a state, it is only spelled with
four letters. All of a sudden there they were in Ohio.

Ohio very likely was as large as that.

Everybody said to Ida and they said it to Frederick too. Smile at
me please smile at me.

Ida smiled.

They settled down in Ohio.

What did they do in Ohio.

Well they did not stay there long.

They went to Texas.

There they really settled down.

It is easier for an officer in the army to settle down in Texas than
in Ohio.

Ida said one day.

Is there anything strange in just walking along.

One day in Texas it was not an accident, believe it or not, a lizard
did sit there. It was almost black all over and curled, with yellow
under and over, hard to tell, it was so curled, but probably
under.

Ida was not frightened, she thought she was thinking. She thought
she heard everybody burst out crying and then heard everybody
calling out, it is not Ohio, it is Texas, it is not Ohio.

Ida was funny that way, it was so important that all these things
happened to her just when and how they did.

She settled down and she and Frederick stayed there until they were not there together or anywhere.

All this time Ida was very careful.

Everything that happened to her was not strange. All along it was not strange Ida was not strange.

It is so easy not to be a mother.

This too happened to Ida.

She never was a mother.

Not ever.

Her life in Ohio which turned out to be her life in Texas went on just like that. She was not a mother. She was not strange. She just knew that once upon a time there was a necessity to know that they would all leave Texas. They did not leave Texas all together but they all left Texas. She left Texas and he left Texas, he was Frederick, and they left Texas. They were all the people they knew when they were in Texas.

As they one and all left Texas, they all fastened their doors and as they fastened their doors nobody saw them leave. That is a way to leave.

Ida always left everywhere in some way. She left Texas in this way. So did they.

She left Texas never to return.

She never went back anywhere so why would she go back to Ohio and to Texas. She never did. Ida never did.

She did not go back to Frederick either.

Ida never did.

She did not remember just how many years she had been with Frederick and in Ohio and in Texas.

She did not remember even when she was with him and there because when she was there she did not count, that is she could count up to ten but it did not give her any pleasure to count then.

How pleasant it is to count one two three four five six seven, and then stop and then go on counting eight nine and then ten or eleven.

Ida just loved to do that but as she certainly was not in Ohio or in Texas that long and certainly not with Frederick that long counting was not anything to do.

Ida liked to be spoken to.

It happened quite often.

How do you do they said and she said it to them and they said it to her. How do you do.

Would you never rather be Ida, they said, never rather be Ida, she laughed, never, they said never rather be Ida.

Of course not, of course she would always rather be Ida and she was.

They all said everybody said, Never rather be Ida, it got to be a kind of a song.

Never, never rather be Ida, never rather be Ida.

Ida never heard anybody sing it. When she heard her name she never heard it. That was Ida.

And so it was all over that is Frederick was all over, Ida left Texas just as it was.

Before she left Texas she talked to Duncan. Old man Duncan they called him but he was quite young. He was forty-five and he had been a policeman and now he was a head of police and not in uniform, of course not, otherwise she would not have been talking to him.

He said to her, where were you before you came to Texas. He asked her that after they had shaken hands several times together and it was evening. It often was evening in Texas.

It is very easy to leave Texas, Ida said, not to Duncan, she just said it.

There is no harm in leaving Texas, no harm at all.

Ida said, I have not left Texas yet, but tell them, you and he, what are you, tell them that he has left Texas and tell them that you and he, well tell them about Texas, you and he.

So then suddenly, she was called away, they thought in Ohio, but she was called away to wherever she was. Just like that Ida was called away.

She was not there any more, because she was called away.

Duncan told her, that is he did not tell her because she was called away, but anyway he told her that he had not left Texas.

Duncan never did leave Texas except once when he went to Tennessee. But by that time he never wanted to leave Texas. No use saying that he only remembered Ida because he didn't.

Once upon a time there was a meadow and in this meadow was a tree and on this tree there were nuts. The nuts fell and then they plowed the ground and the nuts were plowed into the ground but they never grew out.

After Ida left Texas she did not live in the country, she lived in a city. She lived in Washington.

That is the way it went on. Washington is a city and a city well a city is well it is a city. Ida lived there.

Once upon a time every time Ida lived in a city she was careful, she really was. She might lose it lose being careful but really every time she lived in a city she was careful. She was careful in Washington. All who came in would say to her, well Ida how about it.

That is what did happen.

By the time it was all comfortable for Ida and everybody knew better, she knew just what would not be there for her. And it was not. It just was not there for her.

Just then somebody came in and he said here I am. He said to Ida if you were with me I would just say, say she is with me. By golly that is what we are like in Minnesota, Minnesota is just like that.

Hello Ida, said some one. And they said, No Ida we are not. Ida said, no I am not.

Ida felt that way about it. She said well sit down and cry, but nobody did, not just then.

So life began for Ida in Washington.

There were there Ida and two more, Ida kept saying to herself. There whether there whether whether who is not.

That might have been the motto for Minnesota.

She did have to see those who came from Minnesota and hear them say, Minnesota is not old, believe it or not Minnesota is not old.

Ida began a daily life in Washington.

Once upon a time there was a shotgun and there were wooden guinea hens and they moved around electrically, electricity made them move around and as they moved around if you shot them their heads fell off them.

I thought I coughed said Ida and when I coughed I thought I coughed.

Ida said this and he listened to her he was not from Minnesota.

Once upon a time Ida stood all alone in the twilight. She was down in a field and leaning against a wall, her arms were folded and she looked very tall. Later she was walking up the road and she walked slowly.

She was not so young any more. It almost happened that she would be not sad not tired not depressed but just not so young any more.

She looked around her, she was not all alone because somebody passed by her and they said, it is a nicer evening than yesterday evening and she said, it was.

Ida married again. He was Andrew Hamilton and he came from Boston.

It is very usual of them when they come from Boston to be selfish, very usual, indeed. He and Ida sat together before they sat down.

But not, said some one seeing him, and who had heard of Ida, not, he said.

In Boston the earth is round. Believe it or not, in Boston the earth is round. But they were not in Boston, they were in Washington.

In Boston they hear the ocean as well. Not in Washington. There they have the river, the Potomac.

They were being married, it was not exciting, it was what they did. They did get married.

Once upon a time all who had anywhere to go did not go. This is what they did.

Ida was married again this time he came from Boston, she remembered his name. She was good friends with all her husbands.

This one came from Boston. They said Massachusetts, and when they said Massachusetts they remembered how fresh and green they were there, all of it, yes that is what they said.

In Washington it was different.

There it was in Washington it was come carefully and believe what they said.

Who is careful.

Well in a way Ida is.

She lives where she is not.

Not what.

Not careful.

Oh yes that is what they say.

Not careful.

Of course not.

Who is careful.

That is what they said.

And the answer was.

Ida said.

Oh yes, careful.

Oh yes, I can almost cry.

Ida never did.

Oh yes.

They all said oh yes.

And for three days I have not seen her.

That is what somebody did say somebody really somebody has said. For three days I have not seen her.

Nobody said Ida went away.

She was there Ida was.

So was her husband. So was everybody.

PART FIVE

POLITICS

They said, they do not want to buy from Ida. Why should they want to buy.

Ida and he.

He did not come from Louisiana, no. He was that kind. He did not only not come from Louisiana but he had had a carriage hound, a white and black spotted one and he the black and white spotted one was killed not killed but eaten by other dogs, they were all looking at a female dog and no one told him that the dog was nearly dead.

No one told him.

A young woman had silently had a way of giving the dog sugar and when she heard the dog was dead she ate the sugar.

And the man who was not from Louisiana added that, Oh yes he added that.

He and Ida.

He would have bought from Ida bought and well not well yes well no well why why not bought from Ida.

Ida was a friend.

She stayed in Washington.

She came to do what she knew each one of them wanted.

Easy enough in Washington.

She did not sell anything although they all wanted to buy.

Not at Bay Shore.

No not in Louisiana.

But in Carolina.

Not in North Carolina.

But in South Carolina.

Yes he would have bought from Ida in South Carolina but Ida was not there never there. She never was in either North or South Carolina. She was in Washington.

And so well yes so he did he did not buy from Ida.

Only Ida.

Well what did Ida do.

Ida knew just who was who.

She did. She did know.

They did not not an awful lot of them know Ida, just enough knew Ida to make Ida be just the one enough of them knew.

There are so many men.

What do you call them there.

There are so many men.

They did not all know Ida.

Now then.

In Washington, some one can do anything. Little by little it was Ida. She knew Charles and she smiled when she saw him. He wanted her to give him the rest of the morning. The rest of the morning. She was too busy too. She said, she never had anything to do but she did not give him the rest of the morning.

Woodward would not die of chagrin when he did not get what he had bought from Ida.

They all buy twice a day but the morning is the best time to buy. Woodward was a great buyer and he never did die of chagrin.

If he was no longer in Washington would Woodward die of chagrin.

Ida smiled every morning. She rested a good deal, she rested even in the evening.

Would Woodward come in and go out just as he liked.

Now that is a question a great question and Ida might answer, she might answer any question, but she did not find it as interesting as anything.

Would Woodward die of chagrin if he left Washington. Somebody stopped Ida and asked her this thing and she said nothing.

Then she said yes, Yes she said and she said nothing.

Yes they said yes would Woodward die of chagrin if he left Washington.

Almost at a loss Ida said yes, she did stand still and then she went on again.

Nobody ever followed Ida. What was the use of following Ida.

Ida had a dream. She dreamed that they were there and there was a little boy with them. Somebody had given the little boy a large package that had something in it and he went off to thank them. He never came back. They went to see why not. He was not there but there was a lady there and she was lying down and a large lion was there moving around. Where said they is the little boy, the lion ate him the lady said, and the package yes he ate it all, but the little boy came to thank you for it, yes I know but it did happen, I did not want it to happen but it did happen. I am very fond of the lion. They went away wondering and then Ida woke up.

Ida often met men and some of them hoped she would get something for them. She always did, not because she wanted them to have it but because she always did it when it was wanted.

Just when it was not at all likely Ida was lost, lost they said, oh yes lost, how lost, why just lost. Of course if she is lost. Yes of course she is lost.

Ida led a very easy life, that is she got up and sat up and went in and came out and rested and went to bed.

But some days she did rest a little more than on other days.

She did what she could for everybody.

Once in a while a father when he was young did not do it himself but a friend of his did. He took something.

When the policeman came nobody knew him. Most certainly he who later was a father refused to know him. They did not come from Africa, they came from North Carolina and Colorado. Later on the father had a son a young son and the young son began to go with men who stole. They were all then in Michigan so when they did steal they stole it again. The father was so worried, worried lest the police come and say to him your son is stealing, had he not refused when he was young and in North Carolina to recognize a friend who had stolen. He did say to the policeman then that he had never known that man although of course he had. And now, here in Michigan perhaps his own son was stealing. The policeman might come and how could he say he did not know his son. He might say it of course he might, he almost probably would.

Ida said to him I'll ask him. She meant that it was all right, it would be just like that, no trouble to anybody. Ida always did that. She saw the one who was all right and who would say yes yes it is all right and of course it was all right.

Ida did not need to be troubled, all she need do was to rest and she did rest. Just like that.

Once very often every day Ida went away. She could not go away really not, because she had no mother and she had no grandmother no sister and no aunt.

She dreamed that clothes were like Spanish ice-cream. She did not know why she dreamed of Spain. She was married in Washington, there was ice-cream there were clothes, but there was no Spain. Spain never came, but ice-cream and clothes clothes and ice-cream, food and clothes, politics, generals and admirals, clothes and food, she was married and she was in Washington.

She was not away from Washington.

No no more was there any day. She dreamed, if you are old you have nothing to eat, is that, she dreamed in her dream, is that money.

Ida had a companion named Christine. Christine had a little Chinese dog called William. Christine went away taking William. She thought of leaving him behind but she changed her mind.

When Christine went away she accomplished a great deal.

Oh Ida.

Ida was not married any more. She was very nice about it.

All around were what they found. At once they seemed all to like coming.

Ida did not leave Washington.

She rested.

Somebody said. Where is Ida.

Should she go away, somebody said. Go away like what.

Like what, they said.

Like Ida.

No said Christine and for this they thanked her.

All alone in Montana was a little man fragile but he smoked a pipe. Not then but later.

All alone there he was pale. Not tall. Not tall at all. All alone there he went about. He knew nobody was stout in Montana.

For this every little while he tried not to be thinner.

Dear Montana and how he went away.

It does not take long to leave Montana but it takes a long time to get stout, to put flesh on, get rosy and robust, get vaccinated, get everything.

In Montana he was never at a loss. Very likely not because he was careful of Montana.

He knew how to be careful and he was careful of Montana.

And so he plans everything.

He was a great success in Washington. Of course he was.

Politically speaking.

All of a sudden the snow had fallen the mountains were cold and he had left Montana.

That was when he began to smoke his pipe.

That was when he was a success in Washington.

That was when Christine had left him, naturally she had gone again. Now he knew Ida. Not to marry her. It was going to be quite a little while before Ida married again.

Ida moved around, to dance is to move around to move around is to dance, and when Ida moved around she let her arms hang out easily in front of her just like that.

She kept on being in Washington.

Once upon a time, once very often a man was in Washington who was cautious. He came from Wisconsin although he had been born in Washington, Washington city not Washington state.

All right he liked it.

After a little while he was nervous again and then for them it was just as if he was cautious. How do you like it, they said. Then he said no. For that they were very willing that they could just as much as ever they could be used to it.

Oh believe me, he said, and then mountains, he said.

Of course there are no mountains in the city of Washington but there are monuments. Oh believe me, he said, there are mountains in Wisconsin. And everybody believed him.

Once when it happened to snow he stayed at home. I will, he said, I will stay at home and as I am at home I will think and as I am thinking I will say I am thinking. He did, he did stay at home, he did think and as he thought he did think that he would think. He did.

Gradually he wondered what it was he was thinking. He thought how very nice it is and then he said I can not help it.

Of course not of course he could not help it, dear Madison, dear Wisconsin.

He was born in the city of Washington but that just happened.

Ida was in Washington she was not thinking, all the time she was suffering because of his thinking and then he was not thinking about his thinking.

Dear Ida.

Ida very likely Ida was not only in Washington but most likely he would not forget to cry when he heard that Ida was never to leave Washington.

Never to leave Washington.

Of course she finally did.

But in the meantime Ida could not believe that it was best.

To be in Washington.

She knew only knew that she did not rest.

She did it all.

Ida did.

But enough, said some one.

And then Ida came in and sat down and she did rest.

When anybody needed Ida Ida was resting. That was all right that is the way Ida was needed.

Once upon a time there was a city, it was built of blocks and every block had a square in it and every square had a statue and every statue had a hat and every hat was off.

Where was Ida where was Ida.

She was there. She was in Washington and she said thank you very much, thank you very much indeed. Ida was in Washington.

Thank you very much.

While she was in Washington it was a long time.

There it was.

She was kind to politics while she was in Washington very kind. She told politics that it was very nice of them to have her be kind to them. And she was she was very kind.

She really did not get up in the morning. She wished that she could and they wished that she could but it was not at all necessary.

When she was up and she did see them she was kind.

She saw seven, or eight of them and she saw them one or perhaps two and each time it was a very long time. She never went away she always did stay.

This was what they did say.

How do you do, said Ida, how do you feel when I see you, said Ida, and she did say that and they liked it.

Of course they liked it. And then she was not tired but she did lie down in an easy-chair.

It was not really politics really that Ida knew. It was not politics it was favors, that is what Ida liked to do.

She knew she liked to do them.

Everybody knew she liked to do favors for them and wanting to do favors for everybody who wanted to have favors done for them it was quite natural that those who could do the favors did them when she asked them to do them.

It does go like that.

Once upon a time there was a man his name was Henry, Henry Henry was his name. He had told everybody that whatever name they called him by they just had to call him Henry. He came to Washington, he was born in San Francisco and he liked languages, he was not lazy but he did not like to earn a living. He knew that if anybody would come to know about him they would of course call him Henry. Ida did.

She was resting one day and somebody called, it was somebody who liked to call on Ida when she was resting. He might have wanted to marry her but he never did. He knew that everybody sooner or later would know who Ida was and so he brought Henry with him. Henry immediately asked her to do a favor for him, he wanted to go somewhere where he could talk languages and where he would have to do nothing else. Ida was resting. She smiled.

Pretty soon Henry had what he wanted, he never knew whether it was Ida, but he went to see Ida and he did not thank her but he smiled and she smiled and she was resting and he went away.

That was the way Ida was.

In Washington.

When it was a year Ida did not know how much time had passed. A year had passed. She was not married when a year had passed.

She was in Washington when a year had passed.

They asked her to stay with them and she did.

Once upon a time a man was named Eugene Thomas. He was a nice man and not older than Ida. He was waiting after he had been careful about coming in and going out and everybody invited him. They said Eugene are you married and he said perhaps he had been. He never had been. That was the funny part of it he never had been married. He liked to think that Ida had been married and she had, of course she had been.

So that went on.

Ida was not tired, she went on staying in Washington.

Eugene Thomas pretty well stayed there too.

If a house has windows and any house has them anybody can stand at the window and look out.

He was funny Eugene Thomas, he used to say, There is a treasure, That is a pleasure, It is a pleasure to her and to him.

All these things did not really make Ida anxious to see him. Ida was never anxious. Ida was tired. Once in a while she knew all about something and when this happened everybody stood still and Ida looked out of the window and she was not so tired.

It is hard for Ida to remember what Ida said.

She said, I could remember anything I ever said. She did say that.

Eugene Thomas was caught in a flood. And so he did not marry Ida. The flood caught him and carried him away. The flood was in Connecticut and he was so nearly being drowned that he never came back to Washington. But in the meanwhile Ida had begun to wonder, to wonder whether she had perhaps better begin to leave Washington and go elsewhere.

Not that she really went then, she was still resting. She saw a great many who lived in Washington and they looked at her when they saw her. Everybody knew it was Ida, not when they saw her, seeing her did not bring it home to them but hearing about her, hearing that she was Ida, it was that that made them know everything that Ida was to do. It was a pleasant Ida. Even when she was just tired with having besides everything had to come in after she had been out, it was a very pleasant Ida.

And so Ida was in Washington.

One day, it happened again and again some one said something to her, they said Oh Ida, did you see me. Oh yes she said. Ida never did not see anybody, she always saw everybody and said she saw them. She made no changes about seeing then.

So he said to her Ida, your name is Ida isn't it, yes she said, and he said I thought your name was Ida, I thought you were Ida and I thought your name is Ida.

It is, she said.

They sat down.

She did not ask his name but of course he told her. He said his name was Gerald Seaton, and that he did not often care to walk about. He said that he was not too tall nor was he too stout, that he was not too fair and that he often had thought that it was very pleasant to live in Washington. He had lived there but he thought of leaving. What did Ida think. She said she thought that very often it was very well to rest in the afternoon. He said of course, and then they did not leave, they sat there a little longer and they drank something and they thought they would eat something and pretty soon they thought that the afternoon was over which it was not.

How are you Ida said Gerald Seaton and she said, very well I thank you, and she said that they knew that.

Ida was not sure that she did want to marry not that Gerald Seaton had asked her, but then if Ida did want to marry well Gerald Seaton might go away and he might come back again and if while he was away she would want to marry and then when he was back again she still wanted to marry would she marry him.

They neither of them really said anything about any such thing. Gerald Seaton had not yet gone away and Ida had not yet wanted to marry, but but. Ida had friends, she stayed with them and they thought perhaps they thought that Ida would marry again perhaps marry Gerald Seaton.

Who is Gerald Seaton said the husband to his wife, who is any one said the wife to the husband and they liked to sit with Ida while Ida was resting.

Ida could always stay with a married couple, neither the husband nor the wife did not like to have her, they always wanted to make her life easy for her, it always was easy for her and they always wanted her to keep right on going to marry Gerald Seaton or whoever it was, now it was Gerald Seaton and he was going away. Nobody could say that he was not going away.

You see Edith and William are still talking about Ida as everybody is. Does it make any difference to Edith and William. Just enough so that like everybody they go on talking and they talk about Ida.

Edith and William were the married couple with whom Ida was staying.

They were not the ones who were anxious and ambitious, nor were they the ones who collected anything they were a quiet couple even though they were rich and they talked together.

Positively, said Edith, can you go on doing what you do do. Can you go on doing what you did do. This is what Edith told William she had said to Ida.

And William, laughed and then he broke into poetry.

At a glance.

What a chance.

He looked at Edith and laughed and they laughed.

Edith went on being worried and William began again.

That she needs

What she has.

Edith said that William was foolish and Gerald Seaton was going away.

And they have what they are, said William.

Looking at William you never would have thought that he would talk poetry.

He liked to be in a garden.

Edith was worried not really worried but she liked to feel worried and she liked to look as if she felt worried, of course only about Ida.

Oh dear she said, and they have what they are said William chucking her under the chin.

Cheer up Edith he said let us talk about Ida.

And they like where they go
He murmured,
And Edith said Shut up.

Which is all after a while said William and then he and Edith said all right they would talk about Ida and Ida came in, not to rest, but to come in. They stopped it, stopped talking about her.

So Edith and William did not look at Ida, they started talking. What do you think said William what do you think if and when we decide anything what do you think it will be like. This is what William said and Edith looked out of the window. They were not in the same room with Ida but they might have been. Edith liked an opportunity to stand and so she looked out of the window. She half turned, she said to William, Did you say you said Ida. William then took to standing. This was it so they were standing. It is not natural that if anybody should be coming in that they would be standing. Ida did not come in, Edith went away from the window and William stood by the window and saw some one come in, it was not Gerald Seaton because he had gone away.

Let it be a lesson to her said Edith to William, but naturally William had said it first. Life went on very peacefully with Edith and William, it went on so that they were equally capable of seeing Ida all day every day, for which they might not feel it necessary to be careful that they shall after all realize what it is.

It is not early morning nor late in the evening it is just in between.

Edith and William had a mother but not living with them. She was waiting to come to see them but she was not coming any particular day. William had been married before and had a boy, Edith had been married before and had a girl, so naturally they did not have another one. It was very comfortable with them but Ida might go away.

It was a pleasant home, if a home has windows and any house has them anybody can stand at the window and look out.

Ida never did. She rested.

It was summer, it is pretty hot in Washington and Edith and William were going away to the country. Ida did not mind the heat and neither did Gerald Seaton. He was back in Washington.

How hot Washington is in summer and how much everybody in Washington feels the heat to be hot.

It was easy, Ida was Mrs Gerald Seaton and they went away to stay.

It was a long time before they said all they had to say, that is all Washington had to say about Ida and Gerald Seaton. But they were there naturally not since they were man and wife and had gone away.

This was not the only thing to do but they did it. They lived together as man and wife in other places. Which they were they were married, Ida was Mrs Gerald Seaton and Seaton was Gerald Seaton and they both wore their wedding rings.

PART SIX

They lived in a flat not too big not too small. And they lived there almost every day. They were not in Washington, they were far away from Washington, they were in Boston. There they lived almost as if Ida had not been Ida and Gerald Seaton had married any woman. They lived like this for quite a while. Some things did happen one of them was that they left Boston. Ida rested a good deal she liked to live in a smallish flat, she had never lived in a big one because she and Gerald could hear each other from one end of the place to the other and this was a pleasure because Ida liked to hear some one she liked to rest and Gerald Seaton did content her. Almost anything did content Ida although everybody was always talking about her.

Gerald Seaton did not look as if he had any ideas he was just a nice man but he did have some. He was always saying Ida knows a lot of people and if I have known them I have admired the ones I have known and if I have admired the ones I have known I have looked like them that is to say I do not look like them but they are like the ones I have known.

Ida did like to know that Gerald was in the house and she liked to hear him.

Gerald often said, I do not mean, I myself when I say I mean I mean, I do know how much I feel when once in a while I come in and I do. I am very busy, said Gerald and thinking does not take very much of my time, I do not think that is I do not feel that I do not like thinking.

All this would interest Ida also the way he would say I never think about Ida, everybody talks about Ida but I do not talk about Ida nor do I listen when they are all talking about Ida. I am thinking, Gerald would say, I am thinking of another person not any one whom I could possibly think would be at all like Ida not at all. This is what Gerald said and he did say that and that was the way it was.

Ida was not idle but she did not go in and out very much and she did not do anything and she rested and she liked Gerald to be there and to know he was talking.

So they went on living in their apartment but they did not live in Washington and later on they did not live in Boston.

If nobody knows you that does not argue you to be unknown, nobody knew Ida when they no longer lived in Boston but that did not mean that she was unknown.

She went away and she came again and nobody ever said they had enough of that.

What happened. She felt very well, she was not always well but she felt very well.

One day she saw him come, she knew he was there but besides that she saw him come. He came. He said, oh yes I do and she said thank you, they never met again.

Woodward George always worked, and he was always welcome. Ida said do come again. He came very often. When he came he came alone and when he came there were always at least a half dozen there and they all said, oh dear, I wish it was evening.

It almost looked as if Ida and Woodward would always meet, but Woodward went away and as they were not on the same continent, Ida was on one and Woodward was on another it looked as if they would not meet. But a continent can always be changed and so that is not why Ida and Woodward did not always meet.

Very likely Ida is not anxious nor is Woodward. Well said Ida, I have to have my life and Ida had her life and she has her life and she is having her life.

Oh dear said Ida and she was resting, she liked to get up when she was resting, and then rest again.

Woodward started in being a writer and then he became a dressmaker but not in Washington and not in Boston. Ida almost cried when she met his brother. She said what is your name and he answered Abraham George. Oh dear said Ida and she looked at him. Abraham George was a writer and he did not become a dressmaker like his brother and he and Ida talked together all the time. Abraham George even asked her questions, he said, you know I really think you are a very pleasant person to know, and Ida said of course, and she said I do like to do favors for anybody and he said do one for me, and she said what is it, and he said I want to change to being a widower and she said yes of course, and she did not really laugh but she did look very pleasant resting and waiting. Yes she did. After all it was Woodward George who was important to her but he was far far away.

She was still married to Gerald Seaton and houses came and houses went away, but you can never say that they were not together.

One day they went away again, this time quite far away, they went to another country and there they sat down. It was a small house, the place was called Bay Shore, it was a comfortable house to live in, they had friends among others she had a friend whose name was Lady Helen Button. How are you they said to each other. Ida learned to say it like that. How are you.

Ida liked it at Bay Shore. It did not belong to her but she well she did belong to it. How are you, she said when they came to see her.

A good many people did come to see her. Well of course she was married there was Gerald Seaton. How are you, was what they said to her, and they did sometimes forget to say it to Gerald but Gerald was nice and always said, oh yes, do, oh yes do.

She lived there and Gerald Seaton lived there, they lived in the same apartment and they talked to each other when they were dining but not much when they were resting and each in their way was resting.

Ida knew a vacant house when she saw it but she did not look at it, would she be introduced to some one who did look at a vacant house. Never at any time did tears come to Ida's eyes.

Never.

Everybody knew that Andrew was one of two. He was so completely one of two that he was two. Andrew was his name and he was not tall, not tall at all.

And yet it did mean it when he came in or when he went out.

Ida had not known that she would be there when he came in and when he went out but she was.

Ida was.

Andrew, there were never tears in Andrew's voice or tears in his eyes, he might cry but that was an entirely different matter.

Ida knew that.

Slowly Ida knew everything about that. It was the first thing Ida had ever known really the first thing.

Ida somehow knew who Andrew was and leave it alone or not Ida saw him.

If he saw her or not it was not interesting. Andrew was not a man who ever noticed anything. Naturally not. They noticed him.

Feel like that do you said Ida.

Ida was busy resting.

Ida when she went out did not carry an umbrella. It had not rained enough not nearly enough and once a week Ida went walking and today was the once a week when she went walking.

Once a week is two days one following another and this was the second one and Ida was dreaming.

So much for Andrew.

There was hardly any beginning.

There never could be with Andrew when he was there there he was. Anybody could know that and Ida well she just did not know that and Andrew looked about him when she was there and he saw her.

She was married to Gerald and she and Gerald were just as old as ever but that did not bother them. They talked together at least some time every day and occasionally in the evening but that was all and when they talked she called out to him and he did not answer and he called out to her and mostly she did not answer but they were sometimes in their home together. Anyway they were married and had been for quite some time.

Andrew did not notice Ida but he saw her and he went away to meet some one who had been named after a saint, this one was named after a saint called Thomas and so his name was Thomas and so Andrew met Thomas that is to say Andrew went out to meet that is to say he would meet Thomas who was out walking not walking but reading as he was walking which was his habit.

Andrew was there and then Thomas came to him.

Everybody was silent and so were they and then everybody went away. Andrew went away first.

Ida went out walking later on and the rain came down but by that time Ida was at home reading, she was not walking any more. Each one reads in their way and Ida read in her way.

Andrew never read.

Of course not.

Ida was careless but not that way. She did read, and she never forgot to look up when she saw Andrew.

Ida went out walking instead of sitting **in a** garden which was just as well because in this way she often met everybody and stopped and talked with them, this might lead her to meet them again and if it did she sometimes met some one who cried for one reason or another. Ida did not mind anybody crying, why should she when she had a garden a house and a dog and when she was so often visiting. Very often they made four and no more.

This had nothing to do with Andrew who in a way was never out walking and if he was then of course nobody did meet him.

Andrew never disappeared, how could he when he was always there and Ida gradually was always there too. How do you do. That is what she said when she met him.

She did not really meet him, nobody did because he was there and they were there and nobody met him or he them, but Ida did, she met him.

Andrew, she called him, Andrew, not loudly, just Andrew and she did not call him she just said Andrew. Nobody had just said Andrew to Andrew.

Andrew never looked around when Ida called him but she really never called him. She did not see him but he was with him and she called Andrew just like that. That was what did impress him.

Ida liked it to be dark because if it was dark she could light a light. And if she lighted a light then she could see and if she saw she saw Andrew and she said to him. Here you are.

Andrew was there, and it was not very long, it was long but not very long before Ida often saw Andrew and Andrew saw her. He even came to see her. He came to see her whether she was there or whether she was not there.

Ida gradually was always there when he came and Andrew always came.

He came all the same.

Kindly consider that I am capable of deciding when and why I am coming. This is what Andrew said to Ida with some hesitation.

And now Ida was not only Ida she was Andrew's Ida and being Andrew's Ida Ida was more that Ida she was Ida itself.

For this there was a change, everybody changed, Ida even changed and even changed Andrew. Andrew had changed Ida to be more Ida and Ida changed Andrew to be less Andrew and they were both always together.

Second Half

PART ONE

The road is awfully wide.

With the snow on either side.

She was walking along the road made wide with snow. The moonlight was bright. She had a white dog and the dog looked gray in the moonlight and on the snow. Oh she said to herself that is what they mean when they say in the night all cats are gray.

When there was no snow and no moonlight her dog had always looked white at night.

When she turned her back on the moon the light suddenly was so bright it looked like another kind of light, and if she could have been easily frightened it would have frightened her but you get used to anything but really she never did get used to this thing.

She said to herself what am I doing, I have my genius and I am looking for my Andrew and she went on looking.

It was cold and when she went home the fire was out and there was no more wood. There was a little girl servant, she knew that the servant had made a fire for herself with all that wood and that her fire was going. She knew it. She knocked at her door and walked in. The servant was not there but the fire was. She was furious. She took every bit of lighted wood and carried it into her room. She sat down and looked at the fire and she knew she had her genius and she might just as well go and look for her Andrew. She went to bed then but she did not sleep very well. She found out next day that Andrew came to town every Sunday. She never saw him. Andrew was very good looking like his name. Ida often said to herself she never had met an Andrew and so she did not want to see him. She liked to hear about him.

She would if it had not been so early in the morning gone to be a nurse. As a nurse she might seek an Andrew but to be a nurse you have to get up early in the morning. You have to get up early in the morning to be a nun and so although if she had been a nun she could have thought every day about Andrew she never became a nun nor did she become a nurse. She just stayed at home.

It is easy to stay at home not at night-time but in the morning and even at noon and in the afternoon. At night-time it is not so easy to stay at home.

For which reason, Andrew's name changed to Ida and eight changed to four and sixteen changed to twenty-five and they all sat down.

For which all day she sat down. As I said she had that habit the habit of sitting down and only once every day she went out walking and she always talked about that. That made Ida listen. She knew how to listen.

That is what she said.

She did not say Ida knew how to listen but she talked as if she knew that Ida knew how to listen.

Every day she talked the same way and every day she took a walk and every day Ida was there and every day she talked about his walk, and every day Ida did listen while she talked about his walk. It can be very pleasant to walk every day and to talk about the walk and every day and it can be very pleasant to listen every day to him talk about his every-day walk.

You see there was he it came to be Andrew again and it was Ida.

If there was a war or anything Andrew could still take a walk every day and talk about the walk he had taken that day.

For which it made gradually that it was not so important that Ida was Ida.

It could and did happen that it was not so important.

Would Ida fly, well not alone and certainly it was better not to fly than fly alone. Ida came to walking, she had never thought she would just walk but she did and this time she did not walk alone she walked with Susan Little.

For this they did not sing.

Such things can happen, Ida did not have to be told about it nor did she have to tell about it.

There was no Andrew.

Andrew stayed at home and waited for her, and Ida came. This can happen, Andrew could walk and come to see Ida and tell her what he did while he was walking and later Ida could walk and come back and not tell Andrew that she had been walking. Andrew could not have listened to Ida walking. Andrew walked not Ida. It is perhaps best so.

Anybody can go away, anybody can take walks and anybody can meet somebody new. Anybody can like to say how do you do to somebody they never saw before and yet it did not matter. Ida never did, she always walked with some one as if they had walked together any day. That really made Ida so pleasant that nobody ever did stay away.

And then they all disappeared, not really disappeared but nobody talked about them any more.

So it was all to do over again, Ida had Andrew that is she had that he walked every day, nobody talked about him any more but he had not disappeared, and he talked about his walk and he walked every day.

So Ida was left alone, and she began to sit again.

And sitting she thought about her life with dogs and this was it.

The first dog I ever remember seeing, I had seen cats before and I must have seen dogs but the first dog I ever remember seeing was a large puppy in the garden. Nobody knew where he came from so we called him Prince.

It was a very nice garden but he was a dog and he grew very big. I do not remember what he ate but he must have eaten a lot because he grew so big. I do not remember playing with him very much. He was very nice but that was all, like tables and chairs are nice. That was all. Then there were a lot of dogs but none of them interesting.

Then there was a little dog, a black and tan and he hung himself on a string when somebody left him. He had not been so interesting but the way he died made him very interesting. I do not know what he had as a name.

Then for a long time there were no dogs none that I ever noticed. I heard people say they had dogs but if I saw them I did not notice them and I heard people say their dog had died but I did not notice anything about it and then there was a dog, I do not know where he came from or where he went but he was a dog.

It was not yet summer but there was sun and there were wooden steps and I was sitting on them, and I was just doing nothing and a brown dog came and sat down too. I petted him, he liked petting and he put his head on my lap and we both went on sitting. This happened every afternoon for a week and then he never came. I do not know where he came from or where he went or if he had a name but I knew he was brown, he was a water dog a fairly big one and I never did forget him.

And then for some time there was no dog and then there were lots of them but other people had them.

A dog has to have a name and he has to look at you. Sometimes it is kind of bothering to have them look at you.

Any dog is new.

The dogs I knew then which were not mine were mostly very fine. There was a Pekinese named Sandy, he was a very large one, Pekineses should be tiny but he was a big one like a small lion but he was all Pekinese, I suppose anywhere there can be giants, and he was a giant Pekinese.

Sandy was his name because he was that color, the color of sand. He should have been carried around, Pekinese mostly are but he was almost too heavy to carry. I liked Sandy. When he stood up on a table all ruffled up and his tail all ruffled up he did look like a lion a very little lion, but a fierce one.

He did not like climbing the mountains, they were not real mountains, they were made of a man on two chairs and Sandy was supposed to climb him as if he were climbing a mountain. Sandy thought this was disgusting and he was right. No use calling a thing like that climbing the mountains, and if it has been really mountains of course Sandy would not have been there. Sandy liked things

flat, tables, floors, and paths. He liked waddling along as he pleased.
No mountains, no climbing, no automobiles, he was killed by one.
Sandy knew what he liked, flat things and sugar, sugar was flat too,
and Sandy never was interested in anything else and then one day
an automobile went over him, poor Sandy and that was the end of
Sandy.

So one changed to two and two changed to five and the next dog
was also not a big one, his name was Lillieman and he was black
and a French bull and not welcome. He was that kind of a dog he
just was not welcome.

When he came he was not welcome and he came very often. He
was good-looking, he was not old, he did finally die and was buried
under a white lilac tree in a garden but he just was not welcome.

He had his little ways, he always wanted to see something that
was just too high or too low for him to reach and so everything was
sure to get broken. He did not break it but it did just get broken.
Nobody could blame him but of course he was not welcome.

Before he died and was buried under the white lilac tree, he met
another black dog called Dick. Dick was a French poodle and
Lillieman was a French bull and they were both black but they did
not interest each other. As much as possible they never knew the
other one was there. Sometimes when they bumped each other no
one heard the other one bark it was hard to not notice the other one.
But they did. Days at a time sometimes they did.

Dick was the first poodle I ever knew and he was always welcome, round roly-poly and old and gray and lively and pleasant,
he was always welcome.

He had only one fault. He stole eggs, he could indeed steal a
whole basket of them and then break them and eat them, the cook
would hit him with a broom when she caught him but nothing
could stop him, when he saw a basket of eggs he had to steal them
and break them and eat them. He only liked eggs raw, he never
stole cooked eggs, whether he liked breaking them, or the looks of
them or just, well anyway it was the only fault he had. Perhaps
because he was a black dog and eggs are white and then yellow,
well anyway he could steal a whole basket of them and break them
and eat them, not the shells of course just the egg.

So this was Dick the poodle very playful very lively old but full of energy and he and Lillieman the French bull could be on the same lawn together and not notice each other, there was no connection between them, they just ignored each other. The bull Lillieman died first and was buried under the white lilac, Dick the poodle went on running around making love to distant dogs, sometimes a half day's run away and running after sticks and stones, he was fourteen years old and very lively and then one day he heard of a dog far away and he felt he could love her, off he went to see her and he never came back again, he was run over, on the way there, he never got there he never came back and alas poor Dick he was never buried anywhere.

Dogs are dogs, you sometimes think that they are not but they are. And they always are here there and everywhere.

There were so many dogs and I knew some of them I knew some better than others, and sometimes I did not know whether I wanted to meet another one or not.

There was one who was named Mary Rose, and she had two children, the first one was an awful one. This was the way it happened.

They say dogs are brave but really they are frightened of a great many things about as many things as frighten children.

Mary Rose had no reason to be frightened because she was always well and she never thought about being lost, most dogs do and it frightens them awfully but Mary Rose did get lost all the same not really lost but for a day and a night too. Nobody really knew what happened.

She came home and she was dirty, she who was always so clean and she had lost her collar and she always loved her collar and she dragged herself along she who always walked along so tidily. She was a fox-terrier with smooth white hair, and pretty black marks. A little boy brought back her collar and then pretty soon Chocolate came, it was her only puppy and he was a monster, they called him Chocolate because he looked like a chocolate cake or a bar of chocolate or chocolate candy, and he was awful. Nobody meant it but he was run over, it was sad and Mary Rose had been fond of him. Later she had a real daughter Blanchette who looked just like her, but Mary Rose never cared about her. Blanchette was too like her, she was not at all interesting and besides Mary Rose knew that

Blanchette would live longer and never have a daughter and she was right. Mary Rose died in the country, Blanchette lived in the city and never had a daughter and was never lost and never had any worries and gradually grew very ugly but she never suspected it and nobody told her so and it was no trouble to her.

Mary Rose loved only once, lots of dogs do they love only once or twice, Mary Rose was not a loving dog, but she was a tempting dog, she loved to tempt other dogs to do what they should not. She never did what she should not but they did when she showed them where it was.

Little things happen like that, but she had to do something then when she had lost the only dog she loved who was her own son and who was called Chocolate. After that she just was like that.

I can just see her tempting Polybe in the soft moonlight to do what was not right.

Dogs should smell but not eat, if they eat dirt that means they are naughty or they have worms, Mary Rose was never naughty and she never had worms but Polybe, well Polybe was not neglected but he was not understood. He never was understood. I suppose he died but I never knew. Anyway he had his duty to do and he never did it, not because he did not want to do his duty but because he never knew what his duty was.

That was what Polybe was.

He liked moonlight because it was warmer than darkness but he never noticed the moon. His father and his sister danced on the hillside in the moonlight but Polybe had left home so young that he never knew how to dance in it but he did like the moonlight because it was warmer than the dark.

Polybe was not a small dog he was a hound and he had stripes red and black like only a zebra's stripes are white and black but Polybe's stripes were as regular as that and his front legs were long, all his family could kill a rabbit with a blow of their front paw, that is really why they danced in the moonlight, they thought they were chasing rabbits, any shadow was a rabbit to them and there are lots of shadows on a hillside in the summer under a bright moon.

Poor Polybe he never really knew anything, the shepherds said that he chased sheep, perhaps he did thinking they were rabbits, he might have made a mistake like that, he easily might. Another little

little dog was so foolish once he always thought that any table leg was his mother, and would suck away at it as if it was his mother. Polybe was not as foolish as that but he almost was, anyway Mary Rose could always lead him astray, perhaps she whispered to him that sheep were rabbits. She might have.

And then Mary Rose went far away. Polybe stayed where he was and did not remember any one. He never did. That was Polybe.

And he went away tied to a string and he never did try to come back. Back meant nothing to him. A day was never a day to Polybe. He never barked, he had nothing to say.

Polybe is still some place today, nothing could ever happen to him to kill him or to change anything in any way.

The next dog was bigger than any other dog had been.

When a dog is really big he is very naturally thin, and when he is big and thin when he moves he does not seem to be moving. There were two of them one was probably dead before I saw the second one. I did not know the first one but I heard what he could do I saw him of course but when I saw him he came along but he was hardly moving.

It did not take much moving to come along as fast as we were going. There was no other dog there which was lucky because they said that when he saw another dog well he did not move much but he killed him, he always killed any dog he saw although he hardly moved at all to kill him. I saw this dog quite a few times but there was never any other dog anywhere near. I was glad.

The other one well he looked gentle enough and he hardly moved at all and he was very big and he looked thin although he really was not.

He used to walk about very gently almost not at all he was so tall and he moved his legs as if he meant them not to leave the ground but they did, just enough, just a little sideways just enough, and that was all. He lived a long time doing nothing but that and he is still living just living enough.

The next dog and this is important because it is the next dog. His name is Never Sleeps although he sleeps enough.

He was brown not a dark brown but a light brown and he had a lot of friends who always went about together and they all had to be brown, otherwise Never Sleeps would not let them come along. But all that was later, first he had to be born.

It was not so easy to be born.

There was a dog who was an Alsatian wolf-hound a very nice one, and they knew that in the zoo there was a real wolf quite a nice one. So one night they took the dog to see the wolf and they left her there all night. She liked the wolf and the wolf was lonesome and they stayed together and then later she had a little dog and he was a very nice one, and her name was Never Sleeps. She was a gentle dog and liked to lie in the water in the winter and to be quiet in the summer. She never was a bother.

She could be a mother. She met a white poodle he was still young and he had never had a puppy life because he had not been well. His name was Basket and he looked like one. He was taken to visit Never Sleeps and they were told to be happy together. Never Sleeps was told to play with Basket and teach him how to play. Never Sleeps began, she had to teach catch if you can or tag, and she had to teach him pussy wants a corner and she taught him each one of them.

She taught him tag and even after he played it and much later on when he was dead another Basket he looked just like him went on playing tag. To play tag you have to be able to run forward and back to run around things and to start one way and to go the other way and another dog who is smaller and not so quick has to know how to wait at a corner and go around the other way to make the distance shorter. And sometimes just to see how well tag can be played the bigger quicker dog can even stop to play with a stick or a bone and still get away and not be tagged. That is what it means to play tag and Never Sleeps taught Basket how to play. Then he taught him how to play pussy wants a corner, to play this there have to be trees. Dogs cannot play this in the house they are not allowed to and so they have to have at least four trees if there are three dogs and three trees if there are two dogs to play pussy wants a corner. Never Sleeps preferred tag to pussy wants a corner but Basket rather liked best pussy wants a corner.

Ida never knew who knew what she said, she never knew what she said because she listened and as she listened well the moon scarcely the moon but still there is a moon.

Very likely hers was the moon.

Ida knew she never had been a little sister or even a little brother. Ida knew.

So scarcely was there an absence when some one died.

Believe it or not some one died.

And he was somebody's son and Ida began to cry and he was twenty-six and Ida began to cry and Ida was not alone and she began to cry.

Ida had never cried before, but now she began to cry.

Even when Andrew came back from his walk and talked about his walk, Ida began to cry.

It's funny about crying. Ida knew it was funny about crying, she listened at the radio and they played the national anthem and Ida began to cry. It is funny about crying.

But anyway Ida was sitting and she was there and one by one somebody said Thank you, have you heard of me. And she always had. That was Ida.

Even Andrew had he had heard of them, that was the way he had been led to be ready to take his walk every day because he had heard of every one who came in one after the other one.

And Ida did not cry again.

One day, she saw a star it was an uncommonly large one and when it set it made a cross, she looked and looked and she and did not hear Andrew take a walk and that was natural enough she was not there. They had lost her. Ida was gone.

So she sat up and went to bed carefully and she easily told every one that there was more wind in Texas than in San Francisco and nobody believed her. So she said wait and see and they waited.

She came back to life exactly day before yesterday. And now listen.

Ida loved three men. One was an officer who was not killed but he might have been, one was a painter who was not in hospital but he might have been one and one was a lawyer who had gone away to Montana and she had never heard from him.

Ida loved each one of them and went to say good-bye to them.

Good-bye, good-bye she said, and she did say good-bye to them.

She wondered if they were there, of course she did not go away. What she really wanted was Andrew, where oh where was Andrew.

Andrew was difficult to suit and so Ida did not suit him. But Ida did sit down beside him.

Ida fell in love with a young man who had an adventure. He came from Kansas City and he knew that he was through. He was twenty years old. His uncle had died of meningitis, so had his father and so had his cousin, his name was Mark and he had a mother but no sisters and he had a wife and sisters-in-law.

Ida looked the other way when they met, she knew Mark would die when he was twenty-six and he did but before that he had said, For them, they like me for them and Ida had answered just as you say Mark. Ida always bent her head when she saw Mark she was tall and she bent her head when she saw Mark, he was tall and broad and Ida bent her head when she saw him. She knew he would die of meningitis and he did. That was why Ida always bent her head when she saw him.

Why should everybody talk about Ida.

Why not.

Dear Ida.

PART TWO

Ida was almost married to Andrew and not anybody could cloud it. It was very important that she was almost married to Andrew. Besides he was Andrew the first. All the others had been others.

Nobody talked about the color of Ida's hair and they talked about her a lot, nor the color of her eyes.

She was sitting and she dreamed that Andrew was a soldier. She dreamed well not dreamed but just dreamed. The day had been set for their marriage and everything had been ordered. Ida was always careful about ordering, food clothes cars, clothes food cars everything was well chosen and the day was set and then the telephone rang and it said that Andrew was dying, he had not been killed he was only dying, and Ida knew that the food would do for the people who came to the funeral and the car would do to go to the funeral and the clothes would not do dear me no they would not do and all of this was just dreaming. Ida was alive yet and so was Andrew, she had been sitting, he had been walking and he came home and told about his walk and Ida was awake and she was listening and Andrew was Andrew the first, and Ida was Ida and they were almost married and not anybody could cloud anything.

PART THREE

Any ball has to look like the moon. Ida just had to know what was going to be happening soon.

They can be young so young they can go in swimming. Ida had been. Not really swimming one was learning and the other was teaching.

This was being young in San Francisco and the baths were called Lurline Baths. Ida was young and so was he they were both good both she and he and he was teaching her how to swim, he leaned over and he said kick he was holding her under the chin and he was standing beside her, it was not deep water, and he said kick and she did and he walked along beside her holding her chin, and he said kick and she kicked again and he was standing very close to her and she kicked hard and she kicked him. He let go her he called out Jesus Christ my balls and he went under and she went under, they were neither of them drowned but they might have been.

Strangely enough she never thought about Frank, that was his name, Frank, she could not remember his other name, but once when she smelled wild onion she remembered going under and that neither were drowned.

It is difficult never to have been younger but Ida almost was she almost never had been younger.

PART FOUR

And now it was suddenly happening, well not suddenly but it was happening, Andrew was almost Andrew the first. It was not sudden.

They always knew what he could do, that is not what he would do but what they had to do to him. Ida knew.

Andrew the first, walked every day and came back to say where he had walked that day. Every day he walked the same day and every day he told Ida where he had walked that day. Yes Ida.

Ida was just as much older as she had been.

Yes Ida.

One day Ida was alone. When she was alone she was lying down and when she was not alone she was lying down. Everybody knew everything about Ida, everybody did. They knew that when she was alone she was lying down and when she was not alone she was lying down.

Everybody knew everything about Ida and by everybody, everybody means everybody.

It might have been exciting that everybody knew everything about Ida and it did not excite Ida it soothed Ida. She was soothed.

For a four.

She shut the door.

They dropped in.

And drank gin.

I'd like a conversation said Ida.

So one of them told that when his brother was a soldier, it was in summer and he ate an apple off an apple tree a better apple than he he had ever eaten before, so he took a slip of the tree and he brought it home and after he put it into the ground where he was and when he took it home he planted it and now every year they had apples off this apple tree.

Another one told how when his cousin was a soldier, he saw a shepherd dog, different from any shepherd dog he had ever seen and as he knew a man who kept sheep, he took the shepherd dog home with him and gave it to the man and now all the shepherd dogs came from the dog his cousin had brought home with him from the war.

Another one was telling that a friend of his had a sister-in-law and the sister-in-law had the smallest and the finest little brown dog he had ever seen, and he asked the sister-in-law what race it was and where she had gotten it. Oh she said a soldier gave it to me for my little girl, he had brought it home with him and he gave it to my little girl and she and he play together, they always play together.

Ida listened to them and she sighed, she was resting, and she said, I like lilies-of-the-valley too do you, and they all said they did, and one of them said, when his sister had been a nurse in a war she always gathered lilies-of-the-valley before they were in flower. Oh yes said Ida.

And so there was a little conversation and they all said they would stay all evening. They said it was never dark when they stayed all evening and Ida sighed and said yes she was resting.

Once upon a time Ida took a train, she did not like trains, and she never took them but once upon a time she took a train. They were fortunate, the train went on running and Andrew was not there. Then it stopped and Ida got out and Andrew still was not there. He was not expected but still he was not there. So Ida went to eat something.

This did happen to Ida.

They asked what she would have to eat and she said she would eat the first and the last that they had and not anything in between. Andrew always ate everything but Ida when she was alone she ate the first and the last of everything, she was not often alone so it was not often that she could eat the first and the last of everything but she did that time and then everybody helped her to leave but not not to get on a train again.

She never did get on any train again. Naturally not, she was always there or she was resting. Her life had every minute when it was either this or that and sometimes both, either she was there or she was resting and sometimes it was both.

Her life never began again because it was always there.

And now it was astonishing that it was always there. Yes it was. Ida.

Yes it was.

PART FIVE

Any friend of Ida's could be run over by any little thing.

Not Andrew, Andrew was Andrew the first and regular.

Why are sailors, farmers and actors more given to reading and believing signs than other people. It is natural enough for farmers and sailors who are always there where signs are, alone with them but why actors.

Well anyway Ida was not an actress nor a sailor nor a farmer.

Cuckoos magpies crows and swallows are signs.

Nightingales larks robins and orioles are not.

Ida saw her first glow worm. The first of anything is a sign.

Then she saw three of them that was a sign.

Then she saw ten.

Ten are never a sign.

And yet what had she caught.

She had caught and she had taught.

That ten was not a sign.

Andrew was Andrew the first.

He was a sign.

Ida had not known he was a sign, not known he was a sign.

Ida was resting.

Worse than any signs is a family who brings bad luck. Ida had known one, naturally it was a family of women, a family which brings bad luck must be all women.

Ida had known one the kind that if you take a dog with you when you go to see them, the dog goes funny and when it has its puppies its puppies are peculiar.

This family was a mother a daughter and a grand-daughter, well they all had the airs and graces of beauties and with reason, well they were. The grandmother had been married to an admiral and then he died and to a general and then he died. Her daughter was married to a doctor but the doctor could not die, he just left, the granddaughter was very young, just as young as sixteen, she married a writer, nobody knows just how not but before very long she cried, every day she cried, and her mother cried and even her grand-mother and then she was not married any longer to the writer. Then well she was still young and yet twenty-one and a banker saw her and he said he must marry her, well she couldn't yet naturally not the writer was still her husband but very soon he would not be, so the banker was all but married to her, well anyway they went out together, the car turned over the banker was dead and she had broken her collar-bone.

Now everybody wanted to know would the men want her more because of all this or would they be scared of her.

Well as it happened it was neither the one nor the other. It often is not.

The men after that just did not pay any attention to her. You might say they did not any of them pay any attention to her even when she was twenty-three or twenty-four. They did not even ask not any of them. What for.

And so anybody could see that they could not bring good luck to any one not even a dog, no not even.

No really bad luck came to Ida from knowing them but after that anyway, it did happen that she never went out to see any one.

She said it was better.

She did not say it was better but it was better. Ida never said anything about anything.

Anyway after that she rested and let them come in, anybody come in. That way no family would come that just would not happen.

So Ida was resting and they came in. Not one by one, they just came in.

That is the way Andrew came he just came in.

He took a walk every afternoon and he always told about what happened on his walk.

He just walked every afternoon.

He liked to hear people tell about good luck and bad luck.

Somebody one afternoon told a whole lot.

Andrew was like that, he was born with his life, why not. And he had it, he walked every afternoon, and he said something every minute of every day, but he did not talk while he was listening. He listened while he was listening but he did not hear unless he asked to have told what they were telling. He liked to hear about good luck and bad luck because it was not real to him, nothing was real to him except a walk every afternoon and to say something every minute of every day.

So he said, and what were you saying about good luck and bad luck.

Well it was this.

The things anybody has to worry about are spiders, cuckoos goldfish and dwarfs.

Yes said Andrew. And he was listening.

Spider at night makes delight.

Spider in the morning makes mourning.

Yes said Andrew.

Well, said the man who was talking, think of a spider talking.

Yes said Andrew.

The spider says

Listen to me I, I am a spider, you must not mistake me for the sky, the sky red at night is a sailor's delight, the sky red in the morning is a sailor's warning, you must not mistake me for the sky, I am I, I am a spider and in the morning any morning I bring sadness and mourning and at night if they see me at night I bring them delight, do not mistake me for the sky, not I, do not mistake me for a dog who howls at night and causes no delight, a dog says the bright moonlight makes him go mad with desire to bring sorrow to any one sorrow and sadness, the dog says the night the bright moonlight brings madness and grief, but says the spider I, I am a spider, a big spider or a little spider, it is all alike, a spider green or gray, there is nothing else to say, I am a spider and I know and I always tell everybody so, to see me at night brings them delight, to see me in the morning, brings mourning, and if you see me at night, and I am a sight, because I am dead having died up by night, even so dead at night I still cause delight, I dead bring delight to any one who sees me at night, and so every one can sleep tight who has seen me at night.

Andrew was listening and he said it was interesting and said did they know any other superstition.

Yes said the man there is the cuckoo.

Oh yes the cuckoo.

Supposing they could listen to a cuckoo.

I, I am a cuckoo, I am not a clock, because a clock makes time pass and I stop the time by giving mine, and mine is money, and money is honey, and I I bring money, I, I, I. I bring misery and money but never honey, listen to me.

Once I was there, you know everybody, that I I sing in the spring, sweetly, sing, evening and morning and everything.

Listen to me.

If you listen to me, if when you hear me, the first time in the spring time, hear me sing, and you have money a lot of money for you in your pocket when you hear me in the spring, you will be rich all year any year, but if you hear me and you have gone out with no money jingling in your pocket when you hear me singing then you will be poor poor all year, poor.

But sometimes I can do even more.

I knew a case like that, said the man.

Did you said Andrew.

She, well she, she had written a lovely book but nobody took the lovely book nobody paid her money for the lovely book they never gave her money, never never never and she was poor and they needed money oh yes they did she and her lover.

And she sat and she wrote and she longed for money for she had a lover and all she needed was money to live and love, money money money.

So she wrote and she hoped and she wrote and she sighed and she wanted money, money money, for herself and for love for love and for herself, money money money.

And one day somebody was sorry for her and they gave her not much but a little money, he was a nice millionaire the one who gave her a little money, but it was very little money and it was spring and she wanted love and money and she had love and now she wanted money.

She went out it was the spring and she sat upon the grass with a little money in her pocket and the cuckoo saw her sitting and knew she had a little money and it went up to her close up to her and sat on a tree and said cuckoo at her, cuckoo cuckoo, cuckoo, and she said, Oh, a cuckoo bird is singing on a cuckoo tree singing to me oh singing to me. And the cuckoo sang cuckoo cuckoo and she sang cuckoo cuckoo to it, and there they were singing cuckoo she to it and it to her.

Then she knew that it was true and that she would be rich and love would not leave her and she would have all three money and love and a cuckoo in a tree, all three.

Andrew did listen and the man went on.

And the goldfish.

Yes said a goldfish I listen I listen but listen to me I am stronger than a cuckoo stronger and meaner because I never do bring good luck I bring nothing but misery and trouble and all no not at all I bring no good luck only bad and that does not make me sad it makes me glad that I never bring good luck only bad.

They buy me because I look so pretty and red and gold in my bowl but I never bring good luck I only bring bad, bad bad bad.

Listen to me.

There was a painter once who thought he was so big he could do anything and he did. So he bought goldfish and any day he made a painting of us in the way that made him famous and made him say, goldfish bring me good luck not bad, and they better had.

Everything went wonderfully for him, he turned goldfish into gold because everything he did was bold and it sold, and he had money and fame but all the same we the goldfish just sat and waited while he painted.

One day, crack, the bowl where we were fell apart and we were all cracked the bowl the water and the fish, and the painter too crack went the painter and his painting too and he woke up and he knew that he was dead too, the goldfish and he, they were all dead, but we there are always goldfish in plenty to bring bad luck to anybody too but he the painter and his painting was dead dead dead.

We knew what to do.

Andrew was more interested, and the dwarfs he said.

Well this is the way they are they say we are two male and female, if you see us both at once it means nothing, but if you see either of us alone it means bad luck or good. And which is which. Misfortune is female good luck luck is male, it is all very simple.

Oh yes anybody can know that and if they see one of us and it is the female he or she has to go and go all day long until they see a dwarf man, otherwise anything awful could happen to them. A great many make fun of those who believe in this thing but those who believe they know, female dwarf bad luck male dwarf good luck, all that is eternal.

Silence.

Suddenly the goldfish suddenly began to swish and to bubble and squeak and to shriek, I I do not believe in dwarfs neither female nor male, he cried, no not in a cuckoo, no not in spiders, no, the only thing I believe in besides myself is a shoe on a table, oh that, that makes me shiver and shake, I have no shoes no feet no shoes but a shoe on a table, that is terrible, oh oh yes oh ah.

And the cuckoo said,

Oh you poor fish, you do not believe in me, you poor fish, and I do not believe in you fish nothing but fish a goldfish only fish, no I do not believe in you no fish no, I believe in me, I am a cuckoo and I know and I tell you so, no the only thing I believe in which is not me is when I see the new moon through a glass window, I never do because there is no glass to see through, but I believe in that too, I believe in that and I believe in me ah yes I do I see what I see through, and I do I do I do.

No I do not believe in a fish, nor in a dwarf nor in a spider not I, because I am I a cuckoo and I, I, I.

The spider screamed. You do not believe in me, everybody believes in me, you do not believe in spiders you do not believe in me bah. I believe in me I am all there is to see except well if you put your clothes on wrong side to well that is an awful thing to do, and if you change well that is worse than any way and what do I say, if you put your clothes on wrong everything will go well that day but if you change from wrong to right then nothing will go right, but what can I do I am a green spider or a gray and I have the same clothes every day and I can make no mistake any day but I believe oh I believe if you put your clothes on wrong side to everything will be lovely that you do, but anyway everybody has to believe in me, a spider, of course they do, a spider in the morning is an awful warning a spider at night bring delight, it is so lovely to know this is true and not to believe in a fish or in dwarfs or in a cuckoo, ooh ooh, it is I, no matter what they try it is I I. I.

The dwarfs said, And of whom are you talking all of you, we dwarfs, we are in the beginning we have commenced everything and we believe in everything yes we do, we believe in the language of flowers and we believe in lucky stones, we believe in peacocks' feathers and we believe in stars too, we believe in leaves of tea, we believe in a white horse and a red-headed girl, we believe in the moon, we believe in red in the sky, we believe in the barking of a dog, we believe in everything that is mortal and immortal, we even believe in spiders, in goldfish and in the cuckoo, we the dwarfs we believe in it all, all and all, and all and every one are alike, we are, all the world is like us the dwarfs, all the world believes in everything and we do too and all the world believes in us and in you.

Everybody in the room was quiet and Andrew was really excited and he looked at Ida and that was that.

PART SIX

Good luck and bad luck.

No luck and then luck.

Ida was resting.

She was nearly Ida was ready nearly well.

She could tell when she had been settled when she had been settled very well.

Once she had been and she liked it, she liked to be in one room and to have him in another room and to talk across to him while she was resting. Then she had been settled very well. It did not settle everything, nothing was unsettling, but she had been settled very well.

Andrew had a mother.

Some still have one and some do not still have one but Andrew did still have a mother.

He had other things beside

But he had never had a bride.

Flowers in the spring succeed each other with extraordinary rapidity and the ones that last the longest if you do not pick them are the violets.

Andrew had his life, he was never alone and he was never left and he was never active and he was never quiet and he was never sad.

He was Andrew.

It came about that he had never gone anywhere unless he had known beforehand he was going to go there, but and he had, he had gone to see Ida and once he was there it was as if he had been going to see Ida. So naturally he was always there.

Andrew knew that he was the first Andrew.

He had a nervous cough but he was not nervous.

He had a quiet voice but he talked loudly.

He had a regular life but he did what he did as if he would do it and he always did. Obstinate you call him. Well if you like. He said obstinate was not a word.

Ida never spoke, she just said what she pleased. Dear Ida.

It began not little by little, but it did begin.

Who has houses said a friend of Ida's.

Everybody laughed.

But said Andrew I understand when you speak.

Nobody laughed.

It was not customary to laugh.

Three makes more exchange than two.

There were always at least three.

This was a habit with Andrew.

Ida had no habit, she was resting.

And so little by little somebody knew.

How kindly if they do not bow.

Ida had a funny habit. She had once heard that albatrosses which birds she liked the name of always bowed before they did anything. Ida bowed like this to anything she liked. If she had a hat she liked, she had many hats but sometimes she had a hat she liked and if she liked it she put it on a table and bowed to it. She had many dresses and sometimes she really liked one of them. She would put it somewhere then and then she would bow to it. Of course jewels but really dresses and hats particularly hats, sometimes particularly dresses. Nobody knew anything about this certainly not anybody and certainly not Andrew, if anybody knew it would be an accident because when Ida bowed like that to a hat or a dress she never said it. A maid might come to know but naturally never having heard about albatrosses, the maid would not understand.

Oh yes said Ida while she was resting. Naturally she never bowed while she was resting and she was always resting when they were there.

Dear Ida.

It came to be that any day was like Saturday to Ida.

And slowly it came to be that even to Andrew any day came to be Saturday. Saturday had never been especially a day to Andrew but slowly it came to be Saturday and then every day began to be Saturday as it had come to be to Ida.

Of course there was once a song, every day will be Sunday by and by.

Ida knew this about Saturday, she always had, and now Andrew slowly came to know it too. Of course he did walk every day walk even if every day was Saturday. You can't change everything even if everything is changed.

Anybody could begin to realize what life was to Andrew what

life had been to Andrew what life was going to be to Andrew.

Andrew was remarkable insofar as it was all true. Yes indeed it was.

Saturday, Ida.

Ida never said once upon a time. These words did not mean anything to Ida. This is what Ida said. Ida said yes, and then Ida said oh yes, and then Ida said, I said yes, and then Ida said, Yes.

Once when Ida was excited she said I know what it is I do, I do know that it is, yes.

That is what she said when she was excited.

PART SEVEN

Andrew knew that nobody would be so rude as not to remember Andrew. And this was true. They did remember him. Until now. Now they do not remember Andrew. But Andrew knew that nobody would be so rude as not to. And pretty well it was true.

But again.

Andrew never had to think. He never had to say that it was a pleasant day. But it was always either wet or dry or cold or warm or showery or just going to be. All that was enough for Andrew and Ida never knew whether there was any weather. That is the reason they got on so well together.

There was never any beginning or end, but every day came before or after another day. Every day did.

Little by little circles were open and when they were open they were always closed.

This was just the way it was.

Supposing Ida was at home, she was almost at home and when she was at home she was resting.

Andrew had many things to do but then it was always true that he was with Ida almost all day although he never came to stay and besides she was resting.

One of the things Ida never liked was a door.

People should be there and not come through a door.

As much as possible Ida did not let herself know that, they did come through a door.

She did not like to go out to dinner at a house because you had to come in through a door. A restaurant was different there is really no door. She liked a room well enough but she did not like a door.

Andrew was different, he did just naturally come through a door, he came through a door, he was the first to come through a doorway and the last to come through a doorway. Doorways and doors were natural to him. He and Ida never talked about this, you might say they never talked about anything certainly they never talked about doors.

The French say a door has to be open or shut but open or shut did not interest Ida what she really minded was that there was a door at all. She did not really mind standing in a portiere or in a hall, but she did not like doors. Of course it was natural enough feeling as she did about doors that she never went out to see anybody. She went out she liked to go out but not through a doorway. There it was that was the way she was.

One day she was telling about this, she said, if you stand in an open place in a house and talk to somebody who can hear that is very nice, if you are out or in it is very nice but doors doors are never nice.

She did not remember always being that way about doors, she kind of did not remember doors at all, it was not often she mentioned doors, but she just did not care about doors.

One day did not come after another day to Ida. Ida never took on yesterday or tomorrow, she did not take on months either nor did she take on years. Why should she when she had always been the same, what ever happened there she was, no doors and resting and everything happening. Sometimes something did happen, she knew to whom she had been married but that was not anything happening, she knew about clothes and resting but that was not anything happening. Really there really was never anything happening although everybody knew everything was happening.

It was dark in winter and light in summer but that did not make any difference to Ida. If somebody said to her you know they are most awfully kind, Ida could always say I know I do not like that kind. She liked to be pleasant and she was but kind, well yes she knew that kind.

They asked her to a dinner party but she did not go, her husband went, she had a husband then and he wore a wedding ring. Husbands do not often wear wedding rings but he did. Ida knew when he came home that he had worn his wedding ring, she said, not very well and he said oh yes very well.

Three things had happened to Ida and they were far away but not really because she liked to rest and be there. She always was.

Andrew next to that was nothing and everything, Andrew knew a great many people who were very kind. Kind people always like doors and doorways, Andrew did. Andrew thought about Ida and doors, why should he when doors were there. But for Ida doors were not there if they had been she would not have been. How can you rest if there are doors. And resting is a pleasant thing.

So life went on little by little for Ida and Andrew.

It all did seem just the same but all the same it was not just the same. How could anybody know, nobody could know but there it was. Well no there it wasn't.

Ida began talking.

She never began but sometimes she was talking, she did not understand so she said, she did not sit down so she said, she did not stand up so she said, she did not go out or come in, so she said. And it was all true enough.

This was Ida.

Dear Ida.

Ida was good friends with all her husbands, she was always good friends with all her husbands.

She always remembered that the first real hat she ever had was a turban made of pansies. The second real hat she ever had was a turban made of poppies.

For which she was interested in pansies and gradually she was not. She had liked pansies and heliotrope, then she liked wild flowers, then she liked tube-roses, then she liked orchids and then she was not interested in flowers.

Of course she was not interested. Flowers should stay where they grow, there was no door for flowers to come through, they should stay where they grew. She was more interested in birds than in flowers but she was not really interested in birds.

Anything that was given to her she thanked for she liked to thank, some people do not but she did and she liked to be thanked. Yes she said.

She was careful to sit still when she thanked or was thanked, it is better so.

Some people like to stand or to move when they thank or are thanked but not Ida, she was not really resting when she thanked or was thanked but she was sitting.

Nobody knew what Ida was going to do although she always did the same thing in the same way, but still nobody knew what Ida was going to do or what she was going to say. She said yes. That is what Ida did say.

Everybody knew that they would not forget Andrew but was it true.

Not so sure.

You did not have to be sure about any such thing as long as it was happening, which it was not.

Andrew come in said Ida.

Andrew was in.

Andrew do not come in said Ida. Ida said Andrew is not coming in. Andrew came in.

Andrew had not been brought up to come in but little by little he did come in he came in and when Ida said he is not to come in he came in. This was natural as he came to know Ida. Anybody came in who came to know Ida but Ida did not say come in. To Andrew she had said yes come in and Andrew had come in.

It was not a natural life for Andrew this life of coming in and this was what had been happening to Andrew, he had commenced to come in and then he never did anything else, he always came in. He should have been doing something else but he did not he just came in.

Little by little it happened that except that he took his walk in the afternoon he never did anything but come in. This little by little was everything Andrew did.

She tried to stop, not anything but she tried to stop but how could she stop if she was resting how could she stop Andrew from coming in.

And in this way it might happen to come to be true that anybody would forget Andrew.

That would not happen little by little but it could come to be true.

Even in a book they could be rude and forget Andrew but not now. Andrew said not now, and Ida said Andrew said not now and Ida said she said not now but really Ida did not say not now she just said no.

Ida often sighed not very often but she did sigh and when somebody came in she said yes I always say yes, if you say no then you say no but if you say yes then you just say yes.

This was very natural and Ida was very natural.

So much happened but nothing happened to Ida.

To have anything happen you have to choose and Ida never chose, how could she choose, you can choose hats and you can choose other things but that is not choosing. To choose, well to choose, Ida never chose. And then it looked as if it happened, and it did happen and it was happening and it went on happening. How excited, and Ida was excited and so was Andrew and his name might have been William.

He had a great many names Andrew did and one of them was William but when he became Andrew the first he could not be William.

Ida often wished gently that he had been William, it is easier to say William than Andrew and Ida had naturally to say a name. Every time Andrew came in or was there or was anywhere she had to say his name and if his name had been William she could have said it easier. But all the same it was easy enough to say Andrew and she said Andrew.

Sometimes she called him Andy and sometimes she would say Handy Andy it is handy to have Andy, and her saying that did please Andrew. Naturally enough it pleased him.

It is not easy to lead a different life, much of it never happens but when it does it is different.

So Ida and Andrew never knew but it was true they were to lead a different life and yet again they were not.

If one did the other did not, and if the other did then the other did not.

And this is what happened.

If they had any friends they had so many friends.

They were always accompanied, Andrew when he came and went and wherever he was, Ida was not accompanied but she was never alone and when they were together they were always accompanied.

This was natural enough because Andrew always had been and it was natural enough because Ida always had been.

Men were with them and women were with them and men and women were with them.

It was this that made Ida say let's talk.

It was this that made Ida say, I like to know that all I love to do is to say something and he hears me.

It was this that made Ida say I never could though they were not glad to come.

It was this that made Ida say how do you do do come. It was this that made Ida say yes everything I can do I can always ask Andrew and Andrew will always do anything I ask him to do and that is the reason I call him Handy Andy.

Ida never laughed she smiled and sometimes she yawned and sometimes she closed her eyes and sometimes she opened them and she rested. That is what Ida did.

It did look as if nothing could change, nothing could change Ida that was true, and if that was true could anything change Andrew.

In a way nothing could but he could come not to be Andrew and if he were not Andrew Ida would not call him Handy Andy and as a matter of fact when he was not any longer Andrew she never did call him Handy Andy. She called him Andy, and she called him Andrew then but that was not the same thing.

But it was natural enough. Nature is not natural and that is natural enough.

Ida knew that is she did not exactly know then but all the same she did know then some people who always were ready to be there.

The larger the house these people had the more ready they were to be there.

Ida might have come to that but if she did she could not rest.

Oh dear she often said oh dear isn't it queer.

More than that she needed no help, but she might come to need help, and if she would come to need help she would help herself and if she helped herself then she certainly would be needing help.

I let it alone, she told everybody, and she did. She certainly did.

But most gradually Andrew it was true was a way to do, not for Ida, but for Andrew, and that made a lot of trouble, not for Ida, but for Andrew.

What was because was just what was a bother to Ida because she saw that Andrew was across from where he was.

Nobody knew whether it was happening slowly or not. It might be slowly and it might not.

Once in a great while Ida got up suddenly.

When she did well it was sudden, and she went away not far away but she left. That happened once in a way. She was sitting just sitting, they said if you look out of the window you see the sun. Oh yes said Ida, and they said, do you like sunshine or rain and Ida said she liked it best. She was sitting of course and she was resting and she did like it best.

They said, well anybody said, More than enough. Oh yes said Ida, I like it, yes I do, I like it.

Somebody said, well let us go on. No said Ida I always say no, no said Ida. And why not they asked her, well said Ida if you go away. We did not say we were going away, they said. Believe it or not we did not say we were going away, they said. Well said Ida I feel that way too. Do you they said. Yes said Ida I feel that way too.

It was not then that she got up suddenly. It was considerably after. She was not startled, a dog might bark suddenly but she was not startled. She was never startled at once. If she was, well she never was.

But after all, if she got up suddenly, and she did not very often. And once she got up suddenly, she left.

That did not as a matter of fact make very much difference.

More than enough she never really said, but once well really once she did get up suddenly and if she did get up suddenly she went away.

Nobody ever heard Andrew ever mention what he did because he never did it.

Everybody always said something, they said let's have it again, and they always had it again.

For this much they did come in, of course there never really was a beginning, for which it was fortunate.

Ida was mostly fortunate even if it did not matter. It really did not matter, not much.

So whether it was slowly or not was not enough because nobody was scared. They might be careful Ida was careful.

For which reason she was never worried not very likely to be.

She once said when this you see remember me, she liked being like that. Nicely.

For this reason she was rested. She will get up suddenly once and leave but not just now. Not now.

They could exchange well she knew more about hats than cows.

Andrew was interested in cows and horses. But after all there was much more in the way they sat down. Believe it or not they did sit down.

PART EIGHT

Well he said Andrew said that he could not do without Ida. Ida said yes, and indeed when she said yes she meant yes. Yes Andrew could not do without Ida and Ida said yes. She knew she might go away suddenly, but she said yes.

And so it came to be not more exciting but more yes than it had been.

Ida did say yes.

And Andrew was not nervous that is to say Andrew trembled easily but he was not nervous. Ida was nervous and so she said yes. If you are resting and you say yes you can be nervous, and Ida was nervous. There was no mistake about Ida's being nervous. She was not nervous again, she was just nervous. When she said yes she was not nervous. When she was resting she was nervous. Nearly as well as ever she said she was, she said she was nearly as well as ever, but nobody ever asked her if she is well, they always knew she was nearly as well as ever.

It happened that when she went out she came in. Well she did go out and when she went out she came in.

Anyhow went in and went out, but Ida did not.

When she went out she came in.

This was not just in the beginning it came to be more so, the only time that it ever was otherwise was when she got up suddenly and this did happen soon.

And so Andrew well Andrew was not careless nothing ever made Andrew careless.

He was much prepared.

Neither Andrew nor Ida was astonished but they were surprised. They had that in common that they were surprised not suddenly surprised but just surprised.

They were not astonished to learn but they were surprised.

This is what happened.

Ida had an aunt, she remembered she had an aunt but that had nothing to do with Ida nothing at all. Next to nothing to do with Ida.

Her aunt well her aunt sometimes did not feel that way about it but not very often and really it had nothing to do with Ida or with what happened.

What happened was this.

Ida returned more and more to be Ida. She even said she was Ida.

What, they said. Yes, she said. And they said why do you say yes. Well she said I say yes because I am Ida.

It got quite exciting. It was not just exciting it was quite exciting. Every time she said yes, and she said yes any time she said anything, well any time she said yes it was quite exciting.

Ida even was excited, well not altogether but she really was excited. Even Andrew was excited and as for the rest of all of them, all of them were excited.

And in between, well Ida always did have a tendency to say yes and now she did say, she even sometimes said oh yes.

Everybody was excited, it was extraordinary the way everybody was excited, they were so excited that everybody stopped everything to be excited.

Ida was excited but not very excited. At times she was not excited but she did always say yes.

Andrew was excited, he was not excited when he took his walk but he was quite often excited. Ida did say yes.

They went out together of course but it was difficult as the more excited he was the faster he went and the more excited she was the slower she went and as she could not go faster and he could not go slower. Well it was all right.

They lived from day to day. Ida did. So did they all. Some of their friends used to look at clouds, they would come in and say this evening I saw a cloud and it looked like a hunting dog and others would say he saw a cloud that looked like a dragon, and another one would say he saw a cloud that looked like a dream, and another he saw a cloud that looked like a queen. Ida said yes and Andrew said very nicely. They liked people to come in and tell what kind of clouds they had seen. Some had seen a cloud that looked like a fish and some had seen a cloud that looked like a rhinoceros, almost any of them had seen a cloud.

It was very pleasant for Ida that they came and told what the clouds they had seen looked like.

Ida lived from day to day so did they all but all the same a day well a day was not really all day to Ida, she needed only a part of the day and only a part of the night, the rest of the day and night she did not need. They might but she did not.

Andrew did not need day nor night but he used it all he did not use it up but he used it, he used it all of it it was necessary to use all of it and it was always arranged that he did everything that was necessary to do and he did. It was necessary that he used all of the night and all of the day every day and every night. This was right.

Ida chose just that piece of the day and just that piece of the night that she would use.

All right.

They did not say it but she said it and that was why she said yes.

And then something did happen.

What happened was this.

Everybody began to miss something and it was not a kiss, you bet your life it was not a kiss that anybody began to miss. And yet perhaps it was.

Weil anyway something did happen and it excited every one that it was something and that it did happen.

It happened slowly and then it was happening and then it happened a little quicker and then it was happening and then it happened it really happened and then it had happened and then it was happening and then well then there it was and if it was there then it is there only now nobody can care.

And all this sounds kind of funny but it is all true.

And it all began with everybody knowing that they were missing something and perhaps a kiss but not really nobody really did miss a kiss. Certainly not Ida.

Ida was not interested, she was resting and then it began oh so slowly to happen and then there it was all right there it was everybody knew it all right there it was.

Dear Ida.

What happened.

Well what happened was this. Everybody thought everybody knew what happened. And everybody did know and so it was that that happened. Nothing was neglected that is Ida did nothing Andrew did nothing but nothing was neglected.

When something happens nothing begins. When anything begins then nothing happens and you could always say with Ida that nothing began.

Nothing ever did begin.

Partly that and partly nothing more. And there was never any need of excuses. You only excuse yourself if you begin or if somebody else begins but with Ida well she never began and nobody else began. Andrew although he was different was the same, he was restless all day and Ida was resting all day but neither one nor the other had to begin. So in a way nothing did happen.

That was the way it was nothing did happen everybody talked all day and every day about Ida and Andrew but nothing could happen as neither the one of them or the other one ever did begin anything.

It is wonderful how things pile up even if nothing is added. Very wonderful.

Suppose somebody comes in, suppose they say, well how are we today. Well supposing they do say that. It does not make any difference but supposing they do say that. Somebody else comes in and says that too well how are we today. Well if Ida had not answered the first one she could not answer the second one because you always have to answer the first one before you answer the second one.

And if there was still a third one and mostly there was and a fourth one and a fifth one and even a sixth one and each one said well and how are we today, it is natural enough that Ida would have nothing to say. She had not answered the first one and if you are resting you cannot hurry enough to catch up and so she had nothing to say. Yes she said. It is natural enough that she said yes, because she did not catch up with anything and did not interrupt anything and did not begin anything and did not stop anything.

Yes said Ida.

It looks the same but well of course one can run away, even if you are resting you can run away. Not necessarily but you can. You can run away even if you say yes. And if you run away well you never come back even if you are completely followed.

This could be a thing that Ida would do. She would say yes and she was resting and nothing happened and nothing began but she could run away. Not everybody can but she could and she did.

What happened.

Before she ran away.

She did not really run away, she did not go away. It was something in between. She took her umbrella and parasol. Everybody knew she was going, that is not really true they did not know she was going but she went, they knew she was going. Everybody knew.

She went away that is she did get away and when she was away everybody was excited naturally enough. It was better so. Dear Ida.

Little by little she was not there she was elsewhere. Little by little.

It was little by little and it was all of a sudden. It was not entirely sudden because she was not entirely there before she was elsewhere.

That is the way it happened.

Before it happened well quite a while before it happened she did meet women. When they came she was resting, when they went she was resting, she liked it and they did not mind it. They came again and when they came again, she was obliging, she did say yes. She was sorry she was resting, so sorry and she did say yes. She thought they liked it and they did but it was not the same as if she had ever said no or if she had not always been resting.

If she had not always been resting they would not have come nor would they have come again. They said thank you my dear when they went. She had said yes Ida had and she said yes again.

That is the way it was before going away, they had not really come nor had they said Thank you my dear.

That is really the reason that Ida ran away not ran away or went away but something in between. She was ready to be resting and she was ready to say yes and she was ready to hear them say thank you my dear but they had almost not come again.

So Ida was not there. Dear Ida.

She knew she would be away but not really away but before she knew she was there where she had gone to she was really away.

That was almost an astonishment, quite to her, but to all the others not so much so once she was not there.

Of course she had luncheon and dinners to eat on the way.

One of the menus she ate was this.

She ate soft-shell crabs, she had two servings of soft-shell crabs and she ate lobster à la Newburg she only had one helping of that and then she left.

She often left after she ate. That is when she was not resting but she mostly was resting.

And so there she was and where was Andrew, well Andrew moved quickly while Ida moved slowly that is when they were both nervous, when each one of them was nervous. But he was not there yet. Not really.

Ida was resting. Dear Ida. She said yes.

Slowly little by little Andrew came, Andrew was still his name.

He was just as nervous as he was and he walked every afternoon and then he told about his walk that afternoon. Ida was as nervous as she was and she was resting.

For a little time she did not say yes and then she said yes again.

Gradually it was, well not as it had been but it was, it was quite as it was Ida was resting and she was saying yes but not as much as she had said yes. There were times when she did not say yes times when she was not resting not time enough but times.

It is all very confused but more confused than confusing, and later it was not interesting. It was not confused at all, resting was not confused and yes was not confused but it was interesting.

When any one came well they did Ida could even say how do you do and where did you come from.

Dear Ida.

And if they did not come from anywhere they did not come.

So much for resting.

Little by little there it was. It was Ida and Andrew.

Not too much not too much Ida and not too much Andrew.

And not enough Ida and not enough Andrew.

If Ida goes on, does she go on even when she does not go on any more.

No and yes.

Ida is resting but not resting enough. She is resting but she is not saying yes. Why should she say yes. There is no reason why she should so there is nothing to say.

She sat and when she sat she did not always rest, not enough.

She did rest.

If she said anything she said yes. More than once nothing was said. She said something. If nothing is said then Ida does not say yes. If she goes out she comes in. If she does not go away she is there and she does not go away. She dresses, well perhaps in black why not, and a hat, why not, and another hat, why not, and another dress, why not, so much why not.

She dresses in another hat and she dresses in another dress and Andrew is in, and they go in and that is where they are. They are there. Thank them.

Yes.

Gertrude Stein lived in France for over forty years and there experienced both World Wars. During the Second World War she lived in the South East which was at that time Vichy France. Between 1942 and 1944 she kept a journal. This journal was published in 1944 as *Wars I Have Seen*. In the epilogue of the book she considers how she has known two American armies in two different wars and she wonders about the differences between the two generations of Americans – have they changed, has their language changed:

'... the only way the Americans could change their language was by choosing words which they liked better than other words, by putting words next to each other in a different way than the English way, by shoving the language around until at last now the job is done, we use the same words as the English do but the words say an entirely different thing.

'Yes in that sense Americans have changed, I think of the Americans of the last war, they had their language but they were not yet in possession of it, and the children of the depression as that generation called itself it was beginning to possess its language but it was still struggling but now the job is done, the G.I. Joes have this language that is theirs, they do not have to worry about it, they dominate their language and in dominating their language which is now all theirs they have ceased to be adolescents and have become men.

'When I was in America in '34 they asked me if I did not find Americans changed. I said no what could they change to, just to become more American. No I said I could have gone to school with any of them.

'But all the same yes that is what they have changed to they have become more American all American, and the G.I. Joes show it and know it, God bless them.'

Gertrude Stein shows it in *Brewsie and Willie*[1] in which she reconstructs for herself a G.I. language, just as forty years earlier she had reconstructed an American Negro language in her story *Melanctha*.[2] The difference between the two is forty years of creative work and an evolved view of what narrative can be. Gertrude Stein wrote to her friend W. G. Rogers about this book: '... I think in a kind of way it is one of the best things I have ever done. You know how much I have always meditated about narration, how to tell what one has to tell, well this time I have written it, narration as the 20th century sees it.'[3]

Due to the length of *Brewsie and Willie* and its overall evenness, it was decided that five chapters would be sufficient to show the method of the book. They are the first three and the last two chapters. Also included for interest is the short epilogue in which Gertrude Stein speaks directly to Americans.

Brewsie and Willie, written in 1945, was the last book Gertrude Stein wrote. On the day it was published, 22 July 1946, Alice Toklas brought a copy of it to the hospital in Paris where Gertrude Stein lay ill. Five days later she died.[4]

1. Random House, New York, 1946.
2. From *Three Lives*, Grafton Press, New York, 1909.
3. Quoted in *The Third Rose* by John Malcolm Brinnin.
4. Her last work, *The Mother of Us All*, a libretto for a new opera by Vergil Thompson, was completed in March 1946.

29

BREWSIE AND WILLIE

CHAPTER ONE

You know Willie, said Brewsie, I think we are all funny, pretty funny, about this fraternization business, now just listen. They did not have to make any anti-fraternization ruling for the German army in France because although the Germans did their best to fraternize, no French woman would look or speak to them or recognize their existence. I kind of wonder would our women be like French or be like Germans, if the horrible happened and our country was conquered and occupied.

Willie: Well I wouldnt want any American woman to be like a Frenchwoman.

Brewsie: No you would want them to be like the Germans, sleep with the conquerors.

Willie: You get the hell out of here, Brewsie. No American woman would sleep with a foreigner.

Brewsie: But you admire the Germans who do. Which do you want American women to be like.

Willie: I know what I dont want them to be like, I dont want them to be like any lousy foreigner.

Brewsie: But all your fathers and mothers were lousy foreigners.

Willie: You get the hell out of here, Brewsie. What's that to you, I am going to sleep with any German we ich who'll sleep with me and they all will.

Brewsie: Sure they all will but all the same if the horrible happened and our country was defeated and occupied, how about it.

Willie: Well our country isnt going to be defeated and occupied, that's all there is to that.

Brewsie: Yes but you never can tell in a war.

Willie: And that's the reason there aint going to be any more war not if I can help it.

Brewsie: But if you can. help it.

Willie: I'll see to it that I do help it, there aint going to be any more war.

Brewsie: But that's what they said last time and hell here we are.

Willie: Well did I say we werent here, we're here all right, you betcha we're here, and I am going to sleep with any German girl who'll sleep with me, and they all will and that's what I call fraternization, and they let us do it and we're doing it.

Brewsie: But Willie listen.

Willie: Aint I listening, aint I always listening, you're always talking and I am always listening.

Brewsie: Well anyway, Willie, just listen.

While Brewsie talked, it was not alone Willie who sometimes listened, there were others more or less listening, Jo, and Bob and Ralph and Don and there was Brock, he was older, he liked to talk about how his father and mother moved from one house to another and what illnesses they had had and what it did to them and what flowers his mother grew and that she was fond of cooking and eating, and that he was not the only child but they did like him that is to say he was interested in everything they wrote to him and was natural enough because although he had been married, he did not know whether he was married now or not, anyway he did listen to Brewsie, because Brewsie was really very interesting and had a lot to say that was interesting and he, whenever he Brock had time, he did listen to him, he was a good chap Brewsie and had a lot to say that was really interesting.

Listen, said Brewsie, listen to me. I want to know why do you fellows feel the way you do.

Jo: Oh go way Brewsie, dont you know we're disillusioned, that's what we are, disillusioned, that's the word, aint it, fellows, disillusioned.

All of 'em: Sure, that's the word, disillusioned.

Brock: No no I am not disillusioned, as long as my mother is fond of flowers, and she is and fond of cooking as she is and fond of eating as she is, and likes to move into other houses which she does I could never be that word I could never be disillusioned. No, Jo, no, no no, and I think you all know I mean it I do I never could be disillusioned.

Willie: Take me away, that man makes me crazy. I just cant stand another minute of it, take me away.

Brewsie: All right, Willie, let's go. Come along, Jo.

Jo: Yes I got to go to the river to wait on a girl.

Brewsie: Where is she.

Jo: She is gone home to eat but I said I'd sit on the river bank and wait and I'm going to, want to come along.

Willie: There aint two.

Jo: No there aint but one, want to come along.

Brewsie: Let's all three go.

Jo: That's all right with me.

Look, said Willie, there comes a man-eating dog.

It was a dark day but it did not rain. The dog was white and gentle. That is what Willie said.

Brewsie does talk to himself, he said to himself, how can I be interested in how many people will be killed or how much property will be destroyed in the next war, how many people will be killed in the next war.

They went on to the river. It is not always easy to sail a sailboat up a river.

That made them talk about what they did remember, steering an airplane. Some of them sighed, it made them sigh because they liked it. It was like sleeping in a bed, it made them sigh, it did make them sigh because they liked it.

I remember, he said, he said, I remember.

They saw three others coming along, one of them said, what we doing just walking, aint anybody going to buy anything.

Brewsie remembered about buying, there was a time when anybody could buy something that is if he had money with him. Brewsie said that spending money if you had it, well it was just spending money and spending money was not only easy as anything it was more than anything.

I know what you mean, said Willie.

I do too, said Jo, let's go buy something. We aint found anything to buy for the kind of money we got, said Willie, and then the girl came along. If you put your arm all over a girl, well any girl does any girl say, tell him I dont want him, but no girls do because there is chewing gum and tobacco and coffee and chocolate, yes there is.

Does, said Brewsie, does any one want to buy anything if it can be given to them, if they can get it without buying. Nobody answered him, they were busy other ways.

It's a long war but it will end, said Brewsie, and then we will go home. Where's home, said a man just behind him.

What's your name, said Brewsie.

Paul is my name and if it aint Paul it's Donald, what do you want with my name.

I want to know how old you are and where you come from.

Oh get the hell out of here, said Donald Paul and then he sat down.

Let's, said Donald Paul, let's talk about beds. What kind of beds said Brewsie. Oh any kind, the kind you sleep in, the kind you make for yourselves and the kind others make for you. A bed is a bed, just write that down if you know how to read and write, a bed's a bed. When you wish you were dead you always wish for a bed. Yes that's the way it is. Remember you know when they put you in prison they make you make your own bed. I just read about it this evening. Yes, said Brewsie, if there is a bed. Yeah you're right too, if there is a bed. And they both sighed not loud, not really at all. Anybody knows how long a day is when evening comes. They gather that they had rather not be able to sit than not.

Yes, said Brewsie, do be anxious.

It was almost as much aloud as that.

Donald Paul snorted.

Allowed, he said, allowed, what's allowed, anything that is allowed is just what they never said. There are, said Donald Paul, yes there are, said Brewsie. Are what, said Willie. Eight million unemployed any next year, said Jo. Oh go to hell out of here, said Willie and as he spoke he fell asleep just like that.

CHAPTER TWO

Brewsie
 I'm here
 What you doing.
 I'm thinking.
 I am thinking about religion.

What religion.

Well Willie's, somebody said to me today why don't the G.I.'s have the Bible around like the doughboys did, why aint there ever a Bible in a plane.

Why should there be, there aint anything the matter with the plane.

Of course there could be.

Ya but if there could be it would be the fault of the ground men, and if there is any flack then you're taught how to dive in so that it dont hit you and if you dont do it right it does and anyway there is of course there is the calculation of errors. What's the matter with you Brewsie, dont you know all that.

Yes it is kind of funny I know all that, they do say though that the doughboys always had Bibles around, that's what they say.

Well, said Jo, why do you worry.

I don't worry, said Brewsie, I never worry I am kind of foggy in the head and I want to be clear, that's all.

Willie: Well you never will, you just keep on thinking and talking the more foggy you feel. Now you take us, we dont think we know that all America is just so and we are all Americans, that's what we are all Americans.

Brewsie: I wish I was a girl if I was a girl I would be a WAC and if I was a WAC, oh my Lord, just think of that.

Don: Dont you go being funny Brewsie, I been out with a WAC, yes I have, well no she was not an officer WAC although I have been out even with an officer WAC, how can you worry when anything is like that.

Brewsie: Well now boys let's all get together and think.

Willie: All right now how would you want us to get together and think.

Brewsie: Well let's think about how everybody perhaps will get killed in the next war.

Willie: Well they sure will if they fight the war good enough. If you fight a war good enough everybody ought to get killed.

Brewsie: You mean the other side.

Willie: No not the other side, that's only when one side fights good enough, but when they both do, and that can happen too, well when they both do, then everybody will be dead, all dead, fine, then nobody's got to worry about jobs.

Brewsie: But oh dear me, there are the wives and children. Yes there are.

Brock: You know the other day I heard a colored major say, he had no children although he was married nine years and I said, how is that, and he said, is this America any place to make born a Negro child.

Willie: I dont want to hear any talk like that, you know right well Brock I don't want to hear any talk like that.

But Willie, said Brock, Willie you listen to Brewsie and he talks like that and when I talk like Brewsie talks you tell me you dont want me to talk at all like that, that's not right Willie, that's not right, it is not right, Willie, it is not right.

Willie: Oh my God.

While they were talking they did not know what country they were in. If they did know they might talk about it but they did not know what country they were in, and little by little they knew less what country they were in. It was not night yet, it was not even late in the afternoon, they knew that, and sometimes they thought about that, but Brewsie did not talk about that so they did not have to listen about that not that afternoon.

It was early in the morning, and there was anybody there, they never thought that there was anybody there even when there was.

Let's go and have a drink, said Willie, but they could get a drink where they were so they did not go and get a drink, they had a drink where they were.

I was in a hotel, said Willie, and I saw from the window around the corner somebody getting into bed and I could not tell whether it was a little girl or a little woman.

What time was it, said Brewsie.

About half past ten, said Willie.

You couldnt tell by that, said Brewsie, not by that. A little girl could be going to bed then, yes she could.

I know, said Willie, I know, it might have been a little girl and it might have been a round-faced little woman, I kind of think it was a round-faced little woman and I couldnt tell whether she was kneeling to say her prayers or to take make-up off her face, I just couldnt tell.

Was there a mirror in front of her, said Brewsie.

I just couldnt tell, said Willie.

Even a little woman could kneel and say her prayers as well as a little girl, said Brewsie.

Could she, said Willie.

Yes she could, said Brewsie.

Well I dont know, said Willie, it was so around the corner.

Well couldnt you see her the next day.

I tell you it was the back of a house around the corner, how could I tell which house it was next day.

Well, said Brewsie, why didnt you go around that night and see.

I tell you, said Willie, it was around the corner and the front wouldnt be the same as the back.

Well couldnt you count, said Jo waking up.

No not in French how could you count in French around the corner with the back and the front different and not sure it was a girl or a little woman. No I just never did find out.

Well why didnt you go back to the hotel and try again, said Brewsie, try to see her get to bed again.

Because I never have gone back there, said Willie, I never have and when I do get back she will be gone sure she will.

Nobody ever moves in France, said Jo.

No, maybe though it was a hotel.

Well if it was, said Brewsie, it was not a little girl.

I guess you're right Brewsie, I guess it was a little woman, a little round-faced woman and she was taking off her make-up.

Perhaps, said Brewsie, it was a little round-faced woman and she was saying her prayers.

Not likely, said Willie.

CHAPTER THREE

Brewsie: Are we isolationists or are we isolated, are we efficient or are we quick to make up for long preparation, if we were caught without time to get it all in order would we be ready, would we be, well did we be, if Japan had followed up, oh dear me, said Brewsie, oh dear me, are we efficient or are we slow and so we are very quick to make up for being slow, oh dear me, said Brewsie, and do we like the German girls best because we are virgins and they do all the work.

Willie: You get the hell out of here Brewsie, I am no virgin, I never was a virgin, I never will be a virgin.

No, said Brewsie, no, you never were a virgin, well then you dont know the difference perhaps you still are a virgin.

Jo: That sounds funny, Brewsie, that's not the way you talk, Brewsie, what's the matter with you, Brewsie.

Brewsie: I dont know, I kind of feel funny, it is true over half the E. T. O. are virgins, they are they are, and that's why they like the German girls I get so mad I just have to say it, I just get so mad.

Willie: Well I get mad too, if you say I am a virgin.

Jo: Well, Willie, perhaps you are. Brewsie is right, a whole lot of the army are virgins. I dont say they cant but they dont and that's the reason they got to have so many pin-ups and German girls, yes sometimes I guess Brewsie is right, you just bellow, Willie, you just bellow and Brewsie is just foggy so he is but I know, I never say it but I know, a lot of us is just virgins, Willie, just E. T. O. virgins, Willie, all you fellows, are you or are you not E. T. O. Virgins.

Willie: You get the hell out of here, Jo, I can stand what Brewsie says but I wont stand anything you say, I just wont and I warn you right here and now if you call me a virgin again some night or some day you'll die and it wont be any enemy that will have killed you, it will have been just me.

Brock: Oh boys, boys, listen to me, I am older than any of you and I dont know whether I am married or not and I am always interested in what my mother does and I do like to drink but nobody ever thinks of calling me a virgin. You wouldnt, Willie, and you wouldnt, Jo, and you wouldnt, Brewsie, you never would think of calling me a virgin. So dont you be worried, Willie, dont you be worried, you just listen to me and dont you be worried.

Willie: Oh.

Brewsie: But to come back to what is worrying me, to come back to it, are we isolationists or are we isolated.

Willie: You just want to explain, Brewsie, so go ahead, you will anyway so go ahead, we just listen anyway, so just go ahead. Come on, Jo, come on, everybody, Brewsie is thinking.

Brewsie: Well I just am thinking are we isolationists or are we isolated.

Jo: Well what about it.

Well you see, said Brewsie, I kind of like to be liked. Willie likes to be liked, so do you all, well yes I do like to be liked, I just could cry if they dont like me, yes I could. I do like to be liked.

And besides, said Jo, it's dangerous not to be liked, if Willie did not like me I would just be scared.

Brock: I am sure everybody does like me, I do I am sure I do what makes anyone like me.

Oh my God, said Willie, take me away.

All right, said Brewsie, all right where shall we go.

Right back where we started from, said Willie. And the flowers.

Oh come along, said Joe, Brewsie will remember what he wants to say for another day.

No, said Brewsie, I wont remember but I will find it out again.

Let's go, said Willie.

And they went.

The sun was shining and they were all worried, there was nothing to worry about, the sun was shining and they were all worried.

It used to be fine, said Willie, before the war when we used to believe what the newspapers and the magazines said, we used to believe them when we read them and now when it's us they write about we know it's lies, just lies, just bunches of lies, and if it's just bunches of lies, what we going to read when we get home, answer me that, Brewsie, answer me that.

I saw a girl, said Donald Paul, she was saying how can I replace potatoes, how can I take the place of potatoes. My darling, I said, you just cant.

Brewsie: I am going to begin to talk and I am just going on talking, that's what I am going to do.

Sure you are, said Willie.

I say, said Brewsie, and I am just going to be solemn, just as solemn as anything, are we isolationists or are we isolated, do we like Germans because we are greedy and callous like them. Oh dear,

I guess you boys better go away, I might just begin to cry and I'd better be alone. I am a G.I. and perhaps we better all cry, it might do us good crying sometimes does.

Oh get the hell out of here, Brewsie, said Willie.

Crying does good, said Jo, but I dont like it, not anybody's crying.

Where is Donald Paul, said Brewsie.

I told him to go away, said Willie.

If they knew it was Sunday afternoon then it was Sunday afternoon, nicely and quietly Sunday afternoon. Even yesterday was Sunday afternoon, Brewsie said so and they all said, yes, yesterday even yesterday was Sunday afternoon too.

Two majors came along, one was a fat major and one was a thin major, they were in transport, the fat major said, I wonder when we get home, can we make them see that it is just as good not to work seven days a week all day, that railroads get along just as well if you go home for a day and a half a week and work in your garden. The thin major said, I wonder, no I dont wonder about the railroads getting along just as good, I wonder if they'll see it and let us take a day and a half off and perhaps longer and a month for a vacation like they do over here, I wonder. And do you suppose, said the fat major we could retire when we were fifty instead of when we were seventy. I wonder, said the thin major and they went home in the twilight, a nice twilight.

Brewsie when he was awake woke slowly, it was just as well as when he went to sleep, he went to sleep slowly.

Willie never asked him why, Willie knew why.

Said Brewsie, do you remember, Willie, what I was talking about. Well I do, I was talking about a lot of things and I was going to talk a long time and I was going to commence with, Are we isolationists or are we isolated.

Two Red Cross nurses came along, they were lieutenants still they did say, listen he sounds interesting. Tell me, said the fatter and younger, dont you think it is awful that the French have no leaders.

Havent they, said Donald Paul, and if they have why do they want them, a leader is some one who leads you where you dont want to go, where do you want to go, sister, can I lead you.

The older and the thinner said, we were not talking to you, we were talking to him, he sounds interesting.

Donald Paul: Fair sister, you are right, he not only sounds interesting but he is interesting.

Brewsie: I have a great deal to say.

The older one: Yes, that is why we are listening.

Brewsie: If I have a great deal to say it will take a long time to say it.

Yes, said the younger, but how can the French expect to come back if they have no leaders.

Why why why, how how how, said Donald Paul.

How, said Jo, I dont know how.

The older: Yes but he does, you tell us, she said to Brewsie.

Brewsie, said yes, I'll tell you. Leaders, what are leaders, yes was right, a leader either does not lead you or if he does he leads you where you do not want to go. Isnt it so, sisters, isnt it, where do you want to go, where do the French want to go, they dont want to go anywhere, they want enough to eat, a place to sleep, and fuel to keep them warm, that's what they want, leaders never give you that, they kind of scratch around and get it for themselves. No he is right what can leaders do, we always have leaders but where do they lead us. No listen to me and I will tell you about efficiency and about being isolated and why although rich we are poor and why although quick we are slow and how, well leaders better stay at home a while and lead everybody that way.

Chorus of a crowd: Ah yes, let's go home, I want to go home, we want to go home, everybody wants to go home. And then somebody began to sing Home Sweet Home.

Then everybody got quiet.

Do you know, said Donald Paul, I watch all those men all that army going around excursioning in auto-buses, so fat, so well dressed, so taken care of, and I say to myself, they want to go home and I say to myself, do they, and I say to myself, let's go home, and I say to myself, where is home, where you got a bellyful, that's home, where you got no cares, that's home.

Willie: Get the hell out of here, home is home, home is where you come from, that's home, that's fine, that's home.

Jo: You got no imagination, Willie.

Willie: To hell with imagination, I want to go home.

Yes, said the two nurses, you all want to go home, yeah you're all going home.

Yes we all are going home, home, that's where we're going, home.

Donald Paul: All too soon.

Willie: You get the hell out of here. If anybody is going to talk it's Brewsie, Brewsie, you talk.

Brewsie: Not today Willie, not today, I kind of dont understand anything today, I kind of thought I understand everything today, but today I kind of think I dont understand anything today. I aint no leader today, I'm kind of scared of being a leader today.

Willie: Ah you're no leader, Brewsie, you just talk.

Donald Paul: And what do leaders do.

Jo: They talk too, but they talk differently. Orientation, that's the word, said Donald Paul.

Now tell me, said the two nurses, do you all talk like this every day?

Not every day, said Jo.

Mostly every day, said Willie.

I think we will come again, said the younger fatter nurse and the older thinner one was very interested and they went away.

CHAPTER EIGHTEEN

I been thinking, said Brewsie, do we feel alike as well as say alike, do we think alike or dont we think at all. I dont think, said Brewsie, that we feel alike, I think we dont feel alike at all, they say we are sad and I think we are sad because we have different feelings but we articulate all the same. Listen, said Brewsie, you see, said Brewsie, you see I dont think we think, if we thought we could not articulate the same, we couldn't have Gallup polls and have everybody answer yes or no, if you think it's more complicated than that, over here, they wont answer the questions like that, they wont tell you how they are going to think tomorrow but we always know how we gonna think tomorrow because we are all going to think alike, no, said Brewsie, no not think, we are all going to articulate alike, not think, thinking is funnier and more mixed than that, not articulate alike, they ask us G.I.s what we think about Germans yes or no, my gracious, said Brewsie, you cant just think yes or no about Germans or about Russians and yet we all articulate alike about Germans and Russians, just as if it was the Democratic or Republican Party and it isnt, Willie it isnt, it may be life and death to us and we cant all feel alike and we dont think, is it we cant think, is it that we can only articulate, and if you can only articulate and not think, feel different but no way to get it out, because it comes out and it just is a Gallup poll, yes or no, just like that, oh Willie, I get so worried, I know it is just the most dangerous moment in our history, in a kind of a way as dangerous more dangerous than the Civil War, well they didnt all think alike then, they had lots of complications, and they did think, think how they orated, they did think, and then, said Brewsie, the Civil War was over, and everybody stopped thinking and they began to articulate, and instead of that they became job-hunters, and they felt different all the time they were feeling different, but they were beginning to articulate alike, I guess job men just have to articulate alike, they got to articulate yes or no to their bosses, and yes or no to their unions, they just got to articulate alike, and when you begin to articulate alike, you got to drop thinking out, just got to drop it out, you can go on feeling different but you got to articulate the same Gallup poll, yes you do, and it aint no use making it a second ballot, because nobody can think, how can you think when you feel different, you gotta feel different, anybody does have to feel different, but how can you think when you got to articulate alike. Listen to me Willie, listen to me, it's just like that Willie it just is, said Brewsie. I know, said Willie, it's all right, Brewsie, you got it right it's just the way we are, it's just the way it is, but what are you going to do about it Brewsie. Well that's just it, I kind of think, well I kind of feel that our generation, the generation that saw the depression, the generation that saw the war. I did more than see the depression Brewsie, and I did more than see the war, dont you make no mistake about that Brewsie, I did more than see the depression and I did more than see the war. I know Willie, said Brewsie, I know, I know Willie, and there it is, there was the depression and there was the war, yes but back of that, there is job-mindedness, and what can we do about it. No use saying communism communism, it's stimulating to Russians because they discovered it, but it wouldnt stimulate us any not any at all. No, said Willie, it certainly would not stimulate me. No I know Willie, said Brewsie, no I just know just how it wouldnt stimulate you but Willie, what we gonna do, we got to think, and how can we think when we got to jump from feeling different to articulating the same, and if we could think Willie what could we think. But, said Willie, Brewsie you just got to hold out some hope, you just got to hold it out. That's very easy to say, said Brewsie, but how can you hold out hope, until you got hope and how can you get hope unless you can think and how can you think when you got to go right from feeling inside you kind of queer and worried and kind of scared and knowing something ought to be done about it articulating all the same thing every minute they ask you something and every minute you open your mouth even when nobody has asked you anything. They talk about cognac, they talk about wine and women, and even that they say just exactly alike, you know it Willie, you know it. Sure I know it Brewsie, sure I know it, but just all the same Brewsie you got to hold out some kind of hope you just got to Brewsie. Well, Willie, I have got some kind of hope not really got it, but it's kind of there and that is because all of us, yes all of us, yes we kind of learned something from suffering, we learned to feel and to feel different and even when it comes to think well we aint learned to think but we kind of learned that if we could think we might think and perhaps if we did not articulate all alike perhaps something might happen. But, said Willie, how about all that job-mindedness, Brewsie, yes, said Willie, how can you not be job-minded when you all have to look for jobs and either get a job or not get a job but you have to do all the time with jobs, how can you be not job-minded if you dont do anything but breathe in a job, think Brewsie, answer me that, said Willie. Yes, said Brewsie, yes sometimes, said Brewsie, when I know how they all feel. They all feel all right they do all feel, said Willie, they do all feel. Well, said Brewsie, when I see how they all feel, sometimes I almost see something. Well look Brewsie look, look all you can Brewsie, and I'll listen while you are looking Brewsie, count on me I told that Pauline I listened to you and I'll listen to you Brewsie I'll listen.

CHAPTER NINETEEN

Well Brewsie, said Willie, we got 'em, the order has come. Yes I know, said Brewsie. Hullo Jo, said Willie, we got 'em. Sure we got 'em, said Jo. Hullo Willie, said Jimmie. Hullo, said Willie, we got 'em we got orders, we are the boys who are redeployed, in a little boat, on a little shore, and no more will we see a whore whenever we are wherever we are, away so far, it makes me feel funny, kind of funny very funny but it's all right there wont be any thinking over there, no thinking over there, no whores, no thinking, yes Brewsie, nothing but jobs, well do we like it. Yes do we like it, Brewsie, yes do we like it. Well, said John, I am staying, I got no points, so I'll think, do any of you guys want me to think for you. I'll have lots of time, Willie how about you, shall I think the thinks for you. You can stink the stinks for me, but think, well I was gonna say never again, never any thinking, but I dunno, I kind of think I am going to miss thinking, there was that cute Pauline and there was thinking, I kind of think I am going to miss thinking, there'll be no thinking over there, they dont think over there, they got no time to think, they got to get a job, they got to hold the job, they got no time to think over there, yes sometimes I might be kind of lonesome for thinking and I'll be thinking here is John he's got nothing to do, he's having a hell of a good time just thinking. Yes, said Brewsie, yes and yes, and dont you think it was true all we thought over here. Yes, said Willie, of course it was true but it dont do no good, it dont help any, it dont, what we gonna do thinking, what we gonna do. Well I tell you Willie, and if you dont think a little and go on thinking you'll have another awful time. Listen Willie, listen, listen Willie, what's a job, you havent got it, what's a job, you have got it, what's rushing around so fast you cant hear yourself think, what will happen, you'll be old and you never lived, and you kind of feel silly to lie down and die and to never have lived, to have been a job chaser and never have lived. Yes, said Willie, but Brewsie, now honest to God Brewsie, honest to God and it's the last time we all are here, honest to God Brewsie, can you be a job chaser and live at the same time, honest to God Brewsie tell me that can you live and be a job chaser at the same time, honest to God, Brewsie tell me it, honest to God Brewsie, honest to God. Honest to God Willie, said

Brewsie, I just dont know, I just dont know. And if you dont know, said Willie, honest to God who does know. Well, said Jo, I know. What do you know, said Willie. Well, said Jo, I know I am going to. Going to what, said Willie. Honest to God I dont know, said Jo. Well I know, said Jimmie, I dont have to chase jobs, yeah, said Jimmie, because I live in a part of the South where they all live so simple they just cant starve and they live so simple that there aint really much difference between having a job and not having a job, between earning a living and not earning a living, just like these lousy foreigners, said Willie. Well yes perhaps, said Jimmie. And do you think living that way, said Willie. Well, said Jimmie, not so much no and not so much yes, but yes kind of, anyway we can do something that you job chasers cant do, we can listen when other people think and we can sit and wait for them to go on thinking, that's more than you job chasers can do, believe me Willie it's so. Yes, said Willie, I dont say no, yes I know it's so. And said Jo, I know a fellow he is going home to be a bar-keep, he and his brother always wanted to be bar-keeps, and their father never would buy them a bar, and now his brother has been killed in the Pacific and so his father has bought him a bar and is keeping it himself till his son gets home, and the son my God he is fuddled all the time, he is pale and drunk, drunk and pale, my God, said Jo. Well what has that to do with what we got to do, said Jo. Nothing, said Jo, it's just a story. Here we are, said Janet, we heard your crowd were leaving and we came to say good-bye. Good-bye it is sister, said Willie, where is Pauline. She is coming, she said, she wanted to stop and pick you a flower. God bless her for that tender thought, said Willie, God bless her. Yes, said Jo, yes. And said Jimmie, how old is she. What do you want to know that for, said Janet. I just want to know, said Jimmie, if she was her age. Well she aint, said Willie, she's my age. Dear dear, said Janet, isnt that chivalrous unless you are too old. Not so old as that sister, said Willie. And tell me, said Janet, wont you miss talking when you get home, you do know dont you all of you nobody talks like you boys were always talking, not back home. Yes we know, said Jo. Yes we know, said Jimmie. Not Brewsie, said Willie, he'll talk but, said Willie, Brewsie will talk but we wont be there to listen, we kind of will remember that he's talking somewhere but we wont be there to listen, there wont be anybody talking where we will be. But, said Jo, perhaps they will talk now, why you all so sure they wont talk over there, perhaps they will talk over there. Not those on the job they wont, said Willie, not those on the job.

TO AMERICANS

G.I.s and G.I.s and G.I.s and they have made me come all over patriotic. I was always patriotic, I was always in my way a Civil War veteran, but in between, there were other things, but now there are no other things. And I am sure that this particular moment in our history is more important than anything since the Civil War. We are there where we have to have to fight a spiritual pioneer fight or we will go poor as England and other industrial countries have gone poor, and dont think that communism or socialism will save you, you just have to find a new way, you have to find out how you can go ahead without running away with yourselves, you have to learn to produce without exhausting your country's wealth, you have to learn to be individual and not just mass job workers, you have to get courage enough to know what you feel and not just all be yes or no men, but you have to really learn to express complication, go easy and if you cant go easy go as easy as you can. Remember the depression, dont be afraid to look it in the face and find out the reason why, dont be afraid of the reason why, if you dont find out the reason why you'll go poor and my God how I would hate to have my native land go poor. Find out the reason why, look facts in the face, not just what they all say, the leaders, but every darn one of you so that a government by the people for the people shall not perish from the face of the earth, it wont, somebody else will do it if we lie down on the job, but of all things dont stop, find out the reason why of the depression, find it out each and every one of you and then look the facts in the face. We are Americans.

BIBLIOGRAPHY

Principal Publications of Works by Gertrude Stein

Three Lives (1904–5)
 The Grafton Press, New York, 1909
 John Lane the Bodley Head, London, 1915
 The Modern Library, New York, 1933
 Peter Owen, London, 1970
The Making of Americans (1906–8)
 Contact Editions, Paris, 1925
 Harcourt, Brace, New York, 1934 (abridged edition)
  Reissued 1966
 Something Else Press, New York, 1966; Peter Owen, London, 1969
  (photo-copy of the original Contact Editions publication)
Matisse, Picasso and Gertrude Stein (1909–12)
 Plain Edition, Paris, 1933
Tender Buttons (1911)
 Claire-Marie, New York, 1914
 transition No. 14, 1928
 See also *Selected Writings of Gertrude Stein*
Useful Knowledge (1915)
 Payson and Clarke, New York, 1928
 John Lane the Bodley Head, London, 1929
Geography and Plays (1908–20)
 The Four Seas Company, Boston, 1922
 (Introduction by Sherwood Anderson)
Composition as Explanation (1926)
 The Hogarth Press, London, 1926
 Doubleday, Doran & Co., New York, 1928
 See also *Selected Writings of Gertrude Stein*
An Acquaintance with Description (1926)
 Seizin Press, London, 1929
Lucy Church Amiably (1927)
 Plain Edition, Paris, 1930
 Something Else Press, New York, 1969

How To Write (1928–30)
    Plain Edition, Paris, 1931
Before the Flowers of Friendship Faded Friendship Faded (1930)
    Plain Edition, Paris, 1931
Operas and Plays (1913–30)
    Plain Edition, Paris, 1932
The Autobiography of Alice B. Toklas (1932)
    Harcourt, Brace, New York, 1933
    John Lane the Bodley Head, London, 1933
    Random House, New York, 1936
    Penguin Books, Harmondsworth, 1967
    See also *Selected Writings of Gertrude Stein*
Portraits and Prayers (1909–33)
    Random House, New York, 1934
Lectures in America (1934)
    Random House, New York, 1935
    Beacon Press, Boston, 1957 (paperback)
Narration (1935)
    University of Chicago Press, 1935
    (Introduction by Thornton Wilder)
The Geographical History of America or the Relation of Human Nature to the Human Mind (1935)
    Random House, New York, 1936
    (Introduction by Thornton Wilder)
What are Master-pieces (1922–36)
    Conference Press, Los Angeles, 1940
Everybody's Autobiography (1936)
    Random House, New York, 1937
    William Heinemann, London and Toronto, 1938
Picasso (1938)
    Librairie Floury, Paris, 1938
    (French and English)
    Batsford, London, 1938
    Charles Scribner's Sons, New York, 1940
The World is Round (1938)
    William R. Scott, New York, 1939
    Batsford, London, 1939
Paris France (1939)
    Charles Scribner's Sons, New York, 1940
    Batsford, London, 1940
Ida, A Novel (1940)
    Random House, New York, 1941

Wars I Have Seen (1942–4)
  Random House, New York, 1944
  Batsford, London, 1945
Brewsie and Willie (1945)
  Random House, New York, 1946
Selected Writings of Gertrude Stein (1909–44)
  Random House, New York, 1946
  (edited with introduction and notes by Carl Van Vechten)

Posthumous Publications

Four In America (1932–3)
  Yale University Press, New Haven, 1947
  (Introduction by Thornton Wilder)
The Gertrude Stein First Reader and Three Plays (1941–3)
  M. Fridberg, Dublin, 1946
  Houghton Mifflin, Boston, 1948
Last Operas and Plays (1917–46)
  Rinehart and Co., New York, 1949
Things As They Are (1903)
  Banyan Press, Pawlett, Vermont, 1950

The Yale Edition of the Unpublished Work of Gertrude Stein – 8 Volumes
The Yale University Press New Haven

Two: Gertrude Stein and Her Brother (1908–12), published 1951, foreword by Janet Flanner
Mrs Reynolds and Five Earlier Novelettes (1931–42), published 1952, foreword by Lloyd Frankenberg
Bee Time Vine and Other Pieces (1913–27), published 1953, introduction by Vergil Thomson
As Fine as Melanctha (1914–30), published 1954, foreword by Natalie Clifford Barney
Painted Lace and Other Pieces (1914–37), published 1955, introduction by Daniel-Henry Kahnweiler
Stanzas in Meditation and Other Poems (1929–33), published 1956, preface by Donald Sutherland

Alphabets and Birthdays (1915–40), published 1957, introduction by
  Donald Gallup
A Novel of Thank You (1920–26), published 1958, introduction by Carl
  Van Vechten

Biography etc.

W. G. Rogers: *When This You See Remember Me*, Rinehart & Co.,
  New York, 1948
Rosamond S. Miller: *Gertrude Stein: Form and Intelligibility*, Exposition
  Press, New York, 1949
Donald Sutherland: *Gertrude Stein: A Biography of her Work*, Yale
  University Press, New Haven, 1951
Elizabeth Sprigge: *Gertrude Stein: Her Life and Her Work*, Hamish
  Hamilton, London, 1957; Harper, New York, 1957
B. L. Reid: *Art by Subtraction: A Dissenting Opinion of Gertrude Stein*,
  University of Oklahoma Press, 1958
John Malcolm Brinnin: *The Third Rose: Gertrude Stein and her World*,
  Littlebrown, Boston, 1959; Weidenfeld & Nicolson, London, 1960
Donald Gallup (ed.): *The Flowers of Friendship: Letters to Gertrude
  Stein*, Alfred A. Knopf, New York, 1953
Edmund Fuller (ed.): *Journey into the Self: Being the Letters, Papers
  and Journals of Leo Stein*, Crown Publishers, New York, 1950 (paper-
  back)
Richard Bridgman: *Gertrude Stein in Pieces*, Oxford University Press,
  New York, 1971.

The Voice
from
the Whirlwind

The Voice
from
the Whirlwind

The Problem of Evil and the Modern World

Stephen J. Vicchio

Christian Classics, Inc.
Post Office Box 30
Westminster, MD 21157
1989

First published 1989

Library of Congress Catalog Card Number: 89-61356
ISBN: 0-87061-162-3

Printed in the USA

Contents